ALBERTA

Occupational Health and Safety

Act, Regulations and Code

Handbook

Effective July 1, 2009

(6th Printing - December 9, 2011)

Province of Alberta

OCCUPATIONAL HEALTH AND SAFETY ACT

Revised Statutes of Alberta 2000
Chapter O-2

Current as of November 1, 2010

Office Consolidation

© Published by Alberta Queen's Printer

Alberta Queen's Printer
5th Floor, Park Plaza
10611 - 98 Avenue
Edmonton, AB T5K 2P7
Phone: 780-427-4952
Fax: 780-452-0668

E-mail: qp@gov.ab.ca
Shop on-line at www.qp.alberta.ca

Copyright and Permission Statement

Note

All persons making use of this consolidation are reminded that it has no legislative sanction, that amendments have been embodied for convenience of reference only. The official Statutes and Regulations should be consulted for all purposes of interpreting and applying the law.

Amendments Not in Force

This consolidation incorporates only those amendments in force on the consolidation date shown on the cover. It does not include the following amendments:

RSA 2000 c23 (Supp) s1 amends s24.1

2009 cA-31.5 repeals and substitutes s6(4) and (5).

Regulations

The following is a list of the regulations made under the *Occupational Health and Safety Act* that are filed as Alberta Regulations under the Regulations Act

	Alta. Reg.	*Amendments*
Occupational Health and Safety Act		
Farming and Ranching Exemption	27/95	*251/2001*
Occupational Health and Safety	62/2003	*284/2009*
Occupational Health and Safety Code 2009 Order	87/2009	

OCCUPATIONAL HEALTH AND SAFETY ACT

Chapter O-2

Table of Contents

HER MAJESTY, by and with the advice and consent of the Legislative Assembly of Alberta, enacts as follows:

Definitions

1   In this Act,

   (a)   "adopted code" means each code made under section 40.1(1) and adopted under section 40.1(2), including any secondary code adopted or incorporated as referred to in section 40.1(3), that is relevant to the circumstances in question;

   (a.1)   "code of practice" means a code of practice described in section 33;

   (b)   "contractor" means a person, partnership or group of persons who, through a contract, an agreement or ownership, directs the activities of one or more employers involved in work at a work site;

(c) "controlled product" means a substance or material designated in the regulations as a controlled product;

(d) "Council" means the Occupational Health and Safety Council appointed under section 6;

(e) "designated substance" means a substance designated in the regulations as a designated substance;

(f) "Director" means a Director of Inspection, a Director of Medical Services or a Director of Occupational Hygiene;

(g) "Director of Inspection" means a person appointed under section 5 as a Director of Inspection;

(h) "Director of Medical Services" means a physician appointed under section 5 as a Director of Medical Services;

(i) "Director of Occupational Hygiene" means a person appointed under section 5 as a Director of Occupational Hygiene;

(j) "disciplinary action" means an action that adversely affects a worker with respect to terms or conditions of employment;

(k) "employer" means

   (i) a person who is self-employed in an occupation,

   (ii) a person who employs one or more workers,

   (iii) a person designated by an employer as the employer's representative, or

   (iv) a director or officer of a corporation who oversees the occupational health and safety of the workers employed by the corporation;

(l) "hazardous material" means material designated in the regulations as hazardous material;

(m) "hazardous occupation" means an occupation designated in the regulations as a hazardous occupation;

(n) "hazardous work site" means a work site designated in the regulations as a hazardous work site;

(o) "licence" means a licence, certificate or permit issued under this Act;

(p) "Minister" means the Minister determined under section 16 of the *Government Organization Act* as the Minister responsible for this Act;

(q) "new project" means a project defined in the regulations as a new project for the purposes of this Act;

(r) "notifiable disease" means a disease or a state of ill health designated in the regulations as a notifiable disease;

(s) "occupation" means every occupation, employment, business, calling or pursuit over which the Legislature has jurisdiction, except

   (i) farming or ranching operations specified in the regulations, and

   (ii) work in, to or around a private dwelling or any land used in connection with the dwelling that is performed by an occupant or owner who lives in the private dwelling or a household servant of the occupant or owner;

(t) "occupational disease" means a disease or ill health arising out of and directly related to an occupation;

(u) "officer" means a Director or a person appointed under section 5 as an occupational health and safety officer;

(v) "owner" in respect of a work site means the person in legal possession of the work site or, if the person in legal possession does not request the work, the person with an ownership interest in the work site who requests that the work be done;

(w) "peace officer" means a member of the Royal Canadian Mounted Police or a member of a municipal police service;

(x) "prime contractor" means the prime contractor for a work site referred to in section 3;

(y) "project" means

   (i) the construction, demolition, repair, alteration or removal of a structure, building, complex, street, road or highway, pipeline, sewage system or electric, telecommunication or transmission line,

   (ii) the digging of, working in or filling of a trench, excavation, shaft or tunnel,

       (iii)   the installation, modification, repair or removal of any equipment, machinery or plant,

       (iv)   the operation of a manufacturing, industrial or other process, or

       (v)   any work designated by a Director of Inspection or a Director of Occupational Hygiene as a project;

  (z)   "qualifications board" means a qualifications board established under the regulations;

  (aa)   "supplier" means a person who rents, leases, erects, installs or provides any tools, appliances or equipment or who sells or otherwise provides any designated substance or hazardous material to be used by a worker in respect of any occupation, project or work site;

  (aa.1)   "the regulations" means the regulations under section 40(1);

  (bb)   "worker" means a person engaged in an occupation;

  (cc)   "work site" means a location where a worker is, or is likely to be, engaged in any occupation and includes any vehicle or mobile equipment used by a worker in an occupation.

RSA 2000 cO-2 s1;2002 c31 s2

Obligations of employers, workers, etc.

2(1) Every employer shall ensure, as far as it is reasonably practicable for the employer to do so,

  (a)   the health and safety of

       (i)   workers engaged in the work of that employer, and

       (ii)   those workers not engaged in the work of that employer but present at the work site at which that work is being carried out, and

  (b)   that the workers engaged in the work of that employer are aware of their responsibilities and duties under this Act, the regulations and the adopted code.

(2) Every worker shall, while engaged in an occupation,

  (a)   take reasonable care to protect the health and safety of the worker and of other workers present while the worker is working, and

    (b)   co-operate with the worker's employer for the purposes of protecting the health and safety of

        (i)   the worker,

        (ii)   other workers engaged in the work of the employer, and

        (iii)   other workers not engaged in the work of that employer but present at the work site at which that work is being carried out.

(3) Every supplier shall ensure, as far as it is reasonably practicable for the supplier to do so, that any tool, appliance or equipment that the supplier supplies is in safe operating condition.

(4) Every supplier shall ensure that any tool, appliance, equipment, designated substance or hazardous material that the supplier supplies complies with this Act, the regulations and the adopted code.

(5) Every contractor who directs the activities of an employer involved in work at a work site shall ensure, as far as it is reasonably practicable to do so, that the employer complies with this Act, the regulations and the adopted code in respect of that work site.

RSA 2000 cO-2 s2;2002 c31 s3

Prime contractor

3(1) Every work site must have a prime contractor if there are 2 or more employers involved in work at the work site at the same time.

(2) The prime contractor for a work site is

    (a)   the contractor, employer or other person who enters into an agreement with the owner of the work site to be the prime contractor, or

    (b)   if no agreement has been made or if no agreement is in force, the owner of the work site.

(3) If a work site is required to have a prime contractor under subsection (1), the prime contractor shall ensure, as far as it is reasonably practicable to do so, that this Act and the regulations are complied with in respect of the work site.

(4) One of the ways in which a prime contractor of a work site may meet the obligation under subsection (3) is for the prime contractor to do everything that is reasonably practicable to establish and maintain a system or process that will ensure compliance with this Act and the regulations in respect of the work site.

1994 c43 s4

Multiple obligations

4(1) In this section, "function" means the function of prime contractor, contractor, employer, supplier or worker.

(2) If a person has 2 or more functions under this Act in respect of one work site, the person must meet the obligations of each function.

1994 c43 s4

Staff

5(1) In accordance with the *Public Service Act*, there may be appointed one or more Directors of Inspection, Directors of Medical Services, Directors of Occupational Hygiene, occupational health and safety officers and any other employees necessary for the administration of this Act.

(2) The Minister may, in writing, designate

    (a) any employee of the Government as a person who may perform all or part of the duties and responsibilities of a Director of Inspection, a Director of Occupational Hygiene or an officer, or

    (b) any physician employed by the Government or any other physician as a person who may perform all or part of the duties and responsibilities of a Director of Medical Services.

RSA 1980 cO-2 s3;RSA 1980 c15(Supp) s4;
1983 c39 ss4,19;1994 c43 s5

Occupational Health and Safety Council

6(1) There is to be a council called the "Occupational Health and Safety Council" that shall consist of not more than 12 persons appointed by the Lieutenant Governor in Council.

(2) The Minister may designate one of the members of the Council as chair and one or more of the members of the Council as vice-chairs.

(3) The members of the Council shall be appointed for terms not exceeding 3 years.

(4) On the expiration of a member's term of office, that member of the Council may be reappointed.

(5) The members of the Council shall be paid

    (a)   any remuneration that the Lieutenant Governor in Council may prescribe, and

    (b)   their reasonable travelling and living expenses while absent from their ordinary places of residence and in the course of their duties as members of the Council.

RSA 1980 cO-2 s4;1983 cL-10.1 s57

Duties of Council

7 The Council shall

    (a)   advise the Minister on matters concerning this Act, the regulations and the adopted codes and potential changes to them, and the regulations and on matters concerning the health and safety of workers;

    (b)   hear appeals in accordance with this Act;

    (c)   perform any duties and functions assigned to it by the Minister with respect to the administration of this Act, the regulations and the adopted codes.

RSA 2000 cO-2 s7;2002 c31 s4

Inspection

8(1) For the purposes of this Act, an officer may

    (a)   at any reasonable hour enter into or on any work site and inspect that work site;

    (b)   subject to subsection (2), require the production of any records, books, plans or other documents that relate to the health or safety of workers and may examine them, make copies of them or remove them temporarily for the purpose of making copies;

    (c)   inspect, seize or take samples of any material, product, tool, appliance or equipment being produced, used or found in or on the work site that is being inspected;

    (d)   make tests and take photographs or recordings in respect of any work site;

    (e)   interview and obtain statements from persons at the work site.

(2) Only a Director of Medical Services or a person authorized in writing by the Director may require the production of, or examine and make copies of, medical reports or records or remove them temporarily for the purpose of making copies.

(3) When an officer

    (a) removes any records, books, plans or other documents under subsection (1)(b), the officer shall

        (i) give to the person from whom those items were taken a receipt for them, and

        (ii) forthwith make copies of, take photographs of or otherwise record those items and forthwith return them to the person to whom the receipt was given,

  or

    (b) seizes or takes samples of any material, product, tool, appliance or equipment under subsection (1)(c), the officer shall

        (i) give to the person from whom those items were seized or taken a receipt for them, and

        (ii) on that person's request, return those items to that person when they have served the purposes for which they were seized or taken.

(4) If a person refuses to allow an officer to exercise any powers under subsection (1) or interferes or attempts to interfere with the officer in the exercise of those powers, a Director of Inspection may apply to the Court of Queen's Bench for an order restraining that person from preventing or interfering in any manner with the officer in the exercise of those powers.

(5) A statement given under this section is not admissible in evidence for any purpose in a trial, public inquiry under the *Fatality Inquiries Act* or other proceeding except to prove

    (a) non-compliance with this section, or

    (b) a contravention of section 41(3)

in an action or proceeding under this Act.

RSA 2000 cO-2 s8;2009 c53 s122

Order to remedy unhealthy or unsafe conditions

9(1) When an officer is of the opinion that work is being carried out in a manner that is unhealthy or unsafe to the workers engaged in the work or present where the work is being carried out, the officer may in writing order the person responsible for the work being carried out

(a) to stop the work that is specified in the order, and

(b) to take measures as specified in the order that are, in the opinion of the officer, necessary to ensure that the work will be carried out in a healthy and safe manner,

or either of them, within the time limits specified in the order.

(2) When an officer is of the opinion that a person is not complying with this Act, the regulations or the adopted code, the officer may in writing order that person to take such measures, within the time limits specified in the order, as the officer considers necessary to ensure such compliance and specifies in the order.

(3) Measures specified in the order referred to in subsection (2), where the order is made in respect of the failure by a person to comply with section 31(5) or 36, may require one or more of the following:

(a) that the disciplinary action cease;

(b) reinstatement of the worker to the worker's former employment under the same terms and conditions under which the worker was formerly employed;

(c) payment to the worker of money not more than the equivalent of wages that the worker would have earned if the worker had not been dismissed or had not received disciplinary action;

(d) removal of any reprimand or other reference to the matter from the worker's employment records.

(4) If the worker has worked elsewhere while the dismissal or disciplinary action has been in effect, those wages earned elsewhere shall be deducted from the amount payable to the worker under subsection (3)(c).

RSA 2000 cO-2 s9;2002 c31 s5

Danger to persons on work site

10(1) When an officer is of the opinion that a danger to the health or safety of a worker exists in respect of that worker's employment, the officer may at any time enter into or on any work site and do any or all of the following:

(a) order the work or any part of it that is taking place to be stopped forthwith;

    (b)   order any worker or other person present to leave the work site forthwith;

    (c)   in writing order the prime contractor, the contractor or the employer to take measures specified by the officer that the officer considers necessary for the purpose of removing the source of the danger or to protect any person from the danger.

(2) No person shall interfere with an officer in the performance of the officer's duties under this section.

(3) When requested to do so by an officer, a peace officer shall assist the officer in carrying out the officer's duties under this section.

RSA 1980 cO-2 s8;RSA 1980 c15(Supp) ss7,25;1994 c43 s6

Order stopping the use of unsafe tools, appliances, etc.

11(1) When an officer is of the opinion that a tool, appliance or equipment being used or that may be used by a worker

    (a)   is not in safe operating condition, or

    (b)   does not comply with the adopted code,

the officer may in writing order the worker to stop using or to refrain from using that tool, appliance or equipment.

(2) When an officer is of the opinion that a supplier is supplying a tool, appliance or equipment that

    (a)   is not in safe operating condition, or

    (b)   does not comply with the adopted code,

the officer may in writing order the supplier to stop supplying that tool, appliance or equipment for use by any worker.

(3) If an officer makes an order under this section, the officer may rescind that order on being satisfied that the tool, appliance or equipment in respect of which the order was made

    (a)   has been repaired or modified so that it is in safe operating condition, or

    (b)   has been made to comply with the adopted code,

as the case may be.

RSA 2000 cO-2 s11;2002 c31 s6

Improper storage and handling

12(1) When an officer is of the opinion that the storage, handling or use of a substance or material does not comply with the adopted code, the officer may in writing order the person responsible for the storage, handling or use of the substance or material to take the measures specified in the order that are, in the opinion of the officer, necessary to ensure that that code is complied with.

(2) When an officer is of the opinion that a supplier is supplying any substance or material that does not comply with the adopted code, the officer may in writing order the supplier to stop supplying that substance or material.

(3) If an officer makes an order under this section, the officer may in writing rescind that order on being satisfied that the material or substance is being supplied, stored, handled or used in compliance with the adopted code.

RSA 2000 cO-2 s12;2002 c31 s7

Licence

13(1) A licence may be issued in accordance with the regulations.

(2) A Director may, in accordance with the regulations, cancel or suspend a licence.

1983 c39 s7

Protection of workers on a project

14(1) When a person has begun or is about to begin a project and a Director of Inspection or a Director of Occupational Hygiene is of the opinion that the health and safety of any worker who is or will be present at the project is not being or will not be protected, a Director may in writing order that person to stop that project or to refrain from beginning that project, as the case may be.

(2) A Director of Inspection or a Director of Occupational Hygiene shall not rescind an order made under subsection (1) until the Director is satisfied that the person to whom the order was made has taken the measures that, in the opinion of a Director, will protect the health and safety of the workers concerned.

(3) A Director of Inspection or a Director of Occupational Hygiene may require any person who has begun or is about to begin a project to furnish to a Director, within the time specified by a Director, the plans, drawings and specifications that are reasonably necessary for determining whether the health and safety of the workers concerned is being or will be protected.

RSA 1980 cO-2 s10;RSA 1980 c15(Supp) s10;1983 c39 ss19,20

New project

15 A person who intends to begin a new project may be required to file notice in accordance with the regulations.

1983 c39 s8;1988 c36 s15

Appeal

16(1) A person

(a) to whom an order is issued under section 9, 10, 11, 12, 14, 25 or 33, or

(b) whose licence has been cancelled or suspended,

may appeal the order, cancellation or suspension to the Council.

(2) An appeal under subsection (1) shall be commenced by serving a notice of the appeal on a Director of Inspection within 30 days from the date that the order being appealed from was served on the person making the appeal.

(3) After considering the matter being appealed, the Council may by order

(a) confirm, revoke or vary the order being appealed,

(b) confirm the cancellation or suspension,

(c) reinstate the cancelled licence, certificate or permit,

(d) substitute a suspension for a cancellation, or

(e) remove or vary a suspension.

(4) When an appeal is made to the Council under subsection (1), the Council shall hear the appeal and render a decision as soon as practicable.

(5) An appeal lies to the Court of Queen's Bench from an order of the Council on a question of law or a question of jurisdiction and on hearing the matter the Court may make any order, including the awarding of costs, that the Court considers proper.

(6) An appeal under subsection (5) shall be made by way of application within 30 days from the date that the order of the Council is served on the person appealing the order of the Council.

(7) When an appeal is commenced under subsection (1), the commencement of that appeal does not operate as a stay of the order, cancellation or suspension being appealed from except insofar as the chair or a vice-chair of the Council so directs.

(8) When an appeal is commenced under subsection (5), the commencement of that appeal does not operate as a stay of the order of the Council being appealed from except insofar as a judge of the Court of Queen's Bench so directs.

RSA 2000 cO-2 s16;2009 c53 s122

Hearing of appeal

17(1) When the Council hears appeals under this Act, it may, at the direction of the chair, sit in one or more divisions and the divisions may sit simultaneously or at different times.

(2) For the purpose of hearing appeals under this Act, 3 members constitute a quorum of the Council or of a division of the Council.

(3) A division of the Council may exercise and perform all the jurisdiction, powers and duties of the Council with respect to the hearing of appeals under this Act and an order of a division is an order of the Council and binds all members of the Council.

(4) The chair may designate a member of a division of the Council to preside at any sitting of a division at which the chair is not present.

(5) When the Council or a division of the Council is hearing an appeal and one or more members of the Council or division, as the case may be, do not for any reason attend on any day or part of a day, the remaining members present may, if they constitute a quorum under this section, exercise and perform all the jurisdiction, powers and duties of the Council with respect to that hearing.

(6) A decision of a majority of the members of the Council or a division of the Council present and constituting a quorum is the decision of the Council or of the division and in the event that there is a tie vote the chair or the presiding member, as the case may be, may cast a 2nd vote.

(7) The Council may establish rules of procedure respecting the hearing of appeals before it or before a division.

RSA 1980 cO-2 s12;1988 c36 s4

Serious injuries and accidents

18(1) If an injury or accident described in subsection (2) occurs at a work site, the prime contractor or, if there is no prime contractor, the contractor or employer responsible for that work site shall notify a Director of Inspection of the time, place and nature of the injury or accident as soon as possible.

(2) The injuries and accidents to be reported under subsection (1) are

(a) an injury or accident that results in death,

(b) an injury or accident that results in a worker's being admitted to a hospital for more than 2 days,

(c) an unplanned or uncontrolled explosion, fire or flood that causes a serious injury or that has the potential of causing a serious injury,

(d) the collapse or upset of a crane, derrick or hoist, or

(e) the collapse or failure of any component of a building or structure necessary for the structural integrity of the building or structure.

(3) If an injury or accident referred to in subsection (2) occurs at a work site or if any other serious injury or any other accident that has the potential of causing serious injury to a person occurs at a work site, the prime contractor or, if there is no prime contractor, the contractor or employer responsible for that work site shall

(a) carry out an investigation into the circumstances surrounding the serious injury or accident,

(b) prepare a report outlining the circumstances of the serious injury or accident and the corrective action, if any, undertaken to prevent a recurrence of the serious injury or accident, and

(c) ensure that a copy of the report is readily available for inspection by an officer.

(4) The prime contractor, contractor or employer who prepared the report referred to in subsection (3) shall retain the report for 2 years after the serious injury or accident.

(5) A report prepared under this section is not admissible as evidence for any purpose in a trial arising out of the serious injury or accident, an investigation or public inquiry under the *Fatality Inquiries Act* or any other action as defined in the *Alberta Evidence Act* except in a prosecution for perjury or for the giving of contradictory evidence.

(6) Except as otherwise directed by a Director of Inspection, an occupational health and safety officer or a peace officer, a person shall not disturb the scene of an accident reported under subsection (1) except insofar as is necessary in

(a) attending to persons injured or killed,

(b) preventing further injuries, and

(c) protecting property that is endangered as a result of the accident.

RSA 1980 cO-2 s13;RSA 1980 c15(Supp) s12;
1983 c39 ss10,19;1994 c43 s7

Investigation of accident

19(1) If an accident occurs at a work site, an officer may attend at the scene of the accident and may make any inquiries that the officer considers necessary to determine the cause of the accident and the circumstances relating to the accident.

(2) Every person present at an accident when it occurred or who has information relating to the accident shall, on the request of an officer, provide to the officer any information respecting the accident that the officer requests.

(3) An officer may, for the purposes of determining the cause of the accident, seize or take samples of any substance, material, product, tool, appliance or equipment that was present at, involved in or related to the accident.

(4) If an officer seizes or takes samples of any substance, material, product, tool, appliance or equipment under subsection (3), the officer shall

(a) give to the person from whom those items were seized or taken a receipt for those items, and

(b) on that person's request, return those items to that person when those items have served the purposes for which they were seized or taken.

(5) Any statement given under this section is not admissible in evidence for any purpose in a trial, public inquiry under the *Fatality Inquiries Act* or other proceeding except to prove

(a) non-compliance with this section, or

(b) a contravention of section 41(3)

in an action or proceeding under this Act.

(6) A peace officer may assist an officer in carrying out the officer's duties under this section if the officer so requests.

RSA 1980 cO-2 s14;RSA 1980 c15(Supp) s13

Medical examination

20(1) A Director of Medical Services may, for the purposes of determining

(a) the extent of any injury suffered by a worker injured in an accident that occurred in respect of that worker's occupation, or

(b) whether a worker is suffering from an occupational disease that is related to that worker's occupation,

require that worker to be medically examined by a Director of Medical Services or by the worker's physician.

(2) The employer shall pay for a medical examination of a worker under subsection (1).

RSA 1980 cO-2 s15;1983 c39 ss19,20;1988 c36 s5

Time of medical examination

21(1) A medical examination carried out under section 20 shall, when practicable, be performed during the normal hours of employment of the worker being examined.

(2) When a worker examined under section 20

(a) is examined during the worker's normal hours of employment, or

(b) spends time in going to or returning from that examination during the worker's normal hours of employment,

the employer of that worker shall not deduct from that worker any wages, salary or other remuneration or benefits that that worker would have received for working during those normal hours of employment that were spent by that worker in being examined or going to or returning from that examination.

RSA 1980 cO-2 s16

Notice of findings

22 When a physician, in the course of the physician's practice as a physician, finds that a person examined by the physician is affected with or is suffering from a notifiable disease, the physician shall, within 7 days after the diagnosis of that disease, notify a Director of Medical Services in writing of the name, address and place of employment of that person and the name of the notifiable disease.

RSA 1980 cO-2 s17;RSA 1980 c15(Supp) s14;1983 c39 s19

Medical report

23(1) A physician who performs or supervises a medical examination of a worker as required under this Act, the regulations or the adopted code shall, on the request of a Director of Medical Services, furnish any medical reports that a Director may require.

(2) A physician, nurse or first aid attendant who attends a worker who became ill or was injured while engaged in an occupation shall, on the request of a Director of Medical Services, furnish any reports that a Director may require.

RSA 2000 cO-2 s23;2002 c31 s8

Hazards

24(1) If a worker is employed in a hazardous occupation or at a hazardous work site, a Director of Medical Services may

(a) require that the worker's employer shall, within 30 days after the commencement of the worker's employment, register with a Director the worker's name and the location of the work site where the worker is employed,

(b) require the worker to have regular medical examinations,

(c) prescribe the type and frequency of the medical examinations,

(d) prescribe the form and content of medical records to be compiled with respect to that worker, and

(e) prescribe the period of time for which those medical records must be maintained.

(2) When a person registered under subsection (1) terminates the person's employment with the person's employer, the employer shall notify a Director of Medical Services of that termination within 30 days after that termination.

(3) The employer shall pay for medical examinations of a worker under subsection (1).

RSA 1980 cO-2 s19;RSA 1980 c15(Supp) s16;1983 c39 s19;1988 c36 s7

Regular inspection of work sites

25 A Director may, by written order,

(a) require a prime contractor, a contractor or an employer involved in work at a work site to regularly inspect the work site for occupational hazards, and

(b) prescribe the manner, methods and procedures or any of them to be used for carrying out those inspections.

RSA 1980 cO-2 s20;RSA 1980 c15(Supp) s18;1994 c43 s8

Agreements re research and educational programs

26   The Minister may enter into an agreement with any person or government for the purpose of

(a)   carrying out research respecting the health and safety of workers;

(b)   establishing and operating training programs respecting the health and safety of workers;

(c)   establishing and operating programs to train persons in first aid and emergency medical services;

(d)   establishing and operating educational programs respecting the health and safety of workers.

RSA 1980 cO-2 s21

Consultants

27(1)   The Minister may engage the services of experts or persons having special technical or other knowledge to advise the Minister or to inquire into and report to the Minister on matters respecting the health and safety of workers.

(2)   A person whose services are engaged under subsection (1) shall

(a)   be paid any remuneration that the Minister prescribes, and

(b)   be paid the person's reasonable travelling and living expenses while absent from the person's ordinary place of residence and in the course of providing the person's services to the Minister.

RSA 1980 cO-2 s22

Exchange of information

28   The Minister may enter into agreements with The Workers' Compensation Board governing the exchange between the Minister and The Workers' Compensation Board of

(a)   any information or reports respecting any or all of the following:

(i)   any accidents or injuries that occur at work sites;

(ii)   any occupational diseases;

(iii)   any measures taken by prime contractors, contractors or employers to protect the health and safety of workers;

      (iv) any matter concerning the operations of prime contractors, contractors or employers;

and

(b) any statistical information respecting any or all of the following:

      (i) accidents or injuries occurring at work sites;

      (ii) occupational diseases;

      (iii) assessments made by the Board under the *Workers' Compensation Act* and the cost of claims made under that Act.

RSA 1980 cO-2 s23;1994 c43 s9

Publication of information about employers

28.1 The Minister may, in order to enhance the protection of workers and the prevention of work site injuries by encouraging good and discouraging bad work site safety records,

(a) establish indices and measurements of work site injury prevention,

(b) maintain a register consisting of the names of employers and their performance, as determined by the Minister, in relation to those indices and measurements,

(c) publish, or authorize a department or agency of the Government or any other entity to publish, the information contained in that register, and

(d) collect any information needed for that register from another public body that provides the information to the Minister.

2002 c31 s9

Report on designated substances

29(1) If any designated substance is used, stored or manufactured at or on a work site, the person responsible for that work site shall compile a written report with respect to that designated substance containing the information and in the form prescribed by a Director of Occupational Hygiene.

(2) When a person compiles written information under subsection (1), the person shall maintain that information on the work site in a location that is readily accessible to the workers and to other persons who are at that work site.

(3) When a person compiles written information under subsection (1), that person shall, on the request of a Director of Occupational Hygiene, furnish a Director with copies of that written information.

RSA 1980 cO-2 s24;RSA 1980 c15(Supp) s19;1983 c39 s19

Controlled product

30 If a controlled product is used, stored, handled or manufactured at a work site, the prime contractor or, if there is no prime contractor, the contractor or employer responsible for that work site shall ensure that

    (a)   the controlled product is labelled in accordance with the adopted code,

    (b)   a material safety data sheet for the controlled product, containing the information required by the adopted code, is made readily available to workers at the work site, and

    (c)   a worker who works with a controlled product or in proximity to a controlled product receives education, instruction or training with respect to the controlled product in accordance with the adopted code.

RSA 2000 cO-2 s30;2002 c31 s10

Joint work site health and safety committees

31(1) The Minister may, by order, require that there be established at any work site a joint work site health and safety committee that shall

    (a)   identify situations that may be unhealthy or unsafe in respect of the work site,

    (b)   make recommendations to prime contractors, contractors, employers and workers for the improvement of the health and safety of workers at or on the work site,

    (c)   establish and maintain educational programs regarding the health and safety of workers at or on the work site, and

    (d)   carry out those duties and functions provided for by the adopted code.

(2) A joint work site health and safety committee shall consist of workers who represent the workers at the work site and persons who represent the prime contractor, contractors and employers involved in work at the work site.

(3) The number of persons on a joint work site health and safety committee who represent the prime contractor, contractors and employers shall not exceed in total the number of workers on the committee who represent the workers at the work site.

(4) A joint work site health and safety committee shall hold its meetings and carry out its duties and functions during normal working hours.

(5) No disciplinary action shall be taken against a member of a joint work site health and safety committee by reason of that member performing duties and functions as a member of that committee.

RSA 2000 cO-2 s31;2002 c31 s11

Written health and safety policies

32 A prime contractor, contractor or employer, if required by or under the regulations or the adopted code, shall

    (a)   state that person's policy in writing for the protection and maintenance of the health and safety of that person's workers on the work site,

    (b)   state the arrangements to implement that policy, and

    (c)   as far as is reasonably practicable, inform that person's workers of the policy.

RSA 2000 cO-2 s32;2002 c31 s12

Code of practice

33(1) A prime contractor, contractor or employer involved in work at a work site may be required

    (a)   by a written order of a Director, or

    (b)   by the regulations or the adopted code

to establish a code of practice and to supply copies of it to a Director.

(2) A code of practice shall include practical guidance on the requirements of the regulations or the adopted code applicable to the work site, safe working procedures in respect of the work site and other matters as required by a Director, the regulations or the adopted code.

(3) A prime contractor, contractor or employer who establishes a code of practice pursuant to subsection (1) shall ensure that

    (a)   a copy of the code of practice is readily available to the workers and other persons at the work site, and

    (b)   all workers to whom the code of practice applies receive appropriate education, instruction or training with respect to the code so that they are able to comply with its requirements.

(4) A Director may from time to time require that the code of practice be revised.

RSA 2000 cO-2 s33;2002 c31 s13

Acceptances

34(1) A Director may, in accordance with the regulations, issue in writing an acceptance to a prime contractor, contractor or employer if, in the Director's opinion, an alternative tool, appliance, equipment, work process, first aid service or first aid supplies or equipment at a work site provides equal or greater protection than that provided for by the regulations or the adopted code to persons affected by the tool, appliance, equipment, work process, first aid service or first aid supplies or equipment.

(2) A Director may impose terms and conditions the Director considers necessary on the acceptance and those terms and conditions are part of the acceptance.

(3) An acceptance is in effect only during the period prescribed in it and, notwithstanding anything in this Act, the regulations or the adopted code, during that period the terms, conditions or requirements set out in it apply with respect to the tool, appliance, equipment or work process at the work site to which the acceptance applies.

(4) A prime contractor, contractor or employer who is issued an acceptance shall ensure that the acceptance is complied with.

(5) The *Regulations Act* does not apply to an acceptance issued by a Director.

RSA 2000 cO-2 s34;2002 c31 s14

Existence of imminent danger

35(1) No worker shall

    (a)   carry out any work if, on reasonable and probable grounds, the worker believes that there exists an imminent danger to the health or safety of that worker,

    (b)   carry out any work if, on reasonable and probable grounds, the worker believes that it will cause to exist an imminent danger to the health or safety of that worker or another worker present at the work site, or

    (c)   operate any tool, appliance or equipment if, on reasonable and probable grounds, the worker believes that it will cause to exist an imminent danger to the health or safety of that worker or another worker present at the work site.

(2) In this section, "imminent danger" means in relation to any occupation

    (a)   a danger that is not normal for that occupation, or

    (b)   a danger under which a person engaged in that occupation would not normally carry out the person's work.

(3) A worker who

    (a)   refuses to carry out work, or

    (b)   refuses to operate a tool, appliance or equipment

pursuant to subsection (1) shall, as soon as practicable, notify the worker's employer at the work site of the worker's refusal and the reason for the worker's refusal.

(4) On being notified under subsection (3), the employer shall

    (a)   investigate and take action to eliminate the imminent danger,

    (b)   ensure that no worker is assigned to use or operate the tool, appliance or equipment or to perform the work for which a worker has made a notification under subsection (3), unless

        (i)   the worker to be so assigned is not exposed to imminent danger, or

        (ii)   the imminent danger has been eliminated,

    (c)   prepare a written record of the worker's notification, the investigation and action taken, and

    (d)   give the worker who gave the notification a copy of the record described in clause (c).

(5) The employer may require a worker who has given notification under subsection (3) to remain at the work site and may assign the worker temporarily to other work assignments that the worker is reasonably capable of performing.

(6) A temporary assignment under subsection (5), if there is no loss in pay, is not disciplinary action for the purposes of section 36.

(7) If a worker who receives a record under subsection (4)(d) is of the opinion that an imminent danger still exists, the worker may file a complaint with an officer.

(8) An officer who receives a complaint under subsection (7) shall prepare a written record of the worker's complaint, the investigation and the action taken and shall give the worker and the employer a copy of the record.

(9) A worker or an employer who receives a record under subsection (8) may request a review of the matter by the Council by serving a notice of appeal on a Director of Inspection within 30 days from the date of receipt of the record.

(10) After considering the matter, the Council may by order

(a) dismiss the request for a review, or

(b) require the employer to eliminate the imminent danger.

(11) An appeal lies to the Court of Queen's Bench from an order of the Council on a question of law or a question of jurisdiction and on hearing the matter the Court may make any order, including the awarding of costs, that the Court considers proper.

(12) An appeal under subsection (11) shall be made by way of application within 30 days from the date that the order of the Council is served on the person appealing the order of the Council.

(13) The commencement of an appeal under subsection (11) does not operate as a stay of the order of the Council being appealed from except insofar as a judge of the Court of Queen's Bench so directs.

RSA 2000 cO-2 s35;2009 c53 s122

Where disciplinary action prohibited

36 No person shall dismiss or take any other disciplinary action against a worker by reason of that worker acting in compliance with this Act, the regulations, the adopted code or an order given under this Act or the regulations.

RSA 2000 cO-2 s36;2002 c31 s15

Disciplinary action complaint

37(1) A worker who has reasonable cause to believe that the worker has been dismissed or subjected to disciplinary action in contravention of section 31(5) or 36 may file a complaint with an officer.

(2) An officer who receives a complaint under subsection (1) shall prepare a written record of the worker's complaint, the investigation and the action taken and shall give the worker and the employer a copy of the record.

(3) A worker or an employer who receives a record under subsection (2) may request a review of the matter by the Council by serving a notice of appeal on a Director of Inspection within 30 days from the receipt of the record.

(4) After considering the matter, the Council may by order

    (a)   dismiss the request for a review, or

    (b)   require one or more of the following:

        (i)   reinstatement of the worker to the worker's former employment under the same terms and conditions under which the worker was formerly employed;

        (ii)   cessation of disciplinary action;

        (iii)   payment to the worker of money not more than the equivalent of wages that the worker would have earned if the worker had not been dismissed or had not received disciplinary action;

        (iv)   removal of any reprimand or other reference to the matter from the worker's employment records.

(5) If the worker has worked elsewhere while the dismissal or disciplinary action has been in effect, those wages earned elsewhere shall be deducted from the amount payable to the worker under subsection (4)(b)(iii).

(6) An appeal lies to the Court of Queen's Bench from an order of the Council on a question of law or a question of jurisdiction and on hearing the matter the Court may make any order, including the awarding of costs, that the Court considers proper.

(7) An appeal under subsection (6) shall be made by way of application within 30 days from the date that the order of the Council is served on the person appealing the order of the Council.

(8) The commencement of an appeal under subsection (6) does not operate as a stay of the order of the Council being appealed from except insofar as a judge of the Court of Queen's Bench so directs.

RSA 2000 cO-2 s37;2009 c53 s122

Board of inquiry

38(1) The Minister may, when the Minister considers it in the public interest to do so, by order appoint a board of inquiry of one or more persons to inquire into

(a) any matter concerning the health or safety of workers employed

(i) at a particular work site or at several work sites,

(ii) by a particular employer or by a group of employers, or

(iii) in an industry,

or

(b) the circumstances surrounding and the causes of an accident.

(2) A person appointed to a board of inquiry under this section has all the powers of a commissioner appointed under the *Public Inquiries Act*.

RSA 1980 cO-2 s29

Administration costs

39(1) For the purpose of defraying part of the costs of administering this Act,

(a) the Minister shall, if authorized by the regulations, make assessments on employers, or

(b) The Workers' Compensation Board shall, if an agreement is entered into under subsection (2)(b), pay to the Crown amounts that may be prescribed by the Lieutenant Governor in Council.

(2) The Minister and The Workers' Compensation Board may enter into an agreement under which the Board is required to either

(a) collect on behalf of the Crown in right of Alberta assessments made on employers by the Minister, or

(b) pay to the Crown amounts that may be prescribed by the Lieutenant Governor in Council.

RSA 2000 cO-2 s39;2006 c23 s59

Lieutenant Governor in Council regulations

40(1) The Lieutenant Governor in Council may make regulations

(a) establishing general health and safety rules for or in connection with occupations and work sites, including

    (i) reporting, medical and health requirements, and

    (ii) the making available of notices issued by a Director and of orders made under, and other information and documents required by, this Act or the regulations;

(b) providing for any matter or thing which by this Act may or is to be provided for by the regulations;

(c) respecting the establishment, composition and operation of a board dealing with first aid training;

(d) respecting licences and licensing, including qualifications to obtain and hold licences and the maintenance of a registry of licensees;

(e) specifying which work sites are mines or quarries for the purposes of this Act;

(f) respecting fees

    (i) to be paid by the Government to physicians for services performed, and

    (ii) for licences and for services and materials provided

    under this Act, the regulations and the adopted codes;

(g) respecting acceptances referred to in section 34;

(h) establishing and otherwise respecting a system of fixed fines or penalties for contraventions of this Act, the regulations and any adopted code, including mechanisms for administering and enforcing that system and the disposition of the fines or penalties collected under the system;

(i) authorizing the making of orders relating to any matters falling within the scope of clauses (a), (d) or (g) or section 40.1(1)(a);

(j) enabling any particular subject-matter covered by clause (a) to be dealt with by an adopted code.

(2) If regulations are made under subsection (1)(h), those regulations operate notwithstanding anything in the *Financial Administration Act.*

RSA 2000 cO-2 s40;2002 c31 s16

Ministerial orders and codes

40.1(1) The Council may make a code of rules (in this section referred to as an "OHS code")

 (a) respecting specific health and safety matters for or in connection with occupations and work sites, including

  (i) reporting requirements and the maintenance and preservation of documents reported,

  (ii) medical and health requirements,

  (iii) joint work site health and safety committees,

  (iv) the making available of codes of practice and other information and documents required by an adopted code, and

  (v) the instruction, supervision and qualifications of specified persons,

 (b) providing for the prevalence of specified provisions of an adopted code over other specified provisions of an adopted code, and

 (c) providing for any matter or thing which by this Act or the regulations may or is to be provided for by an adopted code.

(2) The Minister may, after consulting with such representatives of employers and of workers in the industries that will be affected by the code as the Minister considers appropriate, make an order adopting any code that is lawfully made by the Council under subsection (1).

(3) An OHS code may itself adopt or incorporate another specific code (in this section referred to as a "secondary code") or part of a secondary code, as that secondary code or part exists as at a particular time, dealing with health and safety matters that are within the Council's jurisdiction under subsection (1).

(4) To avoid doubt, an adopted code is an enactment for the purposes of construing the *Provincial Offences Procedure Act*.

(5) The Minister shall ensure that each adopted code is adequately published in such form as the Minister considers will make it reasonably available, at no expense or at reasonable expense, to all those likely to be affected by it.

(6) To avoid doubt, the *Interpretation Act* applies with respect to an OHS code.

(7) Except to the extent that an OHS code otherwise provides, where there is any conflict between any provisions in an OHS code and any provisions in a secondary code, the former prevail against the latter.

2002 c31 s16

Provisions affecting the regulations and adopted codes

40.2(1) Any provision of the regulations or an adopted code may be made to apply generally or to a particular occupation, work site, prime contractor, owner, employer, contractor, supplier or worker or any class of any such category.

(2) Except to the extent that the regulations otherwise provide, where there is any conflict between any provisions in the regulations and any provisions in an adopted code, the former prevail against the latter.

2002 c31 s16

Offences

41(1) A person who contravenes this Act, the regulations or an adopted code or fails to comply with an order made under this Act or the regulations or an acceptance issued under this Act is guilty of an offence and liable

    (a)   for a first offence,

        (i)   to a fine of not more than $500 000 and in the case of a continuing offence, to a further fine of not more than $30 000 for each day during which the offence continues after the first day or part of a day, or

        (ii)   to imprisonment for a term not exceeding 6 months,

    or to both fines and imprisonment, and

    (b)   for a 2nd or subsequent offence,

        (i)   to a fine of not more than $1 000 000 and in the case of a continuing offence, to a further fine of not more than $60 000 for each day or part of a day during which the offence continues after the first day, or

        (ii)   to imprisonment for a term not exceeding 12 months,

    or to both fines and imprisonment.

(2) Notwithstanding subsection (1), a person who fails to comply with an order made under section 10 or as varied under section 16 is guilty of an offence and liable to a fine of not more than

$1 000 000 or imprisonment for a term not exceeding 12 months or to both fine and imprisonment.

(3) A person who knowingly makes any false statement or knowingly gives false information to an officer or a peace officer engaged in an inspection or investigation under section 8 or 19 is guilty of an offence and liable to a fine of not more than $1000 or to imprisonment for a term not exceeding 6 months or to both fine and imprisonment.

(4) A prosecution under this Act may be commenced within 2 years after the commission of the alleged offence, but not afterwards.

RSA 2000 cO-2 s41;2002 c31 s17

Additional powers of court to make directions

41.1(1) Where a person is convicted of an offence against this Act, in addition or as an alternative to taking any other action provided for in this Act, the court may, having regard to the nature of the offence and the circumstances surrounding its commission, make an order directing the person

    (a)   to establish or to revise

         (i)   the policy referred to in section 32(a) and arrangements referred to in section 32(b), or

        (ii)   a training or educational program regarding the health or safety of workers at the work site,

    (b)   to take specific action to improve health and safety at work sites, or

    (c)   to take any other action specified in the regulations.

(2) The order may contain any substance or conditions that the court considers appropriate.

2002 c31 s18

Enforcement of compliance with order

42 When

    (a)   an order has been made under this Act or the regulations by a Director of Inspection, a Director of Medical Services, a Director of Occupational Hygiene, an officer or the Council, and

    (b)   the person to whom that order has been made is carrying on the work without complying with that order, a Director of Inspection may, notwithstanding that the person to whom the order was made may or may not have been prosecuted under this Act for not complying with that order, apply to the Court of Queen's Bench for an order of the Court requiring that person to comply with the order made by a Director of Inspection, a Director of Medical Services, a Director of Occupational Hygiene, an officer or the Council, as the case may be.

RSA 2000 cO-2 s42;2009 c53 s122

Awarding of costs

43 On an application under section 8(4), 42 or 44, the Court may make any award as to costs that it considers proper.

RSA 1980 cO-2 s34

Service of orders

44(1) When an order is made in writing under this Act or the regulations, that order shall be served

(a) by personal service on the person to whom it is made,

(b) by double registered mail if the post office receipt for the envelope containing the order is signed by the person to whom the order is made, or

(c) as directed by the Court of Queen's Bench on application.

(2) An application under subsection (1)(c) may be made ex parte if the Court considers it proper to do so.

(3) When an order is made orally under section 10(1)(a) or (b), that order is deemed to have been served on the person to whom it is made at the time that the oral order is made to that person.

RSA 2000 cO-2 s44;2009 c53 s122

Grants

45(1) The Minister may make grants if

(a) the Minister is authorized to do so by regulations under this section, and

(b) there is authority available in a supply vote for the purpose for which the grant is to be made.

(2) The Lieutenant Governor in Council may make regulations

(a) authorizing the Minister to make grants;

(b) prescribing the purposes for which grants may be made;

(c) governing applications for grants;

(d) prescribing the persons or organizations or classes of persons or organizations eligible for grants;

(e) specifying the conditions required to be met by any applicant for a grant to render that person eligible for the grant;

(f) prescribing the conditions on which a grant is made and requiring the repayment of it to the Government if the conditions are not met;

(g) providing for the payment of any grant in a lump sum or by instalments and prescribing the time or times at which the grant or the instalments may be paid;

(h) limiting the amount of any grant or class of grant that may be made;

(i) authorizing the Minister to delegate in writing to any employee of the Government any duty, power or function respecting the payment of any grant;

(j) requiring any person receiving a grant to account for the way in which the grant is spent in whole or in part;

(k) authorizing the Minister to enter into an agreement with respect to any matter relating to the payment of a grant.

(3) Any regulation made under subsection (2) may be specific or general in its application.

RSA 1980 cO-2 s36

Act binds Crown

46 The Crown is bound by this Act.

RSA 1980 cO-2 s37

Transitional – regulations

47(1) Notwithstanding section 16 of the *Occupational Health and Safety Amendment Act, 2002* but subject to anything to the contrary in the regulations under section 40(1), any regulation under this Act, as that regulation existed immediately before the commencement of that section, continues in force until it is repealed under this section, and that regulation may be repealed by

(a) an order under section 40.1 dealing with code provisions that deal with subject-matters dealt with by that regulation, or

(b)   the regulations,

as the case may be.

(2) Notwithstanding section 1(aa.1), a regulation continued by subsection (1), while still in force, is included in the term "the regulations" so far as it is not inconsistent with the regulations under section 40(1).

2002 c31 s19

Province of Alberta

OCCUPATIONAL HEALTH AND SAFETY ACT

OCCUPATIONAL HEALTH AND SAFETY REGULATION

Alberta Regulation 62/2003

With amendments up to and including Alberta Regulation 284/2009

Office Consolidation

© Published by Alberta Queen's Printer

Alberta Queen's Printer
5th Floor, Park Plaza
10611 - 98 Avenue
Edmonton, AB T5K 2P7
Phone: 780-427-4952
Fax: 780-452-0668

E-mail: qp@gov.ab.ca
Shop on-line at www.qp.alberta.ca

(Consolidated up to 284/2009)

ALBERTA REGULATION 62/2003

Occupational Health and Safety Act

OCCUPATIONAL HEALTH AND SAFETY REGULATION

Table of Contents

Part 3
Transitional, Coming Into Force and Expiry

Definitions

1 In this Regulation,

(a) "acceptance" means an acceptance issued under section 34 of the Act;

(b) "Act" means the *Occupational Health and Safety Act*;

(c) "asbestos" includes all forms of asbestos;

(d) "blaster's permit" means a permit referred to in section 17;

(e) "blasting area", except at a mine site, means the area extending at least 50 metres in all directions from any place in which explosives are being prepared, fired or destroyed or in which armed charges are known or believed to exist;

(f) "coal dust" means dust that

    (i) results from the mining, transporting or processing of coal,

    (ii) is of a pure or mixed carboniferous, mineralogical composition, and

    (iii) contains 10% or less of free silica calculated by weight;

(g) "competent" in relation to a worker, means adequately qualified, suitably trained and with sufficient experience to safely perform work without supervision or with only a minimal degree of supervision;

(h) "direct supervision" means under the supervision of a competent worker who is

    (i) personally and visually supervising the other worker, and

    (ii) able to communicate readily and clearly with the other worker;

(i) "equipment" means a thing used to equip workers at a work site and includes tools, supplies, machinery and sanitary facilities;

(j) "explosive" means a chemical compound or mixture that by fire, friction, impact, percussion or detonation, may cause a sudden release of gases at a pressure capable of producing destructive effects to adjacent objects or of killing or injuring a person;

(k) "harmful substance" means a substance that, because of its properties, application or presence, creates or could create a danger, including a chemical or biological hazard, to the health and safety of a worker exposed to it;

(l) "lead" includes inorganic and organic compounds of lead;

(m) "mine" means a working, other than a drill hole made while exploring for a mineral, from which coal, metals, precious or semi-precious minerals, industrial minerals, oil sands or any other material could be extracted, whether commercially or otherwise;

(n) "mine site" means a location at which a facility for extracting a mineral by underground, strip, open pit or quarry operations exists or is to be developed, and includes

(i)   a mineral processing plant, storage facility or discard disposal facility that exists or is to be developed in connection with a mine, and

(ii) all connected access roads;

(o)   "mining certificate" means a certificate issued under Part 2;

(p)   "restricted area" means an area of a work site where there is a reasonable chance that the airborne concentration of asbestos, silica, coal dust or lead exceeds the occupational exposure limit under an adopted code;

(q)   "silica" means crystalline silicon dioxide, including quartz, cristobalite, tridymite and tripoli;

(r)   "surface mine" means a mine worked by strip mining, open pit mining or other surface method, including auger mining;

(s)   "underground mine" means a mine other than a surface mine.

Part 1
General

Controlled product

2 For the purposes of section 1(c) of the Act, a product, material or substance specified by the *Controlled Products Regulations* made pursuant to paragraph 15(1)(a) of the *Hazardous Products Act* (Canada) to be included in any of the classes listed in Schedule II to the *Hazardous Products Act* (Canada) is designated as a controlled product.

Hazardous material

3 For the purposes of section 1(l) of the Act, an explosive is designated as a hazardous material.

Hazardous occupation

4 For the purposes of section 1(m) of the Act, the occupation of a person who works with asbestos, silica, coal dust or lead is designated as a hazardous occupation.

Hazardous work site

5 For the purposes of section 1(n) of the Act, a restricted area and a blasting area are each designated as a hazardous work site.

Notifiable diseases

6 The following diseases are notifiable diseases for the purpose of section 22 of the Act:

  (a) asbestosis;

  (b) mesothelioma;

  (c) asbestos-induced lung cancer;

  (d) asbestos-induced laryngeal cancer;

  (e) asbestos-induced gastrointestinal cancer;

  (f) coal worker's pneumoconiosis;

  (g) silicosis;

  (h) lead poisoning; and

  (i) noise-induced hearing loss.

Availability of specifications

7(1) If the Act, a regulation or an adopted code requires work to be done in accordance with a manufacturer's specifications or specifications certified by a professional engineer, an employer must ensure that

  (a) the workers responsible for the work are familiar with the specifications, and

  (b) the specifications are readily available to the workers responsible for the work.

(2) If the Act, a regulation or an adopted code refers to a manufacturer's or employer's specifications or specifications certified by a professional engineer, an employer must ensure that, during the period of time that the matters referred to in the specifications are in use, a legible copy of the specifications is readily available to workers affected by them.

(3) An employer must ensure that the original of the document setting out manufacturer's or employer's specifications or specifications certified by a professional engineer is available in Alberta for inspection by an officer.

Critical documents available

8(1) If an employer is required to make a report or a plan under the Act, it must be in writing and available to the workers at the work site affected by it.

(2) If an employer is required to develop procedures or to put procedures in place under the Act, the procedures must be in writing and available to the workers at the work site affected by them.

Posting orders and notices

9(1) An employer must post a copy of the following at a work site:

   (a)   an order made under the Act that is relevant to the work site;

   (b)   a health and safety notice prepared by or for a Director concerning conditions or procedures at the work site.

(2) The employer must post the copy at a conspicuous place at the work site as soon as the employer receives it.

(3) The employer must keep an order under the Act posted until the conditions specified in the order are met.

(4) Despite subsections (1) to (3), if the work site is mobile and posting is impracticable, the employer must ensure that the information in the order or the notice is brought to the attention of all workers at the work site.

Acceptance

10(1) An application for an acceptance must provide the specific details about the alternative tool, appliance, equipment, work process or first aid service, supplies or equipment that a Director needs to determine if the alternative gives workers equal or greater protection than the original requirement.

(2) An employer must ensure that a copy or a record of an acceptance that applies at a work site is

   (a)   posted at the work site,

   (b)   if applicable, secured to or kept with the equipment to which the acceptance applies, or

   (c)   otherwise communicated to the workers who may be affected by the acceptance.

Notice to a Director

11   If a regulation or an adopted code requires a person to give notice to a Director, the person must use the quickest practical means of communication available.

Equipment

12(1)   An employer must ensure that all equipment used at a work site

(a)   is maintained in a condition that will not compromise the health or safety of workers using or transporting it,

(b)   will safely perform the function for which it is intended or was designed,

(c)   is of adequate strength for its purpose, and

(d)   is free from obvious defects.

(2)   If a worker is required under the Act to use or wear specific equipment, the employer must ensure that the worker uses or wears the equipment at the work site.

General protection of workers

13(1)   If work is to be done that may endanger a worker, the employer must ensure that the work is done

(a)   by a worker who is competent to do the work, or

(b)   by a worker who is working under the direct supervision of a worker who is competent to do the work.

(2)   An employer who develops or implements a procedure or other measure respecting the work at a work site must ensure that all workers who are affected by the procedure or measure are familiar with it before the work is begun.

(3)   An employer must ensure that workers who may be required to use safety equipment or protective equipment are competent in the application, care, use, maintenance and limitations of that equipment.

(4)   If a regulation or an adopted code imposes a duty on a worker, the worker's employer must ensure that the worker performs that duty.

Duties of workers

14(1) A worker who is not competent to perform work that may endanger the worker or others must not perform the work except under the direct supervision of a worker who is competent to perform the work.

(2) A worker must immediately report to the employer equipment that

(a)   is in a condition that will compromise the health or safety of workers using or transporting it,

(b)   will not perform the function for which it is intended or was designed,

(c)   is not strong enough for its purpose, or

(d)   has an obvious defect.

(3) If a regulation or an adopted code imposes a duty on a worker,

(a)   the duty must be treated as applying to circumstances and things that are within the worker's area of occupational responsibility, and

(b)   the worker must perform that duty.

Safety training

15(1) An employer must ensure that a worker is trained in the safe operation of the equipment the worker is required to operate.

(2) An employer must ensure that the training referred to in subsection (1) includes the following:

(a)   the selection of the appropriate equipment;

(b)   the limitations of the equipment;

(c)   an operator's pre-use inspection;

(d)   the use of the equipment;

(e)   the operator skills required by the manufacturer's specifications for the equipment;

(f)   the basic mechanical and maintenance requirements of the equipment;

(g)   loading and unloading the equipment if doing so is a job requirement;

(h)   the hazards specific to the operation of the equipment at the work site.

(3) If a worker may be exposed to a harmful substance at a work site, an employer must

(a)   establish procedures that minimize the worker's exposure to the harmful substance, and

(b)   ensure that a worker who may be exposed to the harmful substance

(i)   is trained in the procedures,

(ii)   applies the training, and

(iii)   is informed of the health hazards associated with exposure to the harmful substance.

(4) A worker must participate in the training provided by an employer.

(5) A worker must apply the training referred to in subsections (1) and (3).

Joint First Aid Training Standards Board

16   If the Minister establishes a Joint First Aid Training Standards Board under section 7 of the *Government Organization Act*, the Board must include members representative of each of the 4 national first aid training standard setting agencies.

Part 2
Permits and Certificates

Blaster's Permits

Issue of blaster's permit

17(1) A worker who handles, prepares, fires, burns or destroys an explosive must hold a blaster's permit issued for that specific type of blasting operation as stated on the permit.

(2) A blaster's permit may be issued by

(a)   a Director of Inspection, or

(b)   an organization that is authorized by a Director of Inspection.

(3) A worker may apply for a blaster's permit in a form approved by a Director of Inspection.

(4) An applicant for a blaster's permit must

    (a)   have successfully completed a course and examination acceptable to the Director of Inspection,

    (b)   have qualifications acceptable to the Director of Inspection,

    (c)   provide the Director of Inspection with written proof that the applicant

        (i)   has, within the previous 36 months, at least 6 months experience in handling, preparing, firing, burning or destroying explosives as a blaster or an assistant to a blaster, and

        (ii)   is, in the opinion of the applicant's employer, competent to carry out the blasting operation,

    or

    (d)   satisfy a Director of Inspection that the applicant holds valid and current documentation from an equivalent certifying authority in another jurisdiction of Canada that is a blaster's permit in that jurisdiction or that is recognized by that Director as the equivalent in that jurisdiction of a blaster's permit issuable under this section.

(5) A Director of Inspection may issue a blaster's permit if the applicant

    (a)   is 18 years of age or older, and

    (b)   complies with subsection (4).

AR 62/2003 s17;284/2009

Expiry

18 A blaster's permit expires 5 years from its date of issue.

Suspension, cancellation

19(1) A Director of Inspection may suspend or cancel a blaster's permit if the holder

    (a)   contravenes the Act, the regulations or an adopted code,

(b) is or was the holder of a permit from another jurisdiction of the same type as the blaster's permit and that permit is suspended or cancelled, or

(c) provided false information to obtain, or assist others to obtain, a blaster's permit.

(2) If a Director of Inspection suspends or cancels a blaster's permit, the suspension or cancellation applies only to the handling, preparation, firing, burning and destruction of explosives in Alberta.

(3) If a Director of Inspection suspends or cancels a blaster's permit issued by an organization referred to in section 17(2)(b), the Director of Inspection must notify the organization of the suspension or cancellation.

(4) A Director of Inspection who suspends or cancels a blaster's permit must give written reasons for the suspension or cancellation to the worker and the worker's employer.

(5) The holder of a blaster's permit must surrender it immediately to a Director of Inspection if it is suspended or cancelled.

Effect at work site

20 If a Director of Inspection suspends or cancels a blaster's permit held by a worker at a work site where explosives are used, all other blaster's permits held by workers at the same work site are suspended until the employer gives the Director proof in writing acceptable to the Director that action has been taken to correct the conditions that led to the initial suspension or cancellation.

Employer records of blaster permits

21 An employer must ensure that a current list of the blasters employed by the employer, listing each blaster's name, the issuer of the permit, permit number and permit expiry date is maintained and readily available for reference by an officer.

Amendment of permit

22(1) A Director of Inspection may amend a blaster's permit.

(2) If a holder of a blaster's permit applies to a Director of Inspection to amend the terms of the blaster's permit to include the experimental use of explosives not otherwise covered by the blaster's permit, the application must include a description of the experimental use including

(a) the explosive to be used,

(b)   the detonator and method of detonation,

(c)   details of the transportation, handling, preparation and loading of the explosives and detonators,

(d)   the name of the supervisor in charge of the operation,

(e)   the name of the blaster, blaster's permit number and the issuer of the permit, and

(f)   any other information a Director of Inspection requires.

Possession of blaster's permit

23 The holder of a blaster's permit must have the original, valid blaster's permit at the work site while a blasting operation is in progress.

Board of Examiners for Mining

Board of Examiners continued

24(1) The Board of Examiners is continued and consists of a Director of Inspection and members appointed by the Minister from the following groups:

(a)   workers who do not perform managerial functions, have at least 5 years of underground mining experience and are currently employed at an underground coal mine;

(b)   workers who perform managerial functions at an underground mine and are the holders of underground coal mine manager's certificates issued under this Part;

(c)   consultants, academics or training professionals who have underground coal mining experience;

(d)   other groups of persons.

(2) The Director is the chair of the Board of Examiners.

(3) The appointment of a person to the Board of Examiners must be for a term set by the Minister.

(4) The fees and expenses payable to a person serving on the Board of Examiners must be in an amount determined by the Minister.

(5) The chair and at least one half of the number of appointed members constitute a quorum of the Board.

Duties

25(1) The Board of Examiners must

(a) determine the eligibility and qualification requirements for candidates applying for a mining certificate,

(b) conduct examinations of candidates seeking mining certificates, and

(c) recommend to a Director of Inspection the candidates to whom a mining certificate should be issued.

(2) The Board of Examiners may recommend to a Director of Inspection that a mining certificate be issued to a candidate who holds a similar document granted by another jurisdiction if the Board is satisfied that the standard of training and examination required to receive that document is equivalent to that required for the issuance of the mining certificate.

Mining Certificates

Underground mine blaster's certificate

26(1) A worker who handles, prepares, fires, burns or destroys an explosive or handles misfires at an underground mine site must hold an underground mine blaster's certificate issued by a Director of Inspection.

(2) A worker may apply for an underground mine blaster's certificate in a form approved by a Director of Inspection.

(3) An applicant for an underground mine blaster's certificate must

(a) either

(i) have not less than 3 years' experience in underground mining,

(ii) produce written evidence of having received adequate instruction and training in underground mine blasting by a worker competent in underground mine blasting, and

(iii) satisfy a Director that the applicant is competent to hold an underground mine blaster's certificate,

or

(b) satisfy a Director of Inspection that the applicant holds valid and current documentation from an equivalent certifying authority in another jurisdiction of Canada that is an underground mine blaster's certificate in that jurisdiction or that is recognized by that Director as the equivalent in that jurisdiction of an underground mine blaster's certificate issuable under this section.

(4) A Director of Inspection may issue an underground mine blaster's certificate to a worker who complies with this section.

AR 62/2003 s26;284/2009

Surface mine blaster's certificate

27(1) A worker who handles, prepares, fires, burns or destroys an explosive or handles misfires at a surface mine site must hold a surface mine blaster's certificate issued by a Director of Inspection.

(2) A worker may apply for a surface mine blaster's certificate in a form approved by a Director of Inspection.

(3) An applicant for a surface mine blaster's certificate must

  (a) either

      (i) have not less than 3 years' experience in surface mining,

      (ii) produce written evidence of having received adequate instruction and training in surface mine blasting by a worker competent in surface mine blasting, and

      (iii) satisfy a Director that the applicant is competent to hold a surface mine blaster's certificate,

    or

  (b) satisfy a Director of Inspection that the applicant holds valid and current documentation from an equivalent certifying authority in another jurisdiction of Canada that is a surface mine blaster's certificate in that jurisdiction or that is recognized by that Director as the equivalent in that jurisdiction of a surface mine blaster's certificate issuable under this section.

(4) A Director of Inspection may issue a surface mine blaster's certificate to a worker who complies with this section.

AR 62/2003 s27;284/2009

Certificate expires

28 An underground or surface mine blaster's certificate expires 5 years from its date of issue.

Suspension, cancellation

29(1) An officer may suspend a surface or underground mine blaster's certificate if the officer has reason to believe that the holder of the mine blaster's certificate

(a) has contravened the Act, the regulations or an adopted code, or

(b) has otherwise used explosives, detonators or equipment in a manner that constitutes a hazard to the holder or other workers.

(2) A mine blaster's certificate may be

(a) suspended by an officer for a period of up to 72 hours, or

(b) suspended by a Director of Inspection for any period of time.

(3) A Director of Inspection may cancel a surface or underground mine blaster's certificate if the Director of Inspection has reason to believe that the holder of the mine blaster's certificate

(a) has contravened the Act, the regulations or an adopted code, or

(b) has otherwise used explosives, detonators or equipment in a manner that constitutes a hazard to the holder or other workers.

(4) The person who suspends or cancels a mine blaster's certificate must give written reasons for the suspension or cancellation to the worker and the worker's employer.

(5) If a mine blaster's certificate is suspended or cancelled, the worker named in the certificate must, on request, surrender it to an officer.

Underground coal mine manager's certificate

30(1) A person may apply in a form approved by a Director of Inspection for an underground coal mine manager's certificate.

(2) A Director of Inspection may issue an underground coal mine manager's certificate to a worker who complies with subsections (3) and (4) or subsection (5).

(3) An applicant must have

    (a)   first aid certification approved under an adopted code and training and knowledge in underground mine rescue procedures, or

    (b)   other training and experience in first aid and underground mine rescue acceptable to the Board of Examiners.

(4) An applicant must

    (a)   be a graduate in mining engineering from a university or college recognized by the Board of Examiners and have experience in underground coal mining totalling not less than 5 years, including one year in work at the working face, or

    (b)   have 10 years of experience in underground coal mining, including 2 years of work at the working face.

(5) Notwithstanding subsections (3) and (4), an applicant is eligible to be issued an underground coal mine manager's certificate if that applicant satisfies a Director of Inspection that the applicant holds valid and current documentation from an equivalent certifying authority in another jurisdiction of Canada that is an underground coal mine manager's certificate in that jurisdiction or that is recognized by that Director as the equivalent in that jurisdiction of an underground coal mine manager's certificate issuable under this section.

AR 62/2003 s30;284/2009

Underground coal mine foreman's certificate

31(1) A person may apply in a form approved by a Director of Inspection for an underground coal mine foreman's certificate.

(2) A Director of Inspection may issue an underground coal mine foreman's certificate to a worker

    (a)   with experience totalling not less than 5 years in an underground coal mine, including one year of working at the working face or its equivalent,

    (b)   who is knowledgeable about blasting procedures,

    (c)   who holds a standard first aider certificate from a training agency, and

    (d)   who has

        (i)   training and qualifications in underground mine rescue procedures, or

(ii)   other training and experience acceptable to the Board of Examiners

or who satisfies a Director of Inspection that the worker holds valid and current documentation from an equivalent certifying authority in another jurisdiction of Canada that is an underground coal mine foreman's certificate in that jurisdiction or that is recognized by that Director as the equivalent in that jurisdiction of an underground coal mine foreman's certificate issuable under this section.

(3) For the purposes of this section, "training agency" means a person or organization that enters into an agreement to deliver first aid training with the Director of Medical Services under the Act.
AR 62/2003 s31;284/2009

Underground coal mine electrical super-intendent's certificate

32(1) A person may apply in a form approved by a Director of Inspection for an underground coal mine electrical superintendent's certificate.

(2) A Director of Inspection may issue an underground coal mine electrical superintendent's certificate to

(a)   a worker who is a graduate in electrical engineering from a university or college recognized by the Board of Examiners and has experience in underground mining totalling at least 2 years,

(b)   a worker who holds a trade certificate in the trade of electrician under the *Apprenticeship and Industry Training Act* or a certificate in the trade of electrician issued by another jurisdiction in Canada bearing an interprovincial standards red seal and has

(i)   3 years of electrical experience in underground coal mining or its equivalent, or

(ii)   4 years of electrical experience, including one year in underground coal mining,

(c)   a worker who has other training and experience acceptable to the Board of Examiners, or

(d)   a worker who satisfies a Director of Inspection that the worker holds valid and current documentation from an equivalent certifying authority in another jurisdiction of Canada that is an underground coal mine electrical superintendent's certificate in that jurisdiction or that is recognized by that Director as the equivalent in that jurisdiction of an underground coal mine electrical superintendent's certificate issuable under this section.

AR 62/2003 s32;284/2009

Expiry and suspension

33(1) The holder of an underground coal mine manager's certificate, an underground coal mine foreman's certificate or an underground coal mine electrical superintendent's certificate must demonstrate, every 5 years to the satisfaction of the Board of Examiners, the holder's knowledge of the Act, the regulations and adopted codes as they relate to mines.

(2) If the holder of an underground coal mine manager's certificate, an underground coal mine foreman's certificate or an underground coal mine electrical superintendent's certificate does not satisfy the Board of Examiners under subsection (1), a Director of Inspection may suspend the certificate until the Board is satisfied.

Provisional certificates

34(1) A Director of Inspection may grant a provisional certificate to a worker who

(a) applies for a mining certificate under this Part,

(b) is qualified to apply for an examination for that mining certificate, and

(c) satisfies the Director regarding the worker's knowledge of the Act, regulations and adopted codes as they apply to the type of mining certificate applied for.

(2) A provisional certificate

(a) is valid for a period of not more than 18 months from the date of its issue,

(b) is subject to cancellation at any time by a Director of Inspection, and

(c) is valid only at the mine specified on the certificate.

(3) A provisional certificate cannot be renewed after the expiry date unless the holder satisfies a Director of Inspection that

(a) the worker is progressing through a course of study to the satisfaction of the Director, or

    (b)   the worker was unable, because of exceptional circumstances, to be present at the scheduled examination referred to in subsection (1)(b) related to the certification.

Fees

Blaster's permit

35 The fee to apply for a blaster's permit

    (a)   is $50, or

    (b)   is $75 if the applicant requests that the application be processed by a Director of Inspection in one work day.

Mining certificates

36(1) The fee to apply for a provisional certificate is $10.

(2) The fee for the issue of a provisional certificate is $50.

(3) The application fee to sit for or challenge an examination listed in this section is $50.

(4) If an application is accepted by a Director of Inspection, the following fees to sit and write an examination are payable:

    (a)   underground coal mine manager's certificate

(i)	Paper 1 - Legislation	$100
(ii)	Paper 2 - Gases, Shot Firing and Explosives	$150
(iii)	Paper 3 - Ventilation - Theory and Practice	$150
(iv)	Paper 4 - Practical	$150
(v)	Paper 5 - Machinery	$150
(vi)	Paper 6 - Surveying, Levelling and Geology	$150

    (b)   underground coal mine foreman's certificate

(i)	Paper 1 - Legislation	$100
(ii)	Paper 2 - Practical	$150

    (c)   underground coal mine electrical superintendent's certificate

Paper 1 - Legislation and Practical $200

(d)   mine blaster's certificate

Paper 1 - Legislation and Practical $100

Part 3
Transitional, Coming into Force and Expiry

Transitional

37(1) A blaster's permit issued under the *Explosives Safety Regulation* (AR 272/76) to a worker by a Director of Inspection before this section comes into force continues as a valid blaster's permit issued under this Regulation and with the same terms and conditions and the same expiry date.

(2) A mining certificate issued under the *Mines Safety Regulation* (AR 292/95) to a worker issued before this Regulation comes into force continues as a valid mining certificate issued under this Regulation and with the same terms and conditions and the same expiry date.

(3) An acceptance issued under the Act that has a term affected by a change under the Act continues with the same terms and conditions.

38 *(This section amends the Mines Safety Regulation (AR 292/95); the amendments have been incorporated into that Regulation.)*

Coming into force

39 This Regulation comes into force on March 31, 2003.

Expiry

40 For the purpose of ensuring that this Regulation is reviewed for ongoing relevancy and necessity, with the option that it may be repassed in its present or an amended form following a review, this Regulation expires on March 31, 2013.

Province of Alberta

OCCUPATIONAL HEALTH AND SAFETY ACT

FARMING AND RANCHING EXEMPTION REGULATION

Alberta Regulation 27/1995

With amendments up to and including Alberta Regulation 251/2001

Office Consolidation

© Published by Alberta Queen's Printer

Alberta Queen's Printer
5th Floor, Park Plaza
10611 - 98 Avenue
Edmonton, AB T5K 2P7
Phone: 780-427-4952
Fax: 780-452-0668

E-mail: qp@gov.ab.ca
Shop on-line at www.qp.alberta.ca

Copyright and Permission Statement

Note

ALBERTA REGULATION 27/95

Occupational Health and Safety Act

FARMING AND RANCHING EXEMPTION REGULATION

Purpose

1 This Regulation is made for the purposes of section 1(s) of the *Occupational Health and Safety Act* to specify the farming and ranching operations that are excluded from the definition of "occupation" under the Act.

AR 27/95 s1;251/2001

Excluded operations

2 The farming and ranching operations that are excluded are the operations that are directly or indirectly involved in the following:

    (a)   the production of crops, including fruits and vegetables, through the cultivation of land;

    (b)   the raising and maintenance of animals or birds;

    (c)   the keeping of bees.

Included operations

3 Despite section 2, the following operations are included in the definition of "occupation" under the Act:

    (a)   operations involved in the processing of food or other products from the operations referred to in section 2;

    (b)   the operation of greenhouses, mushroom farms, nurseries, or sod farms;

    (c)   operations involved in landscaping;

    (d)   operations involved in the raising or boarding of pets.

This page is intentionally blank.

Province of Alberta

OCCUPATIONAL HEALTH AND
SAFETY ACT

OCCUPATIONAL HEALTH AND SAFETY CODE

2009

ALBERTA

Official copies of the *Occupational Health and Safety Code* are available in print from:

Alberta Queen's Printer
5th Floor, Park Plaza
10611 - 98 Avenue NW
Edmonton, AB T5K 2P7
Phone: 780-427-4952   Fax: 780-452-0668
www.qp.alberta.ca

For the purpose of retaining the section numbers of this Code,
those sections which are no longer required and which have
been removed are indicated as **"repealed".**

Table of Contents

Requirements Applicable to Specific Industries and Activities

Schedules

Occupational Health and Safety Act
Occupational Health and Safety Code
Core Requirements Applicable to All Industries
Part 1   Definitions and General Application

Definitions

1   In this Code,

A

"abate" means to encapsulate, enclose or remove asbestos-containing material;

"abnormal audiogram" means an audiogram that indicates

(a) the threshold in either ear is more than 25 dB at 500, 1000 or 2000 Hz,

(b) the threshold in either ear is more than 60 dB at 3000, 4000 or 6000 Hz, or

(c) there is one-sided hearing loss with the difference in hearing threshold level between the better and the poorer ear exceeding the average of 30 dB at 3000, 4000 and 6000 Hz;

"abnormal shift" means a threshold shift, in either ear, of 15 dB at two consecutive test frequencies from 1000 Hz up to and including 6000 Hz when compared to the baseline test;

"acceptance" means an acceptance issued under section 34 of the *Act*;

"Act" means the Occupational Health and Safety Act;

"actively transmitting" with respect to radiofrequency transmitters includes being set to "on" or "standby" mode;

"actuated fastening tool" means a tool that uses a pneumatic, hydraulic, explosive or electric source of energy to bring about its action;

"acute illness or injury" means a physical injury or sudden occurrence of an illness that results in the need for immediate care;

"advanced first aider" means an Emergency Medical Responder, Emergency Medical Technician, nurse or other person who holds a certificate in advanced first aid from an approved training agency;

"aerial device" means a telescoping or articulating unit used for positioning a personnel basket, bucket, platform or other device at an elevated work location;

"all-terrain vehicle" means a wheeled or tracked motor vehicle designed primarily for travel on unprepared surfaces such as open country and marshland, but does not include a snow vehicle, or farming, ranching or construction machinery;

"anchor" means an engineered component for coupling a fall arrest or travel restraint system to an anchorage;

"anchorage" means a structure, or part of a structure, that is capable of safely withstanding any potential forces applied by a fall protection system;

"ANSI" means American National Standards Institute;

"API" means American Petroleum Institute;

"approved to" means that the product bears the approval or certification mark of a nationally accredited third-party testing organization, certifying that the product complies with the referenced standard;

"approved training agency" means a person or organization that enters into an agreement with the Director of Medical Services under section 177;

"asbestos waste" means material that is discarded because there is a reasonable chance that asbestos might be released from it and become airborne, including protective clothing that is contaminated with asbestos;

"ASME" means American Society of Mechanical Engineers;

"ASSE" means American Society of Safety Engineers;

"ASTM" means American Society for Testing and Materials;

"audiometer" means a device meeting the specifications of an audiometer described in ANSI Standard S3.6-2004, *Specification for Audiometers*;

"audiometric technician" means a person who has passed an audiometric technician course approved by the Director of Medical Services, or has been approved by the Director of Medical Services as having the equivalent of an approved audiometric technician course and who, in either case, has passed a requalification examination when requested to do so by the Director of Medical Services;

"authorized worker" in sections 562 to 569 means a competent worker authorized by the employer to install, change or repair electrical equipment;

"AWG" means, with respect to electrical conductors, American Wire Gauge;

B

"biohazardous material" means a pathogenic organism, including a bloodborne pathogen, that, because of its known or reasonably believed ability to cause disease in humans, would be classified as Risk Group 2, 3 or 4 as defined by the Public Health Agency of Canada, or any material contaminated with such an organism;

"blaster" means a worker who holds a valid blaster's permit issued under the *Occupational Health and Safety Regulation*;

"blasting area" means the location at which explosives are being prepared, fired or destroyed or in which armed charges are known or believed to exist, and, except at a mine site, extends at least 50 metres in all directions from the location;

"blasting machine" means a portable device used to initiate detonation;

"blasting mat" means a heavy mat made of woven rope, steel wire or chain, or improvised from other material, placed over loaded holes to prevent earth, rock and debris from being thrown in the air by the detonated explosive;

"boatswain's chair" means a seat that is suspended from ropes, from which one person works on the side of a building;

"body belt" means a body support consisting of a strap with a means for securing it about the waist and attaching it to other components;

"boom" means the part of a structure that is attached to a crane or lifting device superstructure and used to support the upper end of the hoisting tackle;

"boom truck" means a truck that is equipped with a hydraulically driven structure or device that

(a) is mounted on a turret that is secured to a truck,

(b) is supported to provide stability, and

(c) is equipped with a boom that

(i) is telescoping or articulating, and

(ii) can swing or hoist or raise and lower its load;

"bootleg" means that portion of a drill hole or borehole that

(a) is not destroyed after an explosive charge is detonated in it, and

(b) may or may not contain explosives;

"BSI" means British Standards Institute;

"building shaft" means an enclosed vertical opening in a building or structure extending to two or more floors or levels, including an elevator, a ventilation shaft, a stairwell or a service shaft;

"bulk shipment" with respect to a controlled product means a shipment of the controlled product that is contained, without intermediate packaging, in

(a) a vessel with a water volume of more than 454 litres,

(b) a freight container, a road vehicle, a railway vehicle, a portable tank, a freight container carried on a road or railway vehicle, ship or aircraft or a portable tank carried on a road vehicle or railway vehicle, ship or aircraft,

(c) the hold of a ship, or

(d) a pipeline;

"buried facility" means anything buried or constructed below ground level respecting electricity, communications, water, sewage, oil, gas or other substances including, but not limited to, the pipes, conduits, ducts, cables, wires, valves, manholes, catch basins and attachments to them;

C

"Canadian Electrical Code" means CSA Standard C22.1-06, *Canadian Electrical Code, Part 1, Safety Standard for Electrical Installations;*

"CANMET" means the Canadian Explosives Atmospheres Laboratory, Canadian Centre for Mineral and Energy Technology, Natural Resources Canada;

"cantilever hoist" means a hoist in which the car travels on rails that may be an integral part of a vertical mast and on a vertical plane out-board from the mast;

"carabiner" means a connecting component that

(a) generally consists of a trapezoidal or oval body with a self-locking gate that requires at least two consecutive, deliberate actions to open to permit the body to receive an object and that, when released, automatically closes and locks to prevent unintentional opening, and

(b) has an ultimate tensile strength of at least 22.2 kilonewtons;

"CEN" means European Committee for Standardization;

"certified by a professional engineer" means stamped and signed by a professional engineer as described in section 14;

"CGSB" means Canadian General Standards Board;

"chimney hoist" means a hoist used to lift workers, materials or equipment during the construction of a chimney;

"claim for disclosure exemption" means a claim filed under section 408;

"climbable structure' means an engineered or architectural work where the primary method of accessing the structure is by climbing the structure with the principle means of support being the climber's hands and feet;

"close work site" means a work site that is not more than 20 minutes travel time from a health care facility, under normal travel conditions using available means of transportation;

"combustible dust" means a dust that can create an explosive atmosphere when it is suspended in air in ignitable concentrations;

"combustible liquid" means a liquid that has a flash point at or above 37.8°C, as determined by using the methods described in the *Alberta Fire Code* (1997);

"combined operation" in Part 36 means surface and underground mining activity at the same mine site, whether or not the mine material is being extracted from one or more connected or unconnected seams;

"combined ventilation system" in Part 36 means a combination of an exhausting and a forcing ventilation system used in headings to maximize turbulence at the face;

"competent" in relation to a person, means adequately qualified, suitably trained and with sufficient experience to safely perform work without supervision or with only a minimal degree of supervision;

"concrete pump truck" in Part 19 means powered mobile equipment that is comprised of a concrete pump, a distribution boom or mast, delivery pipes and the equipment on which they are mounted;

"confined space" means a restricted space which may become hazardous to a worker entering it because of

    (a)   an atmosphere that is or may be injurious by reason of oxygen deficiency or enrichment, flammability, explosivity, or toxicity,

    (b)   a condition or changing set of circumstances within the space that presents a potential for injury or illness, or

    (c)   the potential or inherent characteristics of an activity which can produce adverse or harmful consequences within the space;

"consultation" means direct and meaningful involvement;

"container" means a bag, barrel, bottle, box, can, cylinder, drum, storage tank or similar package or receptacle;

"contaminant" means a chemical, biological or radiological material in a concentration that will likely endanger the health and safety of a worker if it is inhaled, ingested or absorbed;

"contaminated" means affected by the presence of a harmful substance on workers or at the work site in a quantity sufficient to pose a risk to health;

"contaminated environment" means a work site that contains or may contain a contaminant;

"control system isolating device" means a device that physically prevents activation of a system used for remotely controlling the operation of equipment;

"control zone" means the area within 2 metres of an unguarded edge of a level, elevated work surface that has a slope of no more than 4 degrees;

"controlled product" means a product, material or substance specified by the regulations made under paragraph 15(1)(a) of the *Hazardous Products Act* (Canada) as being included in any of the classes listed in Schedule II to the *Hazardous Products Act* (Canada);

"cow's tail" in Part 41 means a short strap, lanyard or sling connected to the main attachment point of a harness;

"CPSC" means Consumer Products Safety Commission;

"crane" means equipment that is designed to lift loads, lower loads, and move loads horizontally when they are lifted;

"CSA" means Canadian Standards Association;

D

"3 decibel exchange rate" means that when the sound energy doubles, the decibel level increases by three;

"dBA" means a measure of sound level in decibels using a reference sound pressure of 20 micropascals when measured on the A-weighting network of a sound level meter;

"demolition" means the tearing down, destruction, breaking up or razing of the whole or part of a building or structure;

"designated signaller" means a person designated to give signals in accordance with section 191;

"detonator" means a blasting detonator, an electric blasting detonator or a similar device used to detonate explosives;

"detonator leg wire" means an electric wire attached to a detonator;

"detonating cord" means a cord containing explosives of sufficient strength to detonate other explosives;

"Director" in Part 36 means the Director of Inspection whose duties include mines;

"direct supervision" means that a competent worker

    (a) is personally and visually supervising the worker who is not competent, and

    (b) is able to communicate readily and clearly with the worker who is not competent;

"discard" means solid or liquid material that is removed or rejected during mining or processing operations because it has no current use, but that may be of future use;

"distant work site" means a work site that is more than 20 minutes but less than 40 minutes travel time from a health care facility, under normal travel conditions using available means of transportation;

E

"electric blasting detonator" means a shell containing a charge of detonating compound designed to be fired by an electric current;

"electric utility" has the meaning assigned to it by the *Electric Utilities Act*;

"electromagnetic radiation" includes radiation used or found in association with

    (a)   broadcasting,

    (b)   mobile communications systems,

    (c)   remote control signal stations,

    (d)   television and radio transmitters,

    (e)   industrial radiofrequency heaters,

    (f)   equipment used for geophysical surveys,

    (g)   radar,

    (h)   atmospheric electrical storms, and

    (i)   cellular telephone systems;

"emergency first aider" means a person who holds a certificate in emergency first aid from an approved training agency;

"Emergency Medical Responder" means an Emergency Medical Responder under the *Emergency Medical Technicians Regulation* (AR 48/93);

"Emergency Medical Technician" means an Emergency Medical Technician under the *Emergency Medical Technicians Regulation* (AR 48/93);

"Emergency Medical Technician-Paramedic (EMT-P)" means an Emergency Medical Technician-Paramedic under the *Emergency Medical Technicians Regulation* (AR 48/93);

"emergency response plan" means the emergency response plan required under Part 7;

"employer member" means a person appointed to a joint work site health and safety committee under section 197;

"equipment" means a thing used to equip workers at a work site and includes tools, supplies, machinery, instruments and sanitary facilities;

"excavation" in Part 32 means a dug out area of ground but does not include a tunnel, underground shaft or open pit mine;

"excess noise" means noise that exceeds the limits specified in section 218;

"explosive" means a chemical compound or mixture that by fire, friction, impact, percussion or detonation may cause a sudden release of gases at a pressure capable of producing destructive effects to adjacent objects or of killing or injuring a person;

"explosive atmosphere" means an atmosphere that

    (a)   contains a substance in a mixture with air, under atmospheric conditions and at a concentration between the substance's lower explosive limit and upper explosive limit, and

    (b)   is capable of producing destructive effects to adjacent objects or of killing or injuring a person;

"exposed worker" means a worker who may reasonably be expected to work in a restricted area at least 30 work days in a 12-month period:

F

"fall arresting device" means a part of a worker's personal protective equipment that stops the worker's fall and does not allow the worker to fall farther;

"fall protection system" means

(a) a personal fall arrest system,

(b) a travel restraint system,

(c) fabric or netting panels intended for leading edge protection,

(d) a safety net,

(e) a control zone,

(f) use of procedures in place of fall protection equipment, or

(g) another system approved by a Director of Inspection;

"fall restrict equipment" means a component of a fall restrict system that, when combined with other subcomponents and elements, allows the climber of a wood pole to remain at his or her work position with both hands free, and that performs a limited fall arrest function when the climber loses contact between his or her spurs and the pole;

"fall restrict system" means a combination of a work positioning system and fall restrict equipment;

"fibre" means a particulate material with

(a) a diameter equal to or less than 3 micrometres,

(b) a length equal to or greater than 5 micrometres, and

(c) a length to diameter ratio equal to or greater than 3 to 1;

"first aid" means the immediate and temporary care given to an injured or ill person at a work site using available equipment, supplies, facilities or services, including treatment to sustain life, to prevent a condition from becoming worse or to promote recovery;

"first aider" means an emergency first aider, standard first aider or advanced first aider designated by an employer to provide first aid to workers at a work site;

"fixed ladder" means a ladder that is permanently fixed to a supporting structure in a vertical position or at an angle of not more than 15 degrees from vertical and that does not lean back;

"flammable liquid" means a liquid with

(a) a flash point below 37.8°C, and

(b) a vapour pressure of not more than 275.8 kilopascals (absolute), as determined by ASTM Standard D323-06, *Standard Test Method for Vapour Pressure of Petroleum Products (Reid Method);*

"flammable substance" means

(a) a flammable gas or liquid,

(b) the vapour of a flammable or combustible liquid,

(c) dust that can create an explosive atmosphere when suspended in air in ignitable concentrations, or

(d) ignitable fibres;

"flash point" means the minimum temperature at which a liquid in a container gives off vapour in sufficient concentration to form an ignitable mixture with air near the surface of the liquid, as determined by using the methods described in the *Alberta Fire Code* (1997);

"fly form deck panel" means a temporary supporting structure used as a modular falsework that is intended to be, and capable of being, moved from floor to floor and re-used during a construction project;

"free fall distance" means the vertical distance between the point from which a worker falls to the point at which deceleration begins because of the action of a personal fall arrest system;

"fugitive emission" means a substance that leaks or escapes from process equipment, a container, emission control equipment or a product;

"full body harness" means a body support consisting of connected straps designed to distribute force over at least the thighs, shoulders and pelvis, to which a lanyard or lifeline or connecting component can be attached;

G

"gob" means an area of a mine from which coal has been extracted and the roof allowed to cave in;

"grinder accessory" means an abrasive wheel, cutting disc, wire wheel, buffing or polishing disc, or other similar product;

"GVW" means the manufacturer's rated gross vehicle weight;

H

"hand expose zone" means the strip of land

    (a) 1 metre wide on each side of the locate marks for a buried facility other than a high pressure pipeline, or

    (b) 5 metres wide on each side of the locate marks for a high pressure pipeline;

"hand tool" means hand-held equipment that depends on the energy of the worker for its direct effect and does not have a pneumatic, hydraulic, electrical or chemical energy source for its operation;

"handling" with respect to explosives includes preparing, loading, firing, burning or destroying explosives or detonators;

"harmful substance" means a substance that, because of its properties, application or presence, creates or could create a danger, including a chemical or biological hazard, to the health and safety of a worker exposed to it;

"hazard" means a situation, condition or thing that may be dangerous to the safety or health of workers;

"hazard assessment" means an assessment made in accordance with sections 7 or 21;

"hazard information" means information on the correct and safe use, storage, handling and manufacture of a controlled product, including information relating to its toxicological properties;

"hazardous energy" in Part 15 means electrical, mechanical, hydraulic, pneumatic, chemical, nuclear, thermal, gravitational, or any other form of energy that could cause injury due to the unintended motion, energizing, start-up or release of such stored or residual energy in machinery, equipment, piping, pipelines or process systems;

"hazardous location" in Part 10 means a place where fire or explosion hazards may exist due to flammable gases or vapours, flammable or combustible liquids, combustible dust or ignitable fibres or flyings, as described in the *Canadian Electrical Code*;

"hazardous waste" means a controlled product that is intended for disposal, or is sold for recycling or recovery;

"health care facility" means a hospital, medical clinic or physician's office that can dispense emergency medical treatment during the time the workers are at the work site;

"heavy duty scaffold" means a scaffold that

  (a) is designed to support the equivalent of an evenly distributed load of more than 122 kilograms per square metre but not more than 367 kilograms per square metre, and

  (b) has planks with a span of not more than 2.3 metres;

"high hazard work" means work described in Schedule 2, Table 2;

"high pressure pipeline" means a pipeline operating at a pressure of 700 kilopascals or greater;

"hoist" means equipment that is designed to lift and lower loads;

"horizontal lifeline system" means a system composed of a synthetic or wire rope, secured horizontally between 2 or more anchor points, to which a worker attaches a personal fall arrest system or travel restraint system;

"hot tap" means a process of penetrating through the pressure-containing barrier of a pipeline, line, piping system, tank, vessel, pump casing, compressor casing or similar facility that has not been totally isolated, depressurized, purged and cleaned;

"hot work" means work in which a flame is used or sparks or other sources of ignition may be produced, including

  (a) cutting, welding, burning, air gouging, riveting, drilling, grinding and chipping,

  (b) using electrical equipment not classified for use in a hazardous location, and

  (c) introducing a combustion engine to a work process;

"hours of darkness" means the period from 30 minutes after sunset to 30 minutes before sunrise, or any time when, because of insufficient light or unfavourable atmospheric conditions, persons or vehicles cannot be seen at a distance of 150 metres;

I

"IEC" means International Electrotechnical Commission;

"immediately dangerous to life or health" means circumstances in which the atmosphere is deficient in oxygen or the concentration of a harmful substance in the atmosphere

  (a) is an immediate threat to life,

(b) may affect health irreversibly,

(c) may have future adverse effects on health, or

(d) may interfere with a worker's ability to escape from a dangerous atmosphere;

"incombustible dust" means a pulverized inert mine material of light colour,

(a) 100 percent of which passes through a 20 mesh sieve,

(b) not less than 70 percent by weight of which passes, when dry, through a 200 mesh sieve, and

(c) that does not contain more than 5 percent combustible matter or 4 percent free and combined silica;

"industrial power producer" in Part 40 means an employer authorized in Alberta to generate electrical energy as an independent power producer or solely for its own use in manufacturing or in the handling of material;

"industrial rope access work" in Part 41 means work activities at height which incorporate a working line, safety line and full body harness in combination with other devices that allow a worker to ascend, descend and traverse to and from a work area under his or her own control;

"inerting" means to intentionally flood the atmosphere inside a confined space with an inert gas to eliminate the hazard of igniting flammable vapours;

"ionizing radiation" in section 288 means high-energy electromagnetic radiation that is capable of disrupting the structure of atoms or molecules;

"ISO" means International Organization for Standardization;

"isolated" means to have separated, disconnected, de-energized or depressurized;

"isolated work site" means a work site that is 40 minutes or more travel time from the work site to a health care facility under normal travel conditions using available means of transportation;

J

"jib" means an extension to a boom that is attached to the boom tip to provide additional boom length;

"Joint First Aid Training Standards Board" means the Joint First Aid Training Standards Board established under the *Occupational Health and Safety Regulation*;

"joint work site health and safety committee" means a joint work site health and safety committee, if any, established at a work site pursuant to an order under section 31 of the *Act*;

L

"L_{ex}" means the level of a worker's total exposure to noise in dBA, averaged over the entire workday and adjusted to an equivalent 8 hour exposure measured in accordance with section 216 and based on a 3 decibel exchange rate;

"label" includes a mark, sign, device, stamp, seal, sticker, ticket, tag or wrapper;

"laboratory sample" means a sample of a controlled product that is intended solely to be tested in a laboratory, but does not include a sample that is to be used

(a) by the laboratory for testing other products, materials or substances, or

(b) for educational or demonstration purposes;

"ladderjack scaffold" means a scaffold erected by attaching a bracket to a ladder to support the scaffold planks;

"lanyard" means a flexible line of webbing or synthetic or wire rope that is used to secure a full body harness or safety belt to a lifeline or anchor point;

"leading edge" means the edge of a floor, roof, or formwork for a floor or other walking/working surface which changes location as additional floor, roof, decking, or formwork sections are placed, formed or constructed;

"life jacket" means personal protective equipment capable of supporting a person with the head above water in a face-up position without the direct effort of the person wearing the equipment;

"lifeline" means a synthetic or wire rope, rigged from one or more anchor points, to which a worker's lanyard or other part of a personal fall arrest system is attached;

"light duty scaffold" means a scaffold that

(a) is designed to support the equivalent of an evenly distributed load of not more than 122 kilograms per square metre, and

(b) has planks with a span of not more than 3 metres;

"lower explosive limit" means the lower value of the range of concentrations of a substance, in a mixture with air, at which the substance may ignite;

"low hazard work" means work described in Schedule 2, Table 1;

"lumber" means wood that is spruce-pine-fir (S-P-F) or better, of Number 2 grade or better and, if referred to by dimensions, meets the requirements of CSA Standard CAN/CSA-O141-05, *Softwood Lumber*, or the requirements of the NLGA Standard, *Standard Grading Rules for Canadian Lumber* (2003);

M

"machinery" means a combination of mechanical parts that transmits from one part to another, or otherwise modifies, force, motion or energy that comes from hydraulic, pneumatic, chemical or electrical reactions or from other sources, and includes vehicles;

"magazine" with respect to explosives means a building, storehouse, structure or place in which an explosive is kept or stored, but does not include

(a) a vehicle in which an explosive is kept for the purpose of moving the explosive from place to place, or,

(b) a place at which the blending or assembling of the non-explosive component parts of an explosive is allowed;

"manufacturer's rated capacity" means the maximum capacity, speed, load, depth of operation or working pressure, as the case may be, recommended by the specifications of the manufacturer of the equipment for the operation of the equipment under the circumstances prevailing at the time it is operated;

"manufacturer's specifications" means the written specifications, instructions or recommendations, if any, of the manufacturer of equipment or supplies, that describes how the equipment or supplies are to be erected, installed, assembled, started, operated, handled, stored, stopped, calibrated, adjusted, maintained, repaired or dismantled, including a manufacturer's instructions, operating or maintenance manual or drawings for the equipment;

"material hoist" means a hoist that is not designed to lift people;

"material safety data sheet" means a document disclosing the information referred to in paragraph 13(a) of the *Hazardous Products Act* (Canada);

"medical sharp" in Part 35 means a needle device, scalpel, lancet, or any other medical device that can reasonably be expected to penetrate the skin or other part of the body;

"medium hazard work" means work that is neither low hazard work nor high hazard work;

"meets the requirements of" means a manufacturer's self-declaration that the product complies with the referenced standard is acceptable;

"mine" means a working, other than a drill hole, made while exploring for a mineral, from which coal, precious or semi-precious minerals, industrial minerals, oil sands or any other material is being extracted;

"mine blaster" means a surface mine blaster or an underground mine blaster;

"mine entrance" means a surface entrance to a mine at the point above where excavation began or will begin but does not include a mined out area that has been reclaimed;

"mine level" in Part 36 means a horizontal excavation in the ground or in strata of an underground mine that is usable

(a) for drainage or ventilation, or

(b) as an entrance or exit for workers or mine materials to or from a mine or part of a mine;

"mine material" means material that may be taken into or out of a mine including naturally occurring materials, equipment and supplies;

"mine official" means an underground coal mine manager or underground coal mine foreman;

"mine plan" means a map, including a profile or section, of a mine or part of a mine, certified as correct by the mine surveyor;

"mine shaft" in Part 36 means an excavation at an angle of 45 degrees or greater from the horizontal that is usable

(a) for drainage or ventilation, or

(b) as an entrance or exit for workers or mine materials to or from a mine or part of a mine;

"mine site" means a location at which a facility for extracting a mineral by underground, strip, open pit or quarry operations exists or is to be developed, and includes

(a) a mineral processing plant, storage facility or discard disposal facility that exists or is to be developed in connection with a mine, and

(b) all connected access roads;

"mine tunnel" in Part 36 means an excavation at an angle of less than 45 degrees from the horizontal, including inclines and declines, that is usable

(a) for drainage or ventilation, or

    (b)   as an entrance or exit for workers or mine materials to or from a mine or part of a mine;

"mine wall" means the exposed face of an excavation in a surface mine from ground level to the working level;

"misfire" means a drill hole, borehole or device containing an explosive charge that did not explode when detonation was attempted;

"mobile crane" means a crane, other than a boom truck, that

    (a)   incorporates a power driven drum and cable or rope to lift, lower or move loads,

    (b)   is equipped with a lattice or telescoping boom capable of moving in the vertical plane, and

    (c)   is mounted on a base or chassis, either crawler- or wheel-mounted, to provide mobility;

"mobile equipment" means equipment that is

    (a)   capable of moving under its own power or of being pulled or carried, and

    (b)   not intended to be secured to land or a structure;

"musculoskeletal injury" means an injury to a worker of the muscles, tendons, ligaments, joints, nerves, blood vessels or related soft tissues that are caused or aggravated by work, including overexertion injuries and overuse injuries;

N

"NFPA" means National Fire Protection Association;

"NIOSH" means National Institute for Occupational Safety and Health;

"NLGA" means National Lumber Grades Authority;

"noise" means sound energy at a work site;

"non-industrial rope access work" in Part 41 means work activities performed within a recreational or sport context that incorporate a working line and a sit harness or full body harness in combination with other devices during

    (a)   mountaineering, caving and canyoning activities requiring the use of rope access techniques, or

    (b)   climbing on artificial structures designed and built for the purpose of sport climbing;

"nurse" means a registered nurse who is a member of the College and Association of Registered Nurses of Alberta established under the *Health Professions Act* and who is an advanced first aider;

O

"occupational exposure limit (OEL)" with respect to a substance, means the occupational exposure limit established in Schedule 1, Table 2 for that substance;

"occupational rope access" in Part 41 is a term that includes both industrial and non-industrial rope access work;

"operate" with respect to machinery or equipment includes using or handling the machinery or equipment;

"OSHA" means Occupational Safety and Health Administration;

"outlet" in Part 36 means a shaft, slope, incline, decline, adit, tunnel, level or other means of entry to or exit from an underground mine;

"outrigger scaffold" means a supported scaffold that consists of a platform resting on outrigger beams (thrustouts) projecting beyond the wall or face of the building or structure, with inboard ends secured inside the building or structure;

P

"parenteral contact" means piercing mucous membranes or the skin;

"particulate not otherwise regulated" means insoluble particulate composed of substances that do not have an occupational exposure limit;

"permanent" when referring to a structure, process or action, means that it is intended to last indefinitely;

"permanent suspension powered work platform" means a suspension powered work platform that is a permanent part of a building or structure;

"permitted explosive" means an explosive that is listed as such by the Chief Inspector of Explosives, Natural Resources Canada;

"personal fall arrest system" means personal protective equipment that will stop a worker's fall before the worker hits a surface below the worker;

"personal flotation device" means personal protective equipment capable of supporting a person with the head above water, without the direct effort of the person wearing the equipment;

"personal protective equipment" means equipment or clothing worn by a person for protection from health or safety hazards associated with conditions at a work site;

"PIP" means Process Industry Practices;

"pipeline" has the meaning assigned to it by the *Pipeline Act*;

"portable ladder" means any ladder that is not a fixed ladder;

"portable power cables" in Part 36 means portable trailing cables as specified in the applicable sections of CSA Standard CAN/CSA-M421-00 (R2007), *Use of Electricity in Mines*;

"portal" means a structure at the entrance to an underground mine, including any at the surface and any for a distance underground of 30 metres,

    (a)   that is used to support the ground and protect workers, or

    (b)   where outlets, other than vertical shafts, reach the surface;

"powered mobile equipment" means a self-propelled machine or combination of machines, including a prime mover or a motor vehicle, designed to manipulate or move material or to provide a powered aerial device for workers;

"prime" with respect to explosives means to attach a safety fuse assembly or detonator;

"processing plant" in section 532 means a facility where coal, minerals or other products of a mine are cleaned, sized or prepared for sale or use;

"product identifier" with respect to a controlled product, means the brand name, code name or code number specified by a supplier or the product's chemical name, common name, generic name or trade name;

"professional engineer" means a professional engineer under the *Engineering, Geological and Geophysical Professions Act;*

"pulmonary function technician" means a person who

  (a) has passed, or has been approved by a Director of Medical Services as having done the equivalent of passing, a pulmonary function technician course approved by a Director of Medical Services, and

  (b) if so required by a Director of Medical Services, has passed a re-qualification examination approved by such a Director;

"purge" means to remove a substance by displacing it with another substance;

Q

"quarry" means an operation involved in the mining of limestone, sandstone or another industrial mineral;

R

"radiofrequency transmitters" means transmitters that include radio towers, television towers, portable two-way radio base stations and repeaters, portable two-way radios and cellular telephones;

"respirable particulate" means airborne particulate collected and analyzed using NIOSH Method 0600 (Particulates Not Otherwise Regulated, Respirable);

"restricted area" means an area of a work site where there is a reasonable chance that the airborne concentration of asbestos, silica, coal dust or lead exceeds or may exceed the occupational exposure limit for one or more of the substances;

"restricted space" means an enclosed or partially enclosed space, not designed or intended for continuous human occupancy, that has a restricted, limited or impeded means of entry or exit because of its construction;

"rural electrification association" in Part 40 means an association under the *Rural Utilities Act* whose purpose is to supply electricity to its members;

S

"SAE" means Society of Automotive Engineers;

"safeguard" means a guard, shield, guardrail, fence, gate, barrier, toe board, protective enclosure, safety net, handrail or other device designed to protect workers operating equipment or machinery, but does not include personal protective equipment;

"safe patient/client/resident handling" in Part 14 means lifting, transferring, or repositioning by the use of engineering controls, lifting and transfer aids, or assistive devices, by lift teams or other trained staff rather than by sole use of worker body strength;

"safety-engineered medical sharp" in Part 35 means a medical sharp that is designed to, or has a built-in safety feature or mechanism that will, eliminate or minimize the risk of accidental parenteral contact while or after the sharp is used;

"safety fuse" means a train of black powder that

  (a) is tightly wrapped and enclosed in a series of textiles and waterproof materials, and

(b) can be connected to a detonator, and

(c) burns internally at a continuous and uniform rate when ignited;

"safety fuse assembly" means a safety fuse to which a detonator is attached;

"scaffold" means a temporary work platform and its supporting structure used for supporting workers or materials or both, but does not include suspended cages, permanent suspension powered work platforms, boatswain's chairs, elevating platforms, aerial devices, fork-mounted work platforms, temporary supporting structures and fly form deck panels;

"secure" in Part 15 means ensuring that an energy-isolating device cannot be released or activated;

"sharps" means needles, knives, scalpels, blades, scissors and other items that can cut or puncture a person, that may also be contaminated with a biohazardous material;

"shock absorber" means a device intended to reduce the force on a worker when a personal fall arrest system is operating;

"small utility vehicle" in Part 18 means a small vehicle designated for off-road use, equipped with a bench-type seat and a steering wheel, and designed to transport more than one person;

"snow vehicle" means a motor vehicle designated or intended to be driven exclusively or chiefly on snow or ice;

"snubbing" in Part 37 means the act of moving tubulars into or out of a well bore when pressure is contained in the well through the use of stripping components or closed blowout preventers (BOPs), and mechanical force is required to move the tubing in order to overcome the hydraulic force exerted on the tubular in the well bore;

"specifications" other than manufacturer's specifications, includes the written instructions, procedures, drawings or other documents of a professional engineer or employer relating to equipment, supplies and a work process or operation;

"split" in Part 36 means a separate fresh air ventilation circuit in which the intake air comes directly from the main intake airway and the return air goes directly to the main return airway;

"spoil pile" means waste material excavated from an excavation, tunnel or underground shaft;

"standard first aider" means a first aider who holds a certificate in standard first aid from an approved training agency;

"supplier" with respect to a controlled product, means a manufacturer, processor or packager of the controlled product or a person who, in the course of business, imports or sells controlled products;

"supplier label" means the label provided by the supplier of a controlled product under the *Hazardous Products Act* (Canada);

"supplier's material safety data sheet" means the material safety data sheet provided by the supplier of a controlled product under the *Hazardous Products Act* (Canada);

"surface mine" means a mine worked by strip mining, open pit mining or other surface method, including auger mining;

"surface mine blaster" means a worker who holds a valid surface mine blaster's certificate issued under the *Occupational Health and Safety Regulation*;

"suspended scaffold" means a work platform suspended from above by wires or ropes;

"swing drop distance" means, in a fall-arresting action, the vertical drop from the onset of the swinging motion to the point of initial contact with a structure;

T

"temporary" with respect to a structure, process or action, means that it is not intended to last indefinitely;

"temporary protective structure" means a structure or device designed to provide protection to workers, in an excavation, tunnel or underground shaft, from cave ins, collapses or sliding or rolling materials and includes shoring, bracing, piles, planking or cages;

"temporary supporting structures" means falsework, forms, fly form deck panels, shoring, braces or cables that are used to support a structure temporarily or to stabilize materials or earthworks until they are self-supporting or their instability is otherwise overcome, and includes a thrustout materials landing platform;

"total fall distance" means the vertical distance from the point at which a worker falls to the point where the fall stops after all personal fall arrest system components have extended;

"total particulate" means airborne particulate collected and analyzed using NIOSH Method 0500 (Particulates Not Otherwise Regulated, Total);

"tower crane" means a crane that

    (a) is designed to incorporate a power driven drum and cable, a rope and a vertical mast or a tower and jib,

    (b) is of the travelling, fixed or climbing type, and

    (c) is not used to lift people;

"tower hoist" means a hoist

    (a) with a tower that is an integral part of it or supports it,

    (b) that travels between fixed guides, and

    (c) that is not used to lift people;

"travel restraint system" means a type of fall protection system, including guardrails or similar barriers, that prevents a worker from travelling to the edge of a structure or to a work position from which the worker could fall;

"trench" means a long narrow dug out area of ground that is deeper than its width at the bottom;

"tunnel" in Part 36 means an underground passage with an incline of less than 45 degrees from the horizontal;

U

"UIAA" means Union Internationale des Associations d'Alpinisme;

"ULC" means Underwriters' Laboratories of Canada;

"underground coal mine electrical superintendent" means a worker who holds a valid underground coal mine electrical superintendent's certificate issued under the *Occupational Health and Safety Regulation*;

"underground coal mine foreman" means a worker who holds a valid underground coal mine foreman's certificate issued under the *Occupational Health and Safety Regulation*;

"underground coal mine manager" means a worker who holds a valid underground coal mine manager's certificate issued under the *Occupational Health and Safety Regulation*;

"underground mine" means a mine other than a surface mine;

"underground mine blaster" means a worker who holds a valid underground mine blaster's certificate issued under the *Occupational Health and Safety Regulation*;

"underground shaft" means an underground passage with an incline of 45 degrees or more from the horizontal, including a drilled or bored pile or caisson, that is used primarily for the transportation of workers or materials;

"underground shaft hoist" means a hoist used in an underground shaft to gain entry to and exit from a tunnel or underground space, and includes a device for conveying mine material;

"utility employee" in Part 40 means a worker engaged in the work of an electric utility, industrial power producer or rural electrification association;

V

"vehicle" means a device in, on or by which a person or thing may be transported or drawn, and includes a combination of vehicles;

"ventilation stopping" in Part 36 means a structure that directs air flow or separates intake and return air systems;

"violence" whether at a work site or work related, means the threatened, attempted or actual conduct of a person that causes or is likely to cause physical injury;

W

"welding or allied process" in Part 10 means any specific type of electric or oxy-fuel gas welding or cutting process, including those processes referred to in Appendix A of CSA Standard W117.2-06, *Safety in welding, cutting and allied processes;*

"work area" means a place at a work site where a worker is, or may be, during work or during a work break;

"work site label" with respect to a controlled product means a label that discloses

    (a) a product identifier that is identical to that found on the material safety data sheet for the product,

    (b) information for the safe handling of the controlled product, and

    (c) reference to the material safety data sheet for the controlled product;

"work positioning system" means a system of components attached to a vertical safety line and including a full body harness, descent controllers and positioning lanyards used to support or suspend a worker in tension at a work position;

"worker member" means a person elected to a joint work site health and safety committee under section 199;

"working face" means the surface from which mineable material, overburden or waste material is being removed;

"workings" means the area where excavation is occurring in a mine.

Extended application of Code

2(1) If a requirement of this Code imposes a duty on an employer with respect to the design, construction, erection or installation of equipment, and the equipment is erected or installed by or on behalf of a prime contractor, the prime contractor must comply with the requirement as if the requirement were directly imposed on the prime contractor.

(2) Subsection (1) does not relieve the employer or prime contractor from fulfilling other responsibilities under this Code.

Availability of legislation

2.1 An employer must ensure that a current paper or electronic copy of each of the *Occupational Health and Safety Act*, the *Occupational Health and Safety Regulation* and the *Occupational Health and Safety Code* is readily available for reference by workers.

Designated person to prepare plan

2.2 If a requirement of this Code imposes a duty on an employer with respect to the development or preparation of a plan, the employer must ensure that the plan is developed or prepared by a designated person who is competent in the principles and practices of the work described in the plan.

Adoption of standards

3 The following are adopted for the purposes of this Code:

Alberta Energy

Electric Utilities Act (2003)

Alberta Health and Wellness

Ambulance Services Act (2000)

Alberta Municipal Affairs

Code for Electrical Installations at Oil and Gas Facilities (2006)

Alberta Electrical and Communication Utility Code (2002)

Alberta Fire Code (1997)

ANSI Standards

A10.11-1989 (R1998), *Construction and Demolition Operations — Personnel and Debris Nets*

A10.32-2004, *Fall Protection Systems — American National Standard for Construction and Demolition Operations*

A14.1-2007, *American National Standard for Ladders — Wood — Safety Requirements*

A14.2-2007, *American National Standard for Ladders — Portable Metal — Safety Requirements*

A14.5-2007, *American National Standard for Ladders — Portable Reinforced Plastic — Safety Requirements*

A92.3-2006, *Manually Propelled Elevating Aerial Platforms*

A92.5-2006, *Boom-Supported Elevating Work Platforms*

A92.6-2006, *Self-Propelled Elevating Work Platforms*

A92.8-1993 (R1998), *Vehicle-Mounted Bridge Inspection and Maintenance Devices*

A92.9-1993, *Mast-Climbing Work Platforms*

ALCTV-2006, *American National Standard for Automotive Lifts — Safety Requirements for Construction, Testing and Validation*

ALOIM-2000, *Automotive Lifts — Safety Requirements for Operation, Inspection and Maintenance*

B1.20.1-1983 (R2006), *Pipe Threads, General Purpose (Inch)*

S1.25-1991 (R2002), *Specification for Personal Noise Dosimeters*

S1.4-1983 (R2006), *Specification for Sound Level Meters*

S1.43-1997 (R2002), *Specifications for Integrating-Averaging Sound Level Meters*

S3.6-2004, *Specification for Audiometers*

Z26.1 (1996), *Safety Glazing Material for Glazing Motor Vehicles and Motor Vehicle Equipment Operating on Land Highways — Safety Standard*

Z87.1-2003, *Occupational and Educational Personal Eye and Face Protection Devices*

Z87.1-1989, *Practice for Occupational and Educational Eye and Face Protection*

Z89.1-2003, *American National Standard for Industrial Head Protection*

Z359.1-2007, *Safety requirements for personal fall arrest systems, subsystems and components*

API Recommended Practice

RP 4G, *Recommended Practice for Maintenance and Use of Drilling and Well Servicing Structures* (2004)

ASME Standard

B30.9-2006, *Safety Standard for Cableways, Cranes, Derricks, Hoists, Hooks, Jacks and Slings*

B30.20-2006, *Below the Hook Lifting Devices*

B56.1-2000, *Safety Standard for Low Lift and High Lift Trucks*

Association of Canadian Mountain Guides

Climbing Gym Instructor Technical Manual (2003)

Technical Handbook for Professional Mountain Guides (1999)

ASTM Standards

C478-07, *Standard Specification for Reinforced Concrete Manhole Sections*

D323-06, *Standard Test Method for Vapour Pressure of Petroleum Products (Reid Method)*

D2865-06, *Standard Practice for Calibration of Standards and Equipment for Electrical Insulating Materials Testing*

F1447-06 *Standard Specification for Helmets Used in Recreational Bicycling or Roller Skating*

F2413-05, *Specifications for Performance Requirements for Protective Footwear*

Australian Rope Access Association

Industrial Rope Access Technique (2000)

British Columbia Cave Rescue

British Columbia Cave Rescue Companion Rescue Workshop (2005)

BSI Standards

BS 6658: 05, *Specification for Protective Helmets for Vehicle Users*

Canadian Cave Conservancy

Cave Guiding Standards for British Columbia and Alberta (2003)

CEN Standards

EN 341: 1997, *Personal protective equipment against falls from height — Descender devices*

EN 353-2: 2002, *Personal protective equipment against falls from a height — Part 2: Guided type fall arresters including a flexible anchor line*

EN 354: 2002, *Personal protective equipment against falls from a height — Lanyards*

EN 355: 2002, *Personal protective equipment against falls from a height — Energy absorbers*

EN 358: 2000, *Personal protective equipment for work positioning and prevention of falls from a height — Belts for work positioning and restraint and work positioning lanyards*

EN 361: 2007, *Personal protective equipment against falls from a height — Full body harnesses*

EN 362: 2004, *Personal protective equipment against falls from height-Connectors*

EN 397: 2006, *Specification for industrial safety helmets*

EN 567: 1997, *Mountaineering equipment — Rope clamps — Safety requirements and test methods*

EN 813: 1997, *Personal protective equipment for prevention of falls from a height — Sit harnesses*

EN 892: 2004, *Mountaineering equipment — Dynamic mountaineering ropes — Safety requirements and test methods*

EN 1891: 1998, *Personal protective equipment for the prevention of falls from a height — Low stretch kernmantel ropes*

EN 12275: 1998, *Mountaineering equipment — Connectors — Safety requirements and test methods*

EN 12277: 1998, *Mountaineering equipment — Harnesses — Safety requirements and test methods*

EN 12492: 2000, *Mountaineering equipment — Helmets for mountaineers — Safety requirements and test methods*

EN 1677-1: 2000, *Components for slings — Part 1: Forged steel components grade 8*

CGSB Standards

CAN/CGSB 3.16-99 AMEND, *Mining Diesel Fuel*

CAN/CGSB 65.7-M88 AMEND, *Lifejackets, Inherently Buoyant Type*

CAN/CGSB 65.11-M88 AMEND, *Personal Flotation Devices*

CSA Standards

CAN/CSA-B167-96 (R2007), *Safety Standard for Maintenance and Inspection of Overhead Cranes, Gantry Cranes, Monorails, Hoists and Trolleys*

B352.0-95 (R2006), *Rollover Protective Structures (ROPS) for Agricultural, Construction, Earthmoving, Forestry, Industrial and Mining Machines — Part 1: General Requirements*

B352.1-95 (R2006), *Rollover Protective Structures (ROPS) for Agricultural, Construction, Earthmoving, Forestry, Industrial and Mining Machines — Part 2: Testing Requirements for ROPS on Agricultural Tractors*

B352.2-95 (R2006), *Rollover Protective Structures (ROPS) for Agricultural, Construction, Earthmoving, Forestry, Industrial and Mining Machines — Part 3: Testing Requirements for ROPS on Construction, Earthmoving, Forestry, Industrial and Mining Machines*

CAN/CSA-B354.1-04, *Portable elevating work platforms*

CAN/CSA-B354.2-01 (R2006), *Self-Propelled Elevating Work Platforms*

CAN/CSA-B354.4-02, *Self-Propelled Boom-Supported Elevating Work Platforms*

B376-M1980 (R2008), *Portable Containers for Gasoline and Other Petroleum Fuels*

C22.1-06, *Canadian Electrical Code, Part 1, Safety Standard for Electrical Installations*

C22.2 No. 33-M1984 (R2004), *Construction and Test of Electric Cranes and Hoists*

CAN/CSA-C225-00 (R2005), *Vehicle-Mounted Aerial Devices*

CAN/CSA-D113.2-M89 (R2004), *Cycling Helmets*

CAN/CSA-M421-00 (R2007), *Use of Electricity in Mines*

CAN/CSA-M422-M87 (R2007), *Fire-Performance and Antistatic Requirements for Ventilation Materials*

CAN/CSA-M423-M87 (R2007), *Fire-Resistant Hydraulic Fluids*

CAN/CSA-M424.1-88 (R2007), *Flameproof Non-Rail-Bound, Diesel-Powered Machines for Use in Gassy Underground Coal Mines*

CAN/CSA-M424.2-M90 (R2007), *Non-Rail-Bound Diesel-Powered Machines for Use in Non-Gassy Underground Mines*

CAN/CSA-M424.3-M90 (R2007), *Braking Performance — Rubber-Tired, Self-Propelled Underground Mining Machines*

O121-08, *Douglas Fir Plywood*

CAN/CSA-O141-05, *Softwood Lumber*

O151-04, *Canadian Softwood Plywood*

S269.1-1975 (R2003), *Falsework for Construction Purposes*

CAN/CSA-S269.2-M87 (R2003), *Access Scaffolding for Construction Purposes*

W117.2-06, *Safety in welding, cutting and allied processes*

CAN3-Z11-M81 (R2005), *Portable Ladders*

CAN/CSA Z94.1-05, *Industrial Protective Headwear*

Z94.2-02, *Hearing Protection Devices — Performance, Selection, Care, and Use*

Z94.3-07, *Eye and Face Protectors*

Z94.3-02, *Eye and Face Protectors*

Z94.3-99, *Industrial Eye and Face Protectors*

Z94.4-02, *Selection, Use and Care of Respirators*

Z107.56-06, *Procedures for the Measurement of Occupational Noise Exposure*

CAN/CSA-Z150-98 (R2004), *Safety Code on Mobile Cranes*

Z180.1-00 (R2005), *Compressed Breathing Air and Systems*

CAN/CSA-Z185-M87 (R2006), *Safety Code for Personnel Hoists*

Z195-02, *Protective Footwear*

Z248-04, *Code for Tower Cranes*

CAN/CSA-Z256-M87 (R2006), *Safety Code for Material Hoists*

CAN/CSA Z259.1-05, *Body belts and saddles for work positioning and travel restraint*

CAN/CSA-Z259.2.1-98 (R2004), *Fall Arresters, Vertical Lifelines, and Rails*

CAN/CSA-Z259.2.2-98 (R2004), *Self-Retracting Devices for Personal Fall-Arrest Systems*

CAN/CSA-Z259.2.3-99 (R2004), *Descent Control Devices*

Z259.3-M1978 (R2004), *Lineman's Body Belt and Lineman's Safety Strap*

CAN/CSA Z259.10-06, *Full Body Harnesses*

Z259.11-05, *Energy absorbers and lanyards*

Z259.12-01 (R2006), *Connecting Components for Personal Fall Arrest Systems (PFAS)*

Z259.13-04, *Flexible Horizontal Lifeline Systems*

Z259.14-01, *Fall Restrict Equipment for Wood Pole Climbing*

Z259.16-04, *Design of Active Fall-Protection Systems*

CAN/CSA-Z271-98 (R2004), *Safety Code for Suspended Elevating Platforms*

CAN/CSA-Z275.1-05, *Hyperbaric Facilities*

CAN/CSA-Z275.2-04, *Occupational Safety Code for Diving Operations*

CAN/CSA-Z275.4-02, *Competency Standard for Diving Operations*

CAN/CSA-Z321-96 (R2006), *Signs and Symbols for the Workplace*

Z434-03 (R2008), *Industrial Robots and Robot Systems — General Safety Requirements*

CPSC Standard

Title 16 Code of U.S. Federal Regulations Part 1203, *Safety Standard for Bicycle Helmets*

IEC Standards

61672-1 (2002), *Electroacoustics — Sound Level Meters — Part 1: Specifications* 61672-2 (2003), *Electroacoustics — Sound Level Meters — Part 2: Pattern evaluation tests*

International Rope Access Trade Association

General requirements for certification of personnel engaged in industrial rope access methods (2005)

International guidelines on the use of rope access methods for industrial purposes (2001)

ISO Standards

3450: 1996, *Earth-moving machinery — Braking systems of rubber-tyred machines —Systems and performance requirements and test procedures*

3471: 2000, *Earth-moving machinery — Roll-over, protective structures — Laboratory tests and performance requirements*

6165: 2006, *Earth-moving machinery — Basic types — Vocabulary*

NLGA Standard

Standard Grading Rules for Canadian Lumber (2003)

Natural Resources Canada

Blasting Explosives and Detonators — Storage, Possession, Transportation, Destruction and Sale (M82-8/1983), Revised 1993

Storage Standards for Industrial Explosives (M81-7/2001E)

NFPA Standards

30, *Flammable and Combustible Liquids Code*, 2008 Edition

1123, *Code for Fireworks Display,* 2006 Edition

1126, *Standard for the Use of Pyrotechnics Before a Proximate Audience*, 2006 Edition

1971, *Protective Ensemble for Structural Fire Fighting*, 2007 Edition

1977, *Protective Clothing and Equipment for Wildland Fire Fighting*, 2005 Edition

1983, *Standard on Fire Service Life Safety Rope and System Components*, 2006 Edition

OSHA Standard

1928.52, *Protective Frames for Wheel-type Agricultural Tractors — Tests, Procedures and Performance Requirements*

PIP Standard

STF05501 (February 2002), *Fixed Ladders and Cages*, published by the Construction Industry Institute

SAE Standards, Recommended Practices and Reports

J167 (2002), *Overhead Protection for Agricultural Tractors — Test Procedures and Performance Requirements*

J209 (2003), *Instrument Face Design and Location for Construction and Industrial Equipment*

J209 JAN87, *Instrument Face Design and Location for Construction and Industrial Equipment*

J386 (2006), *Operator Restraint System for Off-Road Work Machines*,

J1029 (2007), *Lighting and Marking of Construction, Earthmoving Machinery*

J1042 (2003), *Operator Protection for General-Purpose Industrial Machines*

J1084-APR80 (R2002), *Operator Protective Structure Performance Criteria for Certain Forestry Equipment*

J1194 (1999), *Rollover Protective Structures (ROPS) for Wheeled Agricultural Tractors*

J1511 FEB94/ISO 5010, *Steering for Off-Road, Rubber-Tired Machines*

J2042 (2003), *Clearance, Sidemarker, and Identification Lamps for Use on Motor Vehicles 2032 mm or More in Overall Width*

J2042 July1996, *Clearance, Sidemarker, and Identification Lamps for Use on Motor Vehicles 2032 mm or More in Overall Width*

J2292 (2006), *Combination Pelvic/Upper Torso (Type 2) Operator Restraint Systems for Off-Road Work Machines*

J/ISO 3449 (2005), *Earthmoving Machinery — Falling-Object Protective Structures — Laboratory Tests and Performance Requirements*

Snell Memorial Foundation

B-90A, *1998 Standard for Protective Headgear for Use with Bicycles*

B-95A, *1998 Standard for Protective Headgear for Use with Bicycles*

M2005, *2005 Helmet Standard for Use in Motorcycling*

N-94, *1994 Standard for Protective Headgear For Use in Non-Motorized Sports*

Society of Professional Rope Access Technicians

Certification Requirements for Rope Access Work (2005)

Safe Practices for Rope Access Work (2003)

Transportation Association of Canada

Manual of Uniform Traffic Control Devices for Canada (1998)

UIAA Standards

101: 2004, *Mountaineering and Climbing Equipment — Dynamic Ropes*

105: 2004, *Mountaineering and Climbing Equipment — Harnesses*

106: 2004, *Mountaineering and Climbing Equipment — Helmets*

107: 2004, *Mountaineering and Climbing Equipment — Low Stretch Ropes*

121: 2004, *Mountaineering and Climbing Equipment — Connectors*

126: 2004, *Mountaineering and Climbing Equipment — Rope Clamps*

ULC Standards

C30-1995, *Containers, Safety*

CAN/ULC-60832-99, *Installing Poles (Insulating Sticks) and Universal Tool Attachment (Fittings) for Live Working*

CAN/ULC-D60855-00, *Live Working — Insulating Foam-Filled Tubes and Solid Rods for Live Working*

CAN/ULC-60895-04, *Live Working — Conductive Clothing for Use at Nominal Voltage Up to 800 kV A.C. and +/- 600 kV D.C.*

CAN/ULC-60900-99, *Hand Tools for Live Working up to 1000 V a.c. and 1500 V d.c.*

CAN/ULC-60903-04, *Live Working — Gloves of Insulating Materials*

CAN/ULC-D60984-00, *Sleeves of Insulating Material for Live Working*

CAN/ULC-D61112-01, *Blankets of Insulating Material for Electrical Purposes*

CAN/ULC-D61229-00, *Rigid Protective Covers for Live Working on a.c. Installations*

CAN/ULC-61236-99, *Saddles, Pole Clamps (Stick Clamps) and Accessories for Live Working*

U.S.A. Federal Motor Vehicle Safety Standard

FMVSS 218 *Motorcycle Helmets* 1993 OCT

Previous editions of referenced standards

3.1　　If a standard referenced in this Code applies to equipment manufactured or installed on or after a specified effective date, an employer must ensure that equipment manufactured or installed prior to that date was approved to or, as applicable, met the requirements of, the edition of the referenced standard that was in effect at the time the equipment was manufactured or installed.

Transitional

4　　**Repealed**

Repeal

5　　**Repealed**

Coming into force

6　　This Code comes into force on July1, 2009.

Part 2   Hazard Assessment, Elimination and Control

Hazard assessment

7(1)   An employer must assess a work site and identify existing and potential hazards before work begins at the work site or prior to the construction of a new work site.

7(2)   An employer must prepare a report of the results of a hazard assessment and the methods used to control or eliminate the hazards identified.

7(3)   An employer must ensure that the date on which the hazard assessment is prepared or revised is recorded on it.

7(4)   An employer must ensure that the hazard assessment is repeated

(a)   at reasonably practicable intervals to prevent the development of unsafe and unhealthy working conditions,

(b)   when a new work process is introduced,

(c)   when a work process or operation changes, or

(d)   before the construction of significant additions or alterations to a work site.

7(5)   A prime contractor must ensure that any employer on a work site is made aware of any existing or potential work site hazards that may affect that employer's workers.

Worker participation

8(1)   An employer must involve affected workers in the hazard assessment and in the control or elimination of the hazards identified.

8(2)   An employer must ensure that workers affected by the hazards identified in a hazard assessment report are informed of the hazards and of the methods used to control or eliminate the hazards.

Hazard elimination and control

9(1)   If an existing or potential hazard to workers is identified during a hazard assessment, an employer must take measures in accordance with this section to

(a)   eliminate the hazards, or

(b)   if elimination is not reasonably practicable, control the hazard.

9(2)   If reasonably practicable, an employer must eliminate or control a hazard through the use of engineering controls.

9(3)   If a hazard cannot be eliminated or controlled under subsection (2), the employer must use administrative controls that control the hazard to a level as low as reasonably achievable.

9(4)   If the hazard cannot be eliminated or controlled under subsections (2) or (3), the employer must ensure that the appropriate personal protective equipment is used by workers affected by the hazard.

9(5)   If the hazard cannot be eliminated or controlled under subsections (2), (3) or (4), the employer may use a combination of engineering controls, administrative controls or personal protective equipment if there is a greater level of worker safety because a combination is used.

Emergency control of hazard

10(1) If emergency action is required to control or eliminate a hazard that is dangerous to the safety or health of workers,

(a) only those workers competent in correcting the condition, and the minimum number necessary to correct the condition, may be exposed to the hazard, and

(b) every reasonable effort must be made to control the hazard while the condition is being corrected.

10(2) Sections 7(2) and 7(3) do not apply to an emergency response during the period that emergency action is required.

Health and safety plan

11 If ordered to do so by a Director, an employer must prepare and implement a health and safety plan that includes the policies, procedures and plans to prevent work site incidents and occupational diseases at the work site.

Part 3   Specifications and Certifications

Following specifications

12   An employer must ensure that

(a) equipment is of sufficient size, strength and design and made of suitable materials to withstand the stresses imposed on it during its operation and to perform the function for which it is intended or was designed,

(b) the rated capacity or other limitations on the operation of the equipment, or any part of it, or on the supplies as described in the manufacturer's specifications or specifications certified by a professional engineer, are not exceeded,

(c) modifications to equipment that may affect its structural integrity or stability are performed in accordance with the manufacturer's specifications or specifications certified by a professional engineer, and

(d) equipment and supplies are erected, installed, assembled, started, operated, handled, stored, serviced, tested, adjusted, calibrated, maintained, repaired and dismantled in accordance with the manufacturer's specifications or the specifications certified by a professional engineer.

Manufacturer's and professional engineer's specifications

13(1) If this Code requires anything to be done in accordance with a manufacturer's specifications, an employer may, instead of complying strictly with the manufacturer's specifications, comply with modified specifications certified by a professional engineer.

13(2) If this Code requires anything to be done in accordance with manufacturer's specifications and they are not available or do not exist, an employer must

(a) develop and comply with procedures that are certified by a professional engineer as designed to ensure the thing is done in a safe manner, or

(b) have the equipment certified as safe to operate by a professional engineer at least every 12 calendar months.

Certification by a professional engineer

14(1) If this Code requires that procedures or specifications be certified by a professional engineer, the certification must

(a) be in writing, and

(b) be stamped and signed by the professional engineer.

14(2) Unless the document states otherwise, certification by a professional engineer implies that the procedures or specifications certified are fit and safe for the workers affected by them.

Approved equipment

15   If this Code requires equipment to be approved by a named organization, an employer must use best efforts to ensure that the seal, stamp, logo or similar identifying mark of that organization is on the equipment and legible.

Requirements Applicable to All Industries
Part 4   Chemical Hazards, Biological Hazards and Harmful Substances

General Requirements

Worker exposure to harmful substances

16(1) An employer must ensure that a worker's exposure to any substance listed in Schedule 1, Table 2 is kept as low as reasonably achievable.

16(2) An employer must ensure that a worker's exposure to any substance listed in Schedule 1, Table 2 does not exceed its occupational exposure limits listed in Schedule 1, Table 2.

16(2.1) The amended occupational exposure limit for coal dust as shown in Schedule 1, Table 2 comes into effect on July1, 2010.

16(3) If no occupational exposure limit is established for a harmful substance present at a work site, an employer must ensure that a worker's exposure to that substance is kept as low as reasonably achievable.

16(3.1) A worker may not be exposed to a substance listed in Schedule 1, Table 2 at a concentration exceeding its ceiling limit at any time.

16(4) If no 15-minute occupational exposure limit or ceiling occupational exposure limit is listed for a substance in Schedule 1, Table 2, the employer must

(a) comply with the eight-hour occupational exposure limit, and

(b) ensure that a worker's exposure to that substance does not exceed

(i) three times the eight-hour occupational exposure limit for more than a total of 30 minutes during a continuous 24-hour period, and five times the eight-hour occupational exposure limit, or

(ii) the concentration that is immediately dangerous to life and health,

whichever is lower.

Exposure to multiple substances

17 An employer must take all reasonably practicable steps to ensure that, if a worker is exposed to more than one substance listed in Schedule 1, Table 2 during a single work shift, and the toxicological effects have similar modes of toxic action, the value of D in the formula

$$D = \frac{C_1}{T_1} + \frac{C_2}{T_2} + \ldots + \frac{C_n}{T_n}$$

does not exceed 1, where C_1, C_2,...C_n refer to the airborne concentrations during exposure to contaminants 1, 2,...n, and T_1, T_2,...T_n are their respective occupational exposure limit values expressed in the same units as C_n.

Exposure during shifts longer than 8 hours

18(1) Subject to subsection (3), if a worker is exposed to a substance listed in Schedule 1, Table 2 during a single work shift that is longer than eight hours, the employer must ensure that equivalent protection from adverse health effects is achieved by adjusting the eight-hour exposure limit using the following formulas:

adjusted exposure limit = eight-hour occupational exposure limit x daily reduction factor

$$\text{where the daily reduction factor} = \left\{ \frac{8}{h} x \left(\frac{24-h}{16} \right) \right\}, \text{ and}$$

h = hours worked per day.

18(2) Subsection (1) does not apply to a substance for which the number "3" appears in the "Substance Interaction" column of Schedule 1, Table 2.

18(3) An employer may adjust the eight-hour exposure limit by another method that uses recognized scientific principles and that is approved by a Director of Occupational Hygiene.

Review of exposure limits

19(1) A person may apply to a Director of Occupational Hygiene to request a review of the occupational exposure limit of a substance.

19(2) An application must be in writing and must include reasons for the review, proposed changes and information that supports the request.

19(3) On receipt of a request for a review of an occupational exposure limit, a Director of Occupational Hygiene may review the occupational exposure limit.

Airborne concentration measurements

20(1) If a person measures the airborne concentration of a harmful substance for the purposes of complying with the occupational exposure limits as required by this Code, the person must make the measurement in accordance with any one of

(a) the NIOSH Manual of Analytical Methods, 4th Edition (August 1994), published by the United States Department of Health and Human Services, as amended up to and including the 2nd supplement (January 15, 1998),

(b) Sampling and Analytical Methods published by the U.S. Occupational Safety and Health Administration,

(c) Methods for the Determination of Hazardous Substances guidance published by the Health and Safety Executive of Great Britain,

(d) EPA Test Methods published by the U.S. Environmental Protection Agency (EPA),

(e) Workplace Air Contamination Sampling Guide published by the Institut de recherché Robert-Sauvé en santé et en sécurité du travail (IRRSST),

(f) ISO Standards and Guides of Air Quality published by ISO Technical Committee TC146,

(g) Analyses of hazardous substances in air/DFG Deutsche Forschngsgemeinschaft — Commission for the Investigation of Health Hazards of Chemical Compounds in the Work Area, or

(h) methods or procedures that are approved by a Director of Occupational Hygiene.

20(2) If there is no analytical method or procedure that complies with subsection (1), an employer may use a continuous reading direct-reading instrument to measure airborne concentrations of a harmful substance for the purposes of complying with the occupational exposure limits as required by this Code provided that the instrument is used, calibrated and maintained according to the manufacturer's specifications.

20(2.1) An employer must ensure that the person undertaking airborne measurements is competent to do so.

20(3) If the person is counting fibres, the person must apply NIOSH Method 7400, and only to particles that meet the size criteria for fibres.

20(4) An employer must record the results of the measurements and keep them for 3 years from the date on which the measurements were taken.

Potential worker exposure

21(1) If a worker may be exposed to a harmful substance at a work site, an employer must identify the health hazards associated with the exposure and assess the worker's exposure.

21(2) The employer must ensure that a worker who may be exposed to a harmful substance at a work site

(a) is informed of the health hazards associated with exposure to that substance,

(b) is informed of measurements made of airborne concentrations of harmful substances at the work site, and

(c) is trained in procedures developed by the employer to minimize the worker's exposure to harmful substances, and understands the procedures.

21(3) A worker who is provided with training under subsection (2) must use the procedures appropriately and apply the training.

Worker overexposure

22(1) If a worker may be exposed to an airborne concentration that is more than the occupational exposure limit of a substance, the employer must conduct measurements of the concentrations of that substance at the work site.

22(2) If a worker is exposed to more than the occupational exposure limit of a substance, the employer must immediately

(a) identify the cause of the overexposure,

(b) protect the worker from any further exposure,

(c) control the situation so that no other workers are exposed to the substance at airborne concentrations that are more than the occupational exposure limit, and

(d) explain to the worker the nature and extent of the overexposure.

22(3) As soon as reasonably practicable, an employer must inform the joint work site health and safety committee, if there is one, in writing, that a worker has been exposed to more than the occupational exposure limit of a substance, and of the steps taken to control the overexposure.

Worker decontamination

23   If a worker may be contaminated by a harmful substance at a work site, the employer must

(a) provide the facilities, including showers, the worker needs to remove the contamination before the worker leaves the work site, and

(b) ensure that only those articles and clothing that have been properly decontaminated or cleaned are taken from the work site by the worker.

Emergency baths, showers, eye wash equipment

24 If a worker is present at a work site where chemicals harmful to the eyes or skin are used, the employer must ensure that the worker has immediate access at the work site to emergency baths, showers, eye wash equipment or other equipment appropriate for the potential level of exposure.

Prohibited activities

25(1) An employer must ensure that workers do not eat, drink or smoke tobacco in a part of a work site contaminated by a harmful substance.

25(2) A worker must not eat, drink or smoke tobacco in a part of a work site contaminated by a harmful substance.

Codes of practice

26(1) An employer must have a code of practice governing the storage, handling, use and disposal of a substance listed in Schedule 1, Table 1 that is present at a work site

(a) as pure substance in an amount exceeding 10 kilograms, or

(b) in a mixture in which the amount of the substance is more than 10 kilograms and at a concentration of 0.1 percent by weight or more.

26(2) The code of practice must include measures to be used to prevent the uncontrolled release of the substance and the procedures to be followed if there is an uncontrolled release.

Storage of harmful substances

27 An employer must ensure that a harmful substance used or stored at a work site

(a) is clearly identified, or its container is clearly identified, and

(b) is used and stored in such a way that the use or storage is not a hazard to workers.

General provisions for asbestos, silica, coal dust and lead

28 An employer must

(a) minimize the release of asbestos, silica, coal dust and lead into the air as far as is reasonably practicable,

(b) keep the work site clear of unnecessary accumulations of asbestos, silica, coal dust and lead and waste materials containing any of these substances, and

(c) ensure that the methods used to decontaminate the work area, workers, equipment and protective clothing prevent, as much as is reasonably practicable, the generation of airborne asbestos, silica, coal dust or lead.

Restricted area

29(1) An employer must ensure that only a person authorized by the employer or by law to do so enters a restricted area.

29(2) An employer must post signs that clearly indicate that

(a) asbestos, silica, coal dust or lead are present in the area,

(b) only authorized persons may enter the area, and

(c) eating, drinking and smoking are prohibited in the area.

29(3) Signs posted under subsection (2) must

(a) be in a conspicuous location at the entrances to and on the periphery of each restricted area, as appropriate, and

(b) remain posted until the area is no longer a restricted area.

29(4) An employer must

(a) provide workers in a restricted area with protective clothing that protects other clothing worn by the worker from contamination by asbestos, silica, coal dust or lead,

(b) ensure that workers' street clothing is not contaminated by asbestos, silica, coal dust or lead, and

(c) ensure that a worker does not leave a restricted area until the worker has been decontaminated.

29(5) Subsection (4) does not apply in an emergency if the health or safety of a worker requires the worker to leave a restricted area without being decontaminated.

Protective clothing used in restricted areas containing asbestos or lead

30(1) If clothing used in a restricted area containing asbestos or lead is reused and not discarded, the employer must have the clothing laundered in the appropriate manner and at appropriate intervals to ensure

(a) the clothing is decontaminated, and

(b) there is no cross-contamination of other clothing by asbestos or lead.

30(2) The employer must ensure that clothing contaminated with asbestos or lead that is to be laundered before being reused is stored and transported in sealed containers.

30(3) Containers used in subsection (2) must be clearly labelled

(a) to identify the contents,

(b) to indicate that the contents are a hazard, and

(c) to warn workers that dust from the contents should not be inhaled.

Release of asbestos

31(1) If it is determined that asbestos fibres may be released in a building, the building is in an unsafe condition.

31(2) The employer must take all necessary steps to correct the unsafe condition.

Prohibitions related to asbestos

32(1) A person must not use materials containing crocidolite asbestos in an existing or a new building.

32(2) A person must not apply materials containing asbestos by spraying them.

Asbestos in air distribution systems

33   A person must not use asbestos in an air distribution system or equipment in a form in which, or in a location where, asbestos fibres could enter the air supply or return air systems.

Asbestos in a building to be demolished

34   If a building is to be demolished, the employer must ensure that materials with the potential to release asbestos fibres are removed first.

Encapsulation, enclosure or removal of asbestos

35   If a building is being altered or renovated, the employer must ensure that materials in the area of the alterations or renovations that could release asbestos fibres are encapsulated, enclosed or removed.

Notification of a project

36(1)   An employer who is responsible for removing or abating asbestos or for demolishing or renovating a building or equipment containing asbestos must notify a Director of Inspection of the activity at least 72 hours before beginning the activities that may release asbestos fibres.

36(2)   A person must not remove or abate asbestos or demolish or renovate a building or equipment containing asbestos if a Director of Inspection has not been notified in accordance with subsection (1).

Asbestos worker course

37(1)   An employer must ensure that a worker who works with asbestos receives the training necessary for the worker to perform the work safely.

37(2)   An employer must ensure that a worker who enters a restricted area that is designated as a restricted area due to the presence of asbestos

   (a)   has successfully completed a course of instruction approved by a Director of Occupational Hygiene, and

   (b)   has in the worker's possession the original valid certificate of completion of the course issued to the worker.

Containment and labelling of asbestos waste

38(1)   An employer must ensure that asbestos waste is stored, transported and disposed of in sealed containers that are impervious to asbestos and asbestos waste.

38(2)   An employer must ensure that a container of an asbestos product and asbestos waste is clearly labelled

   (a)   to identify the contents as an asbestos product and carcinogenic, and

   (b)   to warn handlers that dust from the contents should not be inhaled.

Use of crystalline silica in abrasive blasting

39(1)   If conducting abrasive blasting, an employer must, where reasonably practicable, ensure that crystalline silica is replaced with a less harmful substance.

39(2) Repealed

Health assessments for workers exposed to asbestos, silica or coal dust

40(1) This section applies to an exposed worker who may be exposed to asbestos, silica or coal dust.

40(2) A health assessment of the worker must include the following:

    (a) the identity of the worker and the employer;

    (b) the date of the medical examination, chest x-ray and spirogram;

    (c) a 35 centimetres by 43 centimetres postero-anterior view chest x-ray, including a radiologist's report;

    (d) a spirogram, conducted by a pulmonary function technician, including determinations of forced expiratory volume in the first, second and forced vital capacity;

    (e) a history covering

        occupational exposures to asbestos, silica, coal dust or other industrial dusts and carcinogens,

        significant exposures to asbestos, silica, coal dust, other dust and carcinogens during non work-related activities,

        (i) significant symptoms that may indicate silicosis, pneumoconiosis, asbestosis or cancer,

        (ii) past and current medical diagnoses of respiratory disease, and

        (iii) the worker's smoking history,

    (f) a written interpretation and explanation of the results of the assessment by a physician, with particular reference to the worker's exposure to airborne substances.

40(3) The physician must give the written interpretation and explanation of the results of the health assessment to the worker not more than 60 days after the tests are completed.

40(4) The physician must ensure that the records of the health assessment are kept for not less than 30 years.

40(5) The person with custody of the health assessment record must ensure that no person, other than the worker or health professional who conducts the health assessment, the staff supervised by the health professional or another person authorized by law to have access, has access to the exposed worker's health assessment unless

    (a) the record is in a form that does not identify the worker , or

    (b) the worker gives written permission for access by another person.

40(6) An employer must ensure that a worker undergoes a health assessment

    (a) not more than 30 calendar days after the worker becomes an exposed worker, and

    (b) every two years after the first health assessment.

40(7) If an exposed worker received a health assessment from a previous employer within the immediately preceding two years, the worker must inform the present employer of the date or approximate date of that health assessment at the earliest possible time.

40(8) An employer must ensure that an exposed worker has received a health assessment within the immediately preceding two years.

40(9) Despite subsections (7) and (8), exposed workers may refuse to undergo part or all of a health assessment by giving the employer a written statement refusing it.

40(10) An employer must not coerce, threaten or force a worker into refusing part or all of a health assessment.

40(11) An employer must pay the cost of the health assessment, medical interpretation and explanation required by this section.

40(12) An employer must ensure that, if it is reasonably practicable, a health assessment is performed during normal hours of work.

40(13) An employer must not make a deduction from the worker's wages, salary or other remuneration or benefits for the time during which an exposed worker

(a) undergoes a health assessment, or

(b) travels to or from a health assessment.

Lead exposure control plan

41(1) An employer must develop an exposure control plan for lead if

(a) a worker at the work site may be exposed to airborne lead in excess of its occupational exposure limit for more than 30 days in a year, or

(b) a worker's exposure to lead at the work site could result in an elevated body burden of lead through any route of entry.

41(2) The exposure control plan must include at least the following:

(a) a statement of purpose and of the responsibilities of individuals;

(b) methods of hazard identification, assessment and control;

(c) worker education and training;

(d) safe work practices if these are required by the hazard assessment under this Code;

(e) descriptions of personal and work site hygiene practices and decontamination practices;

(f) processes of health monitoring, including biological testing;

(g) methods of documentation and record keeping;

(h) procedures for maintenance of the plan, including annual reviews and updating.

41(3) A worker must follow the exposure control plan and practice the personal and work site hygiene practices established by the employer to minimize lead exposure at the work site.

Lead — air monitoring

42 If a worker may be exposed to lead in harmful amounts at a work site, an employer must ensure that air monitoring and surface testing for lead is regularly conducted to confirm that the controls in place are effective.

Medical monitoring for lead

43(1) An employer must ensure blood lead level testing is available to a worker if the worker at a work site could reasonably be expected to have an elevated body burden of lead.

43(2)   An employer must ensure that a worker exposed to lead is informed of the availability of the blood lead test.

43(3)   The employer must pay the cost of a blood level test.

43(4)   An exposed worker may refuse to undergo a blood level test by giving the employer a written statement refusing it.

43(5)   An employer must not coerce, threaten or force a worker into refusing part or all of the test.

43(6)   Where the worker has a blood level that indicates lead poisoning, an occupational health and safety officer, under the direction of a Director of Medical Services, may require the employer to remove the worker from further lead exposure.

Controlling mould exposure

43.1   Where mould exists or may exist, an employer must ensure that a worker's exposure to the mould is controlled in accordance with section 9.

Part 5　　Confined Spaces

Code of practice

44(1) An employer must have a written code of practice governing the practices and procedures to be followed when workers enter and work in a confined space.

44(2) The code of practice must

    (a) take into account and apply the requirements of this Part and of section 169,

    (b) be maintained and periodically reviewed, and

    (c) identify all existing and potential confined space work locations at a work site.

44(3) A worker involved in any aspect of a confined space entry must comply with the requirements and procedures in the code of practice.

Hazard assessment

45 If a worker will enter a confined space or a restricted space to work, an employer must appoint a competent person to

    (a) identify and assess the hazards the worker is likely to be exposed to while in the confined space or restricted space,

    (b) specify the type and frequency of inspections and tests necessary to determine the likelihood of worker exposure to any of the identified hazards,

    (c) perform the inspections and tests specified,

    (d) specify the safety and personal protective equipment required to perform the work, and

    (e) identify the personal protective equipment and emergency equipment to be used by a worker who undertakes rescue operations in the event of an accident or other emergency.

Training

46(1) An employer must ensure that a worker assigned duties related to confined space or restricted space entry is trained by a competent person in

    (a) recognizing hazards associated with working in confined spaces or restricted spaces, and

    (b) performing the worker's duties in a safe and healthy manner.

46(2) An employer must keep records of the training given under subsection (1).

46(3) An employer must ensure that competence in the following is represented in the workers responding to a confined space or restricted space emergency:

    (a) first aid;

    (b) the use of appropriate emergency response equipment;

    (c) procedures appropriate to the confined space or restricted space.

Entry permit system

47(1) A person must not enter a confined space at a work site without a valid entry permit.

47(2) An employer must establish an entry permit system for a confined space that

(a) lists the name of each worker who enters the confined space and the reason for their entry,

(b) gives the location of the confined space,

(c) specifies the time during which an entry permit is valid,

(d) takes into account the work being done in the confined space, and

(e) takes into account the code of practice requirements for entering, being in and leaving a confined space.

47(3) An employer must ensure that, before a worker enters a confined space, an entry permit is properly completed, signed by a competent person and a copy kept readily available.

47(4) Based on a review of similar confined spaces, an employer may issue an entry permit that can be used for a number of similar confined spaces.

Safety and protection — generally

48(1) An employer must ensure that

(a) if a lifeline is required in a confined space or a restricted space, it is used in a manner that does not create an additional hazard,

(b) the safety and personal protective equipment required under this Code is available to workers entering a confined space or a restricted space,

(c) a worker who enters, occupies or leaves a confined space or restricted space uses the safety and personal protective equipment,

(d) the personal protective equipment and emergency equipment required under this Code is available to workers undertaking rescue operations in a confined space or restricted space,

(e) equipment appropriate to the confined space or restricted space, including personal protective equipment, is available to perform a timely rescue, and

(f) a communication system is established that is readily available to workers in a confined space or a restricted space and is appropriate to the hazards.

48(2) An employer must ensure that all personal protective equipment and emergency equipment required for use in a confined space or a restricted space is inspected by a competent person to ensure the equipment is in good working order before workers enter the confined space or the restricted space.

48(3) An employer must ensure that written records of the inspections required by subsection (2) are retained as required by section 58.

Protection — hazardous substances and energy

49(1) An employer must ensure that workers within a confined space are protected against the release of hazardous substances or energy that could harm them.

49(2) An employer must ensure that a worker does not enter a confined space unless adequate precautions are in place to protect a worker from drowning, engulfment or entrapment.

49(3) An employer must ensure that any hazardous energy in a restricted space is controlled in accordance with Part 15.

Unauthorized entry

50 An employer must ensure that persons who are not authorized by the employer to enter a confined space or a restricted space are prevented from entering.

Traffic hazards

51 An employer must ensure that workers in a confined space or a restricted space are protected from hazards created by traffic in the vicinity of the confined space or restricted space.

Testing the atmosphere

52(1) If the hazard assessment identifies a potential atmospheric hazard and a worker is required or authorized by an employer to enter the confined space, the employer must ensure that a competent worker performs a pre-entry atmospheric test of the confined space to

    (a) verify that the oxygen content is between 19.5 percent and 23.0 percent by volume, and

    (b) identify the amount of toxic, flammable or explosive substance that may be present.

52(2) The employer must ensure that the testing required by subsection (1) is performed using calibrated test instruments appropriate for the atmosphere being tested and the instruments are used in accordance with the manufacturer's specifications.

52(3) The employer must ensure that as often as necessary after the first time a worker enters the confined space, a competent worker

    (a) performs the tests specified in subsection (1), and

    (b) identifies and records any additional hazards.

52(3.1) The employer must ensure that if there is a potential for the atmosphere to change unpredictably after a worker enters the confined space, the atmosphere is continuously monitored in accordance with subsection (2).

52(4) If tests identify additional hazards, the employer must deal with the identified hazards in accordance with this Code.

52(5) The employer must ensure that the procedures and practices put in place under subsection (4) are included in the code of practice.

52(6) The employer must ensure that the results of tests required by this section are recorded.

Ventilation and purging

53(1) If the atmospheric testing under section 52 identifies that a hazardous atmosphere exists or is likely to exist in a confined space, an employer must ensure that the confined space is ventilated, purged or both before a worker enters the confined space.

53(2) If ventilating or purging a confined space is impractical or ineffective in eliminating a hazardous atmosphere, the employer must ensure that a worker who enters the confined space uses personal protective equipment appropriate for the conditions within the confined space.

53(3) If mechanical ventilation is needed to maintain a safe atmosphere in a confined space during the work process, an employer must ensure it is provided and operated as needed.

53(4) If mechanical ventilation is required to maintain a safe atmosphere in the confined space, the employer must ensure that

    (a)   the ventilation system incorporates a method of alerting workers to a failure of the system so that workers have sufficient time to safely leave the confined space, and

    (b)   all workers within the confined space have received training in the evacuation procedures to be used in the event of a ventilation system failure.

53(5) All workers must evacuate a confined space or use an alternative means of protection if a ventilation system fails.

Inerting

54(1) An employer must ensure that a confined space is inerted if it is not reasonably practicable to eliminate an explosive or flammable atmosphere within the confined space through another means.

54(2) If a confined space is inerted, an employer must ensure that

    (a)   every worker entering the confined space is equipped with supplied-air respiratory protection equipment that complies with Part 18,

    (b)   all ignition sources are controlled, and

    (c)   the atmosphere within the confined space stays inerted while workers are inside.

Emergency response

55(1) An employer must ensure that a worker does not enter or remain in a confined space or a restricted space unless an effective rescue can be carried out.

55(2) A worker must not enter or stay in a confined space or restricted space unless an effective rescue can be carried out.

55(3) An employer must ensure that the emergency response plan includes the emergency procedures to be followed if there is an accident or other emergency, including procedures in place to evacuate the confined space or restricted space immediately

    (a)   when an alarm is activated,

    (b)   if the concentration of oxygen inside the confined space drops below 19.5 percent by volume or exceeds 23.0 percent by volume, or

    (c)   if there is a significant change in the amount of hazardous substances inside the confined space.

Tending worker

56(1) For every confined space or restricted space entry, an employer must designate a competent worker to be in communication with a worker in the confined space or restricted space.

56(2) An employer must ensure that the designated worker under subsection (1) has a suitable system for summoning assistance.

56(3) An employer must ensure that a competent worker trained in the evacuation procedures in the emergency response plan is present outside a confined space, at or near the entrance, if

(a) the oxygen content of the atmosphere inside the confined space is less than 19.5 percent by volume,

(b) the oxygen content of the atmosphere inside the confined space is greater than 23.0 percent by volume,

(c) the concentration of a substance listed in Schedule 1, Table 2 inside the confined space is greater than 50 percent of its occupational exposure limit, or

(d) a hazard other than one listed in clauses (a), (b) or (c) is identified by the hazard assessment and the hazard cannot be eliminated or effectively controlled.

56(4) An employer must ensure that the tending worker under subsection (3)

(a) keeps track at all times of the number of workers inside the confined space,

(b) is in constant communication with the workers inside the confined space, and

(c) has a suitable system for summoning assistance.

56(5) A tending worker must not leave the area until all workers have left the confined space or another tending worker is in place.

Entry and exit

57   An employer must ensure that a safe means of entry and exit is available to all workers required to work in a confined space or a restricted space and to all rescue personnel attending to the workers.

Retaining records

58   An employer must ensure that all records respecting entry and work in a confined space, including entry permits and testing under this Part, are retained for not less than

(a) one year if no incident or unplanned event occurred during the entry, or

(b) two years if an incident or unplanned event occurred during the entry.

Part 6   Cranes, Hoists and Lifting Devices

General Requirements

Application
59(1) This Part applies to lifting devices, including cranes and hoists, with a rated load capacity of 2000 kilograms or more.

59(1.1) This Part does not apply to drawworks on equipment that is subject to Part 37.

59(2) Sections 60 to 74 apply to roofer's hoists regardless of their rated load capacity.

59(2.1) A hoist may only be used for vertical lifting or lowering if it complies with this Part and is designed and manufactured for vertical lifting or lowering.

59(3) Despite subsection (2), sections 63, 64(4) and 65 do not apply to roofer's hoists.

59(4) Despite subsection (1), an employer must ensure that a lifting device with a rated load capacity of less than 2000 kilograms has the rated load capacity of the equipment shown on the equipment.

Not commercially manufactured
60   If a lifting device is not commercially manufactured, an employer must ensure that it is fit and safe for use as a lifting device and that it is certified by a professional engineer.

Identification of components
61   An employer must ensure that all major structural, mechanical and electrical components of a lifting device are permanently and legibly identified as being component parts of a specific make and model of lifting device.

Rated load capacity
62(1) An employer must ensure that a lifting device has a plate or weatherproof label permanently secured to it that legibly shows

(a)   the manufacturer's rated load capacity,

(b)   the manufacturer's name, and

(c)   the model, serial number and year of manufacture or shipment date.

62(2) If a lifting device is not commercially manufactured, an employer must ensure that it has a plate or weatherproof label permanently secured to it that legibly shows the rated load capacity according to the professional engineer's certification.

62(3) Subsections (1) and (2) do not apply to A-frames and gin poles.

Load charts
63(1) An employer must ensure that a mobile crane or boom truck is equipped at all times with load charts showing the rated load capacity of the mobile crane or boom truck at all permitted boom angles and boom radii.

63(2) An employer must ensure that a tower crane has a load chart

(a)   conspicuously and permanently secured to the cab, and

(b) showing the manufacturer's rated capacity loads at various radii of a two-part line and a four-part line separately.

Operator requirements

64(1) An employer must ensure that a lifting device is only operated by a competent worker authorized by the employer to operate the equipment.

64(2) At the employer's request, an operator, before operating a lifting device, must be able to demonstrate that the worker is competent in the equipment's operation and knowledgeable about load charts and the code of signals for hoisting operations.

64(3) No worker other than the competent worker authorized by the employer may operate a lifting device.

64(4) Before operating a particular lifting device, the operator must be familiar with all recent entries in its log book.

Log books

65(1) An employer must set up a paper or electronic log book for each lifting device at a work site.

65(1.1) Despite subsection (1), the log book requirement does not apply to manually operated hoists.

65(2) The employer must ensure that

(a) the log book is readily available for inspection by an officer at any time,

(b) the most current log book of a mobile crane accompanies it or is available to the operator at all times, and

(c) if ownership of a lifting device is transferred to a new owner, the log book is transferred to the new owner.

65(3) The employer must ensure that the following details are entered into the log book:

(a) the date and time when any work was performed on the lifting device;

(b) length of time in lifting service

(i) recorded as hours of service if the lifting device is equipped by the manufacturer with an hour-meter, or

(ii) if required by the manufacturer's specifications;

(c) all defects or deficiencies and when they were detected;

(d) inspections, including examinations, checks and tests, that are performed, including those specified in the manufacturer's specifications;

(e) repairs or modifications performed;

(f) a record of a certification under section 73;

(g) any matter or incident that may affect the safe operation of the lifting device;

(h) any other operational information specifically identified by the employer;

(i) in the case of a tower crane, whether or not the weight testing device was lifted for that working day, before the work of lifting loads began.

65(4) The employer must ensure that each entry in a paper log book is signed by the person doing the work.

65(5) The employer must ensure that each entry in an electronic log book identifies the person doing the work.

65(6) In the case of a tower crane, the employer must ensure that a senior representative of the employer at the work site confirms that the entries in the log book are correct every day that the tower crane is in operation.

Preventing an unsafe lift

66 If the operator of a lifting device has any doubts as to the safety of workers in the vicinity of the lift, the operator must not move any equipment or load until the operator is assured that the working conditions are safe.

Preventing collisions

67 An employer must ensure that procedures are developed to prevent collisions if two or more lifting devices are in use and there is the potential for a collision between them, their loads or component parts.

Load weight

68 An employer must ensure that the operator of the lifting device, the rigger supervised by the operator and the person in charge of a lift are provided with all the information necessary to enable them to readily and accurately determine the weight of the load to be lifted.

Lift calculation

68.1 An employer must ensure that a lift calculation is completed for any lift exceeding 75 percent of a crane's rated capacity.

Loads over work areas

69(1) An employer must ensure that work is arranged, if it is reasonably practicable, so that a load does not pass over workers.

69(2) An operator of a lifting device must not pass the load on the device over workers unless

    (a) no other practical alternative exists in the circumstances, and

    (b) the workers are effectively warned of the danger.

69(3) A worker must not stand or pass under a suspended load unless the worker has been effectively warned of the danger and the operator of the lifting device knows the worker is under the suspended load.

69(4) The operator of a lifting device that is travelling with a load must ensure that the load is positioned as close to the ground or grade as possible.

Tag and hoisting lines

70(1) If workers are in danger because of the movement of a load being lifted, lowered or moved by a lifting device, an employer must ensure that

    (a) a worker uses a tag line of sufficient length to control the load,

    (b) the tag line is used in a way that prevents the load from striking the worker controlling the tag line, and

    (c) a tag line is used when it allows worker separation from the load.

70(2) An employer must ensure that tag lines of non-conductive synthetic rope are used when there is a danger of contact with energized electrical equipment.

70(3) An employer must ensure that tag lines are not used in situations where their use could increase the danger to workers.

Hand signals

71   An employer must ensure that hand signals necessary to ensure a safe hoisting operation are given in accordance with section 191 by a competent signaller designated by the employer.

Controls

72(1) Moved to section 95.1

72(2) Repealed

72(3) The employer must ensure that an operator who uses a remote control to operate a lifting device is visually distinguishable from other workers at the work site.

Repairs and modifications

73(1) An employer must ensure that structural repairs or modifications to components of a lifting device are

(a)   made only under the direction and control of a professional engineer, and

(b)   certified by the professional engineer to confirm that the workmanship and quality of materials used has restored the components to not less than their original capacity.

73(2) If structural repairs or modifications are made, the employer must ensure that

(a)   the repaired or modified components are individually and uniquely identified in the log book and on the component, and

(b)   the professional engineer's certification makes reference to those components and their identification.

Containers for hoisting

74(1) An employer must ensure that a container used for a load being lifted by a hoist is designed for that particular purpose and bears a marking to indicate its maximum load rating.

74(2) A person must not use an oil drum or similar container as a container for a load being lifted by a hoist unless the drum or container is hoisted in a cage designed for that purpose.

A-Frames and gin poles

75   An employer must ensure that an A-frame or gin pole

(a)   is not inclined more than 45 degrees from the vertical,

(b)   is equipped with a boom stop, and

(c)   has the sheave and cap of its rigging attached securely enough to the gin pole to withstand any loads to which the assembly may be subjected.

Suspended personnel baskets

75.1(1) An employer must ensure that

(a) a commercially manufactured suspended personnel basket is erected, used, operated and maintained in accordance with the manufacturer's specifications or specifications certified by a professional engineer, or

(b) a suspended personnel basket that is not commercially manufactured is designed and certified by a professional engineer.

75.1(2) Despite section 147, if it is not practicable to provide a separate personal fall arrest system using a vertical lifeline for each worker in the man basket, an employer must ensure that

(a) a separate support is attached between the suspended personnel basket and the hoist line above the hook assembly that is capable of withstanding the weight of the personel basket, materials, equipment and workers should the hook assembly fail, and

(b) each worker within the personnel basket is wearing a separate personal fall arrest system attached to the personnel basket.

Cantilever Hoists

Installation and use

76 An employer must ensure that a cantilever hoist

(a) is anchored to a building or structure at distance intervals that meet the manufacturer's specifications or specifications certified by a professional engineer,

(b) has a foundation that is solid, level and of a size and strength capable of supporting the weight of the hoist and its loads under all working conditions, and

(c) carries loads that do not project beyond the edges of the material landing platform or the skip of the hoist.

Chimney Hoists

Equipment requirements

77 An employer must ensure that a chimney hoist

(a) is equipped with positive drives,

(b) does not have a clutch between the transmission and the hoist drums,

(c) is equipped with a speed-indicating device if the hoist is capable of operating at speeds of more than 0.6 metres per second,

(d) is equipped with at least two independent braking systems, each capable of stopping 150 percent of the manufacturer's rated capacity load, at the manufacture's rated capacity maximum speed,

(e) has a roller or ball bearing swivel installed between the bucket and the rope on the hoist,

(f) is equipped with a communication system that informs the operator when the hoist is to be used to lift or lower workers, and

(g) has a separate safety line attached between the bucket or man basket yoke and the hoist rope above the ball or hook.

Operator responsibilities

78(1) An operator of a chimney hoist must not

(a) lift or lower a worker at a speed of more than 0.6 metres per second,

(b) use the brake alone to control the speed of the chimney hoist when a worker is being lowered,

(c) lift or lower more than two workers at the same time, or

(d) lift or lower materials or equipment at the same time as a worker.

78(2) An operator of a chimney hoist must use safety latch hooks or shackles equipped with safety pins.

Worker in lifting device

79   An employer must ensure that a worker who is lifted or lowered by a chimney hoist uses a personnel basket.

Hand-Operated Hoists

Holding suspended load

80   An employer must ensure that a hand-operated hoist is provided with a device capable of holding the total load suspended safely under all operating conditions.

Material Hoists

Safety code for material hoists

81   A material hoist must meet the requirements of CSA Standard CAN/CSA-Z256-M87 (R2006), *Safety Code for Material Hoists*.

Rider restriction

82(1) A person must not ride on a material hoist.

82(2) An employer must ensure that a worker does not ride on a material hoist.

Gate interlocks

83   An employer must ensure that a material hoist is equipped at each floor or level with devices that prevent

(a) a landing gate from being opened unless the hoist platform is positioned at that landing, or

(b) movement of the hoist platform when a landing gate is open.

Operator responsibilities

84   A material hoist operator must not

(a) leave the hoist controls unattended while the skip, platform or load is in the lifted position, or

(b) move the skip, platform or cage until the operator is informed by a designated signaller that it is safe to do so.

Signal systems

85(1) An employer must ensure that

(a) if a signal system is used to control the movement of a material hoist the signal descriptions are posted at each floor or level and at the operator's station,

(b) the operator of a material hoist, and a designated signaller at the floor or level where loading and unloading is being performed, maintain visual or auditory communication with each other at all times during loading and unloading, and

(c) if an electrical or mechanical signal system has been installed to coordinate the movement of the hoist's skip, platform or cage, the system is arranged so that the hoist operator knows from which floor or level a signal originates.

85(2) An employer must ensure that a material hoist erected at a building that is more than 20 metres high has a signal system that

(a) is installed at each floor or level and at the operator's station,

(b) is designed to allow voice communication between a worker at any floor or level and the operator, and

(c) informs the operator from which floor or level the signal originates.

Hoist brakes

86 An employer must ensure that a material hoist's braking system is capable of stopping and holding the total load suspended safely, under all operating conditions.

Location protected

87 An employer must ensure that

(a) the area around the base of the material hoist is fenced or otherwise barricaded to prevent anyone from entering it if the hoist platform is not at the base level,

(b) a removable guardrail or gate is installed between 600 millimeters and 900 millimetres away from the edge of a floor or level served by the material hoist, and

(c) if the operator controls are not remote from the material hoist, overhead protection is provided for the operator.

Mobile Cranes and Boom Trucks

Safety code for mobile cranes

88 A mobile crane must meet the requirements of CSA Standard CAN/CSA-Z150-98 (R2004), *Safety Code on Mobile Cranes* with the exception of clauses 1.6 and 1.7.

Personnel baskets

88.1 Despite section 88, an employer must ensure that

(a) a personnel basket used with a mobile crane is designed, constructed, maintained and used in accordance with CSA Standard CAN/CSA Z150-98 (R2004), *Safety Code on Mobile Cranes*, clause 5.4.7, or

(b) a personnel basket that is not commercially manufactured is designed and certified by a professional engineer.

Non-destructive testing

89	An employer must ensure that all load-bearing components of a mobile crane undergo non-destructive testing under the direction and control of a professional engineer in accordance with the manufacturer's specifications at 12-month intervals from the date of the mobile crane's most recent certification.

Counterweights and outriggers

90	If outriggers are installed on a mobile crane or boom truck, the employer must ensure the outriggers are extended and supported by solid footings before being used.

Warning device

91	An employer must ensure that a mobile crane is equipped with an effective warning device in addition to the one required by section 267, that

(a)	is readily accessible to the operator,

(b)	is sufficient to warn workers of the impending movement of the crane, and

(c)	if it is an auditory warning device, has a distinct sound that is distinguishable from all other sounds at the work site.

Preventing damage

92(1)	If a boom is fitted on a mobile crane or boom truck and the crane or truck may overturn or flip backwards because of the return movement of the boom, an employer must ensure that

(a)	positive boom stops are installed in the crane or truck in accordance with the manufacturer's specifications, and

(b)	a boom stop limit device is installed to prevent the boom from being drawn back beyond a pre-determined safe boom angle.

92(2)	If a jib is attached to the boom of a mobile crane or boom truck, an employer must ensure that a jib stop device is installed in the crane or truck to prevent the jib from being drawn back over the boom.

92(3)	An employer must ensure that blocking procedures are developed to prevent the collapse or upset of any part of a derrick, mast or boom during the installation, removal or replacement of a derrick or the mast or boom section of a mobile crane or boom truck.

Load blocks

92.1	Despite section 88, an employer must ensure that the load blocks of a mobile crane are maintained and repaired in accordance with the manufacturer's specifications or, if there are no manufacturer's specifications, in accordance with CSA Standard CAN/CSA Z150-98 (R2004), *Safety Code on Mobile Cranes*, clause 4.3.5.2.

Outriggers

92.2	Despite section 88, an employer must ensure that a mobile crane equipped with outriggers is set up with the outriggers on load-bearing floats or pads that are of adequate size, strength and rigidity.

Overhead Cranes

Electrical components and functions

93   A bridge, jib, monorail, gantry or overhead travelling crane must meet the design requirements for electrical components and functions of

(a)   CSA Standard C22.1-06, *Canadian Electrical Code, Part 1, Section 40*, and

(b)   CSA Standard C22.2 No. 33-M1984 (R2004), *Construction and Test of Electric Cranes and Hoists*.

Maintenance and inspection

94   A bridge, jib, monorail, gantry or overhead travelling crane must meet the safety requirements of CSA Standard CAN/CSA-B167-96 (R2007), *Safety Standard for Maintenance and Inspection of Overhead Cranes, Gantry Cranes, Monorails, Hoists and Trolleys*.

Safe movement

95   An employer must ensure that a crane operating on rails, tracks or trolleys

(a)   has a positive stop or limiting device on the crane or on the rails, tracks or trolleys to prevent it from overrunning safe limits or contacting other equipment that is on the same rail, track or trolley,

(b)   is equipped with an overspeed limiting device,

(c)   has positive means of ensuring that the rails, tracks or trolleys cannot be spread or misalign,

(d)   has sweep guards installed to prevent material on the rail, track or trolley from dislodging the crane, and

(e)   has a bed designed to carry all anticipated loads.

Controls

95.1   An employer must ensure that the controls of an overhead crane are of a constant manual pressure type.

Personnel Hoists

Safety code for personnel hoists

96   Except for a personnel hoist used in a mine, a personnel hoist must meet the requirements of CSA Standard CAN/CSA-Z185 (R2006), *Safety Code for Personnel Hoists*.

Roofer's Hoists

Safe use and design

97(1)   An employer must ensure that a roofer's hoist has counterweights

(a)   designed as a component part of the hoist to remain securely attached to the hoist until all lifting is completed, and

(b)   heavy enough to counterbalance four times the maximum weight of the load being lifted.

97(2)   A person must not use roofing materials as a counterweight.

97(3) An employer must ensure that a roofer's hoist is inspected daily by a competent worker designated by the employer.

97(4) An employer must ensure that bolts and pins used to interconnect component parts of a roofer's hoist are equipped with safety pins that prevent them from being dislodged.

97(5) A worker must

(a) use a roofer's hoist only for vertical lifting, and

(b) not exceed the design load limits of the roofer's hoist.

97(6) An employer must ensure that a gallows frame roofer's hoist is constructed of lumber sized as follows, or of material that has the same or greater properties as the lumber used for the same function:

(a) thrustout — 38 millimetres by 184 millimeters lumber;

(b) uprights — 90 millimetres by 90 millimetres lumber;

(c) braces and base plates — 38 millimetres by 140 millimetres.

97(7) An employer must ensure that a gallows frame roofer's hoist

(a) has a hoisting line with a breaking strength of not less than 25 kilonewtons,

(b) has thrustouts placed on their edge that do not overhang more than one-quarter of their length, and

(c) has sheaves securely attached to the thrustouts without using single strand wire or nails.

Tower and Building Shaft Hoists

Protective enclosure

98 An employer must ensure that

(a) a tower hoist is enclosed at ground level with solid walls or equally effective fencing to a height of at least 2 metres on all sides except the loading side,

(b) a hoist shaft inside a building is enclosed on all sides but the landing side at all floors or levels to a height of at least 2 metres with solid walls or equally effective fencing,

(c) a landing gate inside a building does not open unless the hoist platform is positioned at that landing,

(d) the landing side of the hoist shaft inside a building has an access door complete with a lock and an "OPEN SHAFT" sign attached to the enclosure,

(e) a tower or building shaft hoist is braced, guyed or supported at vertical intervals of not more than 6 metres or at the intervals in the manufacturer's specifications and

(f) the bottom pulley block or sheave is securely anchored and the pulley and hoisting ropes to the hoisting engine are enclosed.

Design

99 An employer must ensure that a boom is not installed on a tower hoist unless its design is certified by a professional engineer to the effect that the tower structure can withstand the additional load.

Tower Cranes

Safety code for tower cranes

100 A tower crane manufactured on or after July1, 2009 must meet the requirements of CSA Standard Z248-04, *Code for Tower Cranes*.

Limit devices

101(1) An employer must ensure that a tower crane is equipped with

(a) an overload device consisting of a hoist overload switch that automatically restricts the weight of the load,

(b) a travel limit device consisting of a moment overload switch that automatically restricts the radius within which the load can travel,

(c) a height limit switch that prevents the load from being overwound, and

(d) trolley travel limit devices consisting of a "trolley in" limit switch and a "trolley out" limit switch that prevent the trolley from running to the end of its track and falling off.

101(2) An employer must ensure that the devices described in subsection (1) are adjusted and set in accordance with the manufacturer's specifications and have their limit switches sealed.

Operation

102 An operator of a tower crane must

(a) ensure the safe movement of the crane and its load at all times,

(b) verify at the beginning of each work shift that the mast is plumb, and

(c) verify at least once in each 24 hour period that the limit devices described in section 101 are operational.

Changing components

103(1) An employer must ensure that the major structural, mechanical and electrical components of a tower crane are not interchanged with those of other tower cranes unless

(a) the components are from the same make or model of tower crane,

(b) the components are approved by the manufacturer as suitable for their intended application, or

(c) the components are certified by a professional engineer as suitable for their intended application.

103(2) An employer must ensure that if an operator's cab is attached to the boom of a tower crane, the design of the cab, its position, method of attachment and any structural changes, including changes to the counterweight, capacity and operation of the crane, are in accordance with the manufacturer's specifications or are certified by a professional engineer.

Test weights

104(1) An employer must ensure that if weights are used as a weight testing device on a tower crane,

    (a) the true weight of the test weight is determined and legibly recorded on the weight, and

    (b) when not in use, the test weights rest on supports to prevent the weights from freezing to the ground or creating a vacuum when lifted.

104(2) The employer must ensure that the lifting attachment on a test weight is made of mild steel and of sufficient size and strength to support the weight.

Structural testing and examination

105(1) An employer must ensure that all structural and rigging components of a tower crane undergo non-destructive testing under the direction and control of a professional engineer in accordance with the manufacturer's specifications

    (a) as close as reasonably practicable to the project site,

    (b) before the crane is used for the first time in a project in Alberta, and

    (c) if the crane is moved from project to project, before it is used after the move.

105(2) If a tower crane is in operation on a project for more than one year from the date on which the crane starts operating, the employer must ensure its structural components are examined under the direction and control of a professional engineer after each period of 2000 operating hours or 12 months after the date on which it starts operating, whichever occurs first.

105(3) The employer must ensure that the results of the testing or examination required by subsections (1) and (2) are certified by a professional engineer in a report that clearly identifies the crane and the components to which the information relates.

Wind and temperature limitations

106(1) An employer must ensure that operation of a tower crane is stopped when the wind velocity at the elevation of the crane exceeds the limit recommended in the manufacturer's specifications or, if there are none, in specifications certified by a professional engineer.

106(2) An employer must ensure that operation of a tower crane is stopped when the temperature in the vicinity of the crane is below the limit recommended in the manufacturer's specifications or, if there are none, in specifications certified by a professional engineer.

Multiple cranes

107   If two or more tower cranes are erected in such a manner that the radii of operations overlap,

    (a) the employer must ensure that operators are provided with a visual or auditory means of communicating with each other,

    (b) the operators must be able to communicate with each other when both crane are in operation, and

    (c) the operators must operate the cranes in such a manner that there are no collisions between the cranes or their loads.

Underground Shaft Hoists

Safety requirements

108(1) An employer must ensure that an underground shaft hoist complies with the following:

(a) all supporting parts of the hoist machinery are set on and secured to a substantial foundation;

(b) it is equipped with positive drives for lifting and lowering the hoist cage;

(c) it does not have a clutch between the transmission and the hoist drums;

(d) it has a hoist drum with a spring-activated drum friction brake capable of stopping and holding the total suspended load in a safe manner under all operating conditions;

(e) it has a hoist drum equipped with a positive spring-activated pawl or similar device to lock the drum.

108(2) An employer must ensure that an underground shaft hoist

(a) has a communication system available and working at all times between the hoist operator and workers at landings in the shaft leading to a tunnel or an underground space, and

(b) the controls of the communication system can be operated at all times at every landing in the shaft, on the hoist platform and at the operator's position.

108(3) An employer must ensure that in an emergency an additional means of communication is available and working at all times between the operator of a shaft hoist and workers at the face of the tunnelling operations.

108(4) An employer must ensure that, if a code is used in a communication system in an underground shaft hoist, the code is prominently posted at all times at every landing in the shaft and at the operator's controls.

Operator responsibilities

109(1) The operator of an underground hoist must

(a) ensure that the brake remains on at all times until it is released manually,

(b) hold the hoist drum brake in the "OFF" position when lifting or lowering the hoist cage, and

(c) not lock out or otherwise disable the hoist drum brake when lifting or lowering the hoist cage.

109(2) The operator of an underground hoist must not allow the hoist to travel at more than 1.2 metres per second when a worker is lifted or lowered in the hoist cage.

Hoist cage

110(1) An employer must ensure that

(a) a hoist cage platform is equipped with a car locking device, and

(b) the shaft on which an underground shaft hoist is installed is equipped with guide rails.

110(2) An employer must ensure that a hoist cage has a plate that

(a) states the maximum number of workers and the maximum load for which the hoist cage is designed,

(b) is secured to the hoist cage, and

(c) is clearly visible to the workers in the cage and the operator.

110(3) A person must not use an open hook to attach a hoist cage to the hoisting line.

Unguided suspended cage

111(1) Despite sections 108 to 110, an employer may use a suspended cage that does not have guide rails in an underground shaft if

(a) the movement of the cage is controlled by a crane,

(b) all sides and the top of the cage are enclosed by a screen of sufficient strength to protect any workers being transported in it, and

(c) a designated signaller at the surface has constant effective communication between the cage occupants and the crane operator.

111(2) If a cage referred to in subsection (1) is used in an underground shaft that is more than 30 metres deep, the employer must ensure that the cage is designed and certified by a professional engineer.

111(3) Section 347 does not apply to a cage referred to in subsection (1) or (2) when the cage is transporting workers.

Vehicle Hoists

Safety standards

112 An employer must ensure that a vehicle hoist installed on or after July 1, 2009 meets the requirements of the following:

(a) ANSI Standard ANSI/ALI ALCTV-2006, *American National Standard for Automotive Lifts — Safety Requirements for Construction, Testing and Validation*; or

(b) ANSI Standard ANSI/ALI ALOIM-2000, *Automotive Lifts — Safety Requirements for Operation, Inspection and Maintenance.*

Safe use

113(1) An employer must ensure that a pneumatic or hydraulic vehicle hoist has controls operated by constant manual pressure.

113(2) An employer must ensure that the operator of a vehicle hoist

(a) remains at the controls while the vehicle hoist is in motion, and

(b) does not block the controls during raising and lowering.

113(3) A worker must not be under a suspended load unless the load is supported by

(a) a vehicle hoist designed for that purpose, or

(b) stands or blocks, other than jacks, that are designed, constructed and maintained to support the load and placed on firm foundations.

Winching Operations

Safe practices

114   An operator of a winch must ensure that, before vehicle-mounted winch lines are hooked or unhooked from an object, the vehicle is prevented from moving.

Part 7   Emergency Preparedness and Response

Emergency response plan

115(1) An employer must establish an emergency response plan for responding to an emergency that may require rescue or evacuation.

115(2) An employer must involve affected workers in establishing the emergency response plan.

115(3) An employer must ensure that an emergency response plan is current.

Contents of plan

116   An emergency response plan must include the following:

    (a)   the identification of potential emergencies;

    (b)   procedures for dealing with the identified emergencies;

    (c)   the identification of, location of and operational procedures for emergency equipment;

    (d)   the emergency response training requirements;

    (e)   the location and use of emergency facilities;

    (f)   the fire protection requirements;

    (g)   the alarm and emergency communication requirements;

    (h)   the first aid services required;

    (i)   procedures for rescue and evacuation;

    (j)   the designated rescue and evacuation workers.

Rescue and evacuation workers

117(1) An employer must designate the workers who will provide rescue services and supervise evacuation procedures in an emergency.

117(2) An employer must ensure that designated rescue and emergency workers are trained in emergency response appropriate to the work site and the potential emergencies identified in the emergency response plan.

117(3) The training under subsection (2) must include exercises appropriate to the work site that simulate the potential emergencies identified in the emergency response plan.

117(4) The training exercises referred to in subsection (3) must be repeated at the intervals required to ensure that the designated rescue and evacuation workers are competent to carry out their duties.

Equipment

118(1) An employer must provide workers designated under section 117 with personal protective clothing and equipment appropriate to the work site and the potential emergencies identified in the emergency response plan.

118(2) Workers who respond to an emergency must wear and use personal protective clothing and equipment appropriate to the work site and the emergency.

Part 8   Entrances, Walkways, Stairways and Ladders

Entrances, Walkways, Stairways

Safe entry and exit

119(1) An employer must ensure that every worker can enter a work area safely and leave a work area safely at all times.

119(2) An employer must ensure that a work area's entrances and exits are in good working order.

119(3) An employer must ensure that a work area's entrances and exits are free from materials, equipment, accumulations of waste or other obstructions that might endanger workers or restrict their movement.

119(4) An employer must ensure that, if a worker could be isolated from a primary escape route,

    (a) there is a ready, convenient and safe secondary means of escape from the work area, and

    (b) the secondary escape route is readily useable at all times.

119(5) An employer must ensure that all workers are familiar with escape routes from the work area.

Doors

120(1) An employer must ensure that doors to and from a work area can be opened without substantial effort and are not obstructed.

120(2) An employer must ensure that a door used to enter or leave an enclosed area that poses a hazard to workers entering the area

    (a) is kept in good working order, and

    (b) has a means of opening it from the inside at all times.

Walkways, runways and ramps

121(1) An employer must ensure that a walkway, runway or ramp

    (a) is strong enough to support the equipment and workers who may use it,

    (b) is at least 600 millimetres wide,

    (c) is wide enough to ensure the safe movement of equipment and workers, and

    (d) has the appropriate toe boards and guardrails required by Part 22.

121(2) An employer must ensure that the surface of a walkway, runway or ramp has sufficient traction to allow workers to move on it safely.

Stairways

122(1) An employer must ensure that

    (a) the width of the treads and the height of the rise of a stairway are uniform throughout its length, and

    (b) the treads of a stairway are level.

122(2) An employer must ensure that

    (a) a stairway with 5 or more risers has the appropriate handrail required by this Code, and

(b) a stairway with open sides has a handrail and an intermediate rail or equivalent safeguard on each open side.

122(3) An employer must ensure that temporary stairs are at least 600 millimetres wide.

Handrails on stairways

123(1) This section applies to stairways with 5 or more risers.

123(2) An employer must ensure that a stairway is equipped with a handrail that

(a) extends the entire length of the stairway,

(b) is secured and cannot be dislodged,

(c) is between 800 millimetres and 920 millimetres above the front edge of the treads, and

(d) is substantial and constructed of lumber that is not less than 38 millimetres by 89 millimetres or material with properties the same as or better than those of lumber.

123(3) An employer must ensure that posts supporting a handrail

(a) are spaced not more than 3 metres apart at their vertical centres, and

(b) are constructed of lumber that is not less than 38 millimetres by 89 millimetres or materials with properties the same as or better than those of lumber.

Ladders — General

Restriction on use

124   An employer must ensure that workers do not use a ladder to enter or leave an elevated or sub-level work area if the area has another safe and recognizable way to enter or leave it.

Prohibition on single rail

125   A person must not make a ladder by fastening cleats across a single rail or post.

Prohibition on painting

126(1) Subject to subsection (2), a person must not paint a wooden ladder.

126(2) A wooden ladder may be preserved with a transparent protective coating.

Use near energized electrical equipment

127   An employer must ensure that a ladder used during the servicing of energized or potentially energized electrical equipment is made of non-conductive material.

Ladders on extending booms

128(1) An employer must ensure that

(a) if a ladder is a permanent part of an extending boom on powered mobile equipment, no worker is on the ladder during the articulation, extension or retraction of the boom, and

(b) if outriggers are incorporated in the equipment to provide stability, no worker climbs the ladder until the outriggers are deployed.

128(2) Subsection (1)(a) does not apply to professional fire fighters working on fire fighting equipment.

Crawl Board or Roof Ladder

Safe use

129   An employer must ensure that a crawl board or roof ladder used for roof work

    (a) is securely fastened by hooking the board or ladder over the ridge of the roof or by another equally effective means, and

    (b) is not supported by an eaves trough.

Fixed Ladders

Design criteria

130(1) An employer must ensure that a fixed ladder installed on or after April 30, 2004 meets the requirements of PIP Standard STF05501 (February 2002), *Fixed Ladders and Cages*, published by the Construction Industry Institute.

130(2) Despite the standards referenced in PIP Standard STF05501, an employer may

    (a) use applicable Canadian material and process standards if the employer ensures that the fixed ladder is designed and installed in accordance with established engineering principles, and

    (b) allow the inside diameter of a cage hoop to be as great as 760 millimetres.

130(3) If a fixed ladder is made of a material other than steel, the employer must ensure that the design is certified by a professional engineer as being as strong as or stronger than that required by PIP Standard STF05501.

130(4) The employer must ensure that a self-closing double bar safety gate, or equally effective barrier, is provided at ladderway floor openings and platforms of fixed ladders installed on or after April 30, 2004.

130(5) Subsection (4) does not apply at landings.

130(6) Section 327 applies to an access ladder attached to a scaffold.

Fixed ladders in manholes

131   Despite section 130, fixed ladders used in pre-cast reinforced concrete manhole sections installed on or after July1, 2009 must meet the requirements of ASTM Standard C478-07, *Standard Specification for Reinforced Concrete Manhole Sections*.

Rest platform exemption

132   If each worker working on a drilling rig or service rig on a fixed ladder is equipped with and wears a climb assist device that complies with the manufacturer's specifications or specifications certified by a professional engineer, an employer is not required to

    (a) provide the ladder with rest platforms, or

    (b) have the side rails extend not less than 1050 millimetres above the point at which the workers get on or off.

Portable Ladders

Prohibition

133(1) A worker must not perform work from either of the top two rungs, steps or cleats of a portable ladder unless the manufacturer's specifications allow the worker to do so.

133(2) Despite subsection (1), a worker may work from either of the top two rungs, steps or treads of a stepladder,

    (a) if the stepladder has a railed platform at the top, or

    (b) if the manufacturer's specifications for the stepladder permit it.

Constructed portable ladder

134(1) An employer must ensure that a constructed portable ladder

    (a) is constructed of lumber that is free of loose knots or knot holes,

    (b) with a length of 5 metres or less has side rails constructed of lumber measuring not less than 38 millimetres by 89 millimetres,

    (c) more than 5 metres long has side rails constructed of lumber measuring not less than 38 millimetres by 140 millimetres,

    (d) has side rails that are not notched, dapped, tapered or spliced,

    (e) has side rails at least 500 millimetres apart at the bottom, and

    (f) has rungs that are

        (i) constructed of lumber measuring not less than 21 millimetres by 89 millimetres,

        (ii) held by filler blocks or secured by a single continuous wire, and

        (iii) uniformly spaced at a centre to centre distance of 250 millimetres to 300 millimetres.

134(2) An employer must ensure that a two-way constructed portable ladder that is wide enough to permit traffic in both directions at the same time,

    (a) has a centre structural rail along the length of the ladder,

    (b) is at least one metre wide, and

    (c) is constructed of materials that are substantial enough in size to accommodate the maximum intended load.

Manufactured portable ladder

135 An employer must ensure that a portable ladder manufactured on or after July1, 2009 meets the requirements of

    (a) CSA Standard CAN3-Z11-M81 (R2005), *Portable Ladders,*

    (b) ANSI Standard A14.1-2007, *American National Standard for Ladders — Wood — Safety Requirements,*

    (c) ANSI Standard A14.2-2007, *American National Standard for Ladders — Portable Metal — Safety Requirements, or*

    (d) ANSI Standard A14.5-2007, *American National Standard for Ladders — Portable Reinforced Plastic — Safety Requirements.*

Securing and positioning

136 A worker must ensure that

(a)   a portable ladder is secured against movement and placed on a base that is stable,

(b)   the base of an inclined portable ladder is no further from the base of the wall or structure than one-quarter of the distance between the base of the ladder and the place where the ladder contacts the wall, and

(c)   the side rails of a portable ladder extend at least 1 metre above a platform, landing or parapet if the ladder is used as a means of access to the platform, landing or parapet.

Fall protection

137(1) An employer must ensure that a worker working from a portable ladder from which the worker may fall 3 metres or more uses a personal fall arrest system.

137(2) Subsection (1) does not apply while the worker is moving up or down the portable ladder.

137(3) Despite subsection (1), if it is not reasonably practical to use a personal fall arrest system, a worker may work from a portable ladder without fall protection if

(a)   the work is a light duty task of short duration at each location,

(b)   the worker's centre of balance is at the centre of the ladder at all times even with an arm extended beyond the side rails of the ladder, and

(c)   the worker maintains three-point contact whenever the worker extends an arm beyond a side rail.

Part 9   Fall Protection

Rescue personnel exemption

138   Rescue personnel involved in training or in providing emergency rescue services may use equipment and practices other than those specified in this Part.

General protection

139(1) Subject to subsections (3) through (8), an employer must ensure that a worker is protected from falling at a temporary or permanent work area if a worker may fall

    (a)   a vertical distance of 3 metres or more,

    (b)   a vertical distance of less than 3 metres if there is an unusual possibility of injury, or

    (c)   into or onto a hazardous substance or object, or through an opening in a work surface.

139(2) For the purposes of this section, there is an unusual possibility of injury if the injury may be worse than an injury from landing on a solid, flat surface.

139(3) To meet the requirement under subsection (1), an employer must install an engineering control such as a guardrail.

139(4) Despite subsection (3), an employer must ensure that a worker at a permanent work area is protected from falling by a guardrail if the worker may fall a vertical distance of more than 1.2 metres and less than 3 metres.

139(5) Despite subsections (3) and (4), if the use of a guardrail is not reasonably practicable, an employer must ensure that a worker uses a travel restraint system that meets the requirements of this Part.

139(6) Despite subsection (5), if the use of a travel restraint system is not reasonably practicable, an employer must ensure that a worker uses a personal fall arrest system that meets the requirements of this Part.

139(7) Despite subsection (6), if the use of a personal fall arrest system is not reasonably practicable, an employer must ensure that a worker uses an equally effective fall protection system that meets the requirements of this Part.

139(8) A worker must use or wear the fall protection system the employer requires the worker to use or wear in compliance with this Code.

Fall protection plan

140(1) An employer must develop procedures that comply with this Part in a fall protection plan for a work site if a worker at the work site may fall 3 metres or more and the worker is not protected by guardrails.

140(2) A fall protection plan must specify

    (a)   the fall hazards at the work site,

    (b)   the fall protection system to be used at the work site,

    (c)   the anchors to be used during the work,

    (d)   that clearance distances below the work area, if applicable, have been confirmed as sufficient to prevent a worker from striking the ground or an object or level below the work area,

    (e)   the procedures used to assemble, maintain, inspect, use and disassemble the fall protection system, where applicable, and

(f) the rescue procedures to be used if a worker falls and is suspended by a personal fall arrest system or safety net and needs to be rescued.

140(3) The employer must ensure that the fall protection plan is available at the work site and is reviewed with workers before work with a risk of falling begins.

140(4) The employer must ensure that the plan is updated when conditions affecting fall protection change.

Instruction of workers

141(1) An employer must ensure that a worker is trained in the safe use of the fall protection system before allowing the worker to work in an area where a fall protection system must be used.

141(2) The training referred to in subsection (1) must include the following:

(a) a review of current Alberta legislation pertaining to fall protection;

(b) an understanding of what a fall protection plan is;

(c) fall protection methods a worker is required to use at a work site;

(d) identification of fall hazards;

(e) assessment and selection of specific anchors that the worker may use;

(f) instructions for the correct use of connecting hardware;

(g) information about the effect of a fall on the human body, including

(i)   maximum arresting force,

(ii) the purpose of shock and energy absorbers,

(iii) swing fall,

(iv) free fall;

(h) pre-use inspection;

(i) emergency response procedures to be used at the work site, if necessary; and

(j) practice in

(i)   inspecting, fitting, adjusting and connecting fall protection systems and components, and

(ii) emergency response procedures.

141(3) In addition to the training described in subsection (2), an employer must ensure that a worker is made aware of the fall hazards particular to that work site and the steps being taken to eliminate or control those hazards.

Full body harness

142(1) An employer must ensure that

(a) a full body harness manufactured on or after July 1, 2009 is approved to

(i)   CSA Standard CAN/CSA Z259.10-06, *Full Body Harnesses*,

(ii) ANSI/ASSE Standard Z359.1-2007, *Safety requirements for personal fall arrest systems, subsystems and components*, or

(iii) CEN Standard EN 361: 2007, *Personal protective equipment against falls from a height — Full body harnesses,* and

(b) a worker using a personal fall arrest system wears and uses a full body harness.

142(2) A worker using a personal fall arrest system must wear and use a full body harness.

Body belt

142.1 An employer must ensure that

(a) a body belt manufactured on or after July1, 2009 is approved to

    (i) CSA Standard Z259.1-05, *Body belts and saddles for work positioning and travel restraint,*

    (ii) ANSI/ASSE Standard A10.32-2004, *Fall Protection Systems — American National Standard for Construction and Demolition Operations,* or

    (iii) CEN Standard EN 358: 2000, *Personal protective equipment for work positioning and prevention of falls from a height — Belts for work positioning and restraint and work positioning lanyards,* and

(b) a worker uses a body belt only as part of a travel restraint system or as part of a fall restrict system.

Lanyard

142.2(1) An employer must ensure that a lanyard manufactured on or after July1, 2009 is approved to

(a) CSA Standard Z259.11-05, *Energy absorbers and lanyards,*

(b) ANSI/ASSE Standard Z359.1-2007, *Safety requirements for personal fall arrest systems, subsystems and components,* or

(c) CEN Standard EN 354: 2002, *Personal protective equipment against falls from a height — Lanyards.*

142.2(2) An employer must ensure that a lanyard used by a worker is made of wire rope or other material appropriate to the hazard if a tool or corrosive agent that could sever, abrade or burn a lanyard is used in the work area.

142.2(3) Despite subsection (2), if a worker works near an energized conductor or in a work area where a lanyard made of conductive material cannot be used safely, the employer must ensure that the worker uses another effective means of fall protection.

Shock absorber

142.3(1) An employer must ensure that if a shock absorber or shock absorbing lanyard is used as part of a personal fall arrest system, it is approved to one of the following standards if manufactured on or after July1, 2009:

(a) CSA Standard Z259.11-05, *Energy absorbers and lanyards;*

(b) ANSI/ASSE Standard Z359.1-2007, *Safety requirements for personal fall arrest systems, subsystems and components;* or

(c) CEN Standard EN 355: 2002, *Personal protective equipment against falls from a height — Energy absorbers.*

142.3(2) An employer must ensure that a personal fall arrest system consists of a full body harness and a lanyard equipped with a shock absorber or similar device.

142.3(3) Despite subsection (2), a shock absorber or similar device is not required if the personal fall arrest system is used in accordance with section 151.

142.3(4) Despite subsection (2), a shock absorber is required with a fixed ladder fall arrest system only if it is required by the manufacturer of the system.

Connectors, carabiners and snap hooks

143(1) An employer must ensure that connecting components of a fall arrest system consisting of carabiners, D-rings, O-rings, oval rings, self-locking connectors and snap hooks manufactured on or after July1, 2009 are approved, as applicable, to

  (a) CSA Standard Z259.12-01 (R2006), *Connecting Components for Personal Fall Arrest Systems (PFAS)*,

  (b) ANSI/ASSE Standard Z359.1-2007, *Safety requirements for personal fall arrest systems, subsystems and components*,

  (c) CEN Standard EN 362: 2004, *Personal protective equipment against falls from a height — Connectors*, or

  (d) CEN Standard 12275: 1998, *Mountaineering equipment — Connectors — Safety requirements and test methods.*

143(2) An employer must ensure that a carabiner or snap hook

  (a) is self-closing and self-locking,

  (b) may only be opened by at least two consecutive deliberate manual actions, and

  (c) is marked with

   (i)   its breaking strength in the major axis, and

   (ii) the name or trademark of the manufacturer.

Fall arresters

144   An employer must ensure that a fall arrestor manufactured on or after July1, 2009 is approved to

  (a) CSA Standard Z259.2.1-98 (R2004), *Fall Arresters, Vertical Lifelines, and Rails*,

  (b) ANSI/ASSE Standard Z359.1-2007, *Safety requirements for personal fall arrest systems, subsystems and components*, or

  (c) CEN Standard EN 353-2: 2002, *Personal protective equipment against falls from a height — Part 2: Guided type fall arrestors including a flexible anchor line.*

Self retracting device

145   An employer must ensure that a self-retracting device manufactured on or after July1, 2009 and used with a personal fall arrest system is

  (a) approved to CSA Standard Z259.2.2-98 (R2004), *Self-Retracting Devices for Personal Fall-Arrest Systems*,

  (b) anchored above the worker's head unless the manufacturer's specifications allow the use of a different anchor location, and

  (c) used in a manner that minimizes the hazards of swinging and limits the swing drop distance to 1.2 metres if a worker falls.

Descent control device

146 An employer must ensure that an automatic or manual descent control device manufactured on or after July 1, 2009 and used with a personal fall arrest system is approved to

(a) CSA Standard Z259.2.3-99 (R2004), *Descent Control Devices,*

(b) CEN Standard EN 341: 1997, *Personal protective equipment against falls from a height — Descender devices,* or

(c) NFPA Standard 1983, *Standard on Life Safety Rope and Equipment for Emergency Services,* 2006 edition, classified as general or light duty.

Life safety rope

147(1) An employer must ensure that a life safety rope manufactured on or after July 1, 2009 and used in a fall protection system

(a) is approved to

(i) NFPA Standard 1983, *Standard on Life Safety Rope and Equipment for Emergency Services,* 2006 Edition, as light-use or general-use life safety rope,

(ii) CEN Standard EN 1891: 1998, *Personal protective equipment for the prevention of falls from a height — Low stretch kernmantle ropes,* as Type A rope, or

(b) meets the requirements of

(i) CSA Standard CAN/CSA-Z259.2.1-98 (R2004), *Fall Arresters, Vertical Lifelines, and Rails,* or

(ii) ANSI/ASSE Standard Z359.1-2007, *Safety requirements for personal fall arrest systems, subsystems and components.*

147(2) An employer must ensure that a life safety rope used in a fall protection system

(a) extends downward to within 1.2 metres of ground level or another safe lower surface,

(b) is free of knots or splices throughout the travel portion except for a stopper knot at its lower end,

(c) is effectively protected to prevent abrasion by sharp or rough edges,

(d) is made of material appropriate to the hazard and able to withstand adverse effects, and

(e) is installed and used in a manner that minimizes the hazards of swinging and limits the swing drop distance to 1.2 metres if a worker falls.

147(3) A worker must use a vertical life safety rope in a manner that minimizes the hazards of swinging and limits the swing drop distance to 1.2 metres if a worker falls.

147(4) An employer must ensure that only one worker is attached to a life safety rope at any one time unless the manufacturer's specifications or specifications certified by a professional engineer allow for the attachment of more than one worker.

Adjustable lanyard for work positioning

148   An employer must ensure that an adjustable lanyard manufactured on or after July1, 2009 and used by a worker as part of a work positioning system is approved to

(a) CSA Standard Z259.11-05, *Energy absorbers and lanyards*, as a Class F adjustable positioning lanyard, or

(b) CEN Standard EN 358: 2000, *Personal protective equipment for work positioning and prevention of falls from a height — Belts for work positioning and restraint and work positioning lanyards.*

Rope adjustment device for work positioning

148.1 An employer must ensure that a rope adjustment device manufactured on or after July1, 2009 and used by a worker as part of a work positioning system is approved to

(a) CSA Standard Z259.2.3-99 (R2004), *Descent Control Devices,*

(b) CEN Standard EN 341: 1997, *Personal protective equipment against falls from a height — Descender devices*, or

(c) NFPA Standard 1983, *Standard on Life Safety Rope and Equipment for Emergency Services*, 2006 Edition, classified as general or light duty.

Wood pole climbing

149(1) An employer must ensure that a worker working on or from a wood pole uses fall restrict equipment that is approved to CSA Standard Z259.14-01, *Fall Restrict Equipment for Wood Pole Climbing*, in combination with

(a) a lineman's body belt that

(i)   is approved to CSA Standard Z259.3-M1978 (R2003), *Lineman's Body Belt and Lineman's Safety Strap,* or

(ii) complies with section 142.1, or

(b) a full body harness that complies with subsection 142(1).

149(2) Subsection (1) does not apply to fall restrict equipment or a lineman's body belt in use before April 30, 2004.

Equipment compatibility

150   An employer must ensure that all components of a fall protection system are compatible with one another and with the environment in which they are used.

Inspection and maintenance

150.1 An employer must ensure that the equipment used as part of a fall protection system is

(a) inspected by the worker as required by the manufacturer before it is used on each work shift,

(b) kept free from substances and conditions that could contribute to deterioration of the equipment, and

(c) re-certified as specified by the manufacturer.

Removal from service

150.2(1) An employer must ensure that equipment used as part of a fall protection system is removed from service and either returned to the manufacturer or destroyed if

(a) it is defective, or

(b) it has come into contact with excessive heat, a chemical, or any other substance that may corrode or otherwise damage the fall protection system.

150.2(2) An employer must ensure that after a personal fall arrest system has stopped a fall, the system is removed from service.

150.2(3) An employer must ensure that a personal fall arrest system that is removed from service is not returned to service unless a professional engineer or the manufacturer certifies that the system is safe to use.

Prusik and similar knots

150.3 An employer must ensure that a Prusik or similar sliding hitch knot is used in place of a fall arrester only during emergency situations or during training for emergency situations and only by a competent worker.

Clearance, maximum arresting force and swing

151(1) An employer must ensure that a personal fall arrest system is arranged so that a worker cannot hit the ground, an object which poses an unusual possibility of injury, or a level below the work area.

151(2) An employer must ensure that a personal fall arrest system without a shock absorber limits a worker's free fall distance to 1.2 metres.

151(3) An employer must ensure that a personal fall arrest system limits the maximum arresting force on a worker to 6 kilonewtons, unless the worker is using an E6 type shock absorber in accordance with the manufacturer's specifications, in which case the maximum arresting force must not exceed 8 kilonewtons.

151(4) A worker must limit the vertical distance of a fall by

(a) selecting the shortest length lanyard that will still permit unimpeded performance of the worker's duties, and

(b) securing the lanyard to an anchor no lower than the worker's shoulder height.

151(5) If the shoulder height anchor required by subsection 4(b) is not available, a worker must secure the lanyard to an anchor that is located as high as is reasonably practicable.

151(6) If it is not reasonably practicable to attach to an anchor above the level of a worker's feet, the worker must ensure that the clearance and maximum arresting force requirements of subsections (1) and (3) are met.

Anchors

Anchor strength — permanent

152(1) An employer must ensure that a permanent anchor is capable of safely withstanding the impact forces applied to it and has a minimum breaking strength per attached worker of 16 kilonewtons or two times the maximum arresting force in any direction in which the load may be applied.

152(2) Subsection (1) does not apply to anchors installed before July1, 2009.

152(3) Subsection (1) does not apply to the anchors of flexible horizontal lifeline systems that must meet the requirements of subsection 153(1).

152(4) The employer must ensure that an anchor rated at two times the maximum arresting force is designed, installed and used in accordance with

(a)   the manufacturer's specifications, or

(b)   specifications certified by a professional engineer.

Anchor strength — temporary

152.1(1) An employer must ensure that a temporary anchor used in a travel restraint system

(a)   has a minimum breaking strength in any direction in which the load may be applied of at least 3.5 kilonewtons per worker attached,

(b)   is installed, used and removed according to the manufacturer's specifications or specifications certified by a professional engineer,

(c)   is permanently marked as being for travel restraint only, and

(d)   is removed from use on the earliest of

(i)   the date on which the work project for which it is intended is completed, or

(ii)   the time specified by the manufacturer or professional engineer.

152.1(2) An employer must ensure that a temporary anchor used in a personal fall arrest system

(a)   has a minimum breaking strength in any direction in which the load may be applied of at least 16 kilonewtons or two times the maximum arresting force per worker attached,

(b)   is installed, used and removed according to the manufacturer's specifications or specifications certified by a professional engineer, and,

(c)   is removed from use on the earliest of

(i)   the date on which the work project for which it is intended is completed, or

(ii)   the time specified by the manufacturer or professional engineer.

Duty to use anchors

152.2(1) If a worker uses a personal fall arrest system or a travel restraint system, the worker must ensure that it is safely secured to an anchor that meets the requirements of this Part.

152.2(2) An employer must ensure that a worker visually inspects the anchor prior to attaching a fall protection system.

152.2(3) An employer must ensure that a worker does not use a damaged anchor until the anchor is repaired, replaced or re-certified by the manufacturer or a professional engineer.

152.2(4) An employer must ensure that a worker uses an anchor connector appropriate to the work.

152.2(5) A worker must use an anchor connector appropriate to the work,

Independence of anchors

152.3 An employer must ensure that an anchor to which a personal fall arrest system is attached is not part of an anchor used to support or suspend a platform.

Wire rope sling as anchor

152.4 An employer must ensure that a wire rope sling used as an anchor is terminated at both ends with a Flemish eye splice rated to at least 90 percent of the wire rope's minimum breaking strength.

Flexible and rigid horizontal lifeline systems

153(1) An employer must ensure that a flexible horizontal lifeline system manufactured on or after July1, 2009 meets the requirements of

    (a) CSA Standard Z259.13-04, *Flexible Horizontal Lifeline Systems*, or

    (b) the applicable requirements of CSA Standard Z259.16-04, *Design of Active Fall-Protection Systems*.

153(2) An employer must ensure that a rigid horizontal fall protection system is designed, installed and used in accordance with

    (a) the manufacturer's specifications, or

    (b) specifications certified by a professional engineer.

Installation of horizontal lifeline systems

153.1 An employer must ensure that before a horizontal lifeline system is used, a professional engineer, a competent person authorized by the professional engineer, the manufacturer, or a competent person authorized by the manufacturer certifies that the system has been properly installed according to the manufacturer's specifications or to specifications certified by a professional engineer.

Fixed ladders and climbable structures

154(1) An employer must ensure that if a worker is working from or on a fixed ladder or climbable structure at a height of 3 metres or more and is not protected by a guardrail, continuous protection from falling is provided by

    (a) equipping the fixed ladder or climbable structure with an integral fall protection system that meets the requirements of

        (i) CSA Standard Z259.2.1-98 (R2004), *Fall Arresters, Vertical Lifelines, and Rails,* or

        (ii) ANSI/ASSE Standard Z359.1-2007, *Safety requirements for personal fall arrest systems, subsystems and components*, or

    (b) an alternate fall protection system.

154(2) Subsection (1) applies to fixed ladders and climbable structures constructed and installed after July1, 2009.

Fall protection on vehicles and loads

155(1) If a worker may have to climb onto a vehicle or its load at any location where it is not reasonably practicable to provide a fall protection system for the worker, an employer must

    (a)   take steps to eliminate or reduce the need for the worker to climb onto the vehicle or its load, and

    (b)   ensure that the requirements of subsection 159(2) are met.

155(2) In addition to the requirements of subsection (1), an employer must ensure that if a load is not secured against movement, a worker does not climb onto the load.

155(3) A worker must not climb onto a load if the load is not secured against movement.

Boom-supported work platforms and aerial devices

156(1) An employer must ensure that a worker on a boom-supported elevating work platform, boom-supported aerial device, or forklift truck work platform uses a personal fall arrest system

    (a)   connected to

        (i)   an anchor specified by the manufacturer of the work platform, aerial device or forklift truck, or

        (ii) if no anchor is specified by the manufacturer, an anchor point certified by a professional engineer that meets the requirements of CSA Standard Z259.16-04, *Design of Active Fall-Protection Systems*, and

    (b)   when connected to the anchor, the lanyard, if reasonably practicable, is short enough to prevent the worker from being ejected from the work platform or aerial device but is long enough to allow the worker to perform his or her work.

156(2) An employer must ensure that a worker on a scissor lift or on an elevating work platform with similar characteristics uses a travel restraint system consisting of a full body harness and lanyard

    (a)   connected to an anchor specified by the manufacturer of the scissor lift or elevating work platform, and

    (b)   when connected to the anchor, the lanyard, if reasonably practicable, is short enough to prevent the worker from falling out of the scissor lift or elevating work platform but is long enough to allow the worker to perform his or her work.

156(3) Subsection (2) does not apply if

    (a)   the manufacturer's specifications allow a worker to work from the scissor lift or elevating work platform with similar characteristics using only its guardrails for fall protection, and

    (b)   the scissor lift or elevating work platform is operating on a firm, substantially level surface.

156(4) Despite subsection (2), if a worker's movement cannot be adequately restricted in all directions by the travel restraint system, the employer must ensure that the worker uses a personal fall arrest system.

Water danger

157   An employer must ensure that a worker uses an appropriate fall protection system in combination with a life jacket or personal flotation device if the worker

(a) may fall into water that exposes the worker to the hazard of drowning, or

(b) could drown from falling into the water, from other than a boat.

Leading edge fall protection system

158   An employer using a leading edge fall protection system consisting of fabric or netting panels must ensure that

(a) the system is used only to provide leading edge fall protection,

(b) the system is used and installed according to the manufacturer's specifications,

(c) a copy of the manufacturer's specifications for the system is available to workers at the work site at which the system is being used,

(d) the fabric or netting is

(i) drop-tested at the work site in accordance with the requirements of 29 CFR Section 1926.502(C)4(i) published by the U.S. Occupational Safety and Health Administration, or

(ii) certified as safe for use by a professional engineer, and

(e) all workers using the system are trained in its use and limitations.

Procedures in place of fall protection equipment

159(1) An employer may develop and use procedures in place of fall protection equipment in accordance with subsection (2), if

(a) it is not reasonably practicable to use one of the fall protection systems described in this Part, and

(b) use of procedures in place of fall protection equipment is restricted to the following situations:

(i) the installation or removal of fall protection equipment;

(ii) roof inspection;

(iii) emergency repairs;

(iv) at-height transfers between equipment and structures if allowed by the manufacturer's specifications; and

(v) situations in which a worker must work on top of a vehicle or load and the requirements of section 155 have been met.

159(2) An employer using procedures in place of fall protection equipment must ensure that

(a) a hazard assessment in accordance with the requirements of Part 2 is completed before work at height begins,

(b) the procedures to be followed while performing the work must be in writing and available to workers before the work begins,

(c) the work is carried out in such a way that minimizes the number of workers exposed to a fall hazard while work is performed,

(d) the work is limited to light duty tasks of limited duration,

(e) the worker performing the work is competent to do it,

(f) when used for inspection, investigation or assessment activities, these activities take place prior to the actual start of work or after work has been completed, and

(g) the procedures do not expose a worker to additional hazards.

Work positioning

160(1) An employer must ensure that if a worker uses a work positioning system, the worker's vertical free fall distance in the event of a fall is restricted by the work positioning system to 600 millimetres or less.

160(2) If the centre of gravity of a worker using a work positioning system extends beyond an edge from which the worker could fall or if the work surface presents a slipping or tripping hazard because of its state or condition, an employer must ensure that the worker uses a back-up personal fall arrest system in combination with the work positioning system.

160(3) A worker must use a back-up personal fall arrest system in combination with the work positioning system if the worker's centre of gravity extends beyond an edge from which the worker could fall or if the work surface presents a slipping or tripping hazard because of its state or condition.

Control zones

161(1) If a control zone is used, an employer must ensure that it

(a) is only used if a worker can fall from a surface that has a slope of no more than 4 degrees toward an unguarded edge or that slopes inwardly away from an unguarded edge, and

(b) is not less than 2 metres wide when measured from the unguarded edge.

161(2) An employer must not use a control zone to protect workers from falling from a skeletal structure that is a work area.

161(3) If a worker will at all times remain further from the unguarded edge than the width of the control zone, no other fall protection system need be used.

161(4) Despite section 139, a worker is not required to use a fall protection system when crossing the control zone to enter or leave the work area.

161(5) When crossing a control zone referred to in subsections (3) and (4), to get to or from the unguarded edge, a worker must follow the most direct route.

161(6) An employer must ensure that a control zone is clearly marked with an effective raised warning line or another equally effective method if a worker is working within 2 metres of the control zone.

161(7) An employer must ensure that a worker who must work within a control zone uses

(a) a travel restraint system, or

(b) an equally effective means of preventing the worker from getting to the unguarded edge.

161(8) A person who is not directly required for the work at hand must not be inside a control zone.

Part 10   Fire and Explosion Hazards

Flammable or explosive atmospheres a hazard

161.1 Flammable or explosive atmospheres are considered a hazard for the purposes of Part 2.

General Protection and Prevention

Prohibitions

162(1) A person must not enter or work at a work area if more than 20 percent of the lower explosive limit of a flammable or explosive substance is present in the atmosphere.

162(2) Subsection (1) does not apply to a competent, properly equipped worker who is responding in an emergency.

162(3) A person must not smoke in a work area where a flammable substance is stored, handled, processed or used.

162(3.1)   A person must not use an open flame, except in accordance with section 169, in a work area where a flammable substance is stored, handled, processed or used.

162(4) A person must not mix, clean or use a flammable or combustible liquid at a temperature at or above its flash point in an open vessel if a potential source of ignition is in the immediate vicinity of the activity.

162(5) A person must not use a flammable or combustible liquid at a temperature above its flash point in a washing or cleaning operation, unless the washing or cleaning equipment is specifically designed and manufactured for the use of the liquid.

162(6) A person must not store contaminated rags used to clean or wipe up flammable substances other than in a covered container that has a label that clearly indicates it is to be used for the storage of contaminated rags.

Classification of work sites

162.1(1) If the hazard assessment required by Part 2 determines that a work area is a hazardous location, an employer must ensure that

(a) a professional engineer, or a competent person authorized by a professional engineer, divides and classifies the work area in accordance with section 18 of the *Canadian Electrical Code*,

(b) for any work area falling under the *Code for Electrical Installations at Oil and Gas Facilities*, the area is divided and classified in accordance with rules 19-102 to 19-108 of that Code,

(c) for any work area consisting of facilities described in section 20 of the *Canadian Electrical Code*, the area is divided and classified in accordance with section 20 of the *Canadian Electrical Code*, and

(d) adequate documentation is prepared and maintained by a competent person, outlining the boundaries of the classified area and any specific measures to be taken to prevent the unintentional ignition of an explosive atmosphere.

162.1(2) If the hazard assessment required by Part 2 indicates that the basis of an area classification under subsection (1) has changed, an employer must review and update that classification.

Procedures and precautions

163(1) Repealed

163(2) If the hazard assessment required by Part 2 determines that a work area is not a hazardous location, an employer must ensure that flammable substances stored or used at the work area,

    (a)   will not be in sufficient quantity to produce an explosive atmosphere if inadvertently released,

    (b)   are not stored within 30 metres of an underground shaft,

    (c)   are not stored in the immediate vicinity of the air intake of

        (i)   a ventilation supply system,

        (ii)   an internal combustion engine, or

        (iii)   the fire box of a fired heater or furnace, and

    (d)   are stored only in containers approved to

        (i)   CSA Standard B376-M1980 (R2008), *Portable Containers for Gasoline and Other Petroleum Fuels,*

        (ii)   NFPA Standard 30, *Flammable and Combustible Liquids Code,* 2008 Edition, or

        (iii)   ULC Standard C30-1995, *Containers, Safety,*

        if manufactured on or after July1, 2009.

163(2.1) If the work requires that the contents of metallic or conductive containers be transferred from one container to another, an employer must ensure that static electricity is controlled while the contents are being transferred.

163(3) Moved to section 165(3).

Contaminated clothing and skin

164(1) If a worker's clothing is contaminated with a flammable or combustible liquid, the worker must

    (a)   avoid any activity where a spark or open flame may be created or exists,

    (b)   remove the clothing at the earliest possible time in a manner consistent with clause (a), and

    (c)   ensure that the clothing is decontaminated before it is used again.

164(2) If a worker's skin is contaminated with a flammable or combustible liquid, the worker must wash the skin at the earliest possible time.

Protective procedures and precautions in hazardous locations

165(1) Repealed

165(2) Repealed

165(3) An employer must ensure that in a hazardous location,

    (a)   equipment used will not ignite a flammable substance, and

    (b)   static electricity is controlled,

(i)   in the case of conductive containers for flammable or combustible liquids while the contents are being transferred, by electrically bonding the containers to one another and electrically grounding them, and

(ii) in other cases, by some other effective means.

165(4) An employer must ensure that, if a work area is determined to be a hazardous location, the boundaries of the hazardous location are

(a)   clearly identified to warn workers of the nature of the hazards associated with the presence of the flammable substance in that work area, or

(b)   fenced off to prevent workers or equipment from entering the area without authorization.

165(5) If reasonably practicable, an employer must ensure that procedures and precautionary measures are developed for a hazardous location that will prevent the inadvertent release of

(a)   a flammable substance, or

(b)   oxygen gas if it can contact a flammable substance.

165(6) Despite subsection (5), if it is not reasonably practicable to develop procedures and precautionary measures that will prevent release, an employer must develop procedures and precautionary measures that will prevent an explosive atmosphere from igniting in a hazardous location.

Internal combustion engines

166(1) An employer must ensure that an internal combustion engine in a hazardous location has a combustion air intake and exhaust discharge that are

(a)   equipped with a flame arresting device, or

(b)   located outside the hazardous location.

166(2) An employer must ensure that all the surfaces of an internal combustion engine that are exposed to the atmosphere in a hazardous location are

(a)   at a temperature lower than the temperature that would ignite a flammable substance present in the hazardous location, or

(b)   shielded or blanketed in such a way as to prevent any flammable substance present in the hazardous location from contacting the surface.

166(2.1)   If it is not reasonably practicable to comply with subsection (2), an employer must ensure that another effective safeguard is established.

166(3) Subsections (1) and (2) do not apply to a vehicle that is powered by an internal combustion engine.

166(4) An employer must ensure that a vehicle powered by an internal combustion engine is not located or operated in a hazardous location except in accordance with section 169.

166(5) An employer must ensure that an internal combustion engine is not located in a Zone 0 hazardous location as defined in the *Canadian Electrical Code* or in a part of a Division 1 hazardous location that meets the description of a Zone 0 location as defined in the *Canadian Electrical Code*.

166(6) An employer must ensure that an internal combustion engine is not located in a Zone 1 or Division 1 hazardous location as defined in the *Canadian*

Electrical Code unless it is equipped with combustible gas monitoring equipment in accordance with section 18 of the *Canadian Electrical Code*.

166(7) An employer must ensure that an internal combustion engine is not located in a Class II, Division 1 or a Class III, Division 1 hazardous location as defined in the *Canadian Electrical Code*.

Flare stacks, flare pits and flares

167 An employer must ensure that open flames from flare pits, flare stacks or flares are not less than 25 metres beyond the boundary of a hazardous location.

Industrial furnaces and fired heaters

168(1) An employer must ensure that

(a) a gas or oil fired furnace is designed, operated, monitored, controlled and maintained in a manner that minimizes the possibility of internal explosion of the fire box, and

(b) if the furnace is heating flammable substances, there are no connections between the process medium supply system and the fuel supply system or another system connected to the inside of the fire box of the furnace.

168(2) An employer must ensure that the heated substance systems referred to in subsection (1)(b) are not isolated using inserted blinds or a double block and bleed system.

168(3) A worker must not attempt to ignite a furnace manually, or to re-ignite a furnace after shutdown, until

(a) explosive concentrations of flammable substances are eliminated from the fire box by purging or removed by another effective means, and

(b) tests or procedures are completed that ensure an explosive atmosphere is not present within the furnace.

168(4) An employer must ensure that intakes, exhausts and the fire box of a furnace or fired heater are not located or operated in a Division 1, Zone 0 or Zone 1 hazardous location of any Class as defined in the *Canadian Electrical Code*.

168(5) An employer must ensure that a furnace or fired heater is not located or operated in a Division 2 or Zone 2 hazardous location of any Class as defined in the *Canadian Electrical Code*, unless

(a) the combustion process is totally enclosed except for the combustion air intake and the exhaust discharge,

(b) all surfaces exposed to the atmosphere

(i) operate below the temperature that would ignite a flammable substance present in the hazardous location, or

(ii) are shielded or blanketed in such a way as to prevent a flammable substance in the hazardous location from contacting the surface, and

(c) the combustion air intake and exhaust discharge are equipped with a flame arresting device or are located outside the hazardous location.

168(6) If it is not reasonably practicable to comply with subsection 5(b), an employer must ensure that another effective safeguard is established.

Hot work

169(1) Despite any other section in this Part, an employer must ensure that hot work is done in accordance with subsections (2) and (3) if

(a) the work area is a hazardous location, or

(b) the work area is not normally a hazardous location but an explosive atmosphere may exist for a limited time because

(i) a flammable substance is or may be in the atmosphere of the work area,

(ii) a flammable substance is or may be stored, handled, processed or used in the location,

(iii) the hot work is on or in an installation or item of equipment that contains a flammable substance or its residue, or

(iv) the hot work is on a vessel that contains residue that may release a flammable gas or vapour when exposed to heat.

169(2) An employer must ensure that hot work is not begun until

(a) a hot work permit is issued that indicates

(i) the nature of the hazard,

(ii) the type and frequency of atmospheric testing required,

(iii) the safe work procedures and precautionary measures to be taken, and

(iv) the protective equipment required,

(b) the hot work location is

(i) cleared of combustible materials, or

(ii) suitably isolated from combustible materials,

(c) procedures are implemented to ensure continuous safe performance of the hot work, and

(d) testing shows that the atmosphere does not contain

(i) a flammable substance, in a mixture with air, in an amount exceeding 20 percent of that substance's lower explosive limit for gas or vapours, or

(ii) the minimum ignitable concentration for dust.

169(3) An employer must ensure that the tests referred to in subsection (2)(d) are repeated at regular intervals appropriate to the hazard associated with the work being performed.

Hot taps

170(1) An employer must develop procedures in a hot tap plan specific to the type or class of hot tap work being performed before hot tap work begins.

170(2) The employer must ensure that the plan includes

(a) a site hazard analysis,

(b) a description of the sequence of events,

(c) safety precautions to address the hazards, and

(d) an emergency response plan.

170(3) The employer must ensure that

(a) only competent workers are permitted to carry out a hot tap operation,

(b) the point in the pressure-containing barrier to be hot tapped is checked and strong enough for the hot tap to be done safely,

(c) adequate working space is available at the location of the hot tap,

(d) exit routes are available and their locations known by workers involved in the work,

(e) workers wear appropriate personal protective equipment when a hot tap is performed on equipment containing hydrocarbons, combustible fluids, superheated steam or any other hazardous material,

(f) material being supplied to the equipment being hot tapped can be shut off immediately in an emergency,

(g) the hot tap machine and fittings are of adequate design and capability for the process, conditions, pressure and temperature, and

(h) the pressure in the equipment being hot tapped is as low as practical during the hot tap operation.

170(4) An employer must ensure, where reasonably practicable, that a hot tap is not undertaken if at the proposed hot tap location

(a) the equipment contains a harmful substance,

(b) the equipment is in hydrogen service, or

(c) the equipment contains an explosive mixture.

Spray operations

170.1(1) An employer must ensure that a spray booth used to apply flammable substances is provided with ventilation in accordance with Part 26 and that the ventilation is

(a) adequate to remove flammable vapours, mists, or powders to a safe location, and

(b) interlocked with the spraying equipment so that the spraying equipment is made inoperable when the ventilation system is not in operation.

170.1(2) An employer must ensure that a spray booth will not ignite a flammable substance.

170.1(3)   When spray application of a flammable substance is carried out other than in a spray booth, an employer must ensure that the application is carried out in accordance with the *Alberta Fire Code* (1997), and is

(a) carried out at least 6 metres away from anything that might obstruct ventilation, and

(b) effectively isolated from all machinery and equipment that is, or may become, a source of ignition and that is within 2 metres measured vertically above and 6 metres measured in other directions from the place at which the spray painting substance is being applied.

170.1(4) If it is not reasonably practicable to ensure that the application is carried out as required by subsection (3)(a), an employer must ensure that the work area where the application is carried out is adequately ventilated to remove flammable vapours, mists or powders to a safe location.

170.1(5) An employer must provide a nozzle guard for use with airless spray machinery.

170.1(6) The worker operating airless spray machinery must ensure that the nozzle guard of airless spray machinery is in place at all times when the machinery is being operated.

Compressed and liquefied gas

171(1) An employer must ensure that

    (a) compressed or liquefied gas containers are used, handled, stored and transported in accordance with the manufacturer's specifications,

    (b) a cylinder of compressed flammable gas is not stored in the same room as a cylinder of compressed oxygen, unless the storage arrangements are in accordance with Part 3 of the *Alberta Fire Code* (1997),

    (c) compressed or liquefied gas cylinders, piping and fittings are protected from damage during handling, filling, transportation and storage,

    (d) compressed or liquefied gas cylinders are equipped with a valve protection cap if manufactured with a means of attachment, and

    (e) oxygen cylinders or valves, regulators or other fittings of the oxygen-using apparatus or oxygen distributing system are kept free of oil and grease.

171(2) An employer must ensure that a compressed or liquefied gas system is not exposed to heat sources that generate temperatures that may

    (a) result in the failure or explosion of the contents or the system, or

    (b) exceed the maximum exposure temperatures specified by the manufacturer.

171(3) An employer must ensure that a compressed or liquefied gas system is kept clean and free from oil, grease and other contaminants that may

    (a) cause the system to fail, or

    (b) burn or explode if they come in contact with the contents of the system.

171(4) An employer must ensure that on each hose of an oxygen-fuel system,

    (a) a flashback device is installed at either the torch end or the regulator end, and

    (b) a back-flow prevention device is installed at the torch end.

171(5) An employer must ensure that compressed or liquefied gas cylinders are secured, preferably upright, and cannot fall or roll, unless a professional engineer certifies another method that protects against the hazards caused by dislodgment.

171(6) Despite subsection (5), an employer must ensure that a cylinder containing acetylene is secured and stored upright.

171(7) Moved to section 170.1(5).

171(8) A worker must ensure that

    (a) compressed gas equipment designed to be used with a specific gas is only used with that gas,

    (b) the cylinder valve is shut off and pressure in the hose is released when cutting or welding is not in progress,

    (c) sparks, flames or other sources of ignition are not allowed to come in contact with the cylinders, regulators or hoses of a compressed or liquefied gas system, and

(d) compressed air is not used to blow dust or other substances from clothing.

Welding — general

171.1(1) An employer must comply with the requirements of CSA Standard W117.2-06, *Safety in welding, cutting and allied processes.*

171.1(2) An employer must ensure that welding or allied process equipment is erected, installed, assembled, started, operated, used, handled, stored, stopped, inspected, serviced, tested, cleaned, adjusted, carried, maintained, repaired and dismantled in accordance with the manufacturer's specifications.

171.1(3) An employer must ensure that, before a welding or allied process is commenced, the area surrounding the operation is inspected and

(a) all combustible, flammable or explosive material, dust, gas or vapour is removed, or

(b) alternate methods of rendering the area safe are implemented.

171.1(4) If a welding or allied process is performed above an area where a worker may be present, an employer must ensure that adequate means are taken to protect a worker below the operation from sparks, debris and other falling hazards.

171.1(5) An operator of an electric welding machine must not leave the machine unattended without removing the electrode.

171.1(6) An employer must ensure that appropriate welding and ground leads are used to fasten the electric supply cable securely.

Gas welding or allied process

171.2(1) An employer must ensure that a regulator and its flexible connecting hose are tested immediately after connection to a gas cylinder to ensure that there is no leak of the gas supply.

171.2(2) An employer must ensure that if a leak of the gas supply develops during gas welding or an allied process,

(a) the supply of gas is immediately shut off by the worker performing the welding or allied process, and

(b) the work is not resumed until the leak is repaired.

Welding Services From Vehicles

Storage compartments

172(1) An employer must ensure that welding services provided from vehicles comply with CSA Standard W117.2-01, *Safety in welding, cutting and allied processes* with the exception of Clause G.2 (Cabinets) of Annex G.

172(2) An employer must ensure that gases do not accumulate and reach their lower explosive limit by providing solid-walled storage compartments in which compressed gas cylinders are stored with vents

(a) that have a minimum of 0.18 square metres of free area for every 0.42 cubic metres of compartment volume,

(b) that have the free area split evenly between the top surface and the bottom surface of the storage compartment, and

(c) that are unobstructed under all conditions.

172(3) An employer must ensure that solid-walled storage compartments in which compressed gas cylinders are stored are built so that gases or vapours cannot flow into adjoining compartments.

172(4) An employer must ensure that solid-walled compartments in which compressed gas cylinders are stored use

(a) latching and locking hardware made of non-sparking materials, and

(b) electrical components appropriate for use in an explosive atmosphere, if electrical components are located within the compartment.

172(5) Subsections (1) to (4) apply whether the compressed gas cylinder is stored vertically, horizontally or at an angle.

Horizontal cylinder storage

173(1) An employer must ensure that a compressed gas cylinder that is horizontal when it is transported or used in a vehicle

(a) is in a storage compartment that incorporates a structure of sufficient strength to prevent the cylinder from passing through it should the valve end of the cylinder be damaged and vent its contents in an uncontrolled manner,

(b) is in a storage compartment that incorporates a means of securing the cylinder that stops the cylinder from moving within the compartment and that puts the bottom of the cylinder in direct contact with the structure in clause (a), and

(c) is protected against scoring during insertion into, and removal from, the storage compartment.

173(2) An employer must ensure that the regulator on a compressed gas cylinder that is horizontal when it is transported or used in a vehicle is protected from damage by other equipment in the storage compartment.

173(3) An employer must ensure that a storage compartment on a vehicle from which welding services are provided is certified by a professional engineer as meeting the requirements of subsections (1) and (2).

Handling cylinders

174(1) A worker must not insert or remove a compressed gas cylinder from a storage compartment by holding the valve or valve protection cap.

174(2) A worker must put on and secure to the valve outlet the valve protection cap or plug provided by the manufacturer of a compressed gas cylinder if the cylinder is not secured and not connected to dispensing equipment.

174(3) If a welding service vehicle is not in service for any reason, a worker must

(a) close the compressed gas cylinder valves,

(b) remove the regulators if they are not integral to the cylinders, and

(c) put on and secure the valve protection caps or plugs.

174(4) A worker must shut off the cylinder valve and release the pressure in the hose if a compressed gas cylinder on a welding service vehicle is not in use or if the vehicle is left unattended.

Isolating Pipes and Pipelines

Isolating methods

175   Moved to section 215.4.

Pigging

176   Moved to section 215.5.

Part 11   First Aid

Training standards

177(1) A person or agency that provides training in first aid must enter into an agreement with the Director of Medical Services if the person or agency is to provide training in first aid to workers under this Code.

177(2) An approved training agency that provides the first aid training to candidates for a certificate in emergency first aid, standard first aid or advanced first aid must comply with the terms of the agreement with the Director of Medical Services.

177(3) A worker who successfully completes the training of an approved training agency must meet the standards for a certificate in emergency first aid, standard first aid or advanced first aid that are adopted by the Director of Medical Services in consultation with the Joint First Aid Training Standards Board.

Providing services, supplies, equipment

178(1) An employer must provide first aid services, supplies and equipment and provide a first aid room in accordance with the applicable requirements of Schedule 2, Tables 3 to 7 or an acceptance from the Director of Medical Services.

178(2) A prime contractor must ensure that in accordance with the applicable requirements of Schedule 2, Tables 3 to 7, first aid services, supplies and equipment and a first aid room, are available at the work site suitable for the type of work site and the total number of workers at the work site.

178(3) Despite subsections (1) and (2), the employers and prime contractor at a project may enter into a written agreement to collectively provide first aid services, supplies and equipment and provide a first aid room for workers in accordance with the applicable requirements of Schedule 2, Tables 3 to 7 or an acceptance as allowed by section 34 of the *Act*.

178(4) If a first aid room is a temporary or mobile facility, an employer must ensure that it meets the requirements of Schedule 2, Table 4 except that

(a) the room may be used for other services if it is maintained appropriately to provide first aid, and

(b) where it is not possible or practicable to provide a supply of hot and cold potable water, a supply of cold potable water is acceptable.

Location of first aid

179   An employer and prime contractor must

(a) ensure that first aid services, first aid equipment, supplies and the first aid room required by this Code are

(i)   located at or near the work site they are intended to serve, and

(ii) available and accessible during all working hours;

(b) ensure that first aid equipment and supplies are

(i)   maintained in a clean, dry and serviceable condition,

(ii) contained in a material that protects the contents from the environment, and

(iii) clearly identified as first aid equipment and supplies;

(c) post, at conspicuous places at the work site, signs indicating the location of first aid services, equipment and supplies or, if posting of signs is not practicable, ensure that each worker knows the location of first aid services, equipment and supplies; and

(d) ensure that an emergency communication system is in place for workers to summon first aid services.

Emergency transportation

180(1) Before workers are sent to a work site, the employer must ensure that arrangements are in place to transport injured or ill workers from the work site to the nearest health care facility.

180(2) An employer must ensure that an ambulance service licensed in accordance with the *Ambulance Services Act* is readily available to the work site when travel conditions are normal.

180(3) If an ambulance service licensed in accordance with the *Ambulance Services Act* is not readily available to the work site, or if travel conditions are not normal, an employer must ensure that other transportation is available that

(a) is suitable, considering the distance to be travelled and the types of acute illnesses or injuries that may occur at the work site,

(b) protects occupants from the weather,

(c) has systems that allow the occupants to communicate with the health care facility to which the injured or ill worker is being taken, and

(d) can accommodate a stretcher and an accompanying person if required to.

180(4) An employer must provide a means of communication at the work site to summon an ambulance service licensed in accordance with the *Ambulance Services Act* or transportation described in subsection (3).

180(5) If a worker is acutely ill or injured or needs to be accompanied during transport to a health care facility, an employer must ensure that the worker is accompanied by at least one first aider, in addition to the operator of the transportation.

180(6) Subsection (5) does not apply if there are three or fewer workers at the work site at the time.

First aid providers

181(1) An employer must ensure that the number of first aiders at a work site and their qualifications and training comply with Schedule 2, Tables 5, 6 or 7.

181(2) An employer must ensure that the first aiders at a work site have successfully completed a first aid training course approved by a Director of Medical Services and hold a valid certificate in first aid.

181(3) If a nurse, advanced first aider, or EMT-P is required at a work site, that person must

(a) be based at or near the first aid room, and

(b) when not in the first aid room, be easy to contact or notify if first aid services are required.

181(4) If a nurse, advanced first aider or EMT-P while on duty at the work site, is required to perform non-first aid duties, such duties must be of a type that let the person remain in a fit and clean condition.

181(5) Subsection (4) does not apply if the duties are those of a first aid provider.

181(6) An employer must keep a record of workers at a work site who are first aiders.

Duty to report injury or illness

182 If a worker has an acute illness or injury at the work site, the worker must report the illness or injury to the employer as soon as is practicable.

Record of injury or illness

183(1) An employer must record every acute illness or injury that occurs at the work site in a record kept for the purpose as soon as is practicable after the illness or injury is reported to the employer.

183(2) A record under subsection (1) must include the following:

(a) the name of the worker;

(b) the name and qualifications of the person giving first aid;

(c) a description of the illness or injury;

(d) the first aid given to the worker;

(e) the date and time of the illness or injury;

(f) the date and time the illness or injury was reported;

(g) where at the work site the incident occurred;

(h) the work-related cause of the incident, if any.

183(3) The employer must retain the records kept under this section for three years from the date the incident is recorded.

First aid records access

184(1) This section applies to records of first aid given to a worker.

184(2) Subject to section 8 of the *Act,* a person who has custody of records must ensure that no person other than the worker has access to a worker's records unless

(a) the record is in a form that does not identify the worker,

(b) the worker has given written permission to the person, or

(c) access, use and disclosure of the information is in accordance with an enactment of Alberta or Canada that authorizes or requires the disclosure.

184(3) An employer must give a worker a copy of the records pertaining to the worker if the worker asks for a copy.

Part 12   General Safety Precautions

Housekeeping

185   An employer must ensure that a work site is kept clean and free from materials or equipment that could cause workers to slip or trip.

Lighting

186(1) An employer must ensure that lighting at a work site is sufficient to enable work to be done safely.

186(2) An employer must ensure that a light source above a working or walking surface is protected against damage.

186(3) An employer must ensure that there is emergency lighting at a work site if workers are in danger if the normal lighting system fails.

186(4) Emergency lighting must generate enough light so that workers can

   (a)   leave the work site safely,

   (b)   start the necessary emergency shut-down procedures, and

   (c)   restore normal lighting.

Pallets and storage racks

187(1) An employer must ensure that pallets used to transport or store materials or containers are loaded, moved, stacked, arranged and stored in a manner that does not create a danger to workers.

187(2) An employer must ensure that racks used to store materials or equipment

   (a)   are designed, constructed and maintained to support the load placed on them, and

   (b)   are placed on firm foundations that can support the load.

187(3) A worker must report any damage to a storage rack to an employer as quickly as is practicable.

187(4) The employer and the workers at a work site must take all reasonable steps to prevent storage racks from being damaged to the extent that their integrity as structures is compromised.

Placement of roofing materials

187.1(1) An employer must ensure that supplies and roofing materials stored on the roof of a residential building under construction are located not less than 2 metres from a roof edge.

187.1(2) An employer must ensure that the weight of supplies and roofing materials referred to in subsection (1) is uniformly distributed.

Restraining hoses and piping

188(1) An employer must ensure that a hose or piping and its connections operating under pressure are restrained if workers could be injured by its movement if it fails or if it is disconnected.

188(2) Despite subsection (1), if a hose or piping and its connections operating at a working pressure of 2000 kilopascals or more cannot be restrained, in order to prevent a failure that could injure workers, an employer must ensure that the hose or piping and its connections are designed, installed, used, inspected and maintained

(a)   in accordance with the manufacturer's specifications, or

(b)   in accordance with specifications certified by a professional engineer.

188(3) Subsection (1) does not apply to properly maintained fire hoses used by competent workers.

Securing equipment and materials

189   If a worker may be injured if equipment or material is dislodged, moved, spilled or damaged, both the employer and the worker must take all reasonable steps to ensure the equipment or material is contained, restrained or protected to eliminate the potential danger.

Skeleton structures

190(1) An employer must ensure that the erection drawings and procedures for a project that includes connecting the structural parts of a skeleton structure are prepared and certified by a professional engineer.

190(2) The erection drawings and procedures referred to in subsection (1) must

(a)   show the sequence in which the structure is to be erected,

(b)   show the horizontal and vertical placement of base structures and footings, and

(c)   ensure that the structure is stable during assembly.

190(3) If the erection procedures referred to in subsection (1) must be changed because of site conditions or unanticipated loads on the skeleton structure, the employer must ensure that the changed, additional or alternative procedures are prepared and certified by a professional engineer before they are implemented.

190(4) An employer must ensure that a competent worker at a work site where a skeleton structure is being erected

(a)   coordinates the operation until the structure is permanently stabilized, and

(b)   directs the removal of the temporary supporting structures.

Signallers

191(1) If this Code requires signals to be given by a designated signaller, an employer must designate a competent worker to give the signals.

191(2) An employer must ensure that, if the designated signaller uses hand signals, the signaller wears a highly visible vest, armlet or other piece of clothing that clearly identifies the worker as a designated signaller.

191(3) A designated signaller using hand signals must wear the vest, armlet or other piece of clothing required by the employer under subsection (2).

191(4) Before giving a signal to proceed, a designated signaller must ensure that there are no hazards in the vicinity.

191(5) If a signaller is designated, an equipment operator must take signals only from the designated signaller.

191(6) An employer must ensure that only one designated signaller at a time gives signals to an equipment operator.

191(7) Despite subsections (5) and (6), an equipment operator must take a "STOP" signal from a worker who is not a designated signaller.

191(8) Despite subsections (5) and (6), if signals cannot be transmitted properly between a designated signaller and an equipment operator, an employer must ensure that

    (a)   additional designated signallers are available to transmit signals, or

    (b)   a means of ensuring clear and complete communication other than using designated signallers is provided.

Stabilizing masonry walls

192   An employer must ensure that temporary supporting structures

    (a)   are used to stabilize a masonry wall that is more than 2 metres high during its erection, and

    (b)   are not removed until the wall is permanently stabilized.

Tire servicing

193(1) An employer must ensure that a competent worker services, inspects, disassembles and reassembles a tire or tire and wheel assembly in accordance with the manufacturer's specifications.

193(2) An employer must ensure that the manufacturer's service manuals for tires and wheels serviced by the employer are readily available to workers.

193(3) An employer must ensure that a competent worker inflates a tire mounted on a split-rim or locking ring wheel only if

    (a)   the wheel assembly is in a tire cage or is similarly restrained, and

    (b)   flying parts from split-rim or locking ring failure or tire rupture can be contained.

193(4) An employer must ensure that a worker uses a clamp-on type of connector to inflate split rim and locking ring wheels.

193(5) If a clamp-on type of connector is used to inflate a tire, the employer must ensure that the worker

    (a)   uses an in-line pressure gauge and positive pressure control, and

    (b)   inflates the tire from a safe position out of the immediate danger area.

193(6) A person must not inflate a tire with a clamp-on type of connector unless the person is in a safe position and out of the immediate danger area.

Vehicle traffic control

194(1) If vehicle traffic at a work site is dangerous to workers on foot, in vehicles or on equipment, an employer must ensure that the traffic is controlled to protect the workers.

194(2) An employer must ensure that a worker on foot and exposed to traffic wears a highly visible piece of clothing.

194(3) A worker on foot and exposed to traffic must wear a highly visible piece of clothing.

194(4) If a worker is designated by an employer to control traffic, the employer must ensure that the designated traffic controller wears a highly visible piece of clothing that

    (a)   clearly identifies the worker as a designated traffic controller, and

    (b)   is retroreflective if the worker is controlling traffic in the dark or visibility is poor.

194(5) A worker designated to control traffic must wear a highly visible piece of clothing that complies with subsection (4).

194(6) If a worker is designated by an employer to control traffic, the employer must ensure that the designated traffic controller uses a handheld signal light if it is dark or visibility is poor.

194(7) If traffic on a public highway is dangerous to workers, an employer must protect the workers from the traffic using

    (a) warning signs,

    (b) barriers,

    (c) lane control devices,

    (d) flashing lights,

    (e) flares,

    (f) conspicuously identified pilot vehicles,

    (g) automatic or remote-controlled traffic control systems,

    (h) designated persons directing traffic, or

    (i) methods described in the *Manual of Uniform Traffic Control Devices for Canada* (1998), and its updates, published up to and including June 30, 2009 by the Transportation Association of Canada.

Working on ice

195(1) If a worker is to work on ice and the water beneath the ice is more than 1 metre deep at any point, an employer must ensure the ice will support the load to be placed on it.

195(2) The employer must test the ice for the purposes of subsection (1)

    (a) before work begins, and

    (b) as often during the work as necessary to ensure the safety of the workers.

Part 13   Joint Work Site Health and Safety Committee

Ministerial order
196   This Part applies to a work site that is required to have a joint work site health and safety committee by Ministerial Order under section 31 of the *Act*.

Members
197   A joint work site health and safety committee must have, subject to section 31(3) of the *Act*,

(a)   at least two but not more than six worker members, and

(b)   at least one but not more than six employer members.

Term of membership
198(1) Members of a joint work site health and safety committee hold office for a term of not less than one year and may continue to hold office until their successors are elected or appointed.

198(2) Members of a joint work site health and safety committee may be re-elected or re-appointed for further terms.

198(3) Despite subsection (1), a member of a joint work site health and safety committee may be replaced at any time during that member's term of office by those persons whom the member represents.

Election of worker members
199(1) Worker members of the joint work site health and safety committee must be elected by workers employed at the work site who do not exercise any managerial function on behalf of the employer.

199(2) Despite subsection (1), workers employed at the work site who belong to a trade union or worker association may, in accordance with the constitution or by-laws of the trade union or worker association, elect to the joint work site health and safety committee the number of worker members proportionate to the number of workers at the work site who belong to that trade union or worker association.

199(3) To be eligible to be elected a worker member, a person must work at the work site where the joint work site health and safety committee is established.

Appointment of employer members
200(1) Employer members of a joint work site health and safety committee must be appointed to the committee by the employer or prime contractor.

200(2) To be eligible to be appointed as an employer member, a person must be employed at the work site where the joint work site health and safety committee is established.

Co-chairs of committee
201(1) A joint work site health and safety committee must have two co-chairs.

201(2) Worker members must select one co-chair from among themselves.

201(3) Employer members must select one co-chair from among themselves.

Recording and posting minutes
202   The co-chair selected by employer members must ensure that

    (a) minutes of each meeting of the joint work site health and safety committee are recorded,

    (b) copies of the minutes are given to the employer within seven days after the day the meeting was held, and

    (c) copies of the minutes are posted at the work site within seven days after the day the meeting was held.

Meetings

203(1) The joint work site health and safety committee must meet within 10 days of its establishment and thereafter at least once in each calendar month.

203(2) The joint work site health and safety committee must convene special meetings if requested to do so by a Director of Inspection.

Quorum

204 A quorum of a joint work site health and safety committee is one-half of the members if

    (a) both worker and employer members are present, and

    (b) at least one-half of those present are worker members.

Attendance by an officer

205 An officer may attend a meeting of a joint work site health and safety committee.

Duty to inspect work site

206 A joint work site health and safety committee must perform inspections at the work site at least once before each regular meeting of the committee.

Co-chairs present during inspection

207(1) If an officer inspects a work site, the joint work site health and safety committee co-chairs, or their designates, may be present at that inspection unless the officer asks that they not be there.

207(2) An officer must not make a request under subsection (1) unless, in the officer's opinion, special circumstances exist that would prevent the officer from making a proper inspection if the members of the joint work site health and safety committee or their designates were present during the inspection.

Part 14   Lifting and Handling Loads

Equipment

208(1) An employer must provide, where reasonably practicable, appropriate equipment for lifting, lowering, pushing, pulling, carrying, handling or transporting heavy or awkward loads.

208(2) An employer must ensure that workers use the equipment provided under subsection (1).

208(3) Workers must use the equipment provided for lifting, lowering, pushing, pulling, carrying, handling or transporting heavy or awkward loads.

208(4) For the purposes of this section, a heavy or awkward load includes equipment, goods, supplies, persons and animals.

Adapting heavy or awkward loads

209   If the equipment provided under section 208 is not reasonably practicable in a particular circumstance or for a particular heavy or awkward load, the employer must take all practicable means to

(a)   adapt the load to facilitate lifting, lowering, pushing, pulling, carrying, handling or transporting the load without injuring workers, or

(b)   otherwise minimize the manual handling required to move the load.

Work site design — health care facilities

209.1(1) An employer must ensure that appropriate patient/client/resident handling equipment is adequately incorporated into the design and construction of

(a)   a new health care facility, and

(b)   a health care facility undergoing significant physical alterations, renovations or repairs.

209.1(2) An employer must ensure that any new patient/client/resident handling equipment installed at an existing work site, including vehicles in which patient/client/resident handling occurs, fits adequately in the space intended for it.

209.1(3)   Subsections (1) and (2) do not apply to health care facility construction, alterations, renovations or repairs started before July 1, 2009.

Patient/client/resident handling

209.2(1) An employer must develop and implement a safe patient/client/resident handling program if workers are required to lift, transfer or reposition patients/clients/residents.

209.2(2) The program required by subsection (1) must include an annual evaluation of its effectiveness at preventing worker injuries.

209.2(3) An employer must ensure that workers follow the safe handling program required by subsection (1).

209.2(4) Workers must follow the safe handling program required by subsection (1).

Assessing manual handling hazards

210(1) Before a worker manually lifts, lowers, pushes, pulls, carries, handles or transports a load that could injure the worker, an employer must perform a hazard assessment that considers

    (a) the weight of the load,

    (b) the size of the load,

    (c) the shape of the load,

    (d) the number of times the load will be moved, and

    (e) the manner in which the load will be moved.

210(2) Before a worker performs any manual patient/client/resident handling activities, an employer must perform a hazard assessment that considers the worker's physical and mental capabilities to perform the work.

210(3) If the hazard assessment required by section 7 and subsections (1) and (2) determines that there is a potential for musculoskeletal injury, an employer must ensure that all reasonably practicable measures are used to eliminate or reduce that potential in accordance with section 9.

Musculoskeletal injuries

211 If a worker reports to the employer what the worker believes to be work related symptoms of a musculoskeletal injury, the employer must promptly

    (a) review the activities of that worker, and of other workers doing similar tasks, to identify work-related causes of the symptoms, if any, and

    (b) take corrective measures to avoid further injuries if the causes of the symptoms are work related.

Training to prevent musculoskeletal injury

211.1(1) An employer must ensure that a worker who may be exposed to the possibility of musculoskeletal injury is trained in specific measures to eliminate or reduce that possibility.

211.1(2) An employer must ensure that the training referred to in subsection (1) includes

    (a) identification of factors that could lead to a musculoskeletal injury,

    (b) the early signs and symptoms of musculoskeletal injury and their potential health effects, and

    (c) preventive measures including, where applicable, the use of altered work procedures, mechanical aids and personal protective equipment.

Part 15   Managing the Control of Hazardous Energy

Isolation

212(1) If machinery, equipment or powered mobile equipment is to be serviced, repaired, tested, adjusted or inspected, an employer must ensure that no worker performs such work on the machinery, equipment or powered mobile equipment until it has come to a complete stop and

(a) all hazardous energy at the location at which the work is to be carried out is isolated by activation of an energy-isolating device and the energy–isolating device is secured in accordance with section 214, 215, or 215.1 as designated by the employer, or

(b) the machinery, equipment or powered mobile equipment is otherwise rendered inoperative in a manner that prevents its accidental activation and provides equal or greater protection than the protection afforded under (a).

212(2) An employer must develop and implement procedures and controls that ensure the machinery, equipment or powered mobile equipment is serviced, repaired, tested, adjusted or inspected safely if

(a) the manufacturer's specifications require the machinery, equipment or powered mobile equipment to remain operative while it is being serviced, repaired, tested, adjusted, or inspected, or

(b) there are no manufacturer's specifications and it is not reasonably practicable to stop or render the machinery, equipment or powered mobile equipment inoperative.

212(3) If piping, a pipeline or a process system containing a harmful substance under pressure is to be serviced, repaired, tested, adjusted or inspected, an employer must ensure that no worker performs such work on the piping, pipeline or process system until flow in the piping, pipeline or process system has been stopped or regulated to a safe level, and the location at which the work is to be carried out is isolated and secured in accordance with section 215.4.

Verifying isolation

213   A worker must not perform work on machinery, equipment or powered mobile equipment to be serviced, repaired, tested, adjusted or inspected until

(a) the actions required by subsection 212(1) are completed,

(b) the machinery, equipment, or powered mobile equipment is tested to verify that it is inoperative, and

(c) the worker is satisfied that it is inoperative.

Securing Isolation

Securing by individual workers

214(1) Once all energy-isolating devices have been activated to control hazardous energy in accordance with section 212(1), an employer must ensure that a worker involved in work at each location requiring control of hazardous energy secures each energy-isolating device with a personal lock.

214(2) Once each energy-isolating device is secured as required by subsection (1), the worker must verify that the hazardous energy source has been effectively isolated.

214(3) If more than one worker is working at each location requiring hazardous energy to be controlled,

(a) each worker must attach a personal lock to each energy-isolating device, and

(b) the first worker applying a lock must verify that the hazardous energy source has been effectively isolated.

214(4) If a worker who has placed a personal lock is reassigned before the work is completed, or the work is extended from one shift to another, an employer must ensure that

(a) another worker, authorized by the employer to do so, attaches a personal lock to the energy-isolating device prior to removal of the reassigned or departing worker's lock, or

(b) there is an effective and orderly transfer of control of the reassigned or departing worker's lock.

214(5) An employer must ensure that each personal lock used has a unique mark or identification tag on it to identify it as belonging to the worker to whom it is assigned.

214(6) An employer must ensure that the name of the worker to whom a personal lock or identification tag is assigned is readily available during the time a hazardous energy source is isolated.

214(7) Upon completing the work requiring isolation of hazardous energy, an employer must ensure that the machinery, equipment or powered mobile equipment is returned to operation in accordance with section 215.3.

Securing by a group

215(1) If a large number of workers is working on machinery, equipment or powered mobile equipment, or a number of energy-isolating devices must be secured, an employer may use a group procedure in accordance with subsections (2) through (6).

215(2) An employer must ensure that the group procedure referred to in subsection (1) is readily available to workers at the work site where the group procedure is used.

215(3) Once all required energy-isolating devices have been activated in accordance with section 212(1) by a worker designated by the employer, an employer must ensure that a designated worker has

(a) secured all energy-isolating devices,

(b) secured any keys for the devices used under clause (a) to a key securing system such as a lock box,

(c) completed, signed and posted a checklist that identifies the machinery or equipment covered by the hazardous energy control procedure, and

(d) verified and documented that all sources of hazardous energy are effectively isolated.

215(4) Each worker working at each location requiring control of hazardous energy must apply a personal lock to the key securing system referred to in subsection (3)(b) before working on the machinery, equipment or powered mobile equipment.

215(5) If a worker who has placed a personal lock is reassigned before the work is completed, or the work is extended from one shift to another, an employer must ensure that there is an effective and orderly transfer of control of the reassigned or departing worker's personal lock.

215(6) Upon completing the work requiring isolation of hazardous energy, a worker referred to in subsection (4) must remove his or her personal lock from the key securing system.

215(7) Upon completing the work requiring isolation of hazardous energy, an employer must ensure that the machinery, equipment, or powered mobile equipment is returned to operation in accordance with section 215.3.

Securing by complex group control

215.1(1) If it is not reasonably practicable to secure energy-isolating devices in accordance with sections 214 or 215 because of

    (a)   the physical size and extent of the machinery, equipment, piping, pipeline, or process system,

    (b)   the relative inaccessibility of the energy-isolating devices,

    (c)   the number of workers involved in the work requiring hazardous energy control,

    (d)   the number of energy-isolating devices involved,

    (e)   the extended length of time of the required isolation, or

    (f)   the interdependence and interrelationship of the components in the system or between different systems,

an employer may use a complex group control process approved by a Director of Inspection.

215.1(2) Prior to initiating a complex group control process, an employer must complete a hazard assessment to identify the type and location of hazardous energy sources.

215.1(3) If using a complex group control process, an employer must ensure that

    (a)   procedures are implemented to ensure continuous safe performance of the work requiring isolation of hazardous energy,

    (b)   a work permit or master tag procedure is implemented so that

        (i)   each involved worker personally signs on the job before commencing the work and signs off the job upon completing the work, or

        (ii) a crew leader signs on and off the job for a crew or team of workers,

    (c)   a worker designated by the employer

        (i)   has activated all required energy-isolating devices to control hazardous energy in accordance with section 212(1), and

        (ii) has secured the energy-isolating devices, and

(d) another worker designated by the employer has verified that all sources of hazardous energy are effectively isolated.

215.1(4) If a complex group control process is being used and provided that the isolation point is reasonably accessible and isolation is required for the work being undertaken by the worker, each involved worker may place personal locks on the energy-isolating devices and verify effective isolation.

215.1(5) Upon completing the work requiring isolation of hazardous energy, an employer must ensure that the machinery, equipment, piping, pipeline or process system is returned to operation in accordance with section 215.3

Securing remotely controlled systems

215.2(1) If securing an energy-isolating device as required by section 212(1) is not reasonably practicable on a system that remotely controls the operation of machinery, equipment, piping, a pipeline or a process system, an employer must ensure that control system isolating devices and the procedures for applying and securing them provide equal or greater protection than the protection afforded under section 212(1)(a).

215.2(2) Upon completing the work requiring isolation of hazardous energy, an employer must ensure that the system is returned to operation in accordance with section 215.3.

Returning to operation

215.3(1) A person must not remove a personal lock or other securing device unless

(a) the person is the worker who installed it,

(b) the person is the designated worker under section 215(3) or section 215.1(3)(c), or

(c) the person is acting in accordance with the procedures required under section 215.2

215.3(2) Despite subsection (1), in an emergency or if the worker who installed a lock or other securing device is not available, a worker designated by the employer may remove the lock or other securing device in accordance with a procedure that includes verifying that no worker will be in danger due to the removal.

215.3(3) An employer must ensure that securing devices are not removed until

(a) each involved worker is accounted for,

(b) any personal locks placed by workers under sections 214, 215(4) or 215.1(4) are removed,

(c) procedures are implemented to verify that no worker is in danger before a worker under section 214(1), designated under section 215(3), designated under section 215.1(3)(c), or in accordance with procedures under section 215.2 removes the securing devices and the machinery, equipment, powered mobile equipment, piping, pipeline or process system is returned to operation.

215.3(4) An employer must ensure that each involved worker follows the procedures under subsection (3)(c).

Piping and Pigging

Isolating piping

215.4(1) To isolate piping or a pipeline containing harmful substances under pressure, an employer may use

(a) a system of blanking or blinding, or

(b) a double block and bleed isolation system providing

    (i) two blocking seals on either side of the isolation point, and

    (ii) an operable bleed-off between the two seals.

215.4(2) An employer must ensure that piping that is blanked or blinded is clearly marked to indicate that a blank or blind is installed.

215.4(3) An employer must ensure that, if valves or similar blocking seals with a bleed-off valve between them are used to isolate piping, the bleed-off valve is secured in the "OPEN" position and the valves or similar blocking seals in the flow lines are functional and secured in the "CLOSED" position.

215.4(4) An employer must ensure that the device used to secure the valves or seals described in subsection (3) is

(a) a positive mechanical means of keeping the valves or seals in the required position, and

(b) strong enough and designed to withstand inadvertent opening without the use of excessive force, unusual measures or destructive techniques.

215.4(5) If it is not reasonably practicable to provide blanking, blinding or double block and bleed isolation, an employer must ensure that an alternate means of isolation that provides adequate protection to workers, certified as appropriate and safe by a professional engineer, is implemented.

Pigging and testing of pipelines

215.5(1) A person who is not directly involved in a pigging and testing operation must not be in the immediate area of piping exposed during the operation.

215.5(2) An employer must ensure that

(a) a pigcatcher on a pipeline is isolated from the pipeline and depressurized before the pig is removed, and

(b) there are no workers at the end of the pipe or in the immediate vicinity of the pigcatcher if the pipe or pigcatcher is under pressure during the operation.

Part 16　Noise Exposure

Duty to reduce

216　An employer must ensure that all reasonably practicable measures are used to reduce the noise to which workers are exposed in areas of the work site where workers may be present.

Noise control design

217(1) An employer must ensure that the following are designed and constructed in such a way that the continuous noise levels generated are not more than 85 dBA or are as low as reasonably practicable:

(a)　a new work site;

(b)　significant physical alterations, renovations or repairs to an existing work site or work area;

(c)　a work process introduced to the work site or work area;

(d)　significant equipment introduced to the work site or work area.

217(2) Subsection (1) does not apply to alterations, renovations or repairs begun or work processes or equipment introduced before April 30, 2004.

Worker exposure to noise

218　An employer must ensure that a worker's exposure to noise does not exceed

(a)　the noise exposure limits in Schedule 3, Table 1, and

(b)　85 dBA L_{ex}.

Noise exposure assessment

219(1) If workers are, or may be, exposed to noise at a work site in excess of 85 dBA L_{ex} and the noise exposure limits in Schedule 3, Table 1, an employer must do a noise exposure assessment under section 7.

219(2) A person who assesses noise exposure at a work site must measure the noise in accordance with CSA Standard Z107.56-06, *Procedures for the Measurement of Occupational Noise Exposure.*

219(3) A person who measures noise exposure at a work site must use

(a)　a sound level meter meeting the requirements for a Type 2 instrument as specified by ANSI Standard S1.4-1983 (R2006), *Specification for Sound Level Meters,*

(b)　a noise dosimeter meeting the requirements for a Type 2 instrument as specified by ANSI Standard S1.25-1991 (R1997), *Specification for Personal Noise Dosimeters*, and set at

(i)　a criterion level of 85 dBA with a 3 dB exchange rate,

(ii)　a threshold level at or below 80 dBA or "off," and

(iii) slow response,

(c)   an integrating sound level meter meeting the requirements as specified by ANSI Standard S1.43-1997, Specifications for *Integrating-Averaging Sound Level Meters*, or IEC Standard 61672-1 (2002), *Electroacoustics — Sound Level Meters — Part 1: Specifications* and IEC Standard 61672-2 (2003), *Electroacoustics — Sound Level Meters — Part 2: Pattern evaluation tests*, or

(d)   equipment approved by a Director of Occupational Hygiene.

219(4) An employer must ensure that a noise exposure assessment is

(a)   conducted and interpreted by a competent person, and

(b)   updated if a change in equipment or process affects the noise level or the length of time a worker is exposed to noise.

Results recorded

220(1) An employer must ensure that results of noise exposure measurements are recorded and include

(a)   the dates of measurements,

(b)   the workers or occupations evaluated,

(c)   the type of measuring equipment used,

(d)   the sound level readings measured, and

(e)   the work location evaluated.

220(2) An employer must ensure that

(a)   a copy of the results of the noise exposure assessment is available on request to an affected worker or an officer, and

(b)   the record of the noise exposure assessment is retained for as long as the employer operates in Alberta.

Noise management program

221(1) If a noise exposure assessment confirms that workers are exposed to excess noise at a work site, the employer must develop and implement a noise management program that includes policies and procedures.

221(2) The employer must ensure that the noise management program includes the following:

(a)   a plan to educate workers in the hazards of exposure to excess noise and to train workers in the correct use of control measures and hearing protection;

(b)   the methods and procedures to be used when measuring or monitoring worker exposure to noise;

(c)   the posting of suitable warning signs in any work area where the noise level exceeds 85 dBA;

(d)   the methods of noise control to be used;

(e)   the selection, use and maintenance of hearing protection devices to be worn by workers;

(f)   the requirements for audiometric testing and the maintenance of test records;

(g)   an annual review of the policies and procedures to address

(i)   the effectiveness of the education and training plan,

(ii)   the need for further noise measurement, and

(iii)   the adequacy of noise control measures.

221(3) A worker who is subject to noise management must cooperate with the employer in implementing the policies and procedures.

Hearing protection

222(1) An employer must ensure that hearing protection equipment provided to workers exposed to excess noise

(a)   meets the requirements of CSA Standard Z94.2-02, *Hearing Protection Devices — Performance, Selection, Care, and Use,* and

(b)   is of the appropriate class and grade as described in Schedule 3, Table 2.

222(2) An employer must

(a)   provide workers with training in the selection, use and maintenance of hearing protection equipment required to be used at a work site in accordance with the manufacturer's specifications, and

(b)   ensure that affected workers wear the required hearing protection equipment.

222(3) Workers who are provided with hearing protection equipment must wear and use the equipment in accordance with the training provided by the employer.

Audiometric testing

223(1) An employer must provide, at the employer's expense, the following audiometric tests for a worker exposed to excess noise:

(a)   an initial baseline test as soon as is practicable, but not later than six months after the worker is employed or within six months after a worker is exposed to excess noise because of a change in the worker's duties or process conditions,

(b)   not more than 12 months after the initial baseline test, and

(c)   at least every second year after the test under clause (b).

223(2) An employer must ensure that audiometric tests are administered by an audiometric technician who must

(a)   work in consultation with a physician, audiologist or occupational health nurse designated by the employer,

(b)   maintain a log book for each audiometer being used that

(i)   contains the audiometer's written calibration records, and

(ii)   remains with the audiometer throughout its useful lifetime,

(c)   conduct the tests in a location where background noise levels do not exceed those specified in Schedule 3, Table 3,

(d)   record the results of the audiometric tests,

(e)   provide a copy of the test results to the worker,

(f)   retain the records of the audiometric tests for a period of not less than 10 years, and

(g)   ensure that the medical history information is under the sole control of the person designated under subsection (2)(a).

223(3) If the results of an audiometric test indicate an abnormal audiogram or show an abnormal shift, the audiometric technician must

(a) advise the worker of the test results,

(b) request the worker to provide, and the worker must provide, relevant medical history, and

(c) forward the results that indicate an abnormal audiogram or an abnormal shift, the medical history and the baseline audiogram to a physician or audiologist designated by the employer to receive this information.

223(4) If the physician or audiologist designated by the employer confirms the audiogram as abnormal or the occurrence of the abnormal shift, the physician or audiologist must

(a) advise the worker to that effect within 30 days,

(b) with the written consent of the worker, provide results of the audiometric tests to the worker's physician,

(c) advise the employer as to the effectiveness of the noise management program in place at the work site, and

(d) retain the records of the audiometric test for a period of not less than 10 years.

223(5) A person must not release records of audiometric tests conducted on a worker or medical history received from a worker as required by this section to any person without the worker's written permission except in accordance with this section.

Credit of time

224 If it is not reasonably practicable for a worker to undergo audiometric testing during the worker's normal working hours, the employer must

(a) credit the time the worker spends to get the test done as time at work, and

(b) ensure that the worker does not lose any pay or other benefits because the worker was tested.

Part 17   Overhead Power Lines

Safe limit of approach distances

225(1) An employer must contact the power line operator before work is done or equipment is operated within 7.0 metres of an energized overhead power line

(a)   to determine the voltage of the power line, and

(b)   to establish the appropriate safe limit of approach distance listed in Schedule 4.

225(1.1) Except as provided for in subsection (2), an employer must ensure that the safe limit of approach distance, as established in subsection (1), is maintained and that no work is done and no equipment is operated at distances less than the established safe limit of approach distance.

225(2) An employer must notify the operator of an energized overhead power line before work is done or equipment is operated in the vicinity of the power line at distances less than the safe limit of approach distances listed in Schedule 4, and obtain the operator's assistance in protecting workers involved.

225(3) An employer must ensure that earth or other materials are not placed under or beside an overhead power line if doing so reduces the safe clearance to less than the safe limit of approach distances listed in Schedule 4.

225(4) A worker must follow the direction of the employer in maintaining the appropriate safe clearance when working in the vicinity of an overhead power line.

Transported loads, equipment and buildings

226   The safe limit of approach distances listed in Schedule 4 do not apply to a load, equipment or building that is transported under energized overhead power lines if the total height, including equipment transporting it, is less than 4.15 metres.

Utility worker and tree trimmer exemption

227   Section 225 does not apply to utility workers, qualified utility workers or utility tree trimmers working in accordance with the requirements of the *Alberta Electrical and Communication Utility Code* (2002).

Part 18   Personal Protective Equipment

Duty to use personal protective equipment

228(1) If the hazard assessment indicates the need for personal protective equipment, an employer must ensure that

    (a)   workers wear personal protective equipment that is correct for the hazard and protects workers,

    (b)   workers properly use and wear the personal protective equipment,

    (c)   the personal protective equipment is in a condition to perform the function for which it was designed, and

    (d)   workers are trained in the correct use, care, limitations and assigned maintenance of the personal protective equipment.

228(2) A worker must

    (a)   use and wear properly the appropriate personal protective equipment specified in this Code in accordance with the training and instruction received,

    (b)   inspect the personal protective equipment before using it, and

    (c)   not use personal protective equipment that is unable to perform the function for which it is designed.

228(3) An employer must ensure that the use of personal protective equipment does not itself endanger the worker.

Eye Protection

Compliance with standards

229(1) If a worker's eyes may be injured or irritated at a work site, an employer must ensure that the worker wears properly fitting eye protection equipment that

    (a)   is approved to

        (i)   CSA Standard Z94.3-07, *Eye and Face Protectors*,

        (ii)   CSA Standard Z94.3-02, *Eye and Face Protectors*, or

        (iii)   CSA Standard Z94.3-99, *Industrial Eye and Face Protectors*, and

    (b)   is appropriate to the work being done and the hazard involved.

229(2) Prescription eyewear may be worn if it

    (a)   is safety eyewear,

    (b)   meets the requirements of

        (i)   CSA Standard Z94.3-07, *Eye and Face Protectors*,

        (ii)   CSA Standard Z94.3-02, *Eye and Face Protectors*, or

        (iii)   CSA Standard Z94.3-99, *Industrial Eye and Face Protectors*, and

    (c)   is appropriate to the work and the hazard involved.

229(2.1)   Prescription safety eyewear having glass lenses must not be used if there is danger of impact unless it is worn behind equipment meeting the requirements of subsection (1).

229(2.2)   If the use of plastic prescription lenses is impracticable, and there is no danger of impact, a worker may use lenses made of treated safety glass meeting the requirements of

(a) ANSI Standard Z87.1-2003, *Occupational and Educational Personal Eye and Face Protection Devices*, or

(b) ANSI Standard Z87.1-1989, *Practice for Occupational and Educational Eye and Face Protection.*

229(2.3) Despite subsection (2), prescription safety eyewear may consist of frames that meet the requirements of ANSI Standard Z87.1-2003, *Occupational and Educational Personal Eye and Face Protection Devices* provided the lenses meet the requirements of CSA Standard Z94.3-07, *Eye and Face Protectors.*

229(3) If a worker must wear a full face piece respirator and the face piece is intended to prevent materials striking the eyes, an employer must ensure that the face piece

(a) meets the requirements of

    (i) CSA Standard Z94.3-07, *Eye and Face Protectors*, or

    (ii) CSA Standard Z94.3-02, *Eye and Face Protectors*, or

(b) meets the impact and penetration test requirements of section 9 of

    (i) ANSI Standard Z87.1-2003, *Occupational and Educational Personal Eye and Face Protection Devices*, or

    (ii) ANSI Standard Z87.1-1989, *Practice for Occupational and Educational Eye and Face Protection.*

Contact lenses

230 An employer must ensure that, if wearing contact lenses poses a hazard to the worker's eyes during work, the worker is advised of the hazards and the alternatives to wearing contact lenses.

Electric arc welding

231 A worker must not perform electric arc welding if it is reasonably possible for another worker to be exposed to radiation from the arc unless the other worker is wearing suitable eye protection or is protected by a screen.

Flame Resistant Clothing

Use of flame resistant clothing

232(1) If a worker may be exposed to a flash fire or electrical equipment flashover, an employer must ensure that the worker wears flame resistant outerwear and uses other protective equipment appropriate to the hazard.

232(2) A worker must ensure that clothing worn beneath flame resistant outerwear and against the skin is made of flame resistant fabrics or natural fibres that will not melt when exposed to heat.

Foot Protection

Footwear

233(1) An employer must ensure that a worker uses footwear that is appropriate to the hazards associated with the work being performed and the work site.

233(2) If the hazard assessment identifies that protective footwear needs to have toe protection, a puncture resistant sole, metatarsal protection, electrical protection, chainsaw protection or any combination of these, the employer must ensure that the worker wears protective footwear that is approved to

(a) CSA Standard Z195-02, *Protective Footwear*, or

(b) ASTM Standard F2413-05, *Specification for Performance Requirements for Protective Footwear,*

if the protective footwear was manufactured on or after July 1, 2009.

233(3) Despite subsection (2), if a worker is likely to be exposed to a hazard other than those referred to in subsection (2), the employer must ensure that the worker uses footwear appropriate to the hazard.

233(4) If a worker is unable, for medical reasons, to wear protective footwear that complies with subsection (2), the worker may substitute external safety toecaps if the employer ensures that

(a)   the safety toecaps meet the impact force requirements of

(i)   CSA Standard Z195-02, *Protective Footwear,* or

(ii) ASTM Standard F2413-05, *Specification for Performance Requirements for Protective Footwear,*

(b)   metatarsal protection is not needed to protect the feet from injury,

(c)   the hazard assessment confirms that the worker will not be exposed to any sole penetration hazards, and

(d)   wearing the safety toecaps does not itself create a hazard for the worker.

233(5) An employer must ensure that a fire fighter wears safety footwear that is approved to

(a)   CSA Standard Z195-02, *Protective Footwear,*

(b)   NFPA Standard 1971, *Protective Ensemble for Structural Fire Fighting,* 2007 Edition, or

(c)   NFPA Standard 1977, *Protective Clothing and Equipment for Wildland Fire Fighting,* 2005 Edition,

if the safety footwear was manufactured on or after July 1, 2009.

Head Protection

Industrial headwear

234(1) Subject to sections 235, 236 and 237, if there is a foreseeable danger of injury to a worker's head at a work site and there is a significant possibility of lateral impact to the head, an employer must ensure that the worker wears industrial protective headwear that is appropriate to the hazards and meets the requirements of

(a)   CSA Standard CAN/CSA-Z94.1-05, *Industrial Protective Headwear,* or

(b)   ANSI Standard Z89.1-2003, *American National Standard for Industrial Head Protection,* for Type II head protection,

if the protective headwear was manufactured on or after July 1, 2009.

234(2) Subject to sections 235, 236 and 237, if there is a foreseeable danger of injury to a worker's head at a work site and the possibility of lateral impact to the head is unlikely, an employer must ensure that the worker wears industrial protective headwear that is appropriate to the hazard and meets the requirements of

(a) CSA Standard CAN/CSA-Z94.1-05, *Industrial Protective Headwear*, or

(b) ANSI Standard Z89.1-2003, *American National Standard for Industrial Head Protection*,

if the protective headwear was manufactured on or after July1, 2009

Bicycles and skates

235(1) An employer must ensure that a worker who is riding a bicycle or using in-line skates or a similar means of transport wears a safety helmet

(a) that is approved to one of the following standards for bicycle safety helmets if the helmet was manufactured on or after July1, 2009:

(i) CSA CAN/CSA-D113.2-M89 (R2004), *Cycling Helmets;*

(ii) CPSC, Title 16 Code of U.S. Federal Regulations Part 1203, *Safety Standard for Bicycle Helmets*;

(iii) Snell Memorial Foundation B-90A, 1998 Standard for Protective Headgear for Use with Bicycles;

(iv) Snell Memorial Foundation B-95A, 1998 Standard for Protective Headgear for Use with Bicycles;

(v) Snell Memorial Foundation N-94, 1994 Standard for Protective Headgear in Non-Motorized Sports;

(vi) ASTM F1447-06, Standard Specification for Helmets Used in Recreational Bicycling or Roller Skating;

(vii) **Repealed**;

(viii) **Repealed**;

(ix) **Repealed**;

(x) **Repealed**; and

(b) that is free of damage or modification that would reduce its effectiveness.

235(2) Despite subsection (1), if workers at a work site normally wear industrial protective headwear in accordance with section 234, that protective headwear may be worn by workers using a bicycle or similar means of transport at the work site if

(a) the worker travels at a speed of not more than 20 kilometres per hour, and

(b) the protective headwear is worn with a fastened chin strap.

All-terrain vehicles, snow vehicles, motorcycles

236(1) An employer must ensure that a worker riding an all-terrain vehicle, snow vehicle, motorized trail bike or motorcycle or, subject to subsection (2), a small utility vehicle at a work site wears a safety helmet approved to one of the following standards:

(a) U.S.A. Federal Motor Vehicle Safety Standard FMVSS 218, *Motorcycle Helmets* 1993 OCT;

(b) BSI Standard BS 6658: 05, *Specification for Protective Helmets for Vehicle Users;*

(c) Snell Memorial Foundation Standard M2005, *2005 Helmet Standard for Use in Motorcycling,*

if the safety helmet was manufactured on or after July1, 2009.

236(1.1) Subsection (1) does not apply to small utility vehicles equipped with seat belts and rollover protection.

236(2) Protective headwear in good condition that meets the requirements of an earlier version of a standard listed in subsection (1) may be used unless it is damaged.

236(3) Subsection (1) does not apply if the vehicle is equipped with rollover protective structures that comply with section 270 and seat belts or restraining devices that comply with section 271.

236(4) A worker who wears protective headwear under subsection (1) and who uses an all-terrain vehicle, snow vehicle, motorized trail bike or motorcycle to travel to a remote work site may continue to wear that protective headwear while working at the work site if

(a) the work does not subject the worker to potential contact with exposed energized electrical sources, and

(b) the work is done for a short period of time.

Fire fighters

237   Despite section 234, an employer may permit a fire fighter to wear protective headwear that meets the requirements of the following standards considering the nature of the hazard:

(a) NFPA Standard 1971, *Protective Ensemble for Structural Fire Fighting,* 2007 Edition, or

(b) NFPA Standard 1977, *Protective Clothing and Equipment for Wildland Fire Fighting,* 2005 Edition,

if the protective headwear was manufactured on or after July1, 2009.

Bump hat

238   Despite section 234, an employer may permit a worker to wear a bump hat at the work site if the danger of injury is limited to the worker's head striking a stationary object.

Exemption from wearing headwear

239(1) Despite section 234, if it is impractical for a worker to wear industrial protective headwear during a particular work process,

(a) the employer must ensure that the worker's head is protected using an adequate alternative means of protection during the work process, and

(b) the worker may conduct the work while the alternative means of protection is in place.

239(2) A worker must wear industrial protective headwear if the foreseeable danger of injury to the worker's head persists immediately after completing the work process referred to in subsection (1).

Life Jackets and Personal Flotation Devices

Compliance with standards

240(1) An employer must ensure that a life jacket is approved to CGSB Standard CAN/CGSB 65.7-M88 AMEND, *Lifejackets, Inherently Buoyant Type*, and any amendments for approved small vessel life jackets.

240(2) An employer must ensure that a personal flotation device is approved to CGSB Standard CAN/CGSB 65.11-M88 AMEND, *Personal Flotation Device*, and any amendments for personal flotation devices, type 1 (inherently buoyant).

Use of jackets and flotation devices

241(1) If there is a foreseeable danger that a worker could be exposed to the hazard of drowning, an employer must ensure that the worker wears a life jacket.

241(2) A worker who could be exposed to the hazard of drowning must wear a life jacket.

241(2.1) Subsections (1) and (2) do not apply if other safety measures are in place that will protect a worker from the hazard of drowning.

241(3) Despite subsections (1) and (2), if a worker performs work from a boat for an extended period of time, the worker may wear a personal flotation device if the employer ensures that there is also a life jacket readily accessible to each worker on the boat.

Limb and Body Protection

Limb and body protection

242 If there is a danger that a worker's hand, arm, leg or torso may be injured, an employer must ensure that the worker wears properly fitting hand, arm, leg or body protective equipment that is appropriate to the work, the work site and the hazards identified.

Skin protection

243 An employer must ensure that a worker's skin is protected from a harmful substance that may injure the skin on contact or may adversely affect a worker's health if it is absorbed through the skin.

Respiratory Protective Equipment

Respiratory dangers

244(1) An employer must determine the degree of danger to a worker at a work site and whether the worker needs to wear respiratory protective equipment if

    (a) a worker is or may be exposed to an airborne contaminant or a mixture of airborne contaminants in a concentration exceeding their occupational exposure limits,

    (b) the atmosphere has or may have an oxygen concentration of less than 19.5 percent by volume, or

    (c) a worker is or may be exposed to an airborne biohazardous material.

244(2) In making a determination under subsection (1), the employer must consider

   (a) the nature and exposure circumstances of any contaminants or
        biohazardous material,

   (b) the concentration or likely concentration of any airborne contaminants,

   (c) the duration or likely duration of the worker's exposure,

   (d) the toxicity of the contaminants,

   (e) the concentration of oxygen,

   (f) the warning properties of the contaminants, and

   (g) the need for emergency escape.

244(3) Based on a determination under subsection (1), the employer must

   (a) subject to subsection 3(b), provide and ensure the availability of the
        appropriate respiratory protective equipment to the worker at the work
        site, and

   (b) despite section 247, when the effects of airborne biohazardous
        materials are unknown, provide and ensure the availability of
        respiratory protective equipment appropriate to the worker's known
        exposure circumstances.

244(3.1)   Subsection (3) does not apply when an employer has developed and
implemented procedures that effectively limit exposure to airborne biohazardous
material.

244(4) A worker must use the appropriate respiratory equipment provided by the
employer under subsection (3).

Code of practice

245(1) If respiratory protective equipment is used at a work site, an employer
must prepare a code of practice governing the selection, maintenance and use of
respiratory protective equipment.

245(2) In the case of a health care worker who may be exposed to airborne
biohazardous material, an employer must ensure that the code of practice
required under subsection (1) includes training on at least an annual basis.

Approval of equipment

246   An employer must ensure that respiratory protective equipment required
at a work site is approved

   (a) by NIOSH, or

   (b) by another standards setting and equipment testing organization, or
        combination of organizations, approved by a Director of Occupational
        Hygiene.

Selection of equipment

247   An employer must ensure that respiratory protective equipment used at a
work site is selected in accordance with CSA Standard Z94.4-02, *Selection, Use
and Care of Respirators*.

Storage and use

248(1) An employer must ensure that respiratory protective equipment kept ready
to protect a worker is

   (a) stored in a readily accessible location,

(b) stored in a manner that prevents its contamination,

(c) maintained in a clean and sanitary condition,

(d) inspected before and after each use to ensure it is in satisfactory working condition, and

(e) serviced and used in accordance with the manufacturer's specifications.

248(2) An employer must ensure that respiratory protective equipment that is not used routinely but is kept for emergency use is inspected at least once every calendar month by a competent worker to ensure it is in satisfactory working condition.

Quality of breathing air

249(1) An employer must ensure that air used in a self-contained breathing apparatus or an air line respirator

(a) is of a quality that meets the requirements of Table 1 of CSA Standard Z180.1-00 (R2005), *Compressed Breathing Air and Systems,* and

(b) does not contain a substance in a concentration that exceeds 10 percent of its occupational exposure limit.

249(2) Subsection (1)(b) does not apply to substances listed in Table 1 of CSA Standard Z180.1-00 (R2005), *Compressed Breathing Air and Systems.*

Effective facial seal

250(1) An employer must ensure that respiratory protective equipment that depends on an effective facial seal for its safe use is correctly fit tested and tested in accordance with

(a) CSA Standard Z94.4-02, *Selection, Use and Care of Respirators,* or

(b) a method approved by a Director of Occupational Hygiene.

250(2) An employer must ensure that, if a worker is or may be required to wear respiratory protective equipment and the effectiveness of the equipment depends on an effective facial seal, the worker is clean shaven where the face piece of the equipment seals to the skin of the face.

Equipment for immediate danger

251 If an employer determines under section 244 that breathing conditions at a work site are or may become immediately dangerous to life or health, the employer must ensure that a worker wears self-contained breathing apparatus or an air line respirator that

(a) is of a type that will maintain positive pressure in the face piece,

(b) has a capacity of at least 30 minutes unless the employer's hazard assessment indicates the need for a greater capacity,

(c) provides full face protection in situations where contaminants may irritate or damage the eyes,

(d) in the case of an air line respirator, is fitted with an auxiliary supply of respirable air of sufficient quantity to enable the worker to escape from the area in an emergency, and

(e) in the case of a self-contained breathing apparatus, has an alarm warning of low pressure.

Equipment — no immediate danger

252 An employer must ensure that a worker wears self-contained breathing apparatus or an air line respirator having a capacity of at least 30 minutes if

(a) the employer determines under section 244 that conditions at the work site are not or cannot become immediately dangerous to life or health but

(i) the oxygen content of the atmosphere is or may be less than 19.5 percent by volume, or

(ii) the concentration of airborne contaminants exceeds or may exceed that specified by the manufacturer for air purifying respiratory equipment, and

(b) the complete equipment required by section 251 is not provided.

Air purifying equipment

253 An employer may permit workers to wear air purifying respiratory protective equipment if

(a) the oxygen content of the air is, and will continue to be, 19.5 percent or greater by volume,

(b) the air purifying equipment used is designed to provide protection against the specific airborne contaminant, or combination of airborne contaminants, present, and

(c) the concentration of airborne contaminants does not exceed the maximum concentration specified by the manufacturer for the specific type of air purifying equipment, taking into consideration the duration of its use.

Emergency escape equipment

254(1) Despite sections 251 and 252, if normal operating conditions do not require the wearing of respiratory protective equipment but emergency conditions may occur requiring a worker to escape from the work area, the employer may permit the escaping worker to wear

(a) a mouth bit and nose-clamp respirator if

(i) the respirator is designed to protect the worker from the specific airborne contaminants present, and

(ii) the oxygen content of the atmosphere during the escape is 19.5 percent or greater by volume, or

(b) alternative respiratory protective equipment that can be proven to give the worker the same or greater protection as the equipment referred to in clause (a).

254(2) Before permitting a worker to use the equipment referred to in subsection (1), the employer must consider the length of time it will take the worker to escape from the work area.

Abrasive blasting operations

255 If a worker is performing abrasive blasting, the employer must ensure that the worker wears a hood specifically designed for abrasive blasting, supplied with air that is at a positive pressure of not more than 140 kilopascals.

Part 19   Powered Mobile Equipment

Operator responsibilities

256(1) A worker must not operate powered mobile equipment unless the worker

(a) is trained to safely operate the equipment,

(b) has demonstrated competency in operating the equipment to a competent worker designated by the employer,

(c) is familiar with the equipment's operating instructions, and

(d) is authorized by the employer to operate the equipment.

256(2) Subsections (1)(a), (b) and (c) do not apply if a worker in training operates the equipment under the direct supervision of a competent worker designated by the employer.

256(3) The operator of powered mobile equipment must

(a) report to the employer any conditions affecting the safe operation of the equipment,

(b) operate the equipment safely,

(c) maintain full control of the equipment at all times,

(d) use the seat belts and other safety equipment in the powered mobile equipment,

(e) ensure that passengers in the powered mobile equipment use the seat belts and other safety equipment in the powered mobile equipment, and

(f) keep the cab, floor and deck of the powered mobile equipment free of materials, tools or other objects that could interfere with the operation of the controls or create a tripping or other hazard to the operator or other occupants of the equipment.

Visual inspection

257(1) Before operating powered mobile equipment, the operator must complete a visual inspection of the equipment and the surrounding area to ensure that the powered mobile equipment is in safe operating condition and that no worker, including the operator, is endangered when the equipment is started up.

257(2) While powered mobile equipment is in operation, the operator must complete a visual inspection of the equipment and surrounding area at the intervals required by the manufacturer's specifications or, in the absence of manufacturer's specifications, the employer's operating procedures.

257(3) Despite subsections (1) and (2), if the powered mobile equipment is continuously operated as part of an ongoing work operation, the operator may visually inspect the equipment during the work shift or work period as required by the employer's operating procedures.

257(4) A person must not start powered mobile equipment if the visual inspection under subsection (1) is not completed.

Dangerous movement

258(1) If the movement of a load or the cab, counterweight or any other part of powered mobile equipment creates a danger to workers,

(a) an employer must not permit a worker to remain within range of the moving load or part, and

(b) the operator must not move the load or the equipment if a worker is exposed to the danger.

258(2) If the movement of a load or the cab, counterweight or any other part of powered mobile equipment creates a danger to workers, a worker must not remain within range of the moving load or part.

258(3) If a worker could be caught between a moving part of a unit of powered mobile equipment and another object, an employer must

(a) restrict entry to the area by workers, or

(b) require workers to maintain a clearance distance of at least 600 millimetres between the powered mobile equipment and the object.

Pedestrian traffic

259(1) An employer must ensure that, if reasonably practicable,

(a) walkways are designated that separate pedestrian traffic from areas where powered mobile equipment is operating,

(b) workers use the designated walkways.

259(2) If it is not reasonably practicable to use designated walkways, an employer must ensure that safe work procedures are used to protect workers who enter areas where powered mobile equipment is operating.

Inspection and maintenance

260(1) An employer must ensure that powered mobile equipment is inspected by a competent worker for defects and conditions that are hazardous or may create a hazard.

260(2) An inspection under subsection (1) must be made in accordance with the manufacturer's specifications.

260(3) If an inspection under subsection (1) indicates that powered mobile equipment is hazardous or potentially hazardous, an employer must ensure that

(a) the health and safety of a worker who may be exposed to the hazard is protected immediately,

(b) the powered mobile equipment is not operated until the defect is repaired or the condition is corrected, and

(c) the defect is repaired or the unsafe condition corrected as soon as reasonably practicable.

260(4) Despite subsection (3), if an inspection under subsection (1) indicates that the powered mobile equipment is potentially hazardous but the equipment can be operated safely, an employer must ensure that

(a) the operator is made aware of the potential hazard, and

(b) the defect or condition is repaired as soon as reasonably practicable.

260(5) An employer must ensure that a record of the inspections and maintenance carried out as required by subsections (1) and (2) is kept at the work site and readily available to a worker who operates the powered mobile equipment.

Maintenance on elevated parts

261   An employer must ensure that if elevated parts of powered mobile equipment are being maintained or repaired by workers, the parts and the powered mobile equipment are securely blocked in place and cannot move accidentally.

Starting engines

262(1) Subject to subsection (3), an employer must ensure that a worker does not start the power unit of powered mobile equipment if the drive mechanisms and clutches of the equipment are engaged.

262(2) A worker must not start the power unit of powered mobile equipment if the drive mechanisms and clutches of the equipment are engaged.

262(3) An employer must ensure that no worker, including the operator, can be injured due to the movement of powered mobile equipment or any part of it, if

    (a) its power unit can be started from a location other than the equipment's control platform or cab seat, or

    (b) it is not reasonably practicable to disengage its drive mechanism or clutches.

Unattended equipment

263(1) A person must not leave the controls of powered mobile equipment unattended unless the equipment is secured against unintentional movement by an effective method of immobilizing the equipment.

263(2) A person must not leave the controls of powered mobile equipment unattended unless a suspended or elevated part of the powered mobile equipment is either landed, secured in a safe position, or both.

Lights

264(1) An employer must ensure that powered mobile equipment operated during hours of darkness or when, due to insufficient light or unfavourable atmospheric conditions, workers and vehicles are not clearly discernible at a distance of at least 150 metres, is equipped with lights that illuminate

    (a) a direction in which the equipment travels,

    (b) the working area around the equipment, and

    (c) the control panel of the equipment.

264(2) An employer must ensure that the lights on earthmoving construction machinery installed on or after July 1, 2009 complies with SAE Standard J1029 (2007), *Lighting and Marking of Construction, Earthmoving Machinery.*

Windows and windshields

265(1) An employer must ensure that glazing used as part of the enclosure for a cab, canopy or rollover protective structure on powered mobile equipment is safety glass or another non-shattering material providing at least equivalent protection.

265(2) An employer must ensure that the glazing installed on or after July 1, 2009 on an enclosure of powered mobile equipment is approved to ANSI Standard ANSI/SAE Z26.1 (1996), *Safety Glazing Material for Glazing Motor Vehicles and Motor Vehicle Equipment Operating on Land Highways — Safety Standard.*

265(3) An employer must ensure that broken or cracked glazing that obstructs an operator's view from powered mobile equipment is replaced as soon as is reasonably practicable.

265(4) An employer must ensure that a windshield on powered mobile equipment has windshield wipers of sufficient size and capacity to clean matter that obstructs the operator's view from the windshield.

Other safety equipment

266   An employer must ensure that powered mobile equipment has

(a)   a device within easy reach of the operator that permits the operator to stop, as quickly as possible, the power unit, drawworks, transmission or any ancillary equipment driven from the powered mobile equipment, including a power take-off auger or digging, lifting, or cutting equipment,

(b)   an effective means of warning workers of the presence, general dimensions and movement of the equipment if the presence, dimensions or movement may be a danger to a worker,

(c)   seats or other installations sufficient to ensure the safety of the operator and other workers who may be in or on the equipment while it is in motion, and

(d)   safety clips on the connecting pins if the powered mobile equipment is equipped with a trailer hitch.

Warning signal

267(1) An employer must ensure that, if a powered mobile equipment operator's view of the equipment's path of travel is obstructed or cannot be seen directly or indirectly in a direction, the powered mobile equipment has

(a)   an automatic audible warning device that

(i)   activates if the equipment controls are positioned to move the equipment in that direction, and

(ii)   is audible above the ambient noise level,

(b)   a warning device or method appropriate to the hazards of the work site, or

(c)   an automatic system that stops the equipment if a worker is in its path.

267(2) If it is impractical to equip powered mobile equipment in accordance with subsection (1), the operator must ensure that the operator and other workers are protected from injury before moving the equipment by

(a)   doing a visual inspection on foot of the area into which the equipment will move,

(b)   following the directions of a traffic control or warning system,

(c)   getting directions from a designated signaller or other worker who

(i)   has an unobstructed view of the area into which the equipment will move, or

(ii)   is stationed in a safe position in continuous view of the operator, or

(d)   ensuring all other workers are removed from the area into which the equipment will move.

Bulkheads

268   An employer must install a bulkhead or provide other effective means to protect the operator of a vehicle transporting equipment or materials that may shift during an emergency stop.

Guards and screens

269   An employer must ensure that powered mobile equipment has a cab, screen, shield, grill, deflector, guard or other adequate protection for the operator if the hazard assessment indicates there is a significant possibility that the operator may be injured by flying or projecting objects.

Rollover protective structures

270(1) An employer must ensure that the following types of powered mobile equipment weighing 700 kilograms or more have rollover protective structures:

    (a)   tracked (crawler) or wheeled bulldozers, loaders, tractors or skidders, other than those operating with side booms;

    (b)   back hoes with a limited horizontal swing of 180 degrees;

    (c)   motor graders;

    (d)   self-propelled wheeled scrapers;

    (e)   industrial, agricultural and horticultural tractors, including ride-on lawnmowers;

    (f)   wheeled trenchers.

270(2) An employer must ensure that a rollover protective structure installed on or after July1, 2009 complies with the applicable requirements of

    (a)   CSA Standard B352.0-95 (R2006*), Rollover Protective Structures (ROPS) for Agricultural, Construction, Earthmoving, Forestry, Industrial and Mining Machines — Part 1: General Requirements*, and

        (i)   CSA Standard B352.1-95 (R2006), *Rollover Protective Structures (ROPS) for Agricultural, Construction, Earthmoving, Forestry, Industrial and Mining Machines — Part 2: Testing Requirements for ROPS on Agricultural Tractors*, or

        (ii) CSA Standard B352.2-95 (R2006), *Rollover Protective Structures (ROPS) for Agricultural, Construction, Earthmoving, Forestry, Industrial and Mining Machines — Part 3: Testing Requirements for ROPS on Construction, Earthmoving, Forestry, Industrial and Mining Machines,*

    (b)   SAE Standard J1042 (2003), *Operator Protection for General-Purpose Industrial Machines,*

    (c)   SAE Standard J1194 (1999), *Rollover Protective Structures (ROPS) for Wheeled Agricultural Tractors,*

    (d)   ISO Standard 3471: 2000, *Earth-moving machinery — Roll-over protective structures — Laboratory tests and performance requirements*, or

    (e)   OSHA Standard 1928.52, *Protective Frames for Wheel-type Agricultural Tractors — Tests, Procedures and Performance Requirements.*

270(3) If powered mobile equipment is not referred to in subsection (1) and a hazard assessment identifies rollover as a potential hazard, the employer must

(a) equip the powered mobile equipment with a rollover protective structure that is either supplied by the manufacturer or certified by a professional engineer as being suited to that equipment, or

(b) institute safe work procedures that eliminate the possibility of rollover.

Equipment with rollover protection

271(1) An employer must ensure that the powered mobile equipment fitted with a rollover protective structure manufactured on or after July 1, 2009 has seat belts for the operator and passengers that comply with

(a) SAE Standard J386 (2006), *Operator Restraint System for Off-Road Work Machines*, or

(b) SAE Information Report J2292 (2006), *Combination Pelvic/Upper Torso (Type 2) Operator Restraint Systems for Off-Road Work Machines*.

271(2) Despite subsection (1), if the work process makes wearing the seat belts in the powered mobile equipment impracticable, the employer may permit workers to wear shoulder belts or use bars, screens or other restraining devices designed to prevent the operator or a passenger from being thrown out of the rollover protective structure.

Falling objects protective structures

272(1) If the hazard assessment identifies that an operator of powered mobile equipment is exposed to falling objects, the employer must ensure that the powered mobile equipment is equipped with a falling objects protective structure.

272(2) A falling objects protective structure installed on or after July 1, 2009 must comply with the appropriate requirements of

(a) SAE Standard J167 (2002), *Overhead Protection for Agricultural Tractors — Test Procedures and Performance Requirements*,

(b) SAE Standard J/ISO 3449 (2005), *Earthmoving Machinery — Falling-Object Protective Structures—Laboratory Tests and Performance Requirements*, or

(c) SAE Standard J1042 (2003), *Operator Protection for General-Purpose Industrial Machines*.

272(3) An employer, instead of using a falling objects protective structure that complies with subsection (2), may use equipment that is certified by a professional engineer as providing the equivalent or better protection.

Recertification after modification

273 An employer must ensure that any addition, modification, welding or cutting of a rollover protective structure or a falling objects protective structure is done in accordance with the instructions of, and is re-certified as restored to its original performance requirements by, the equipment manufacturer or a professional engineer.

Fuel tank in cab

274 An employer must ensure that a fuel tank located in the enclosed cab of a unit of powered mobile equipment has a filler spout and vents

(a) extending outside the cab, and

(b) that are sealed to prevent vapours from entering the enclosed cab.

Worker transportation

275(1) An employer must ensure that no part of an operator's or passenger's body extends beyond the side of a vehicle or powered mobile equipment while it is in operation.

275(2) An employer must ensure that equipment or material in a vehicle or unit of powered mobile equipment is positioned or secured to prevent injury to the operator and passengers, if any.

275(3) An employer must ensure that sufficient protection against inclement weather is provided for workers travelling in a vehicle or unit of powered mobile equipment.

275(4) If a vehicle or unit of powered mobile equipment with an enclosed body is used to transport workers, an employer must ensure that the equipment's exhaust gases do not enter the enclosed body.

Riding on loads

276 A person must not ride on top of a load that is being moved.

Hazardous loads

277(1) An employer must ensure that workers are not servicing or maintaining a vehicle while flammable, combustible or explosive materials are

(a) being loaded into or unloaded from the vehicle, or

(b) in the vehicle, other than in the vehicle's fuel tank or a portable fuel tank that is approved to the appropriate ULC standard for that tank.

277(2) For the purposes of subsection (1), servicing and maintaining a vehicle does not include checking or topping up fluid levels or air pressure.

277(3) A worker must not service or maintain a vehicle in contravention of subsection (1).

Tank trucks

278(1) The operator must ensure that a tank truck containing flammable, combustible or explosive materials is bonded and grounded while

(a) its loading lines are connected or disconnected, and

(b) the contents of the tank truck are being transferred.

278(2) Section 277 does not apply to a commercial tank truck designed to transport flammable, combustible or explosive materials.

Refuelling

279(1) An employer must ensure that a worker does not

(a) smoke within 7.5 metres of a vehicle while it is being refuelled,

(b) refuel a vehicle when there is a source of ignition within 7.5 metres of that vehicle, or

(c) dispense flammable fuels into the fuel tank of a motor vehicle or watercraft while its engine is running.

279(2) A person must not

(a) smoke within 7.5 metres of a vehicle while it is being refuelled,

(b) refuel a vehicle when there is a source of ignition within 7.5 metres of that vehicle, or

(c) dispense flammable fuels into the fuel tank of a motor vehicle or watercraft while its engine is running.

279(3) An employer must ensure that a worker dispensing flammable fuel

(a) takes precautions to prevent the fuel from overflowing or spilling,

(b) does not knowingly overfill the fuel system, and

(c) does not use an object or device that is not an integral part of the hose nozzle valve assembly to maintain the flow of fuel.

279(4) Subsections (1)(c) and (2)(c) do not apply to the fuelling system of the motor vehicle or watercraft if its manufacturer or a professional engineer certifies

(a) it is safe to refuel while the engine is running, and

(b) the safe work practices to be used during the refuelling.

All-Terrain Vehicles and Snow Vehicles

Three-wheeled all-terrain cycles

280   A person must not use a three-wheeled all-terrain vehicle at a work site.

Operator's manual

281   An employer must ensure that the operator's manual for an all-terrain vehicle or snow vehicle is kept in a secure place with the vehicle or at another location readily accessible to the operator.

Load and slope limitations

282(1) The operator of an all-terrain vehicle or snow vehicle must ensure that, if it is used to move a load, the load conforms to the weight, height and other limits specified by the manufacturer of the all-terrain vehicle or snow vehicle.

282(2) If the manufacturer has not set limits for operation of the all-terrain vehicle or snow vehicle on sloping ground, the employer must implement safe work procedures appropriate for the slopes on which the equipment is used.

Forklift Trucks

Load chart

283   An employer must ensure that a forklift truck has a durable and legible load rating chart that is readily available to the operator.

Seat belt

284   If a forklift truck is equipped with a seat belt by the original equipment manufacturer or a seat belt is added to the equipment at some later date, an employer must ensure that the seat belt is present and in useable condition.

Pile Driving Equipment and Practices

Chocking

285 The operator of pile driving equipment must ensure that a pile hammer is securely chocked while suspended by the hammer line if the equipment is not operating.

Pile hoisting

286(1) The operator of pile driving equipment must ensure that pilings are not hoisted in the leads if workers who are not directly involved in the pile hoisting are on the superstructure or within range of a falling pile.

286(2) A worker must not

(a) remain or ride on a load or part of a load being moved, raised or lowered by pile driving equipment, or

(b) be on the superstructure of pile driving equipment or within range of a falling pile if the worker is not directly involved in the pile hoisting.

Restraining hoses and connections

287 An employer must ensure that the pressure hoses of pile driving equipment with pressure hammers have, on the pressure side of all hose connections, safety chains or ropes designed to protect workers should the hoses or connections fail.

Brake bands and clutches

288 An employer must ensure that

(a) at the beginning of a work shift, the brake bands and clutches of pile driving equipment are inspected by a competent worker designated by the employer, and

(b) if the worker finds contamination by oil or grease, the contaminated units are dismantled and cleaned or replaced before they are used.

Timber piles

289 The employer must ensure that

(a) workers in the area of a timber pile being struck by a pile driver are protected from any danger that may result from the pile shattering, and

(b) before piles are placed in position for driving, pile heads are cut square and timber piles are free of debris, bark and splintered wood.

Crane boom inspection

290(1) An employer must ensure that a crane boom used for driving piles with a vibratory hammer is

(a) inspected

(i) at the intervals specified in the manufacturer's specifications or specifications certified by a professional engineer, or

(ii) annually or every 600 operating hours, whichever comes first, and

(b) certified by a professional engineer as safe for continued use.

290(2) An employer must ensure that a crane boom with a vibratory pile extractor is

(a) inspected

  (i) at the intervals specified in the manufacturer's specifications or specifications certified by a professional engineer, or

  (ii) annually or every 200 operating hours, whichever comes first, and

(b) certified by a professional engineer as safe for continued use.

290(3) An employer must ensure that a crane boom used for dynamic compaction is

(a) inspected

  (i) at the intervals specified in the manufacturer's specifications or specifications certified by a professional engineer, or

  (ii) annually or every 200 operating hours, whichever comes first, and

(b) certified by a professional engineer as safe for continued use.

Personal Vehicle for Work Purposes

Licensing and mechanical inspection

290.1 If a worker uses a personal vehicle for work purposes,

(a) an employer must ensure that the worker complies with section 256(1) by complying with the appropriate licensed driver requirements of provincial legislation, and

(b) the worker must ensure that the vehicle is maintained in sound mechanical condition.

Concrete Pump Trucks

Safety requirements

290.2(1) An employer must ensure that all load bearing components of a concrete pump truck undergo non-destructive testing under the direction and control of a professional engineer in accordance with the manufacturer's specifications at 12-month intervals from the date of the concrete pump truck's most recent certification.

290.2(2) An employer must ensure that the operator of a concrete pump truck visually inspects all load bearing components and safety and control devices of the concrete pump truck before each use.

290.2(3) Before using a concrete pump truck at a work site, an employer must ensure that the outriggers of the equipment are extended in accordance with the manufacturer's specifications.

290.2(4) While a concrete pump truck is in use at a work site, an employer must ensure that no worker or other person is positioned under a distribution boom or mast connected to the concrete pump truck.

290.2(5) An employer must ensure that a concrete pump truck is not moved when its distribution boom or mast is partially or full extended, unless the truck is designed to be moved with its distribution boom or mast partially or fully extended.

Part 20   Radiation Exposure

Prevention and protection

291   If workers may be exposed to ionizing radiation at a work site, an employer must

    (a) develop and implement safe work practices and procedures to be used when the workers deal with or approach the radiation source,

    (b) if practicable, involve the workers in the development and implementation of the safe work practices and procedures, and

    (c) inform the workers of the potential hazards of ionizing radiation and the radiation source.

Part 21 Rigging

Breaking strength

292(1) An employer must ensure that rigging is not subjected to a load of more than

    (a) 10 percent of the breaking strength of the weakest part of the rigging, if a worker is being raised or lowered,

    (b) subject to section 292.1, 20 percent of the ultimate breaking strength of the weakest part of the rigging in all other situations unless the manufacturer has fatigue rated the rigging in accordance with CEN Standard EN 1677-1: 2000, *Components for slings — Part 1: Forged steel components grade 8*, and

    (c) subject to section 292.1, if the rigging is fatigue rated in accordance with CEN Standard EN 1677-1: 2000 and a worker is not being raised or lowered, the maximum load must not exceed 25 percent of the ultimate breaking strength.

292(2) Despite subsection (1), an employer may use a dedicated rigging assembly designed and certified for a particular lift or project by a professional engineer, but the dedicated rigging assembly must be re-rated to comply with subsection (1) before it is used for another lift or project.

Safety factors

292.1(1) Subject to section 292, an employer must ensure that rigging components are rated relative to their ultimate breaking strength in accordance with the following safety factors:

    (a) running lines   3.5 to 1;

    (b) non-rotating hoist lines   5 to 1;

    (c) tugger lines/blocks for pulling   3 to 1;

    (d) pendant lines/guy lines   3 to 1; and

    (e) winch lines   2 to 1.

292.1(2) An employer must ensure that rigging components or hoisting lines that are used in any towing operation are not used for any hoisting operation.

Load ratings

293(1) An employer must ensure that the maximum load rating of the rigging, as determined by the rigging manufacturer or a professional engineer, is legibly and conspicuously marked on the rigging.

293(2) Despite subsection (1), if it is not practicable to mark the rigging, the employer must ensure the maximum load rating of the rigging is available to the workers at the work site.

Inspection

294 An employer must ensure that rigging to be used during a work shift is inspected thoroughly prior to each period of continuous use during the shift to ensure that the rigging is functional and safe.

Prohibition

295 A worker must not use rigging that does not comply with this Part.

Rigging protection

296   An employer must ensure that sharp edges on loads to be hoisted are guarded to prevent damage to the slings or straps of the rigging.

Standards

297(1) An employer must ensure that wire rope, alloy steel chain, synthetic fibre rope, metal mesh slings and synthetic fibre slings manufactured on or after July 1, 2009 meet the requirements of ASME Standard B30.9-2006, *Safety Standard for Cableways, Cranes, Derricks, Hoists, Hooks, Jacks and Slings.*

297(2) An employer must ensure that below-the-hook lifting devices, other than slings, meet the requirements of ASME Standard B30.20-2006, *Below the Hook Lifting Devices.*

297(3) Despite subsection (2), an employer may use a capacity data sheet to label a spreader bar with its rated capacity.

297(4) Where a capacity data sheet is used in accordance with subsection (3), an employer must ensure that the data sheet and corresponding spreader bar are identified by a unique numbering system.

Slings

298(1) An employer must ensure that synthetic fibre slings are permanently and legibly marked or appropriately tagged with the following:

    (a)   the manufacturer's name or trade mark;

    (b)   the manufacturer's code or stock number;

    (c)   the safe working load for the types of hitches permitted; and

    (d)   where appropriate, the type and material of construction.

298(2) An employer must ensure that slings at a worksite are not subjected to pull tests beyond 100 percent of their rated load capacity.

Rope wound on drum

299(1) An employer must ensure that rope on a winding drum is securely fastened to the drum.

299(2) An employer must ensure that the number of wraps of rope remaining at all times on a drum

    (a)   complies with the manufacturer's specifications for the rope and the drum, or

    (b)   if there are no manufacturer's specifications, is not less than 5 full wraps.

Cable clips

300(1) An employer must ensure that U-bolt type clips used for fastening wire rope are installed

    (a)   so that the U-bolt section of the clip bears on the short or "dead" side of the rope,

    (b)   so that the saddle of a clip bears on the long or "live" side of the rope, and

    (c)   using the number and with the spacing that complies with the specifications in Schedule 5.

300(2) An employer must ensure that cable clips used for fastening wire rope are installed, and torqued to the manufacturer's specifications or, in the absence of manufacturer's specifications, to the values specified in Schedule 5.

300(3) An employer must ensure that double-saddle clips (fist clips) used for fastening wire rope are installed using the number and the spacing and torque that complies with the specifications in Schedule 5.

300(4) An employer must ensure that double base clips used for fastening wire rope are installed with a spacing that is not less than 6 times the diameter of the rope.

Ferrules

301(1) If a ferrule is used to form an eye loop in a wire rope and

    (a)   the ends of the splice are visible beneath the ferrule, or

    (b)   the ferrule is identified as covering a "Flemish eye" splice,

the employer must ensure that the ferrule is commercially manufactured of steel and properly swaged onto the splice.

301(2) Despite subsection (1), if an aluminum alloy ferrule must be used, an employer must ensure that the ferrule is

    (a)   commercially manufactured,

    (b)   identified as being made of aluminum alloy, and

    (c)   properly swaged onto the splice.

Matching components

302(1) An employer must ensure that the wire ropes, sheaves, spools and drums used in rigging have a diameter of not less than the diameter specified by the manufacturer for use in that circumstance.

302(2) An employer must ensure that the rope used in rigging is of the correct size for the sheave, spool or drum over which the rope passes.

302(3) An employer must ensure that the grooving of wire rope sheaves is of the correct size for the wire rope used.

302(4) An employer must ensure that end fittings and connectors used on a wire rope conform to the manufacturer's specifications as to number, size and method of installation.

302(5) An employer must ensure that rigging blocks are constructed and installed so that the ropes cannot jump off the sheaves.

Safety latches

303(1) An employer must ensure that a hook has a safety latch, mousing or shackle if the hook could cause injury if it is dislodged while in use.

303(2) Despite subsection (1), if a competent worker disconnecting the hook would be in danger if the hook has a safety latch, mousing or shackle, the employer may use another type of hook.

303(3) Despite subsection (1), an employer may use a sorting hook for hoisting a skeleton steel structure or for performing similar operations if a sorting hook is safer to use than a hook with a safety latch, mousing or shackle.

303(4) During a hoisting operation in a caisson, an employer

    (a)   must not use a spring-loaded safety latch hook, and

(b) must use a shackle assembly consisting of a pin fully shouldered into the eyes of the shackle and secured by a nut that is prevented from rotating by a cotter pin.

Makeshift rigging and welding

304 An employer must ensure that rigging does not have

(a) makeshift fittings or attachments, including those constructed from reinforcing steel rod, that are load bearing components,

(b) rigging and fittings that are repaired by welding unless they are certified safe for use by a professional engineer after the repair is completed, or

(c) alloy steel chain that is welded or annealed.

Rejection Criteria

Synthetic fibre slings

305(1) An employer must ensure that a synthetic fibre web sling is permanently removed from service if it is damaged or worn as follows:

(a) the length of the edge cut exceeds the web thickness;

(b) the depth of an abrasion is more than 15 percent of the webbing thickness, taken as a proportion of all plies;

(c) the total depth of the abrasion on both sides of the webbing is more than 15 percent of the webbing thickness, taken as a proportion of all plies;

(d) the depth of the warp thread damage is up to 50 percent of the webbing thickness and the damage

(i) is within 25 percent of the sling width of the edge, or

(ii) covers 25 percent of the sling width,

(e) the warp thread damage is as deep as the sling is thick

(i) in an area that is within 25 percent of the sling width of the edge, or

(ii) over an area that is more than 12.5 percent of the width of the sling;

(f) weft thread damage allows warp threads to separate over an area that is wider than 25 percent of the sling width and longer than twice the sling width.

305(2) An employer must ensure that a synthetic fibre web sling is permanently removed from service if

(a) part of the sling is melted, charred or damaged by chemicals,

(b) stitches in load bearing splices are broken or worn, or

(c) end fittings are excessively pitted or corroded, cracked, distorted or broken.

305(3) An employer must ensure that a synthetic fibre web sling is permanently removed from service if it is damaged in such a way that the total effect of the damage on the sling is approximately the same as the effect of any one of the types of damage referred to in subsections (1) or (2).

305(4) An employer must ensure that a synthetic fibre web sling that is permanently removed from service under this section is physically altered to prevent its further use as a sling.

Wire rope

306(1) An employer must ensure that wire rope is permanently removed from service if

    (a)   wear or corrosion affects individual wires over more than one third of the original diameter of the rope,

    (b)   there is evidence that the rope structure is distorted because of bulging, kinking, bird-caging or any other form of damage,

    (c)   there is evidence of heat or arc damage, or

    (d)   the normal rope diameter is reduced, from any cause, by more than

        (i)   0.4 millimetres if the normal rope diameter is 8 millimetres or less,

        (ii)   1 millimetre if the normal rope diameter is more than 8 millimetres and less than 20 millimetres,

        (iii)   2 millimetres if the normal rope diameter is 20 millimetres or more and less than 30 millimetres, and

        (iv)   3 millimetres if the normal rope diameter is 30 millimetres or more.

306(2) An employer must ensure that a running wire rope is permanently removed from service

    (a)   if six or more randomly distributed wires are broken in one rope lay, or

    (b)   if three or more wires are broken in one strand in one rope lay.

306(3) An employer must ensure that a stationary wire rope such as a guy line is permanently removed from service

    (a)   if three or more wires are broken in one rope lay in sections between end connections, or

    (b)   if more than one wire is broken within one rope lay of an end connection.

306(4) An employer must ensure that wire rope that does not rotate because of its construction is permanently removed from service

    (a)   if there is evidence of the damage referred to in subsection (1),

    (b)   if two randomly distributed wires are broken in six rope diameters, or

    (c)   if four randomly distributed wires are broken in 30 rope diameters.

Metal mesh slings

307   An employer must ensure that a metal mesh sling is removed from service if

    (a)   there is a broken weld or a broken brazed joint along the sling edge,

    (b)   a wire in any part of the mesh is broken,

    (c)   corrosion has reduced a wire diameter by 15 percent,

    (d)   abrasion has reduced a wire diameter by 25 percent,

    (e)   there is a loss of flexibility because the mesh is distorted,

(f) the depth of the slot is increased by more than 10 percent because the choker fitting is distorted,

(g) the width of the eye opening is decreased by more than 10 percent because either end fitting is distorted,

(h) the original cross-sectional area of metal is reduced by 15 percent or more at any point around the hook opening or end fitting,

(i) either end fitting is distorted, or

(j) an end fitting is cracked.

Electric arc damage

308   An employer must ensure that a component of rigging that has been contacted by an electric arc is removed from service unless a professional engineer certifies that it is safe to use.

Damaged hooks

309   An employer must ensure that a worn, damaged or deformed hook is permanently removed from service if the wear or damage exceeds the specifications allowed by the manufacturer.

Part 22   Safeguards

Safeguards

310(1) Repealed

310(2) An employer must provide safeguards if a worker may accidentally, or through the work process, come into contact with

    (a) moving parts of machinery or equipment,

    (b) points of machinery or equipment at which material is cut, shaped or bored,

    (c) surfaces with temperatures that may cause skin to freeze, burn or blister,

    (d) energized electrical cables,

    (e) debris, material or objects thrown from machinery or equipment,

    (f) material being fed into or removed from process machinery or equipment,

    (g) machinery or equipment that may be hazardous due to its operation, or

    (h) any other hazard.

310(2.1)   Repealed

310(3) Subsection (2) does not apply to machinery that already has a safeguard that

    (a) automatically stops the machinery if a worker comes into contact with a moving part or a point at which material is cut, shaped or bored,

    (b) prevents a worker from coming into contact with a hazard referred to in subsection (2), or

    (c) eliminates the hazards referred to in subsection (2) before a worker can be injured.

310(4) If an employer determines that an effective safeguard cannot be provided in the circumstances, the employer must ensure that an alternative mechanism or system or a change in work procedure is put into place to protect workers from being exposed to hazards that exist if there is no safeguard.

310(5) An alternative mechanism or system or a change in work procedure put into place under subsection (4) must offer protection to workers that is equal to or greater than the protection from a safeguard referred to in subsection (3).

310(6) An employer must place warning signs on machinery that starts automatically

    (a) on a clearly visible location at a point of access to the machinery, and

    (b) that give clear instructions to workers on the nature of the hazard.

Tampering with safeguards

311(1) A person must not remove a safeguard from a machine that is operating if the safeguard is not designed to be removed when the machine is operating.

311(2) A person must not remove a safeguard or make it ineffective unless removing it or making it ineffective is necessary to perform maintenance, tests, repairs, adjustments or other tasks on equipment.

311(3) If a worker removes a safeguard or makes it ineffective, the worker must ensure that

    (a) alternative protective measures are in place until the safeguard is replaced,

    (b) the safeguard is replaced immediately after the task is completed, and

    (c) the safeguard functions properly once replaced.

311(4) If a safeguard for machinery is removed or made ineffective and the machinery cannot be directly controlled by a worker, the worker who removes the safeguard or makes it ineffective must lock out or lock out and tag the machinery or render it inoperative.

No safeguards

312(1) Despite other sections in this Part, an employer may allow the machinery to be operated without the safeguards if

    (a) safeguards are normally required by this Code for machinery, and

    (b) the machinery cannot accommodate or operate with these safeguards.

312(2) If machinery in subsection (1) is operated without safeguards, the employer must ensure workers operating or in the vicinity of the machine wear personal protective equipment that

    (a) is appropriate to the hazard, and

    (b) offers protection equal to or greater than that offered by the safeguards.

Building shafts

313(1) An employer must ensure that if a work platform is necessary to ensure the safety of workers in a building shaft, there is

    (a) a main work platform that is completely decked and designed to support any anticipated load, and

    (b) a second platform not more than 4 metres below the main work platform.

313(2) An employer must ensure that if there is no work platform at a doorway or opening to a building shaft

    (a) the doorway or opening is enclosed,

    (b) the enclosure is not less than 2 metres high, and

    (c) there is an access door opening out from the enclosed area.

313(3) An employer must ensure that, while a building shaft is being constructed, at least one warning sign indicating the presence of an open building shaft is placed at each point of entry to the shaft.

Covering openings

314(1) An employer must ensure that an opening or hole through which a worker can fall is protected by

    (a) a securely attached cover designed to support an anticipated load, or

    (b) guardrails and toe boards.

314(2) If a person removes a cover, guardrail or toe board, or any part thereof, protecting an opening or hole for any reason, an employer must ensure a temporary cover or other means of protection replaces it immediately.

314(3) If a temporary cover is used to protect an opening or hole, an employer must ensure a warning sign or marking clearly indicating the nature of the hazard

(a)   is posted near or fixed on the cover, and

(b)   is not removed unless another effective means of protection is immediately provided.

Guardrails

315(1) An employer must ensure that a guardrail required by this Code

(a)   has a horizontal top member installed between 920 millimetres and 1070 millimetres above the base of the guardrail,

(b)   has a horizontal, intermediate member spaced mid-way between the top member and the base,

(c)   has vertical members at both ends of the horizontal members with intermediate vertical supports that are not more than 3 metres apart at their centres, and

(d)   is constructed of lumber that is 38 millimetres by 89 millimetres or of material with properties the same as or better than those of lumber.

315(2) Despite subsection (1), a temporary guardrail does not require a horizontal intermediate member if it has a substantial barrier positioned within the space bounded by the horizontal top member, toe board and vertical members, that prevents a worker from falling through the space.

315(3) An employer must ensure that a guardrail is secured so that it cannot move in any direction if it is struck or if any point on it comes into contact with a worker, materials or equipment.

Hoppers, bins and chutes

316   If a worker can access materials in hoppers, bins or chutes, an employer must ensure the hoppers, bins or chutes have horizontal bars, screens or equally effective safeguards that prevent a worker from falling into the hoppers, bins or chutes.

Machine failure

317   If a worker may be injured if a machine fails, an employer must install safeguards on the machine strong enough to contain or deflect flying particles of material, broken parts of machinery and a shock wave.

Protection from falling objects

318(1) An employer must ensure that workers in a work area where there may be falling objects are protected from the falling objects by an overhead safeguard.

318(2) An employer must ensure that a safeguard used under subsection (1) is designed to withstand the shock loads from objects that may fall onto it.

318(3) Despite subsection (1), if the danger from falling objects is in a location in a work site where workers go intermittently or incidentally to their regular duties, an employer may place appropriate and adequate warning signs, horns, flashing lights or similar devices at the location to warn workers of the hazard.

318(4) An employer must ensure that a safeguard used on a hoist or scaffold under subsection (1)

(a) is made of wire mesh or an enclosure material that is equally or more efficient at containing equipment and materials,

(b) is not less than 1 metre high from the floor, platform or working level of the safeguard, and

(c) encloses all sides of a cantilever hoist platform or skip, except the side adjacent to the building.

318(5) If the material being hoisted or lowered is of a kind that prevents the sides of a cantilever hoist platform or skip from being enclosed as required by subsection (4), an employer must provide another effective alternative safeguard against falling materials for the workers.

318(6) An employer must ensure that a safeguard around the surface opening of an underground shaft serving a tunnel

(a) is made of wire mesh or an enclosure material that is equally or more effective at containing equipment and materials, and

(b) is not less than 1 metre high from the surface.

318(7) An employer must ensure that a safeguard is installed on all sides of

(a) the cage of a building shaft hoist or a tower hoist, or

(b) a hoist cage in an underground shaft serving a tunnel.

318(8) An employer must ensure that a safeguard used on a cage under subsection (7) is made of

(a) wire mesh, or

(b) an enclosure material that is equally or more effective at containing equipment and materials and at protecting workers from hazards associated with the movement of a cage in a shaft.

Push stick or block

319 If a worker may be injured while feeding materials into cutting or shaping machinery, an employer must ensure the machine worker uses a push stick, push block or other similar means of feeding the material.

Safety nets

320(1) An employer must ensure that a safety net

(a) meets the requirements of ANSI Standard A10.11-1989 (R1998), *Construction and Demolition Operations — Personnel and Debris Nets,*

(b) has safety hooks or shackles of drawn, rolled or forged steel with an ultimate tensile strength of not less than 22.2 kilonewtons,

(c) has joints between net panels capable of developing the full strength of the web,

(d) extends not less than 2.4 metres beyond the work area,

(e) extends not more than 6 metres below the work area, and

(f) is installed and maintained so that the maximum deflection under impact load does not allow any part of the net to touch another surface.

320(2) An employer must ensure that the supporting structure to which a personnel safety net is attached is certified by a professional engineer as being capable of withstanding any load the net is likely to impose on the structure.

320(3) Subsection (1) does not apply to properly maintained rescue nets used by fire fighters and other emergency services personnel.

Toe boards

321(1) An employer must ensure that

    (a)   a toe board required by this Code is not less than 140 millimetres in height above the surface of the work area, and

    (b)   the space between the bottom of the toe board and the surface of the work area is not more than 6 millimetres high.

321(2) An employer must ensure that toe boards are installed at the outer edge above the work area if a worker may be under a permanent floor, platform, mezzanine, walkway, ramp, runway or other permanent surface where

    (a)   guardrails are installed, or

    (b)   materials can fall more than 1.8 metres.

321(3) An employer must ensure that toe boards are installed at the outer edge above the work area of temporary scaffolding or a temporary work platform if materials can fall more than 3.5 metres.

321(4) An employer must ensure that toe boards are installed around the top of a pit containing a machine with exposed rotating parts if workers may be working in the pit.

321(5) Subsection (1) does not apply to

    (a)   the entrance of a loading or unloading area if the employer takes other precautions to ensure that materials do not fall from the permanent surface, or

    (b)   the entrance to a ladder.

Wire mesh

322   An employer must ensure that wire mesh used in a safeguard required by this Code is

    (a)   fabricated of wire at least 1.6 millimetres in diameter, and

    (b)   spaced to reject a ball 40 millimetres in diameter.

Part 23   Scaffolds and Temporary Work Platforms

Scaffolds

CSA Standard applies

323   Subject to sections 324 and 325, an employer must ensure that scaffolds erected to provide working platforms during the construction, alteration, repair or demolition of buildings and other structures comply with CSA Standard CAN/CSA-S269.2-M87 (R2003), *Access Scaffolding for Construction Purposes.*

Design

324(1) An employer must ensure that a single pole or double pole scaffold is

    (a)   supported against lateral movement by adequate bracing,

    (b)   anchored by one tie-in for each 4.6 metre vertical interval and one tie-in for each 6.4 metre horizontal interval,

    (c)   anchored by one tie-in for each 3 metre vertical interval and one tie-in for each 3 metre horizontal interval if the scaffold is hoarded, and

    (d)   set plumb on a base plate, jackscrew or other load dispersing device on a stable service.

324(2) An employer must ensure that ropes or wire ropes used in scaffolding are

    (a)   protected against fraying or other damage, and

    (b)   made of heat or chemical resistant material if there is a possibility of exposure to heat or chemicals.

324(3) An employer must ensure that wooden scaffolds are constructed of unpainted dressed lumber.

324(4) Despite subsection (1)(c), an employer must ensure that hoarded masonry walk-through scaffold frames are

    (a)   anchored by not less than one tie-in for each 9 square metres of hoarding surface area, and

    (b)   have vertical tie-ins spaced at least 2 metres apart but not more than 3 metres apart.

324(5) If scaffolding or a temporary work platform can be damaged by powered mobile equipment or a vehicle contacting it, an employer must take reasonable measures to protect the scaffolding or temporary work platform from being contacted.

Load

325(1) An employer must ensure that a scaffold is designed and constructed to support at least 4 times the load that may be imposed on it.

325(2) An employer must ensure that the load to which a scaffold is subjected never exceeds the equivalent of one-quarter of the load for which it is designed.

325(3) An employer must ensure that a scaffold used to carry the equivalent of an evenly distributed load of more than 367 kilograms per square metre is

    (a)   designed and certified by a professional engineer, and

    (b)   constructed, maintained and used in accordance with the certified specifications.

325(4) Subsection (3) applies to a type of scaffold that is not otherwise specifically referred to in this Code.

325(5) An employer must ensure that all workers on a scaffold are informed of the maximum load that the scaffold is permitted to carry.

Tagging requirements

326(1) An employer must ensure that a scaffold is colour coded using tags at each point of entry indicating its status and condition as follows:

    (a) a green tag with "Safe for Use," or similar wording, to indicate it is safe for use;

    (b) a yellow tag with "Caution: Potential or Unusual Hazard," or similar wording, to indicate the presence of a potential or unusual hazard;

    (c) a red tag with "Unsafe for Use," or similar wording, to indicate it is not safe to use.

326(2) An employer must ensure that a bracket scaffold, double-pole scaffold, needle-beam scaffold, outrigger scaffold, single-pole scaffold, suspended scaffold or swingstage scaffold erected but not immediately put into service, or not used for more than 21 consecutive calendar days, has a red tag at each point of entry until it is inspected and tagged by a competent worker for use.

326(3) An employer must ensure that a bracket scaffold, double-pole scaffold, needle-beam scaffold, outrigger scaffold, single-pole scaffold, suspended scaffold or swingstage scaffold is inspected and tagged by a competent worker before it is used for the first time and at intervals of not more than 21 calendar days while workers work from the scaffold or materials are stored on it.

326(4) A tag attached to a scaffold under this section expires 21 calendar days after the date of the inspection it records.

326(5) A tag required by this section must include

    (a) the duty rating of the scaffold,

    (b) the date on which the scaffold was last inspected,

    (c) the name of the competent worker who last inspected the scaffold,

    (d) any precautions to be taken while working on the scaffold, and

    (e) the expiry date of the tag.

326(6) A worker must not use a scaffold if it has

    (a) a red tag,

    (b) a green or yellow tag that has expired, or

    (c) no tag at all.

326(7) Subsection (6) does not apply to a competent worker who is involved in the erection, inspection or dismantling of a scaffold.

Vertical ladder on scaffold

327(1) An employer must ensure that a vertical ladder that gives access to a working level of a scaffold is used by a worker only to move up or down between levels of the scaffold.

327(2) Workers moving between levels of a scaffold on a vertical ladder

    (a) must not extend a part of their body, other than an arm, beyond the side rails of the ladder, and

(b) must maintain a three-point stance on the ladder at all times.

327(3) The employer must ensure that a ladder attached to a scaffold and providing access to a working level of a scaffold

(a) is securely fastened to the scaffold,

(b) does not lean away from the scaffold,

(c) extends at least 1 metre above the uppermost working level of the scaffold,

(d) has rungs that are uniformly spaced at a centre-to-centre distance of 250 millimetres to 305 millimetres,

(e) has a maximum unbroken length of 9.1 metres measured from the ground or between working levels, and

(f) is equipped with a ladder cage that begins within 2.4 metres of the ground or working level if the ladder is more than 6.1 metres in height.

327(4) The employer must ensure that the ladder cage required by subsection (3)(f) is

(a) circular with an inside diameter that measures no more than 760 millimetres, or

(b) square with inside dimensions that measure no more than 760 millimetres by 760 millimetres.

327(5) Despite subsections (3)(e) and (3)(f), the ladder may have a maximum unbroken length of more than 9.1 metres and does not require a ladder cage if a fall protection system complying with Part 9 is used.

Working from a ladder

328(1) An employer must ensure that no worker performs work from a ladder that is used to give access to the working levels of a scaffold.

328(2) A worker must not perform work from a ladder that is used to give access to the working levels of a scaffold.

Scaffold planks

329(1) An employer must ensure that a commercially manufactured scaffold plank is used, stored, inspected and maintained according to the manufacturer's specifications.

329(2) An employer must ensure that a solid sawn lumber scaffold plank is

(a) graded as scaffold grade or better, and

(b) sized 51 millimetres by 254 millimetres.

329(3) An employer must ensure that a solid sawn lumber scaffold plank

(a) is used, stored, inspected and maintained according to the manufacturer's specifications, or

(b) if there are no manufacturer's specifications, is made of at least number one grade lumber that is 51 millimetres by 254 millimetres with a wane limited to 20 percent of the width of the wide face of the plank and the warp limited to ensure a flat surface.

329(4) An employer must ensure that a scaffold plank

(a) is visually inspected by a competent worker before it is installed in a scaffold, (b)　is subjected to and passes a load test before it is installed in a scaffold if a visual inspection reveals damage that could affect its strength or function,

    (c)　extends not less than 150 millimetres and not more than 300 millimetres beyond a ledger, and

    (d)　is secured to prevent movement in any direction that may create a danger to a worker.

329(5) Despite subsection (4)(c), an employer must ensure that an overlapping scaffold plank extends not less than 300 millimetres beyond a ledger.

Scaffold platform

330(1) An employer must ensure that the platform of a scaffold

    (a)　is a minimum width of 500 millimetres, except that a nominal 300 millimetre wide platform may be used with ladderjacks, pump jacks or similar systems,

    (b)　does not have an open space between the platform and a structure that is greater than 250 millimetres in width,

    (c)　if not level, is designed to ensure adequate footing for workers using the platform, and

    (d)　is continuous around obstructions that would create openings into or through which a worker might step or fall through.

330(2) Repealed

Metal scaffolding

331　An employer must ensure that

    (a)　metal scaffolding is erected, used, inspected, maintained and dismantled in accordance with the manufacturer's specifications or specifications certified by a professional engineer, and

    (b)　the structural parts of metal scaffolding are securely fastened together as required by the manufacturer.

Bracket scaffolds

332(1) An employer must ensure that a bracket scaffold

    (a)　is constructed, installed and used in accordance with the manufacturer's specifications or specifications certified by a professional engineer,

    (b)　is securely attached to the support wall in a manner that prevents the bracket from dislodging, and

    (c)　is used only as a light duty scaffold.

332(2) An employer must ensure that the brackets on a bracket scaffold are spaced at intervals of not more than 3 metres.

Double-pole scaffolds

333(1) An employer must ensure that uprights and ledgers

    (a)　of light duty double-pole scaffolds are spaced not more than 3 metres apart, and

    (b)　of heavy duty double-pole scaffolds are spaced not more than 2.3 metres apart.

333(2) An employer must ensure that the dimensions of parts of wooden double-pole scaffolds are not less than those specified in Schedule 6, Tables 1, 2, 3 and 4.

Free-standing or rolling scaffolds

334(1) An employer must ensure that

(a) the height of a free-standing or rolling scaffold is not more than 3 times its smallest base dimension,

(b) if outriggers are used to attain the 3 to 1 ratio, the outriggers are firmly attached and ensure the stability of the scaffold,

(c) if a vehicle is used instead of scaffold wheels to form a rolling scaffold, all parts of the scaffold are securely fastened together and the scaffold is securely attached to the vehicle,

(d) if outriggers are required to maintain the stability of a vehicle-mounted scaffold, the outriggers are securely attached to the frame of the vehicle, and

(e) a rolling scaffold is equipped with locking wheels or there are blocks for the wheels.

334(2) A worker must not remain on a rolling scaffold while it is being moved unless

(a) the height of its work platform is not more than twice its smallest base dimension, and

(b) the surface over which it travels is firm, level and free of hazards that may cause the scaffold to topple.

334(3) A worker using a rolling scaffold must engage the wheel locking devices or block the scaffold against movement while the scaffold is stationary and a worker is working from the scaffold.

Half-horse scaffolds

335(1) An employer must ensure that

(a) a half-horse scaffold is used only as a light duty scaffold,

(b) half-horse scaffold ledgers are not more than 3 metres apart, and

(c) half-horse scaffold legs are not spliced or more than 5 metres high.

335(2) An employer must ensure that the parts of a half-horse scaffold are not less than the lumber sizes specified in Schedule 6, Tables 5 or 6.

335(3) If a part of a half-horse scaffold is not made of lumber, an employer must ensure that the part is made of a material that has properties equal to or greater than those of lumber.

Ladderjack scaffolds

336(1) An employer must ensure that ladders used for ladderjack scaffolds are

(a) erected in accordance with the manufacturer's specifications, or

(b) if there are no manufacturer's specifications, are not more than 3 metres apart.

336(2) An employer must ensure that brackets in a ladderjack scaffold are designed to

(a) be supported by the side rails of the ladder, or

(b)   have at least 90 millimetres of width resting on the ladder rung.

336(3) An employer must ensure that a ladderjack scaffold is not more than 5 metres high.

336(4) An employer must ensure that there are not more than two workers at a time on a ladderjack scaffold.

336(5) Despite sections 329 and 330, an employer may use a single commercially manufactured extendable painter's plank or a commercially manufactured aluminum or laminated plank on a ladderjack scaffold.

Needle-beam scaffolds

337(1) An employer must ensure that beams supporting a needle-beam scaffold

(a)   are constructed of lumber, or a material that has properties equal to or greater than those of lumber,

(b)   are not less than 89 millimetres by 140 millimetres, and

(c)   are placed on their edge.

337(2) An employer must ensure that planks forming the working platform of a needle-beam scaffold are pinned to prevent shifting.

337(3) An employer must ensure that ropes supporting a needle-beam scaffold have

(a)   a breaking strength of at least 39 kilonewtons, and

(b)   a diameter of not less than 16 millimetres.

337(4) An employer must ensure that beam ends of a needle-beam scaffold are provided with stops to prevent the ropes from slipping off the beam.

Outrigger scaffolds

338(1) This section applies to outrigger scaffolds, including suspended outrigger scaffolds.

338(2) If a reference in this section is made to lumber, a material that has properties equal to or greater than those of lumber may be used in its place.

338(3) An employer must ensure that

(a)   thrustouts are constructed of lumber that is 89 millimetres by 140 millimetres and placed on their edge,

(b)   thrustouts do not extend more than 2 metres beyond the edge of the bearing surface,

(c)   thrustouts are securely braced at the fulcrum point against movement or upset,

(d)   the inboard ends of thrustouts are securely anchored against horizontal or vertical movement or upset,

(e)   the inboard portion from the fulcrum point to the point of anchorage is not less than 1.5 times the length of the outboard portion,

(f)   the maximum distance between thrustouts is 2.3 metres,

(g)   if a working platform is suspended or thrust out, the platform is

(i)   supported by vertical lumber hangers that are 38 millimetres by 140 millimetres or larger and not more than 3 metres long secured to the side of each thrustout and extending at least 300 millimetres above the top of each thrustout, and

> (ii) secured to a block that rests on the top edge of each thrustout as an additional support,

(h) a suspended platform is supported by lumber beams that are 38 millimetres by 140 millimetres and that are

> (i) secured to the vertical hangers at least 300 millimetres above the bottom of the hangers, and

> (ii) resting on blocks that are secured to the side of the hangers below each beam as an additional support,

(i) working platforms are completely planked between the hangers, and

(j) a suspended platform is braced to prevent swaying.

338(4) An employer must ensure that

(a) counterweights are not used,

(b) stops to prevent lateral movement of the hangers are fixed to

> (i) the thrustout and block referred to in subsection 3(g)(ii),

> (ii) the ledgers and the blocks referred to in subsection (3)(h), and

(c) materials are not stored on outrigger scaffolds.

Roofing brackets

339 An employer must ensure that a roofing bracket is

(a) constructed to support the loads that may be put on it,

(b) provided with effective non-slip devices, and

(c) secured to the roof with nails.

Single-pole scaffolds

340 An employer must ensure that

(a) a wooden single-pole scaffold is used only as a light duty scaffold and is not more than 9 metres in height,

(b) the uprights on a wooden single-pole scaffold are spaced not more than 3 metres apart, and

(c) the dimensions and/or strength of members of single-pole scaffolds are not less than those specified in Schedule 6, Tables 7 and 8.

Suspended scaffolds

341(1) This section applies to suspended scaffolds other than suspended outrigger scaffolds or suspended swingstage scaffolds.

341(2) An employer must ensure that

(a) a commercially manufactured suspended scaffold is erected, used, operated and maintained in accordance with the manufacturer's specifications or specifications certified by a professional engineer, and

(b) a suspended scaffold that is not commercially manufactured is designed and certified by a professional engineer.

341(3) An employer must ensure that

(a) the upper end of the suspension rope terminates in a spliced loop in which a steel thimble or eye is securely inserted,

(b) the suspension rope is secured to a thrustout by a bolt passing through the shackle, the steel thimble or the eye and the bolt is drawn up tightly to the end plate of the shackle by a securing nut,

(c) the planks of the platform are laid tightly together and overlap the supporting ledgers at each end of the scaffold by at least 300 millimetres, and

(d) working platforms are not less than 1 metre wide.

341(4) An employer must ensure that all parts of a suspended scaffold are inspected daily.

341(5) An employer must ensure that

(a) thrustouts are securely anchored to the building,

(b) counterweights are not used for anchoring a thrustout, and

(c) a stop bolt is placed at the outer end of each thrustout.

341(6) An employer must ensure that the working parts of a hoisting mechanism are left exposed so that

(a) defective parts of the mechanism can be easily detected, and

(b) an irregularity in the operation of the mechanism can be easily detected.

341(7) An employer must ensure that a suspended scaffold platform has an enclosure that

(a) is on the three sides of the platform that are not adjacent to the building,

(b) is made of wire mesh that complies with section 322 or another material that is at least as effective at containing materials or equipment, and

(c) extends not less than 1 metre above the platform.

Swingstage scaffolds

342(1) An employer must ensure that

(a) a commercially manufactured swingstage scaffold is erected, used, operated and maintained in accordance with the manufacturer's specifications or specifications certified by a professional engineer,

(b) a swingstage scaffold that is not commercially manufactured is designed and certified by a professional engineer, and

(c) operating procedures are developed for a swingstage scaffold referred to in clause (b).

342(2) If it is necessary for the safe operation of a swingstage scaffold with a platform, an employer must ensure that the platform is designed to prevent the swingstage scaffold from swinging or swaying away from the building or structure.

Requirements for swingstage scaffold

343(1) An employer must ensure that a swingstage scaffold is used only as a light duty scaffold.

343(2) An employer must ensure that a swingstage scaffold is suspended by at least two upper attachment points placed so that the suspension ropes are parallel.

343(3) An employer must ensure that a platform is at least 500 millimetres wide and fastened to the stirrups.

343(4) An employer must ensure that a platform is equipped with rollers or fenders that bear against the side of the building or structure to hold the platform at a distance from the wall sufficient to avoid an obstacle, but not so far as to allow a worker to fall through the space between the wall and the platform.

343(5) An employer must ensure that a thrustout, clamp or parapet hook is tied back or otherwise secured to a solid part of the structure and cannot move or be dislodged.

343(6) An employer must ensure that counterweights

    (a)   are firmly attached to the thrustouts,

    (b)   are heavy enough to counterbalance four times the maximum weight likely to be on the scaffold, and

    (c)   do not consist of bagged or loose material.

343(7) An employer must ensure that power units on a swingstage scaffold are equipped with

    (a)   manually operated constant pressure controls, and

    (b)   positive drives for raising and lowering the scaffold.

343(8) An employer must ensure that a swingstage scaffold platform has an enclosure that

    (a)   is on the three sides of the platform that are not adjacent to the building,

    (b)   is made of wire mesh that complies with section 322 or another material that is at least as effective at containing materials or equipment, and

    (c)   extends not less than 1 metre above the platform.

Safety on swingstage scaffolds

344(1) An employer must ensure that if workers are required to be on a swingstage scaffold, the hoisting equipment is equipped with automatically operating locking mechanisms so that the suspension ropes cannot slip or run free.

344(2) An employer must ensure that if workers are required to be on a manually operated swingstage scaffold,

    (a)   the hoisting mechanism is securely locked in a positive drive position, and

    (b)   the scaffold has a secondary anti-fall device that connects the scaffold to the suspension rope at a point above the hoisting mechanism.

344(3) An employer must ensure that a powered swingstage scaffold has a manually operated secondary mechanism or an escape device, other than the vertical lifeline used for fall protection, if workers cannot reach a safe exit when there is a mechanical failure or power failure.

344(4) An employer must ensure that a worker on the stage of a swingstage scaffold can use the manually operated secondary mechanism or escape device referred to in subsection (3) to move the scaffold to a point at which the worker can exit safely.

344(5) An employer must ensure that a suspension rope is long enough to reach the next working surface below the scaffold.

344(6) An employer must ensure that the end of a suspension rope is doubled back and held securely by a cable clamp so that the hoisting machine cannot run off the end of the rope.

344(7) An employer must ensure that two or more swingstage scaffolds are not linked together by bridging the distance between them.

Workers on swingstage scaffolds

345(1) Before starting to work on a swingstage scaffold, a worker must inspect the scaffold to ensure that

    (a)   the thrustouts or parapet hooks are secured in accordance with section 343, and

    (b)   counterweights meet the requirements of section 343.

345(2) A worker on a swingstage scaffold must ensure that

    (a)   all ropes from the scaffold that extend to the ground or a landing are prevented from tangling, and

    (b)   when the scaffold is being moved up or down on its suspension ropes, the stage is not out of level by more than 10 percent of its length.

345(3) A person on a swingstage scaffold must

    (a)   remain between the stirrups at all times,

    (b)   not bridge the distance between the scaffold and any other scaffold,

    (c)   not use a vertical lifeline used for fall protection as a means of entering or leaving a swingstage, and

    (d)   not use bagged or loose materials as counterweights on the scaffold.

345(4) An employer must ensure that if a worker may fall 3 metres or more while working from a suspended swingstage scaffold, the worker's personal fall arrest system is connected to a vertical lifeline.

345(5) Despite subsection (4), an employer may allow a worker using a swingstage scaffold to connect a personal fall arrest system to a horizontal lifeline or anchorage on the swingstage scaffold if the failure of one suspension line will not substantially alter the position of the swingstage scaffold.

Elevating Platforms and Aerial Devices

Worker safety

346(1) An employer must ensure that a worker is not travelling in a basket, bucket, platform or other elevated or aerial device that is moving on a road or work site if road conditions, traffic, overhead wires, cables or other obstructions create a danger to the worker.

346(2) A person must not travel in a basket, bucket, platform or other elevated or aerial device that is moving on a road or work site if road conditions, traffic, overhead wires, cables or other obstructions create a danger to the person.

Standards

347(1) An employer must ensure that a self-propelled work platform manufactured on or after July 1, 2009 with a boom-supported elevating platform that telescopes, articulates, rotates or extends beyond the base dimensions of the platform meets the requirements of

(a) CSA Standard CAN/CSA-B354.4-02, *Self-Propelled Boom-Supported Elevating Work Platforms,* or

(b) ANSI Standard ANSI/SIA A92.5-2006, *Boom-Supported Elevating Work Platforms.*

347(2) Subsection (1) does not apply to a work platform mounted on a motor vehicle.

347(3) An employer must ensure that a self-propelled integral chassis elevating work platform manufactured on or after July 1, 2009 with a platform that cannot be positioned laterally completely beyond the base and with its primary functions controlled from the platform meets the requirements of

(a) CSA Standard CAN/CSA-B354.2-01 (R2006), *Self-Propelled Elevating Work Platforms,* or

(b) ANSI Standard ANSI/SIA A92.6-2006, *Self-Propelled Elevating Work Platforms.*

347(4) An employer must ensure that a manually propelled, integral chassis elevating work platform manufactured on or after July 1, 2009 with a platform that cannot be positioned laterally completely beyond the base, that may be adjusted manually or using power and that must not be occupied when moved horizontally meets the requirements of

(a) CSA Standard CAN3-B354.1-04, *Portable elevating work platforms,* or

(b) ANSI Standard ANSI/SIA A92.3-2006, *Manually Propelled Elevating Aerial Platforms.*

347(5) An employer must ensure that a telescopic aerial device, aerial ladder, articulating aerial device, vertical tower, material-lifting aerial device or a combination of any of them, when mounted on a motor vehicle, whether operated manually or using power, meets the requirements of CSA Standard CAN/CSA-C225-00 (R2005), *Vehicle-Mounted Aerial Devices.*

347(6) An employer must ensure that a mast climbing elevating work platform that may be adjusted manually or using power meets the requirements of ANSI Standard ANSI/SIA A92.9-1993, *Mast-Climbing Work Platforms.*

347(7) An employer must ensure that a vehicle-mounted bridge inspection and maintenance elevating work platform meets the requirements of ANSI Standard ANSI/SIA A92.8-1993 (R1998), *Vehicle-Mounted Bridge Inspection and Maintenance Devices.*

347(8) An employer must ensure that an order picker meets the requirements of ASME Standard B56.1-2000, *Safety Standard for Low Lift and High Lift Trucks.*

347(9) An elevating work platform of a type not referred to in subsections (1) to (8) must meet a standard the use of which is approved by a Director of Inspection.

Permanent suspension powered work platforms

348(1) An employer must ensure that the platform of a permanent suspension powered work platform

    (a) is constructed, installed, operated, tested, inspected, maintained, altered and repaired in accordance with CSA Standard CAN/CSA-Z271-98 (R2004), *Safety Code for Suspended Elevating Platforms*, or

    (b) if it was installed before April 30, 2004, is certified by a professional engineer.

348(2) For the purposes of subsection (1), the "rated capacity" in CSA Standard CAN/CSA-Z271-98 (R2004) is to be taken to mean the total weight of

    (a) workers and hand tools, with a minimum aggregate weight of 115 kilograms per worker, and

    (b) water and other equipment that the work platform is designed to lift at the rated speed.

Fork-mounted work platforms

349(1) An employer must ensure that a cage or work platform mounted on the forks of powered mobile equipment and intended to only support material is so designed and constructed that it is securely attached to the lifting carriage or forks of the powered mobile equipment, so that the cage or platform cannot accidentally move laterally or vertically and so that the powered mobile equipment cannot tip.

349(2) An employer must ensure that a work platform mounted on the forks of powered mobile equipment and intended to support a worker

    (a) is commercially manufactured or, if not commercially manufactured, is designed and certified by a professional engineer,

    (b) has guardrails and toe boards, and

    (c) has a screen or similar barrier that prevents a worker from touching any drive mechanism.

349(3) An employer must ensure that the operator of the powered mobile equipment remains at the controls while a worker is on the elevated fork-mounted work platform.

349(4) A person must not be on a fork-mounted work platform while the powered mobile equipment to which the platform is attached is moving horizontally.

Suspended man baskets

350   **Moved to section 75.1**

Boatswain's chairs

351(1) An employer must ensure that

    (a) a commercially manufactured boatswain's chair is assembled, used and maintained in accordance with the manufacturer's specifications or specifications certified by a professional engineer, or

    (b) a boatswain's chair that is not commercially manufactured is designed and certified by a professional engineer.

351(2) An employer must ensure that a boatswain's chair provides stable support for the user.

351(3) An employer must ensure that a rope used to suspend a boatswain's chair is

(a) made of synthetic fibre with a breaking strength of at least 27 kilonewtons, and

(b) is compatible for use with the rigging hardware in the suspension system.

351(4) An employer must ensure that a wire rope used to suspend a boatswain's chair is

(a) of a type recommended for suspending boatswain's chairs by the rope manufacturer, and

(b) is suitable for the hoist being used.

Temporary supporting structures

352(1) An employer must ensure that a temporary supporting structure and every part of it, including metal scaffold components, are designed, constructed and braced in accordance with CSA Standard S269.1-1975 (R2003), *Falsework for Construction Purposes*.

352(2) Subsection (3) applies to a temporary supporting structure unless the requirements of CSA Standard S269.1-1975 (R2003), *Falsework for Construction Purposes* are more stringent.

352(3) An employer must ensure that a temporary supporting structure is certified by a professional engineer if the temporary supporting structure

(a) consists of shoring that is more than 3.7 metres in height,

(b) may transmit loads to another part of the structure that may not provide adequate support, or

(c) is designed to act as a unit composed of parts so connected to one another that a load applied to any part of it may alter the stresses induced in other parts.

352(4) A professional engineer certification for the purposes of subsection (3) must show

(a) the size and specifications of the temporary supporting structure, including the type and grade of all materials for its construction,

(b) the loads for which the temporary supporting structure is designed,

(c) the sequence of loading or unloading the temporary supporting structure, if the loading or unloading sequence is critical to its stability, and

(d) the shoring sequence, as necessary, after the temporary supporting structure is stripped.

Fly form deck panels

353(1) An employer must ensure that a fly form deck panel

(a) is capable of resisting a minimum horizontal load of 3.6 kilonewtons applied in any direction at the upper edge,

(b) has a safety factor against overturning of at least 2 to 1, and

(c) has a safety factor against sliding of at least 1.5 to 1.

353(2) An employer must ensure that attachments to the panel are completed and secured before the fly form deck panel is detached from the hoist used to position the panel.

353(3) An employer must ensure that erection drawings and procedures respecting a fly form deck panel are readily available to the workers who will assemble, fly, use, dismantle or reuse the panel.

353(4) The erection drawings and procedures referred to in subsection (3) must include

    (a)   a plan view, longitudinal section and cross section of the panel,

    (b)   the calculated position of the panel's centre of gravity,

    (c)   step-by-step procedures for all phases of assembly, flying, use, dismantling, repair and reuse of the panel,

    (d)   procedures for installing the panel on non-typical floors, and

    (e)   any supplementary specifications for using the panels that are prepared by the manufacturer, a professional engineer or the employer.

353(5) An employer must ensure that no person is on a fly form deck panel while it is being flown.

353(6) A person must not be on a fly form deck panel while it is being flown.

Part 24   Toilets and Washing Facilities

Restrictions by employer

354   An employer must not place unreasonable restrictions on a worker's use of, or access to, any of the facilities required by this Part.

Drinking fluids

355(1) An employer must ensure that an adequate supply of drinking fluids is available to workers at a work site.

355(2) The drinking fluids available at a work site must include potable water.

355(3) Unless water is provided by a drinking fountain, the employer must ensure that an adequate supply of single-use drinking cups is provided in a sanitary container located by the water supply.

355(4) If there are outlets at a work site for both potable water and non-potable fluid, the employer must ensure that the outlet for potable water has a prominent label that clearly indicates drinking water.

Exception

356   Sections 357 to 361 do not apply to

(a) a food establishment or other work site for which there are specific regulations under the *Public Health Act*, or

(b) a mobile or temporary work site at which work is being performed for a period of not more than five working days if the employer has arranged for workers to use local toilet facilities during that period.

Toilet facilities

357(1) Subject to subsection (2), an employer must ensure that a work site has the number of toilets for each sex that are required by Schedule 7, in separate toilet facilities.

357(2) A work site may have only one toilet facility for the use of both sexes if

(a) the total number of workers at the work site is never more than 10, and

(b) the door to the toilet facility can be locked from the inside.

357(3) If three or more toilets are required for men, an employer may substitute not more than two thirds of the toilets with urinals.

357(4) If two toilets are required for men, an employer may substitute one of them with a urinal.

356(5) An employer must ensure that a toilet facility is located so that it is readily accessible to the workers who may use it.

Water and drainage

358(1) If a work site is connected to a public or municipal water main and sanitary drainage system, the employer must ensure that the toilets are connected to that system.

358(2) If a work site is not connected to a public or municipal water main and sanitary drainage system, the employer must ensure that the toilets are self-contained units or connected to a septic tank.

358(3) An employer must ensure that a toilet that is a self-contained unit is emptied and serviced at regular intervals to ensure the unit does not overflow.

Hand cleaning facilities

359(1) An employer must ensure that at least one wash basin or hand cleaning facility is provided in a toilet facility.

359(2) An employer must ensure that there is one wash basin or hand cleaning facility for every two toilets in addition to the wash basin or hand cleaning facility required under subsection (1) if three or more toilets are required in a toilet facility.

359(3) An employer may substitute circular wash fountains for wash basins or hand cleaning facilities required by subsections (1) and (2) on the basis that each 500 millimetres of the fountain's circumference is equivalent to one wash basin or hand cleaning facility.

Supplies and waste receptacle

360   An employer must ensure that a toilet facility at a work site has

(a)   toilet paper available at each toilet,

(b)   hand cleaning agents and single-use towels of cloth or paper, or air hand drying equipment, at each wash basin or hand cleaning facility, and

(c)   a covered disposal container for feminine hygiene products near each toilet used by women.

Condition of facilities

361(1) An employer must ensure that a lunch room, change room, toilet, urinal, wash basin, hand cleaning facility, circular wash fountain or shower at a work site is clean and sanitary, and operational.

361(2) An employer must ensure that changing rooms, lunch rooms, toilet facilities and rooms in which a wash basin or shower are located are not used as storage areas for materials unless the storage facilities are properly constructed for those materials.

Part 25   Tools, Equipment and Machinery

Contact by clothing, etc.

362(1) If contact between moving parts of machinery, electrically energized equipment or part of the work process and a worker's clothing, jewellery or hair is likely, an employer must ensure that

   (a)   the worker's clothing fits closely to the body,

   (b)   the worker does not wear bracelets, rings, dangling neckwear, a wristwatch or similar articles, and

   (c)   the worker's head and facial hair is short or confined and cannot be snagged or caught.

362(2) If contact between moving parts of machinery, electrically energized equipment or part of the work process and a worker's clothing, jewellery or hair is likely, a worker must

   (a)   wear clothing that fits closely to the body,

   (b)   not wear bracelets, rings, dangling neckwear, a wristwatch or similar articles, and

   (c)   have head and facial hair that is short or confined and cannot be snagged or caught.

362(3) Despite subsections (1) and (2), a worker may wear a medical alert bracelet that has a breakaway or tear away band.

Machines close together

363   An employer must ensure that a worker is not in danger because the machines installed at a work site are close to each other or to a worker.

Moving workers

364   An employer must ensure that machinery or equipment used to move, raise or lower workers is designed by the manufacturer or certified by a professional engineer as being appropriate for that purpose.

Starting machinery

365(1) An employer must ensure that an alarm system is installed if

   (a)   a machine operator does not have a clear view of the machine or parts of it from the control panel or operator's station, and

   (b)   moving machine parts may endanger workers.

365(2) The alarm system must effectively warn workers that the machine is about to start.

Preventing machine activation

366   An employer must install a positive means to prevent the activation of equipment if

   (a)   a worker is required, during the course of the work process, to feed material into the machine, or

   (b)   a part of the worker's body is within the danger zone of the machine.

Operator responsibilities

367(1) Before starting machinery, an operator must ensure that starting the machinery will not endanger the operator or another worker.

367(2) While operating machinery, an operator must ensure that its operation will not endanger the operator or another worker.

Controls

368 An employer must ensure that an operational control on equipment

(a) is designed, located or protected to prevent unintentional activation, and

(b) if appropriate, is suitably identified to indicate the nature or function of the control.

Immobilizing machinery

369 A worker must not leave a machine, or a part of or extension to a machine, unattended or in a suspended position unless the machine is immobilized and secured against accidental movement.

Drive belts

370(1) A worker must not shift a drive belt on a machine manually while the machine or motor is energized.

370(2) An employer must ensure that a permanent drive belt shifter

(a) is provided for all loose pulleys on a machine, and

(b) is constructed so that the drive belt cannot creep back onto the driving pulley.

Continuous-feed machinery

371 An employer must ensure that the drive mechanism of a powered, continuously-fed feeder device permits the feeder mechanism to be stopped independently of the processing mechanism.

Elevated conveyor belts

372(1) If an elevated conveyor belt passes over a walkway, an employer must ensure that the conveyor

(a) has side walls high enough to prevent materials from falling from it, and

(b) runs in a trough strong enough to carry the weight of a broken chain, rope, belt or other material that falls from the conveyor.

372(2) A worker must use a walkway to cross over a conveyor belt if

(a) the conveyor belt is moving, or

(b) the conveyor belt is motionless but has not been locked out in accordance with Part 15.

372(3) A worker must not cross under a moving conveyor belt except at a walkway.

Crossing conveyor belts

373(1) A worker must cross over a conveyor belt using a bridge that is at least 1 metre wide and has adequate guardrails.

373(2) Despite subsection (1), a worker may cross over a conveyor belt at a location other than a bridge if the belt is locked out.

373(3) A worker must cross under a moving conveyor belt at a designated place where the worker is protected from moving parts of the conveyor and from material falling from the belt.

Actuated fastening tools

374   A worker must not permit the trigger of an actuated fastening tool to be mechanically held in the "ON" position unless the manufacturer's specifications permit the tool to be used that way.

Grinders

375(1) An employer must ensure that

    (a)   a grinder is operated in accordance with the manufacturer's specifications, and subject to subsection (2), equipped with a grinder guard,

    (b)   the maximum safe operating speed of the grinder accessory in revolutions per minute is equal to or greater than the maximum speed of the grinder shaft in revolutions per minute, and

    (c)   if a hand-held grinder is used, the object being ground cannot move.

375(2) An employer must ensure that the guard of a hand-held grinder covers the area of the grinder accessory contained within an arc of at least 120 degrees of the accessory's circumference.

375(3) An employer must ensure that if a tool rest is installed on a fixed grinder, the manufacturer's specifications are followed if they exist, or the tool rest is

    (a)   installed in a manner compatible with the work process,

    (b)   securely attached to the grinder,

    (c)   set at or within 3 millimetres of the face of the wheel, and

    (d)   set at or above the centre line of the wheel.

375(4) A worker must not

    (a)   grind material using the side of an abrasive wheel unless the wheel has been designated for that purpose, or

    (b)   adjust a tool rest while a grinder accessory is in motion.

Chainsaws

376(1) An employer must ensure that a chain saw

    (a)   is operated, adjusted and maintained in accordance with the manufacturer's specifications, and

    (b)   is designed or equipped with a mechanism that minimizes the risk of injury from kickback when the saw is in use.

376(2) A worker must not adjust the chain of a chain saw while the saw's motor is idling.

Circular saw blades

377(1) An employer must ensure that a circular saw blade with a crack of any size adjacent to the collar line, or with a crack elsewhere that exceeds the limits specified in Schedule 8, Table 1, is

(a) removed from service, and

(b) replaced or repaired.

377(2) If a circular saw blade has a crack near the periphery that does not exceed the limits specified in Schedule 8, Table 1, an employer must ensure that

(a) the blade is removed from service and replaced,

(b) the crack in the blade is repaired, or

(c) the crack is prevented from getting longer by slotting, centre punching, drilling or another effective means.

377(3) An employer must ensure that a circular saw that is repaired under subsection (1) or (2) is retensioned as necessary by a competent worker.

Band saw blades

378(1) An employer must ensure that a band saw blade, other than a shake band saw blade, with a crack that exceeds the limits specified in Schedule 8, Table 2, is

(a) removed from service and replaced, or

(b) the crack in the blade is repaired.

378(2) An employer must ensure that a band saw blade, other than a shake band saw blade, with a crack that does not exceed the limits specified in Schedule 8, Table 2, is

(a) removed from service until the crack is repaired, or

(b) the crack is prevented from getting longer by centre punching or another means.

378(3) An employer must ensure that a band saw that is repaired under subsection (1) or (2) is retensioned as necessary by a competent worker.

378(4) A worker must not use a shake band saw blade that is cracked.

Band saw wheels

379(1) Unless a manufacturer specifies or a professional engineer certifies otherwise, an employer must ensure that a cast steel band saw wheel measured 25 millimetres inboard from the rim edge has a minimum rim thickness

(a) of 14 millimetres for wheels up to and including 1.8 metres in diameter,

(b) of 16 millimetres for wheels more than 1.8 metres in diameter and up to and including 2.75 metres in diameter, and

(c) of 17.5 millimetres for wheels more than 2.75 metres in diameter.

379(2) An employer must ensure that a band saw wheel that is more than 1.2 metres in diameter is tested for cracks at least once every 12 calendar months by a competent worker.

379(3) An employer must ensure that a band saw wheel that has been exposed to excessive heat is removed from service until the wheel manufacturer or a professional engineer certifies it is safe for continued use.

Power-fed circular saws

380(1) An employer must ensure that a power fed circular rip saw with horizontal power-driven infeed rolls has a sectional non-kickback device located in front of the saw blade across the full width of the feed rolls.

380(2) An employer must ensure that a power fed circular resaw has

(a) a splitter that is as high as the top of the saw, and

(b) a cover.

Cut-off saws

381(1) An employer must ensure that a hand-operated cut-off saw, other than a radial arm saw, is equipped with a device that returns the saw automatically to the back of the table when the saw is released at any point in its travel.

381(2) An employer must ensure that a limit device is used to prevent a swing or sliding cut-off saw from travelling past the outside edge of the cutting table.

Sawmill head rig

382(1) An employer must ensure that a circular head saw has adjustable guides and a splitter that

(a) is located not more than 75 millimetres from the back of the head saw, and

(b) extends not less than 250 millimetres above the carriage bench.

382(2) An employer must ensure that the upper half of a top saw on a circular head rig is covered.

382(3) An employer must ensure that circular head saw guide adjustment controls are operated remotely from the guides.

Sawmill log carriage

383(1) An employer must ensure that a sawmill log carriage has

(a) a substantial buffer stop at each end of the carriage travel,

(b) a carriage with a safety device that keeps the head blocks not less than 30 millimetres from the saw,

(c) each head block equipped with a dog, and

(d) sweepers at the front and back of the carriage to clear obstructions from the track.

383(2) A worker must not use frayed or worn rope, whether fibre or wire, on carriage drives.

383(3) An employer must ensure that a sawyer's lever, operating the carriage drive mechanism, is designed and constructed to operate in the opposite direction from the direction the carriage travels if the operator's position with respect to the carriage could put the operator in danger.

383(4) An employer must ensure that

(a) a sawmill with a device for turning logs has a hold-down device installed on the carriage, and

(b) a secure restraining device maintains the carriage drive control mechanism and the log-turning control in neutral if the operator is not at the controls.

Robots

384(1) An employer must ensure that the design, construction, installation, testing, start-up, operation and maintenance of an industrial robot system comply with CSA Standard Z434-03 (R2008), *Industrial Robots and Robot Systems — General Safety Requirements.*

384(2) Repealed

384(3) Repealed

384(4) Repealed

384(5) Repealed

384(6) Repealed

384(7) Repealed

384(8) Repealed

Teaching a robot

385   If a worker is teaching a robot, an employer must ensure that

(a)   only the worker teaching the robot is allowed to enter the restricted work envelope,

(b)   the robot system is under the sole control of the worker teaching the robot,

(c)   if the robot is under drive power, it operates at slow speed only or at a speed that is deliberately selected and maintained by the worker teaching the robot,

(d)   the robot cannot respond to a remote interlock or signal that would activate the robot, and

(e)   the worker is outside the restricted work envelope before the robot is returned to automatic operation.

Part 26   Ventilation Systems

Application

386   This Part applies to work sites if a mechanical ventilation system controls worker exposure to

(a) an airborne contaminant that exceeds or is likely to exceed the occupational exposure limits prescribed in this Code,

(b) a biological contaminant that exceeds or is likely to exceed the occupational exposure limits prescribed in this Code,

(c) potentially hazardous dust, fumes, gas, mist, aerosol, smoke, vapour or other particulate of a kind or quantity that is given off by a process,

(d) an atmosphere that has flammable levels of gases, vapours, liquids or solids, or

(e) an atmosphere that has less than 19.5 percent or more than 23 percent by volume of oxygen.

Design

387(1) An employer must ensure that a ventilation system is

(a) designed, installed and maintained in accordance with established engineering principles, and

(b) maintained and operated according to the manufacturer's specifications.

387(2) An employer must ensure that

(a) externally exhausted air from a ventilation system is, if reasonably practicable, prevented from entering a work site,

(b) make up air of a volume that does not compromise the effectiveness of the ventilation system and other ventilation systems is provided, and

(c) if it is a recirculating air system, the concentration of a contaminant controlled by the ventilation system and discharged within the work site from the system, if reasonably practicable, does not exceed 10 percent of the contaminant's occupational exposure limit.

Safety

388(1) An employer must ensure that provision is made to warn workers immediately if a ventilation system fails, and to provide for their protection.

388(2) An employer must ensure that workers at the work site

(a) are trained in the correct use of the ventilation system,

(b) participate in the training, and

(c) use the ventilation system properly.

Part 27   Violence

Hazard assessment

389   Workplace violence is considered a hazard for the purposes of Part 2.

Policy and procedures

390   An employer must develop a policy and procedures respecting potential workplace violence.

Instruction of workers

391   An employer must ensure that workers are instructed in

(a)   how to recognize workplace violence,

(b)   the policy, procedures and workplace arrangements that effectively minimize or eliminate workplace violence,

(c)   the appropriate response to workplace violence, including how to obtain assistance, and

(d)   procedures for reporting, investigating and documenting incidents of workplace violence.

Response to incidents

392(1) Sections 18(3) to (6) and 19 of the *Act* apply to an incident of workplace violence.

392(2) An employer must ensure that a worker is advised to consult a health professional of the worker's choice for treatment or referral if the worker

(a)   reports an injury or adverse symptom resulting from workplace violence, or

(b)   is exposed to workplace violence.

Part 28   Working Alone

Application

393(1) This Part applies if

(a)   a worker is working alone at a work site, and

(b)   assistance is not readily available if there is an emergency or the worker is injured or ill.

393(2) Working alone is considered a hazard for the purposes of Part 2.

Precautions required

394(1) An employer must, for any worker working alone, provide an effective communication system consisting of

(a)   radio communication,

(b)   landline or cellular telephone communication, or

(c)   some other effective means of electronic communication

that includes regular contact by the employer or designate at intervals appropriate to the nature of the hazard associated with the worker's work.

394(1.1) Despite subsection (1), if effective electronic communication is not practicable at the work site, the employer must ensure that

(a)   the employer or designate visits the worker, or

(b)   the worker contacts the employer or designate at intervals appropriate to the nature of the hazard associated with the worker's work.

394(2) Repealed

394(3) Repealed

Part 29 Workplace Hazardous Materials Information System (WHMIS)

Application

395(1) Subject to subsections (3), (4) and (5), this Part applies to controlled products at a work site.

395(2) An employer must ensure that a controlled product is used, stored, handled or manufactured at a work site in accordance with this Part.

395(3) This Part does not apply if the controlled product is

    (a) wood or a product made of wood,

    (b) tobacco or a tobacco product,

    (c) a hazardous waste, or

    (d) a manufactured article,

        (i) that is formed to a specific shape or design during manufacture,

        (ii) that has a shape or design that determines its use in whole or in part, and

        (iii) that, under normal use, will not release or otherwise cause a person to be exposed to chemicals emanating from it.

395(4) Except for section 407, this Part does not apply if the controlled product is a dangerous good, under the *Dangerous Goods Transportation and Handling Act*, to the extent that its handling, offering for transport or transport is subject to that *Act*.

395(5) Sections 398, 403, 404, 405, 406, 407 and 408 do not apply if the controlled product is

    (a) an explosive governed by the *Explosives Act* (Canada),

    (b) a cosmetic, device, drug or food governed by the *Food and Drug Act* (Canada),

    (c) a product governed by the *Pest Control Products Act* (Canada),

    (d) a nuclear substance governed by the *Nuclear Safety and Control Act* (Canada), or

    (e) a product, material or substance packaged

        (i) as a consumer product, and

        (ii) in a quantity normally used by a member of the general public.

Hazardous waste

396 If a controlled product is a hazardous waste generated at the work site, an employer must ensure that it is stored and handled safely using a combination of

    (a) any means of identification, and

    (b) instruction of workers on the safe handling of the hazardous waste.

Training

397(1) An employer must ensure that a worker who works with or near a controlled product or performs work involving the manufacture of a controlled product is trained in

(a) the content required to be on a supplier label and a work site label and the purpose and significance of the information on the label,

(b) the content required to be on a material safety data sheet and the purpose and significance of the information on the material safety data sheet,

(c) procedures for safely storing, using and handling the controlled product,

(d) if applicable, the procedures for safely manufacturing the controlled product,

(e) if applicable, the methods of identification referred to in section 402,

(f) the procedures to be followed if there are fugitive emissions, and

(g) the procedures to be followed in case of an emergency involving the controlled product.

397(2) An employer must develop and implement the procedures referred to in subsection (1) in consultation with the joint work site health and safety committee if there is one.

Label required

398(1) Subject to subsection (4), an employer must ensure that a controlled product or its container at a work site has a supplier label or a work site label on it.

398(2) An employer must not remove, modify or alter a supplier label on a container in which a controlled product is received from a supplier if any amount of the controlled product remains in the container.

398(3) If the supplier label on a controlled product or its container is illegible or is removed or detached, an employer must immediately replace the label with another supplier label or a work site label.

398(4) Despite section 395(2), an employer may store a controlled product that does not have a supplier label or a work site label on it for not more than 120 days if the employer

(a) is actively seeking the supplier label or the information required for a work site label,

(b) posts a placard that complies with section 401, and

(c) ensures that a worker who works with or in proximity to the stored controlled product

(i) knows the purpose of the placard and the significance of the information on it,

(ii) is trained in the procedures to be followed if there are fugitive emissions, and

(iii) is trained in the procedures to be followed in case of an emergency involving the controlled product.

398(5) If a controlled product is received at a work site in a multi-container shipment and the individual containers do not have supplier labels on them, the employer must apply to each individual container a work site label.

398(6) If a controlled product imported under section 23 of the *Controlled Products Regulations* (Canada) (SOR/88-66) is received at a work site without a supplier label, the employer must apply a label disclosing the information and displaying the hazard symbols referred to in paragraph 13(b) of the *Hazardous Products Act* (Canada).

398(7) If a bulk shipment of a controlled substance is received at a work site, the employer must

(a) if a supplier label is provided, apply the supplier label to the controlled product or its container, or

(b) if a material safety data sheet or a statement in writing is transmitted in accordance with section 15 of the *Controlled Products Regulations* (SOR/88-66) and a supplier label is not provided, apply a work site label to the controlled product or its container.

Production or manufacture

399 If an employer produces or manufactures a controlled product for use at a work site, the employer must ensure that the controlled product or its container has, at a minimum, a work site label on it.

Decanted products

400(1) If a controlled product is decanted at a work site into a container other than the container in which it was received from a supplier, the employer must ensure that a work site label is applied to the container.

400(2) Subsection (1) does not apply to a portable container that is filled directly from a container that has a supplier label or a work site label if all of the controlled product is required for immediate use and the controlled product is

(a) under the control of and used exclusively by the worker who filled the portable container,

(b) used only during the shift during which the portable container is filled, and

(c) the contents of the portable container are clearly identified on the container.

Placards

401(1) Sections 398, 399 and 400 do not apply if an employer posts a placard respecting a controlled product that

(a) is not in a container,

(b) is in a container or in a form intended for export from Canada, or

(c) is in a container that

(i) is intended to contain the controlled product for sale or other disposition, and

(ii) is labelled, or is about to be labelled, in an appropriate manner having regard to the intended disposition.

401(2) A placard referred to in subsection (1) must

(a) have the information required to be on a work site label printed large enough to be read by workers,

(b) be big enough to be conspicuous, and

(c) be located in a conspicuous place at the work area where the controlled product is stored.

Transfer of controlled products

402 Sections 398, 399 and 400 do not apply to a controlled product at a work site if

(a) the controlled product is contained or transferred in

(i) a piping system that includes valves,

(ii) a reaction vessel, or

(iii) a tank car, tank truck, ore car, conveyor belt or similar conveyance, and

(b) the employer identifies the controlled product by using colour coding, labels, placards or some other means of effective identification.

Laboratory samples

403(1) Section 398 does not apply to a controlled product in a laboratory sample if

(a) the sale or importation of the controlled product is exempt from the application of paragraph 13(a) or (b) or paragraph 14(a) or (b) of the *Hazardous Products Act* (Canada) by the *Controlled Products Regulations* (Canada) (SOR/88-66), and

(b) the container for the laboratory sample is labelled in accordance with paragraph 10(b) or 17(b) of the *Controlled Products Regulations* (Canada) (SOR/88-66).

403(2) An employer must ensure that a laboratory sample brought into the laboratory is packaged in a container that has a label with the following information printed on it:

(a) the product identifier;

(b) the chemical identity or generic chemical identity of an ingredient of the controlled product referred to in paragraph 13(a) of the *Hazardous Products Act* (Canada), if it is known to the supplier or the employer;

(c) the name of the supplier or other person providing the sample;

(d) the emergency telephone number of the person providing the sample;

(e) the statement "Hazardous Laboratory Sample. For hazard information or in an emergency call," followed by the emergency telephone number of the person providing the sample.

403(3) An employer must ensure that using the emergency telephone number required under subsection (2)(d) provides

(a) the user with hazard information in respect of the controlled product, and

(b) a medical professional with information in respect of the controlled product that

(i) is referred to in paragraph 13(a) of the *Hazardous Products Act* (Canada) and in the possession of the person who is providing the laboratory sample, and

(ii) may be required for a medical diagnosis or treatment in an emergency.

403(4) Where a controlled product is in a container other than the container in which it was received from the supplier, the employer is exempt from section 400 if the controlled product is used in a laboratory and is clearly identified.

403(5) Where a controlled product is manufactured and used in a laboratory, the employer is exempt from section 399 if the controlled product is clearly identified.

403(6) Where a controlled product is produced at the work site and is in a container for the sole purpose of use, analysis, testing or evaluation in a laboratory, the employer is exempt from section 400 if the controlled product is clearly identified and the provisions of section 397 are complied with.

Material safety data sheet — supplier

404(1) An employer who acquires a controlled product for use at a work site must obtain a supplier material safety data sheet for that controlled product unless the supplier is exempted from the requirement to provide a material safety data sheet by section 9 or 10 of the *Controlled Products Regulations* (Canada) (SOR/88-66) and complies with that section.

404(2) Despite section 395(2), an employer may store a controlled product for which there is no supplier material safety data sheet for not more than 120 days if the employer is actively seeking the supplier material safety data sheet.

Material safety data sheet — employer

405(1) An employer must prepare a material safety data sheet for a controlled product produced or manufactured at a work site.

405(2) Subsection (1) does not apply to a fugitive emission or an intermediate product undergoing reaction within a reaction vessel.

405(3) An employer may provide a material safety data sheet in a format different from the supplier material safety data sheet or containing additional hazard information if

    (a) the supplier material safety data sheet is available at the work site, and

    (b) the material safety data sheet, subject to section 408,

        (i) includes the information required for a supplier material safety data sheet, and

        (ii) states that the supplier material safety data sheet is available at the work site.

Information current

406(1) If the most recent supplier material safety data sheet for a controlled product at a work site is 3 years from its latest revision, an employer must, if possible, obtain an up-to-date supplier's material safety data sheet for the controlled product.

406(2) If an employer is unable to obtain a supplier's material safety data sheet that is less than 3 years old, the employer must review, and revise if necessary, the existing supplier's material safety data sheet on the basis of the ingredients disclosed on the sheet.

406(3) An employer must update a material safety data sheet referred to in section 405(1)

(a) not more than 90 days after new hazard information becomes available to the employer, and

(b) at least every 3 years.

Availability of material safety data sheet

407 An employer must ensure that the material safety data sheet required by this Part is readily available at a work site to workers who may be exposed to a controlled product and to the joint work site health and safety committee if there is one.

Claim for disclosure exemption

408 An employer may file a claim with the Hazardous Materials Information Review Commission that the following information is confidential business information and should be exempt from disclosure on a label or a material safety data sheet required under this Part:

(a) the chemical identity or concentration of an ingredient of a controlled product;

(b) the name of a toxicological study that identifies an ingredient of a controlled product;

(c) the chemical name, common name, generic name, trade name or brand name of a controlled product;

(d) information that could be used to identify a supplier of a controlled product.

Interim non-disclosure

409(1) Subject to subsection (2), an employer who claims an exemption from the Hazardous Materials Information Review Commission may,

(a) delete the information that is the subject of the claim for exemption from the material safety data sheet for the controlled product, and

(b) remove a supplier label and replace it with the work site label that complies with this Part.

409(2) An employer may delete confidential business information and remove the documents from the date the employer files the claim for exemption until its determination by the Commission, if the employer discloses on the material safety data sheet, and where applicable, on the label of the product or its container,

(a) the date on which the claim for exemption was filed, and

(b) the registry number assigned to the claim for exemption under the *Hazardous Materials Information Review Act* (Canada).

409(3) An exemption is valid for three years after the date the Commission determines the information is confidential business information.

Exemption from disclosure

410(1) If an employer is notified by the Hazardous Materials Information Review Commission that a claim for exemption under section 408 is valid, the employer may, subject to subsection (2),

(a) remove the supplier label and replace it with a work site label that complies with this Part, and

(b) delete the confidential business information from the material safety data sheet for the controlled product.

410(2) An employer may delete confidential business information from a controlled product's material safety data sheet label if the employer includes on its material safety data sheet and, if applicable, on its label or the container in which it is packaged,

(a) a statement that an exemption from disclosure has been granted,

(b) the date of the Hazardous Materials Information Review Commission's decision granting the exemption, and

(c) the registry number assigned to the claim for exemption under the *Hazardous Materials Information Review Act* (Canada).

410(3) The information referred to in subsection (2) must be included for a period of 3 years beginning not more than 30 days after the final disposition of the claim for exemption.

Duty to disclose information

411(1) An employer who manufactures a controlled product must give, as quickly as possible under the circumstances, the source of toxicological data used in preparing a material safety data sheet on request to

(a) an officer,

(b) a concerned worker at the work site,

(c) the joint work site health and safety committee, or

(d) if there is no joint work site health and safety committee, a representative of concerned workers at the work site.

411(2) The *Hazardous Materials Information Review Act* (Canada), applies to the disclosure of information under subsection (1).

Information — confidential

412(1) If an officer or other official working under the authority of the *Hazardous Products Act* (Canada) obtains information from the Hazardous Materials Information Review Commission under paragraph 46(2)(e) of the *Hazardous Materials Information Review Act* (Canada), the officer or other official

(a) must keep the information confidential, and

(b) must not disclose it to any person except in accordance with this Part and for the purposes of the administration or enforcement of the *Hazardous Products Act* (Canada) or the *Occupational Health and Safety Act.*

412(2) A person to whom information is disclosed under subsection (1)(b)

(a) must keep the information confidential, and

(b) must not disclose it to any person except in accordance with this Part and for the purposes of the administration or enforcement of the *Hazardous Products Act* (Canada) or the *Occupational Health and Safety Act.*

Information to medical professional

413(1) An employer must give information that the employer has, including confidential business information exempted from disclosure under this Part, to a medical professional for the purpose of making a medical diagnosis or treating a worker in an emergency.

413(2) A person to whom confidential business information is given under subsection (1) must not give the information to another person except for the purpose of treating a worker in an emergency.

413(3) A person to whom confidential business information is given under subsection (2) must keep the information confidential.

Limits on disclosure

414(1) A person must not use or disclose confidential business information exempted from disclosure under this Part except in accordance with sections 412 and 413.

414(2) Subsection (1) does not apply to a person who makes a claim for exemption or to a person acting with that person's consent.

Requirements Applicable to Specific Industries and Activities
Part 30   Demolition

Worker in charge
415   An employer must ensure that a competent worker designated by the employer is in charge of the demolition work at all times while work is in progress.

Location of equipment
416   An employer must ensure that temporary offices and tool boxes are outside of the range of falling materials.

Hazardous substances
417   Before demolition begins and while demolition work continues, an employer must ensure that

(a)   all chemical and biological substances that may be hazardous to workers during demolition are removed from the structure or the part of the structure that is being demolished, and

(b)   existing concrete at the work site is not disturbed or removed until any embedded facilities have been isolated or their location marked in accordance with section 447.

Use of explosives
418   If a structure is to be demolished using explosives, an employer must ensure that a competent person develops a demolition procedure to protect the health and safety of workers.

Disconnecting services
419   An employer must ensure that

(a)   all utilities are disconnected before demolition begins, and

(b)   written confirmation of the disconnection by the person who disconnects the utilities is available at the work site.

Materials chute
420(1) An employer must ensure that a materials chute that is at an angle of more than 45 degrees from the horizontal is totally enclosed.

420(2) An employer must ensure that

(a)   workers cannot enter an area into which material is dropped, thrown or conveyed by a materials chute, and

(b)   conspicuous warning signs in the area advise of the danger.

Dismantling buildings
421(1) An employer must ensure that if a building or structure is being demolished,

(a)   all glass and windows on the exterior walls of the building or structure and adjacent to a public walkway are removed before demolition begins,

    (b) if the demolition may affect the stability of an adjoining building or structure, the demolition is carried out in accordance with procedures certified by a professional engineer that safeguard the stability of the adjoining structure,

    (c) if tensioned steel cables or bars are known to be in the building or structure, demolition procedures are certified and supervised by a professional engineer,

    (d) if there are workers in the building or structure during the demolition, the demolition is performed floor by floor from the top down,

    (e) steel structures are dismantled column length by column length and tier by tier,

    (f) a structural member that is being removed

        (i)   is not under stress, other than its own weight, and

        (ii) is secured or supported to prevent unintentional movement, and

    (g) unless it is being demolished at the time, a wall or other part of the building or structure is not left unstable or in danger of collapsing unintentionally.

421(2) A person must not allow materials or debris to accumulate in a building or structure being demolished if the accumulation could result in the collapse of a part of the building or structure.

Building shaft demolitions

422   An employer must ensure that a free-standing scaffold is used in the demolition of a building shaft from the inside of the shaft.

Part 31   Diving Operations

Application

423(1) This Part applies to diving operations performed by workers who are diving at a work site.

423(2) This Part does not apply to sport or recreational diving or to a person instructing others in sport or recreational diving.

423(3) If the requirements of this Part conflict with a requirement under another Part, the requirements of this Part prevail.

Employer responsibilities

424   An employer must ensure that diving operations meet the requirements of

    (a) CSA Standard CAN/CSA-Z275.1-05, *Hyperbaric Facilities,*

    (b) CSA Standard CAN/CSA-Z275.2-04, *Occupational Safety Code for Diving Operations,* and

    (c) CSA Standard CAN/CSA-Z275.4-02, *Competency Standard for Diving Operations.*

Dive crew
425   Repealed

Diver's supervisor or tender
426   Repealed

Surface supply dive crew
427   Repealed

Two divers as mutual tenders
428   Repealed

Divers
429   Repealed

Diver's personal logs
430   Repealed

Medical certificate
431   Repealed

Diving equipment
432   Repealed

Warning devices
433   Repealed

Breathing media
434   Repealed

SCUBA diving
435   Repealed

SCUBA diving — prohibitions

436　　Repealed

Intakes, pipes and tunnels

437　　Despite Clause 3.5.3.4 of CSA Standard Z275.2-04, *Competency Standard for Diving Operations*, an employer must ensure that the flow through the intake of a pipe, tunnel, duct or similar installation in the vicinity of a dive

(a)　is stopped and the intake mechanism is locked out before the dive begins, and

(b)　is not restarted until after the diver leaves the water.

Contaminated environments

438　　Repealed

Diving equipment

439　　Repealed

Contaminated equipment

440　　Repealed

Part 32　Excavating and Tunnelling

Disturbing the ground

441　For the purpose of this Part, ground is disturbed if a work operation or activity on or under the existing surface results in a disturbance or displacement of the soil, but not if the disturbance or displacement is a result only of

(a)　routine, minor road maintenance,

(b)　agricultural cultivation to a depth of less than 450 millimetres below the ground surface over a pipeline, or

(c)　hand-digging to a depth of no more than 300 millimetres below the ground surface, so long as it does not permanently remove cover over a buried facility.

Classification of soil type

442(1) For the purpose of this Part, soil is classified as "hard and compact" if it closely exhibits most of the following characteristics:

(a)　it is hard in consistency and can be penetrated only with difficulty by a small, sharp object;

(b)　it is very dense;

(c)　it appears to be dry;

(d)　it has no signs of water seepage;

(e)　it is extremely difficult to excavate with hand tools;

(f)　if has not been excavated before.

442(2) For the purpose of this Part, soil is classified as "likely to crack or crumble" if

(a)　it has been excavated before but does not exhibit any of the characteristics of "soft, sandy or loose" soil, or

(b)　it closely exhibits most of the following characteristics:

(i)　it is stiff in consistency and compacted;

(ii)　it can be penetrated with moderate difficulty with a small, sharp object;

(iii)　it is moderately difficult to excavate with hand tools;

(iv)　it has a low to medium natural moisture content and a damp appearance after it is excavated;

(v)　it exhibits signs of surface cracking;

(vi)　it exhibits signs of localized water seepage.

442(3) For the purposes of this Part, soil is classified as "soft, sandy or loose" if it closely exhibits most of the following characteristics:

(a)　it is firm to very soft in consistency, loose to very loose;

(b)　it is easy to excavate with hand tools;

(c)　it is solid in appearance but flows or becomes unstable when disturbed;

(d)　it runs easily into a well-defined conical pile when dry;

(e)　it appears to be wet;

(f) it is granular below the water table, unless water has been removed from it;

(g) it exerts substantial hydraulic pressure when a support system is used.

442(4) If an excavation contains soil of more than one soil type, for the purposes of this Part an employer must operate as if all of it is the soil type with the least stability.

Soil stabilization

443(1) Subject to subsection (2), an employer must stabilize the soil in

(a) an excavation by shoring or cutting back, or

(b) a tunnel, underground shaft or open pit mine by shoring.

443(2) An employer may stabilize the soil in an excavation, tunnel, underground shaft or open pit mine using an artificial soil stabilization technique, including freezing soil by artificial means or grouting if the process used is

(a) designed by a professional engineer to control soil conditions, and

(b) performed in accordance with the professional engineer's specifications.

443(3) A person must not use natural freezing of the soil as an alternative or partial alternative to a temporary protective structure, or to stabilize the soil in an excavation, tunnel or underground shaft.

Marking an excavation

444   If there is a danger of a worker or equipment falling into an excavation, an employer must ensure that workers are made aware of the excavation through flagging, marking, safeguards or other appropriate and effective means.

Water hazard

445   An employer must ensure that an excavation that a worker may be required or permitted to enter is kept free of an accumulation of water that may pose a hazard to the worker.

Worker access

446(1) An employer must provide workers with a safe means of entering and leaving an excavation, tunnel or underground shaft.

446(2) An employer must ensure that a worker does not enter an excavation, tunnel or underground shaft that does not comply with this Part.

446(3) A worker must not enter an excavation, tunnel or underground shaft that does not comply with this Part.

Locating buried or concrete-embedded facilities

447(1) Before the ground is disturbed or existing concrete is removed at a work site, an employer must

(a) contact the owner or the owner's designate of

(i) a pipeline that is within 30 metres of the work site, and

(ii) any other buried or concrete-embedded facility that may be affected by the ground disturbance or removal of existing concrete,

(b) advise the owner or the owner's designate of the proposed activities,

(c) ask the owner or the owner's designate to identify and mark the location of the buried or concrete-embedded facility, and

(d) not begin disturbing the ground or removing the existing concrete until buried or concrete-embedded facilities have been identified and their locations marked.

447(2) An employer must ensure that workers are aware of locate marks for buried or concrete-embedded facilities.

447(3) An employer must ensure that steps are taken to re-establish the locate marks for buried or concrete-embedded facilities if activities at the work site move or destroy the locate marks.

447(4) Despite subsection (1), an employer may use as-built record drawings of the buried or concrete-embedded facilities for locating the buried or concrete-embedded facilities if

(a) the work does not require excavation or removal of the soil, ground, or existing concrete, and

(b) the ground is penetrated to a depth of 1 metre or less or the existing concrete is penetrated to a depth of 150 millimetres or less.

447(5) The as-built record drawings referred to in subsection (4) must be certified by the owner of the buried or concrete-embedded facility as the most current drawings of record that indicate the constructed location of the buried or concrete-embedded facility.

Exposing buried facilities

448(1) An employer must ensure that work with mechanical excavation equipment is not permitted within the hand expose zone of a buried facility until the buried facility has been exposed to sight

(a) by hand digging,

(b) by a non-destructive technique acceptable to the owner of the buried facility, or

(c) by a method equivalent to clause (a) or (b).

448(2) Despite subsection (1), an employer may use mechanical excavation if doing so does not present a hazard and

(a) if the buried facility is an electrical cable or conduit, the employer must ensure that

(i) it is grounded and isolated so that its disconnection is visible, and

(ii) the owner of the electrical cable or conduit is notified of the operation before it begins, or

(b) if the buried facility is not an electrical cable or conduit, the employer ensures that

(i) it is no longer in use, and

(ii) the owner of the buried facility gives the employer written consent to excavate or remove the facility.

(c) **Repealed**

(d) **Repealed**

(e) **Repealed**

448(3) An employer may reduce the width of a hand expose zone for a high pressure pipeline to within 1 metre on each side of the pipeline locate marks if

    (a)   the high pressure pipeline is not governed by the *Pipeline Act*, and

    (b)   the employer obtains written approval from the owner of the high pressure pipeline.

448(4) If the ground that will be disturbed lies within a pipeline right-of-way, an employer must

    (a)   contact the operator or licensee of the pipeline, and

    (b)   get their consent to disturb the ground.

448(5) An employer must not allow the use of mechanical excavation equipment within 600 millimetres of a buried pipeline unless the use of the equipment is under the direct supervision of a representative of the owner of the buried pipeline.

448(5.1)   If an employer, on behalf of an electric utility, undertakes emergency work that

    (a)   involves ground disturbance to a depth of no more than 500 millimetres below the ground surface,

    (b)   is on the horizontal alignment or right-of-way of an electric utility structure, and

    (c)   is determined by the employer to be in a location where no buried facilities are present in the area affected by the work,

the employer is exempt from the requirements of subsections (1) through (5).

448(6) An employer must ensure that any exposed buried facilities are protected and supported so that workers are not injured.

448(7) If a pipeline is exposed during a work operation, an employer must notify the pipeline operator or licensee before backfilling the excavation.

Exemption

449   Sections 450 to 459 and sections 461 to 464 do not apply to an excavation if a professional engineer certifies that the ground formation is and will remain stable, free from cave-ins, sliding or rolling materials and other hazards associated with the workings that may compromise worker safety.

Methods of protection

450(1) Before a worker begins working in an excavation that is more than 1.5 metres deep and closer to the wall or bank than the depth of the excavation, an employer must ensure that the worker is protected from cave-ins or sliding or rolling materials by

    (a)   cutting back the walls of the excavation to reduce the height of the remaining vertical walls, if any, to no more than 1.5 metres for "hard and compact soil" and "likely to crack or crumble soil,"

    (b)   installing temporary protective structures, or

    (c)   using a combination of the methods in clauses (a) and (b).

450(2) Subsection (1) does not apply if a trench is constructed in solid rock throughout the entire trench.

Cutting back walls

451   If the walls of an excavation are cut back, an employer must ensure that

    (a)   if the soil is classified as "hard and compact soil," the walls are sloped to within 1.5 metres of the bottom of the excavation at an angle of not less than 30 degrees measured from the vertical,

    (b)   if the soil is classified as "likely to crack or crumble soil" the walls are sloped to within 1.5 metres of the bottom of the excavation at an angle of not less than 45 degrees measured from the vertical, and

    (c)   if the soil is classified as "soft, sandy or loose soil" the walls are sloped from the bottom of the excavation at an angle of not less than 45 degrees measured from the vertical.

Loose materials

452   An employer must ensure that loose materials are scaled and trimmed from the sides of an excavation if workers may be on or near the sides.

Spoil piles

453   An employer must ensure that a spoil pile is piled so that

    (a)   the leading edge of the pile is at least 1 metre away from the edge of the excavation,

    (b)   the slope of a spoil pile adjacent to the excavation is at an angle of not more than 45 degrees from the horizontal, and

    (c)   loose materials are scaled and trimmed from the spoil pile.

Power pole support

454   An employer must ensure that work that disturbs the ground in the vicinity of an overhead power line is performed in a manner that does not reduce the original support provided for power line poles.

Safe entry and exit

455(1) An employer must ensure that if a worker is required to enter a trench that is more than 1.5 metres deep, a safe point of entering and leaving is located not more than 8 metres from the worker.

455(2) An employer must ensure that if a worker is in a trench that is more than 1.5 metres deep, the trench is supported or sloped so that the worker can reach the safe point in order to enter and leave.

Temporary protective structures

456(1) An employer must ensure that temporary protective structures in an excavation

    (a)   3 metres deep or less are of sufficient strength to prevent the walls of the excavation from caving in or otherwise moving into the excavation, and

    (b)   more than 3 metres deep are designed, constructed and installed in accordance with the specifications of a professional engineer.

456(2) The specifications of a professional engineer for subsection (1)(b) must include

    (a)   the size and specifications of the structure, including the type and grade of materials used in its construction, and

(b) the loads for which the structure is designed.

456(3) An employer must ensure that, before beginning an excavation, a foundation that may be affected by the excavation is supported by a temporary protective structure designed, constructed and installed in accordance with the specifications of a professional engineer.

Alternatives to temporary protective structures

457(1) Despite section 456, an employer may install the following as temporary protective structures in trenches:

(a) if the trenches vary in depth from 1.5 metres to 6 metres, shoring, stringers and bracing constructed of lumber that complies with Schedule 9, or a material that has equal or greater properties to those of the lumber;

(b) exterior grade plywood as a substitute for 38 millimetre shoring elements if

(i) the plywood meets the requirements of CSA Standard O121-08, *Douglas Fir Plywood* or CSA Standard O151-04, *Canadian Softwood Plywood*,

(ii) the plywood is at least 19 millimetres thick,

(iii) the trench is not more than 2.7 metres deep,

(iv) uprights are installed at intervals of not more than 600 millimetres centre-to-centre,

(v) cross braces do not bear directly on the plywood, and

(vi) cross braces bearing on uprights or walers are located at all joints in the plywood sheathing.

457(2) Despite subsection (1)(a), screw jacks, hydraulic equipment or other apparatus may be used as shoring, stringers or bracing if they are at least equivalent in strength and reliability to the shoring, stringers or bracing described in Schedule 9.

457(3) Despite subsection (1)(a) if the trench is less than 2.4 metres deep and in soil classified as "hard and compact" an employer does not have to use stringers.

457(4) Despite section 456, an employer may install additional protection certified by a professional engineer in trenches to compensate for passing vehicular traffic, working machinery or a heavy object placed within a distance equal to the depth of the trench, measured from the near edge of the bottom of the trench to the traffic, machinery or heavy object.

457(5) Despite section 456, an employer may install additional protection certified by a professional engineer in a trench to compensate for the stress created because the trench is adjacent to or abuts a building or other structure.

Installation of shoring, stringers or bracing

458(1) An employer must ensure that a worker who installs shoring, stringers or bracing uses a ladder and works down from the top of the trench, installing each brace in descending order.

458(2) An employer must ensure that a worker who removes shoring, stringers or bracing uses a ladder and works upward from the bottom of the trench, removing each brace in ascending order.

458(3) A worker must install shoring, stringers or bracing in accordance with subsection (1) and remove them in accordance with subsection (2).

458(4) Despite subsections (2) and (3), if the quality of the ground in which a trench has been dug has deteriorated during operations to the extent that it is unsafe to use the method of removal required by subsection (2), an employer must ensure that the shoring, stringers or bracing are removed using a method that does not require the worker to be in the trench.

Access for powered mobile equipment

459 An employer must ensure that the open side of an excavation or a route used by powered mobile equipment to gain access to an excavation has a barrier high enough to stop the equipment from sliding or rolling into the excavation.

Dumping block

460 An employer must ensure that if powered mobile equipment may go over a bank or enter a dump opening while it is discharging its load, the equipment is effectively stopped or controlled by

(a) an anchored block,

(b) a ridge of material acting as a backstop, or

(c) a designated signaller with a stop signal.

Underground shafts

461(1) An employer must ensure that, during the excavation of an underground shaft that is between 1.5 metres and 6 metres deep, the walls of the shaft from the top down are retained by temporary protective structures strong enough to prevent the walls from collapsing or caving in.

461(2) An employer must ensure that, during the excavation of an underground shaft 6 metres or more deep, the walls of the shaft from the top down are retained by temporary protective structures certified by a professional engineer as strong enough to prevent the walls from collapsing or caving in.

461(3) An employer must ensure that

(a) a solid fence or equally effective means of preventing workers, materials and equipment from falling into the shaft is provided around an underground shaft opening, and

(b) gates not less than 1 metre high are installed at each entrance of an underground shaft and are kept closed when they are not being used.

461(4) Workers must keep a gate to the entrance of an underground shaft closed when it is not being used.

461(5) An employer must ensure that an underground shaft is provided with suitable and efficient machinery or another device for keeping the shaft free of accumulations of water.

Drilled or bored underground shaft

462(1) An employer must ensure that

(a) a worker who is required to enter a drilled or bored underground shaft is protected by a casing or temporary protective structure, and

(b) the casing or temporary protective structure extends and remains at least 300 millimetres above surface of the ground where the shaft is drilled or bored.

462(2) An employer must ensure that a casing or temporary protective structure referred to in subsection (1) is certified by a professional engineer as having sufficient strength to resist the shifting of the surrounding materials.

462(3) Subject to subsection (4), if a worker in a belled area of an underground shaft is exposed to falling materials and is unable to stand clear of the area, an employer must ensure that the worker precedes each load of excavated material to the surface.

462(4) If a worker referred to in subsection (3) cannot precede each load to the surface, an employer must ensure that

(a) the worker accompanies each load if the equipment is designed to safely transport both the worker and the excavated material simultaneously, and

(b) safe work procedures are prepared that include the procedures to be followed when the worker and the excavated material are moved simultaneously.

Prohibition

463   A worker must not enter a belled area of a drilled or bored underground shaft if the worker is not protected by temporary protective structures.

Tunnel

464(1) An employer must ensure that, during the excavation of a tunnel, the walls of the tunnel from the top down are retained by temporary protective structures certified by a professional engineer as strong enough to prevent the walls from collapsing or caving in.

464(2) An employer must ensure that a tunnel is provided with suitable and efficient machinery or another device for keeping the tunnel free from accumulations of water.

Part 33   Explosives

Application

465(1) This Part applies to the use of explosives at a work site other than a mine site.

465(2) This Part applies to the industrial use of explosives for the high energy welding of materials, including pipe and power transmission lines.

465(3) This Part does not apply to the use of explosive actuated fastening tools at a work site.

Burning material

466(1) An employer must ensure that no person smokes tobacco or burns material with 15 metres of an explosive.

466(2) A person must not smoke tobacco or burn material within 15 metres of an explosive.

Safe work procedures

467(1) An employer must prepare safe work procedures specific to the blasting activities undertaken by the employer.

467(2) The safe work procedures for the handling of pyrotechnic and special effects devices and explosives must be based on

    (a)   NFPA Standard 1123, *Code for Fireworks Display* (2006 Edition), and

    (b)   NFPA Standard 1126, *Standard for the Use of Pyrotechnics Before a Proximate Audience* (2006 Edition).

Blasters

468(1) An employer must ensure that a worker who handles, prepares, loads, fires, burns or destroys an explosive is

    (a)   a blaster, or

    (b)   under the direct supervision of a blaster.

468(2) An employer must ensure that a blasting area and all supplies and equipment in the blasting area are under the direction and control of a blaster before blasting operations are allowed to begin and during blasting operations.

468(3) If there are 2 or more blasters working at a blasting area, the employer must designate the responsibility under subsection (2) to one of them.

468(4) A blaster in charge of a blasting operation must

    (a)   ensure that the blasting operation is carried out in accordance with the employer's safe work procedures and this Code, and

    (b)   exercise direct control of the blasting area.

Reporting incidents involving explosives

469   An employer must include the following in a report under section 18(1) of the *Act* on an incident arising from an unplanned or uncontrolled explosion or fire:

    (a)   the name of the blaster;

    (b)   the blaster's permit number, if any, and the issuer of the permit;

    (c)   the date, time and place of the incident;

    (d)   the make, type and date code of the explosives;

    (e)   the type and method of detonation;

    (f)   the purpose for which the explosives were being used;

    (g)   the make, type and size of detonator used;

    (h)   the conditions at the site;

    (i)   the names of injured persons, if any;

    (j)   the names and addresses of witnesses.

Handling Explosives

Canadian guidelines

470(1) An employer must ensure that a blaster complies with, and a blaster must comply with, *Blasting Explosives and Detonators Storage, Possession, Transportation, Destruction and Sale* (M82-8/1983), Revised 1993, published by Natural Resources Canada.

470(2) An employer must ensure that a magazine is constructed in accordance with *Storage Standards for Industrial Explosives* (M81-7/2001E) published by Natural Resources Canada.

Intermittent storage

471 An employer and a blaster must ensure that explosives are returned to the appropriate magazine between periods of work.

Light sources in magazines

472 An employer must ensure that artificial light sources used in a magazine are of such closed and protected construction, position or character that they will not cause a fire or explosion when lit or if they are dropped.

Transporting explosives

473(1) An employer must ensure workers comply with the *Dangerous Goods Transportation and Handling Act* and the *Explosives Act* (Canada) when transporting explosives.

473(2) An employer must ensure that only the person authorized by the employer drives or is a passenger in a vehicle that is transporting explosives or detonators.

473(3) An employer and a blaster must ensure that the leg wires of electric detonators are shunted and folded while they are being transported.

473(4) An employer must ensure that vehicles transporting explosives have fire extinguishers that are

    (a)   in good working order,

    (b)   located and attached to the vehicle in such a manner as to be readily available for use at all times, and

    (c)   in the quantity and with the rating set out in Schedule 10, Table 1.

Oldest used first

474 A blaster must ensure that the oldest explosive is taken from a magazine first and is used first.

Deteriorated or damaged explosive

475 An employer must ensure that a deteriorated or damaged explosive is

    (a) not used in any blasting operation, and

    (b) destroyed or disposed of safely by a blaster.

Unused explosives

476 An employer must ensure that unused explosives, fuse assemblies or detonators are

    (a) stored in accordance with this Code, or

    (b) destroyed or disposed of safely by a blaster.

Appropriate quantities

477(1) An employer must ensure that explosives are brought to a work site in charge strengths appropriate to the blasting operation at the work site.

477(2) A blaster must not remove from the magazine more explosives than are required to complete each task.

477(3) A blaster must ensure that a charge is sectioned or cut only if there is no reasonable alternative available.

Cutting or piercing

478 An employer and a blaster must ensure that an explosive is sectioned, cut or pierced only

    (a) with tools made of non-sparking material, and

    (b) on a clean, wooden surface free from grit or other foreign matter.

Cartridge explosives

479(1) An employer must ensure that cartridge explosives are not removed from their original outer cover.

479(2) A person must not remove a cartridge explosive from its original outer cover.

Tools

480 An employer must provide workers with standard crimping tools and a safe location for

    (a) crimping detonators to detonating cord, and

    (b) cutting fuses.

Priming

481(1) A blaster must ensure that

    (a) a charge is primed only at the blasting site, and

    (b) all explosives, other than the total charge to be loaded, are kept in a magazine.

481(2) A blaster must ensure that a charge is not primed in a magazine or a place where other explosives are stored.

481(3) An employer and a blaster must ensure that workers do not assemble primed charges before the hole drilling operation is complete.

481(4) An employer and a blaster must ensure that workers prepare and load one charge at a time, and then only for the drill hole or bore hole at which they are working.

Length of safety fuse assemblies

482 A blaster must ensure that safety fuse assemblies used in a blasting operation are at least 1 metre long.

Detonators

483 A blaster must ensure that detonators made by different manufacturers are not used together in a single blasting circuit.

Storms

484 An employer and a blaster must ensure that a blasting operation using electric detonators is not performed during or on the approach of an electrical storm or a severe dust storm.

Drilling

Drilling location

485 An employer and a blaster must ensure that a worker does not drill in or adjacent to a drill hole or bore hole that contains, or may contain, an explosive that could be detonated by the drilling operation.

Bootleg

486(1) An employer and a blaster must ensure that a worker examines a bootleg and, if possible, it is washed out or blown out before a worker drills in that area.

486(2) If a worker finds an explosive in a bootleg, the employer and blaster must ensure that a charge is promptly inserted and detonated to destroy the explosive in the bootleg.

Size of drill hole

487 An employer and a blaster must ensure that a drill hole or borehole is big enough to allow a worker to insert the explosive charge without using excessive force.

Prohibition

488(1) A person must not look directly into a drill hole during a blasting operation.

488(2) An employer and a blaster must ensure that a worker does not look directly into a drill hole during a blasting operation.

Loading

Unwinding detonator leg wires

489(1) An employer and a blaster must ensure that a worker unravels or unwinds detonator leg wires slowly when a charge is lowered into a drill hole or borehole.

489(2) A worker must not unravel or unwind detonator leg wires by

    (a) throwing them on the ground, or

    (b) dragging them along the ground.

Static electricity

490   An employer and a blaster must ensure that the build-up of static electricity is minimized at a work site where workers are handling explosives.

Tamping explosives

491(1) An employer must ensure that loading poles, tamping poles and pole extension fittings are made of non-sparking, anti-static material.

491(2) A blaster must ensure that a worker does not use excessive force when tamping explosives.

Sequential firing

492   A blaster must ensure that detonating connectors used to provide sequential firing are delayed to minimize misfires resulting from cutting off holes.

Detonation within 30 days

493   An employer must ensure that workers detonate all loaded drill holes or bore holes within 30 calendar days of the date they are loaded unless a Director of Inspection approves the extension of that period.

Detonator leg wires

494(1) An employer and a blaster must ensure that detonator leg wires of loaded drill holes and bore holes

    (a)   are not exposed for more than 600 millimetres above ground level,

    (b)   are shunted, and

    (c)   are wrapped on a wooden or plastic lath or a wire pin flag.

494(2) The employer must ensure that the position of the drill hole or bore hole is marked by setting the base of the wooden or plastic lath or wire pin flag in the drill hole or bore hole.

Testing detonators and circuits

495(1) An employer and a blaster must ensure that all electric detonators and the complete firing circuit are tested with a galvanometer or circuit tester before firing.

495(2) An employer must ensure that workers test detonators and firing circuits only with galvanometers or circuit testers designed for use with detonators.

Damaged leads and wires

496   An employer and a blaster must ensure that workers do not use damaged leads and damaged connecting wires in blasting circuits.

Connecting down lines to trunk cords

497   A blaster must ensure that a worker who is using detonating cord with explosives connects or attaches down lines to trunk cords only after all the drill holes and boreholes are loaded.

Firing

Community protection

498   If an employer or a blaster is conducting blasting operations in the vicinity of a city, town, village, hamlet, inhabited campsite, other inhabited area, building, railway or road, the employer and the blaster must take adequate precautions against possible injury to persons and damage to property by

    (a)   limiting the explosive charge to the minimum required to do the job,

    (b)   using a blasting mat or other suitable protective device over the drill hole, bore hole or blasting area,

    (c)   closing roads, trails, paths and other approaches to the blasting area during blasting operations, and

    (d)   placing warning signs or barricades or using flag persons to ensure that no unauthorized person enters or remains in the area that is potentially dangerous.

Safe distance

499(1) When the blasting is being done, a blaster must ensure that

    (a)   all workers at the work site are protected from falling rocks, flying debris, mud and anything else that is disturbed, agitated or displaced by the blast, and

    (b)   no worker fires a charge until all workers are protected by suitable cover or are at a safe distance from the blast.

499(2) For seismic blasting operations, the minimum safe distance referred to in subsection (1)(b) is 30 metres.

499(3) For the purposes of operations involving pyrotechnic and special effects devices and explosives, the minimum blasting distances are those in

    (a)   NFPA Standard 1123, *Code for Fireworks Display* (2006 Edition), and

    (b)   NFPA Standard 1126, *Standard for the Use of Pyrotechnics Before a Proximate Audience* (2006 Edition).

Stray electric currents

500   An employer and a blaster must prevent sources of stray electric currents from prematurely detonating electric detonators.

Overhead power line

501(1) If a worker is blasting within 60 metres of an overhead power line, an employer and a blaster must ensure that the worker uses

    (a)   detonating cord as a down line to the explosive charge, and

    (b)   a short leg-wire detonator to initiate the detonating cord.

501(2) The employer and the blaster must ensure that the leg wire referred to in subsection (1) is shorter than the distance from the overhead power line to the nearest ground level in the vicinity of the blasting operation.

Above-ground charge

502   An employer and a blaster must ensure that if a detonator discharges above the surface of the ground, the detonator is covered by a blasting mat or other protective device that confines fragments of debris created by the discharge.

Radiofrequency transmitters

503(1) Subject to subsections (2) and (4), a worker must not load, prime or fire a charge using electric detonators in the vicinity of an actively transmitting radiofrequency transmitter unless the distance from the drill hole or borehole closest to the base of the nearest transmitter antenna is at least the distance required by Schedule 10, Table 2 or Table 3 as is applicable.

503(2) An employer and a blaster must ensure that detonator leg wires are shunted directly or through a blasting machine if a radiofrequency transmitter is used within the minimum separation distance limits specified by Schedule 10, Table 2 or Table 3 as is applicable.

503(3) A person who brings a cellular telephone within 50 metres of an electric detonator must

    (a)   turn the cellular telephone off before advising the blaster of the presence of the telephone, and

    (b)   follow the blaster's instructions respecting the use of cellular telephones.

503(4) An employer and a blaster must ensure that detonator leg wires are shunted directly or through a blasting machine if there is an actively transmitting cellular telephone within the minimum separation distance limits specified by Schedule 10, Table 3.

Length of fuse assembly

504   A blaster must ensure that all safety fuse assemblies are long enough to

    (a)   protrude from the collar of the borehole, and

    (b)   allow the blaster to reach a safe location after the blaster ignites the safety fuse.

Blasting machine

505(1) An employer and blaster must ensure that workers use blasting machines designed for use with explosives in all electrically controlled blasting operations.

505(2) A worker must not use a battery system for electric blasting.

505(3) Repealed

Shunting the firing line

506   Before and after a charge is fired, a blaster must ensure that

    (a)   the firing line is shunted if the blasting machine is not connected to the firing line, or

    (b)   the blasting machine is set to its "safe" or "unarmed" position if it is connected to the firing line.

Loaded hole

507   If a loaded hole cannot be immediately detonated safely within a reasonable time after it is loaded, an employer and a blaster must ensure that clearly visible signs are posted in the location of the loaded hole warning of the presence of the loaded hole.

Destroying Explosives

Standards

508   An employer must ensure that explosives are destroyed in accordance with the recognized safe practices set out in the guideline *Blasting Explosives* *and Detonators — Storage, Possession, Transportation, Destruction and Sale* (M82-8/1983), Revised 1993, published by Natural Resources Canada.

Misfire waiting period

509(1) If a blaster fired a charge using a safety fuse assembly and delay detonators and suspects a misfire, the employer and the blaster must ensure that no worker returns to or is permitted to approach the blasting area before the end of the longer of the following periods:

   (a)   30 minutes after the last charge was fired or should have fired; or

   (b)   the period recommended by the manufacturer.

509(2) If a blaster fired a charge using electric detonators and suspects a misfire, the employer and the blaster must ensure that no worker returns to or is permitted to approach the blasting area before the end of the longer of the following periods:

   (a)   10 minutes after the last charge was fired or should have fired; or

   (b)   the period recommended by the manufacturer.

Withdrawing a misfire

510(1) If a blaster fires a charge and there is a misfire, the blaster must ensure that no worker attempts to withdraw the charge.

510(2) Subsection (1) does not apply to a misfire that occurs during oil well blasting and perforating operations.

Destroying a misfire

511(1) Subject to section 512, an employer and a blaster must ensure that the blaster inserts a charge on top of or beside a misfire and detonates it.

511(2) If a misfire cannot be detonated immediately, an employer and a blaster must

   (a)   ensure that clearly visible signs are posted in the location of the misfire warning of the presence of the misfire, and

   (b)   detonate it in accordance with subsection (1) as soon as reasonably practicable.

Abandoned charge

512(1) An employer must ensure that a misfire or misfired charge is abandoned only if it cannot be detonated safely.

512(2) If a blaster cannot safely detonate a misfire or an unfired charge in a drill hole, the employer and the blaster may abandon it if

   (a)   the blaster cuts its detonator lead wires and places them in the drill hole beneath the surface,

   (b)   the drill hole is covered with surface cuttings,

   (c)   the drill hole's location is marked, and

   (d)   a permanent record of the misfire and its location is kept by the employer.

Removal of waste

513   Before abandoning a blasting area, an employer and a blaster must ensure that the following are destroyed or removed for destruction:

(a) all pieces of charges that have blown from the shot hole;

(b) all wrappings or boxes used in the handling of explosives;

(c) all other waste from the blasting operations.

Loss or theft

514   An employer must ensure that the loss or theft of explosives from a work site is immediately reported to the nearest Royal Canadian Mounted Police detachment and the Chief Inspector of Explosives, Natural Resources Canada.

Specific Blasting Activities

Avalanche control

515(1) This section applies to blasting used to control avalanches.

515(2) Despite section 481, during avalanche control activities involving the hand deployment of explosive charges,

(a) a blaster may prime charges away from the blasting site, and

(b) may prime more than one charge at a time.

515(3) An employer must ensure that charges are primed by a blaster during avalanche control activities

(a) as close to the control route as possible, and

(b) in a safe, sheltered location from which the public are excluded.

515(4) An employer and a blaster must ensure that a worker does not carry primed charges and their pull-wire fuse lighters in the same container.

515(5) A blaster must ensure that the pull-wire fuse lighter is not connected to the safety fuse assembly of a primed charge until immediately before the charge is placed.

Oil well blasting

516(1) This section applies to oil well blasting and perforating.

516(2) An employer must ensure that perforating activities are done in accordance with practices approved by a Director of Inspection.

516(3) A competent worker who is not a blaster may load perforating explosives, other than detonators, into a perforating gun or a down hole tool if the worker has readily available access to a blaster.

516(4) An employer must ensure that a blaster is available to assist the worker referred to in subsection (3).

516(5) An employer must ensure that a blaster

(a) detonates perforating explosives, including using a drop bar in a tubing-conveyed perforating firing system, and

(b) retrieves a perforating firing system from the well bore.

516(6) Before and after a charge is fired, a blaster must ensure that the blasting machine is disconnected from the firing circuit by switching it to its "safe" or "unarmed" position.

516(7) In the event that an armed explosive device is at the surface, a blaster must ensure that all power and electronic transmitting devices within 20 metres of the explosive device are turned off.

Seismic blasting and drilling

517(1) This section applies to seismic blasting and drilling.

517(2) Despite section 466, a worker may use an open flame to warm water on a seismic drill if

    (a)   the flame is used by a worker under the direct supervision of a blaster or by a competent worker designated by the blaster,

    (b)   propane is the fuel source of the flame, and

    (c)   the propane compressed gas cylinder used has a regulator.

517(3) Before a worker uses an open flame to warm water on a seismic drill, the blaster must ensure that

    (a)   all explosives not used in the particular seismic activity are returned to magazines on the drill rig,

    (b)   all magazines are closed and locked,

    (c)   the water tank, piping or valve being heated and the flame end of the torch are at least 600 millimetres away from the closest magazine,

    (d)   all compressed gas cylinders are secured and located at least 600 millimetres from the closed magazine,

    (e)   all combustible materials are removed from the vicinity of the magazines and the open flame, and

    (f)   a fire extinguisher is readily available to the worker.

Part 34   Forestry

Felling and bucking

518(1) Before a tree is felled, a faller must ensure that there is a clear path of retreat and sufficient space to work for the faller and the faller's trainee, if any.

518(2) An employer must ensure that workers, except a hand faller and the hand faller's trainee, if any, remain a distance of not less than twice the height of the tallest tree away from the immediate area in which the felling is taking place.

518(3) If a self-propelled mechanized feller is operating, an employer must ensure that workers remain at least the minimum distance prescribed by the manufacturer of the feller away from the immediate area in which felling is taking place.

518(4) A worker cutting timber must

   (a) fall or remove snags and trees that create a danger to workers as the cutting progresses,

   (b) when felling a tree, make a correct notch not less than one-quarter and not more than one-third of the diameter of the tree at the butt,

   (c) ensure that the undercut is complete and cleaned out,

   (d) leave sufficient uncut wood in the felling cut to control the direction in which the tree falls,

   (e) not work on hillsides immediately below another worker if skidding, sliding or rolling trees or logs may be dangerous,

   (f) carry and use wedges for hand felling, and

   (g) closely trim logs before they are put onto a truck, log deck or rollway.

518(5) A worker who is bucking must

   (a) take measures to protect other workers from the movement of trees during bucking,

   (b) clear away all brush and other objects that may catch the saw before starting the bucking, and

   (c) work on the upper side of logs lying on inclines.

518(6) An employer must ensure that a worker complies with subsections (4) and (5).

Hand felling

519   An employer must ensure that workers do not do hand felling during environmental conditions that may be hazardous to workers.

Mechanized feller or limber

520   An employer must ensure that a mechanized feller or limber

   (a) has a cab for the operator with two exits through which the operator can readily escape, and

   (b) is designed and equipped to direct the fall of the tree away from the mechanized feller.

Operator protective structures

521   An employer must ensure that skidders, grapple skidders and crawlers used in the harvesting of trees meet the requirements of SAE Recommended

Practice J1084-APR80 (R2002), *Operator Protective Structure Performance Criteria for Certain Forestry Equipment.*

Road warnings

522   A worker must not fell a tree within the range of a road travelled by other workers or the public unless

   (a)   a designated signaller is on the road to warn those approaching and to stop traffic until the tree is down and it is safe to continue, or

   (b)   there are two flags or warning signs at the side of the road at a distance of 30 metres to 90 metres from each approach to the place where the tree is to be felled.

Partially cut trees

523   An employer must ensure that a partially cut tree is not left standing.

Logging trucks

524(1) Repealed

524(2) Repealed

524(3) An employer may operate a logging truck with a load that exceeds the manufacturer's specifications for the maximum weight of the load if the employer

   (a)   prepares a written assessment of the hazards relating to the operation of the logging truck, and

   (b)   implements controls that ensure the safe operation of the truck.

Traffic safety

525(1) An employer must ensure that bridges, elevated platforms and other structures used by vehicles transporting workers, logs or other forest products in forestry operations are constructed and maintained to permit safe transit.

525(2) If two or more vehicles may simultaneously use a section of road that is too narrow to permit them to pass each other, an employer must ensure that a traffic control system is installed on the road.

525(3) A traffic control system under subsection (2) must use

   (a)   turnouts if they are necessary for safety,

   (b)   warning signs at locations where they are needed, and

   (c)   instructional signs giving

      (i)   the kilometre markings,

      (ii)   the road names or number markings, and

      (iii) the radio frequency, if any, used for traffic control.

525(4) The traffic control system under subsection (2) must require vehicles to operate with their headlights turned on at all times.

Part 35 Health Care and Industries with Biological Hazards

Exposure control

525.1 An employer must ensure that a worker's exposure to blood borne pathogens or other biohazardous material is controlled in accordance with section 9.

Medical sharps

525.2(1) Subsections (2) and (3) come into effect on July1, 2010.

525.2(2) An employer must provide and ensure that any medical sharp is a safety-engineered medical sharp.

525.2(3) Subsection (2) does not apply if

(a) use of the required safety-engineered medical sharp is not clinically appropriate in the particular circumstances, or

(b) the required safety-engineered sharp is not available in commercial markets.

525.2(4) An employer must develop and implement safe work procedures for the use and disposal of medical sharps if a worker is required to use or dispose of a medical sharp.

525.2(5) An employer must ensure that a worker who is required to use and dispose of a medical sharp is trained in the safe work procedures required by subsection (4) and such training must include

(a) the hazards associated with the use and disposal of medical sharps,

(b) the proper use and limitations of safety-engineered medical sharps,

(c) procedures to eliminate accidental contact with medical sharps, and

(d) any other relevant information.

525.2(6) A worker must use and dispose of a medical sharp in accordance with the training provided by the employer.

Sharps containers

526(1) An employer must provide sharps containers and ensure that they are located as close as is reasonably practicable to where sharps are used.

526(2) A worker must use the sharps container provided.

526(3) An employer must ensure that a sharps container has a clearly defined fill line and is sturdy enough to resist puncture under normal conditions of use and handling.

Recapping needles

527 A person must not recap waste needles.

Policies and procedures

528(1) An employer must establish policies and procedures dealing with storing, handling, using and disposing of biohazardous materials.

528(2) An employer must ensure that workers are informed of the health hazards associated with exposure to the biohazardous material.

Limited exposure

    529   An employer must ensure that worker exposure to biohazardous materials is kept as low as reasonably practicable.

Post-exposure management

    530   An employer must establish policies and procedures for the post-exposure management of workers exposed to biohazardous material.

Part 36   Mining

Division 1:   General

Application
  531   This Part applies to mines and mine sites.

Building safety
  532   An employer must ensure that a processing plant, other facility or building at a mine is
   (a)   kept as free as is reasonably practicable of dust, and
   (b)   cleaned often enough to prevent any dust from becoming a health or safety hazard.

Mine plans
  533   An employer at a mine site must keep mine plans that include
   (a)   the workings surveyed, current to within three months of the previous survey,
   (b)   extensions to the workings sketched in, current to within one month of the previous survey,
   (c)   the general direction and inclination of the strata and thickness of the bed or strata being worked,
   (d)   the legal description of the land making up the mine operating property,
   (e)   a right of way on the land for a pipeline or other utility corridor, and
   (f)   exploration drill holes drilled for any purpose.

Record retention
  534   An employer must keep the records of an inspection required under this Part for not less than 12 months after the inspection unless a section requires them to be kept for a longer period.

Excavation
  535(1) An employer at a surface mine must ensure that there is no excavation within
   (a)   10 metres of a boundary of a mine operating property,
   (b)   20 metres of a right of way for a highway or a thoroughfare,
   (c)   30 metres of an oil or gas well, or
   (d)   30 metres of a right of way for a pipeline or other utility corridor.
  535(2) An employer at a surface mine must ensure that the walls of excavations are designed to ensure the distances prescribed in subsection (1) are maintained.

Open stockpiles
  536   An employer must ensure that stockpiles of mine materials that are open to the atmosphere or accessible to workers are constructed and marked in such a way that workers are not endangered by any surface or sub-surface instability of the stockpiles.

Dust from drills

537(1) An employer must ensure that if a blast hole drill, rotary drill or other drill is used, the dust released is controlled.

537(2) If drilling is intermittent and dust cannot be effectively controlled, an employer may apply to the Director for an acceptance approving an alternate means of protecting workers from dust.

Light metal alloys

538(1) An employer must ensure that, if it is reasonably practicable, workers do not take into an underground coal mine or other hazardous location light metal alloys that

   (a) contain more than 15 percent aluminum by mass of the alloy or more than 15 percent aluminum, magnesium and/or titanium, taken together, by mass of the alloy, or

   (b) contain more than 6 percent magnesium and/or titanium taken together or separately, by mass of the alloy.

538(2) Despite subsection (1), an employer may permit workers to take and use equipment that contains light metal alloys into a hazardous location if the equipment has protective design features that minimize the potential for incendiary friction or sparking.

538(3) An employer must ensure that fan blades for auxiliary or booster fans to be used in an underground coal mine and that do not comply with subsection (1) are

   (a) adequately coated with non-sparking material,

   (b) inspected by a competent person each time they are moved, or at least every 6 months, and a record of these inspections is kept at the mine,

   (c) taken out of service if the coating is damaged.

538(4) This section also applies to hazardous locations at the surface of an underground mine.

Surface haul roads

539(1) An employer must ensure that a haul road is built and maintained so that a vehicle can travel safely into or out of a mine.

539(2) An employer must ensure that a haul road with a gradient of more than 5 percent has emergency escape routes that

   (a) are spaced throughout the length of the haul road, and

   (b) allow a runaway vehicle to be stopped safely.

539(3) An employer must ensure that

   (a) any portion of a surface haul road that exposes mobile equipment to a vertical fall of greater than 3 metres is protected by a berm that is equivalent to at least one-half the height of the largest haulage truck tire in use on that haul road, and

   (b) any breaks in the berms of a surface haul road must not be greater than the width of the smallest haul truck in regular service on that road.

Discard from mines

540   An employer must ensure that a dump or impoundment used for disposing of the following is stable:

    (a)   discard from the mine;

    (b)   refuse from the plant;

    (c)   rock and soil from the mine operation;

    (d)   mine and plant effluent.

Mine walls

541(1) An employer must establish and put in place specifications and procedures, certified by a professional engineer, for the safe control of mine walls, including the overall slope of walls.

541(2) An employer must ensure that

    (a)   undermining is not carried out in unconsolidated or blasted mine material,

    (b)   the working face is less than 1.5 metres above the maximum height that the excavation equipment can reach,

    (c)   unconsolidated mine material lying within 2 metres of the crest of a working face is removed,

    (d)   unconsolidated mine material lying more than 2 metres from the crest of a working face is stabilized so that it does not create a hazard to workers working near the working face, and

    (e)   safety berms are constructed and maintained so that accumulations of loose rock or other mine material do not create a hazard to workers on working benches.

Dumping block

542   An employer must ensure that if powered mobile equipment may go over a bank or enter a dump opening while it is discharging its load, the equipment is effectively stopped or controlled by

    (a)   an anchored block,

    (b)   a ridge of material acting as a backstop, or

    (c)   a designated signaller with a stop signal.

Environmental monitoring of hazardous gases

543(1) An employer must ensure that appropriate flammable gas monitors are installed in a hazardous location and are continuously monitored via a remote monitoring and control system in a permanently attended surface communication station.

543(2) An employer must ensure that the flammable gas monitors required by subsection (1)

    (a)   are installed in an appropriate place in each hazardous location, and

    (b)   **Repealed**

    (c)   will cause an alarm to sound in a permanently attended surface communication station if the content of the atmosphere exceeds 20 percent of the lower explosive limit of the gas being monitored.

Reporting dangerous occurrences

544(1) An employer must notify the Director as soon as possible if any of the following occur:

(a) an unexpected major ground fall or subsidence that endangers or may endanger workers, equipment or facilities;

(b) an unplanned stoppage of the main underground ventilation system, if it lasts more than 30 minutes;

(c) a vehicle that goes out of control;

(d) ignition of flammable gas, combustible dust or other material underground;

(e) workers are withdrawn from a hazardous location under emergency conditions;

(f) electrical equipment failures or incidents that cause, or threaten to cause, injury to workers or damage to equipment or facilities;

(g) any other unusual incident or unexpected event that could have caused serious injury to a worker;

(h) outbursts and inrushes; or

(i) an incident involving a hoist, sheave, hoisting rope, shaft conveyance, shaft, shaft timbering or headframe structure.

544(2) An employer must notify the Director as soon as possible if any of the following occur and the integrity of a dam or dike is affected:

(a) cracking or evidence of weakening or subsidence of a dam or impoundment dike;

(b) unexpected seepage or the appearance of springs on the outer face of a dam or dike;

(c) the freeboard of a dam or dike is less than adequate; or

(d) there is a washout or significant erosion to a dam or dike.

Fire Prevention and Emergency Response

Emergency response station

545(1) An employer must establish, maintain and operate an emergency response station and provide facilities for conducting rescue operations and other emergency work at a mine, unless the Director exempts the mine from this section.

545(2) An employer must ensure that adequate rescue equipment and apparatus are available for immediate use at an emergency response station.

545(3) An employer must ensure that there are sufficient workers at a mine site who are trained in the use and maintenance of rescue equipment.

Emergency response team

546(1) An employer must appoint a competent worker to be responsible for the training of workers designated under section 117.

546(2) An employer must ensure that the emergency response workers referred to in subsection (1)

(a) are competent to perform the tasks assigned to them,

(b) are medically fit to perform rescue operations and other emergency work at a mine,

(c) qualify as standard first aiders in accordance with Part 11, and

(d) have completed training approved by the Director.

546(3) An employer must ensure that the designated members of the emergency response team

(a) practice at least every two months, and

(b) make periodic tours of all of the workings so that they are familiar with the complete mine layout and the location of entrances and exits to work areas.

546(4) At an underground coal mine, the underground coal mine manager must establish and maintain appropriately trained and equipped rescue teams as follows:

(a) if the number of workers underground at one time is less than 50, but greater than 10, a minimum of one team;

(b) if the number of workers underground at one time is greater than 50, a minimum of two teams;

(c) if the number of workers underground at one time is less than 10,

(i) maintain on site appropriately trained and equipped personnel to provide a first response and assessment capability, and

(ii) establish mutual aid agreements with external agencies to provide additional appropriately trained and equipped personnel.

Fire fighting training

547(1) An employer at an underground coal mine must ensure that

(a) all workers newly employed at the mine receive training in the use of fire fighting equipment during the first three months of their employment, and

(b) all workers continually employed underground receive a practical course in the use of fire fighting equipment every two years.

547(2) An employer must keep a record of the workers attending fire fighting training.

Fire precautions

548(1) An employer at an underground coal mine must ensure that

(a) not more than 700 litres of flammable liquid is stored in the mine unless the flammable liquid is stored in a fireproof receptacle or chamber,

(b) mine material likely to cause a fire does not accumulate in any working part of the mine,

(c) mine material likely to cause a fire is kept in fireproof containers that are removed and disposed of at regular intervals,

(d) flammable construction material is not used in an area of the mine in which stationary compressors or other stationary equipment capable of producing more than 400 kilowatts is installed,

(e) tarred or other building paper is not used in the mine, and

(f) propane is not used in the mine except in mine heaters in portal structures.

548(2) An employer at an underground coal mine must ensure that the following are constructed of non-flammable material or treated to make them fire resistant:

(a) underground portals;

(b) main fan installations;

(c) booster fan installations;

(d) ventilation air crossings;

(e) stoppings, regulators and doors.

548(3) An employer at an underground coal mine must ensure that workers use dust-suppression devices if concentrations of dust may be hazardous.

548(4) An employer at an underground coal mine must ensure that unattended conveyor belt transfer points have automatic fire warning devices that sound an alarm in the manned surface control room.

548(5) An employer at an underground coal mine must ensure that equipment brought into the mine by workers uses fire resistant hydraulic fluids that meet the requirements of CSA Standard CAN/CSA-M423-M87 (R2007), *Fire-Resistant Hydraulic Fluids*.

548(6) Subsection (5) does not apply to the following vehicle components:

(a) axles;

(b) fluid couplings;

(c) braking systems that employ totally enclosed friction elements immersed in a cooling liquid; or

(d) braking systems whose hydraulics are independent of any other hydraulic system.

548(7) Despite subsections (5) and (6), the Director may approve a vehicle that uses an automatic fire suppression system and associated automatic engine shutdown provided the mine uses a continuous fire detection and gas-monitoring system.

Fireproofing of roadways

549(1) An employer at an underground coal mine must ensure that, from not less than 5 metres on the air intake side to not less than 10 metres on the return air side, the roadway support and lining of a conveyor transfer or loading point installed in the mine is constructed

(a) of fire resistant materials, or

(b) subject to subsection (2), with the minimum amount possible of combustible materials.

549(2) If reasonably practicable, an employer must ensure that combustible materials in a mine are treated with a fire resistant coating.

Conveyor clearance

550 An employer at an underground coal mine must ensure that

(a) a clearance is maintained between the bottom rollers of conveyor belt systems and the floor of the roadway that permits workers to remove combustible material, and

(b) if the clearance is obtained by mounting the conveyor belt system on pillars, the pillars are of non-flammable material.

Fire detection systems

551(1) An employer at an underground coal mine must ensure that

(a) one or more fire detection systems are installed in the mine, and

(b) the system automatically activates an audible alarm in a permanently attended surface control room if the system stops working.

551(2) The Director may require an employer to install a fire detection system at a specific location in an underground coal mine.

Emergency warning system

552 An employer at an underground coal mine must

(a) establish an effective emergency warning system that warns all workers at a work area of an emergency that requires prompt evacuation of the area, and

(b) ensure that the emergency warning system is tested at least once in every 12 month period and the results of that test, including remedial actions to address any identified deficiencies, are recorded in a logbook or electronic record that is maintained at the mine for that purpose for a period of three years and is available to an Officer upon request.

Evacuation

553 An employer at an underground mine must

(a) prepare procedures for safe evacuation of the mine,

(b) post copies of the procedures at conspicuous places on the surface and underground,

(c) ensure that all workers

(i) are instructed in the procedures,

(ii) recognize the emergency warning, and

(iii) are familiar with the emergency escape routes,

(d) ensure that a mock exercise for evacuation of the mine is conducted with all workers annually,

(e) prepare a report of the exercise identifying remedial actions to address any deficiencies, and

(f) ensure that a copy of the report is kept at the mine and is available to an Officer upon request.

Fire fighting equipment

554(1) An employer at an underground coal mine must ensure that fire fighting equipment is provided

(a) at or near every structure where fire may endanger life, and

(b) at all underground locations where a fire hazard may exist.

554(2) An employer at an underground coal mine must ensure that if there is a fire, the direction of the mine ventilation air flow will not prevent or hamper the effective use of the fire fighting equipment.

554(3) An employer at an underground coal mine must ensure that fire fighting equipment

(a) is inspected once a month,

(b) except for fire extinguishers, is tested once in every three month period, and

(c) the results of the inspection are recorded in a log book maintained for that purpose.

Fire extinguishers

555 An employer at an underground coal mine must ensure that there are at least two suitable fire extinguishers

(a) at each stationary electric or diesel motor or transformer in the mine, and

(b) at each switchgear in use in the mine.

Location of equipment

556(1) An employer at an underground coal mine must ensure that there is a mine plan that shows the location of all fire fighting pipelines, water control valves, fire stations and fire cabinets in the mine.

556(2) The employer at an underground coal mine must ensure that the mine plan is

(a) reviewed at intervals of not more than three months and updated as required, and

(b) readily available to workers in a work area during an emergency.

Water supply

557 An employer at an underground coal mine must ensure that the water supply meets the following:

(a) the supply of available water intended for fire fighting is not less than 100 cubic metres;

(b) the system can supply water to any part of the mine at the pressure and volume necessary for fire fighting;

(c) if electric pumps are used to maintain the water supply, there is a standby pumping system whose power supply is not dependent on the main electrical system for the mine; and

(d) if the main fire fighting water supply is located in a return air roadway, then supply control valves must be located at appropriate intervals in the intake air roadway(s).

Water control valves

558(1) An employer at an underground mine must ensure that fire fighting water control valves meet the requirements of this section and are located

(a) on the intake side of conveyor loading points, transfer points and main junctions,

(b) along fire ranges so that the distance between valves is not more than 100 metres,

(c) at points central to room and pillar workings, and

(d)　as close as is reasonably practicable to longwall faces.

558(2) An employer at an underground coal mine must ensure that the fire fighting system and water control valves are capable of delivering a flow of not less than 4 litres per second.

558(3) An employer at an underground mine must ensure that the following are as close as is reasonably practicable to each fire fighting water control valve:

(a)　nozzles with a minimum internal diameter of 38 millimetres;

(b)　hoses

(i)　long enough to cover the distances between the valves,

(ii)　with a minimum internal diameter of 38 millimetres, and

(iii)　with a working pressure of 1000 kilopascals.

Refuge stations

559(1) An employer at an underground coal mine must ensure that there are refuge stations located at strategic places in the mine.

559(2) A refuge station must

(a)　be big enough to accommodate all workers working in the vicinity during one shift,

(b)　have water, air and a system that communicates effectively with the surface, and

(c)　be separated from adjoining workings by closeable fireproof doors arranged and equipped to prevent gases from entering the refuge station.

559(3) An employer at an underground coal mine must ensure that the number of workers that can be accommodated in a refuge station is posted outside of the entrance to the station.

559(4) The Director may exempt an underground coal mine or part of a mine from subsection (1).

Electrical Systems

Electrical standards

560　Subject to sections 561 to 572, an employer must ensure that the installation, maintenance and operation of electrical equipment meets the requirements of CSA Standard CAN/CSA-M421-00 (R2007), *Use of Electricity in Mines*.

Notice to Director

561(1) An employer must notify the Director before

(a)　electrical energy is installed and used at a mine,

(b)　**Repealed**

(c)　electrical equipment is placed, installed or modified in an underground coal mine or a hazardous location, or

(d)　an electrical distribution system is disconnected from the power source when a mine is to be abandoned or left unattended.

561(2) An employer must ensure that a system referred to in subsection (1)(a) or (c) is not energized until written approval is given by the Director.

561(3) A notification under subsection (1) must show the parts of the mine where the electrical energy is to be transmitted and used.

Electrical installations

562(1) An employer must ensure that electrical installations, repairs and modifications are made by an authorized worker.

562(2) An employer must ensure that records of the installation of and repairs and modifications to electrical equipment are

(a) kept at the mine for two years following the activity, and

(b) available for inspection at the mine by an officer.

Surface facilities

563(1) An employer must ensure that all electrical equipment in a hazardous location on the surface is approved by the manufacturer or a professional engineer for use in the presence of the specific gas, vapour or dust that is or may be in the location.

563(2) An employer must ensure that electrical equipment is repaired, adjusted or replaced in a hazardous location at a surface mine only

(a) after the equipment is disconnected from the power supply and is confirmed as disengaged, and

(b) if the electrician performing the work is satisfied that no dangerous concentration of flammable gas is present.

Underground coal mine

564(1) An employer must ensure that electrical equipment is operated in an underground coal mine only after an underground coal mine electrical superintendent approves it.

564(2) An employer must ensure that electrical equipment used in an underground coal mine is installed, re-installed, repaired, maintained and tested under the supervision of an underground coal mine electrical superintendent.

564(3) An employer must ensure that electrical equipment is repaired, adjusted or replaced in an underground coal mine only

(a) after the equipment is disconnected from the power supply and is confirmed as disengaged, and

(b) if the electrician performing the work is satisfied that no dangerous concentration of flammable gas is present.

Equipment supply systems

565(1) An employer must ensure that supply systems for mobile electrical equipment are tested to ensure the effectiveness of the ground fault tripping and ground conductor monitoring circuits

(a) before the equipment is put into service, and

(b) every 12 months while the equipment is in service.

565(2) An employer must ensure that a record of the tests required under subsection (1) is

(a) kept at the mine for two years after the test, and

(b) available for inspection at the mine by an officer.

Batteries

566(1) An employer must ensure that battery charging stations in an underground mine are

(a) ventilated by intake air to ensure gases are diffused and the contaminated air is discharged directly into the return airway, and

(b) approved by the Director.

566(2) An employer must ensure that workers do not repair batteries in an underground coal mine or other hazardous location.

Overhead power lines

567   An employer must ensure that the cable supplying a moveable switch house or substation from an overhead line

(a) is not more than 25 metres long unless

(i)   the ampacity of the cable is at least one-third of the overcurrent protection setting of the supply, or

(ii) properly sized overcurrent protective devices are installed at the point of cable termination to the overhead line,

(b) has at the overhead line end

(i)   a separate means of disconnection located on a power pole, or

(ii) subject to the approval of the Director, an alternative means of disconnection arranged to prevent switching errors or incorrect isolation,

(c) is continuous, without cable couplers or junction boxes, and

(d) has conductors connected directly through suitable cable glands to the supply terminals of the switch house or substation.

Ground fault protection

568   An employer must ensure that in an underground coal mine the current of portable power cables supplying moveable electrical equipment and submersible pumps operating at a voltage exceeding 125 volts

(a) is automatically interrupted if there is a ground fault, and

(b) cannot be restored until the ground fault is removed.

Switchgear

569(1) An employer must ensure that

(a) the surface of an underground mine has electrical distribution switchgear for isolating all underground electrical circuits, and

(b) an authorized worker is available to operate the switchgear whenever the circuits are energized.

569(2) An employer must ensure that electrical distribution switchgear is not located nearer to the working face in an underground coal mine than the last ventilated cross-cut.

Grounding

570(1) An employer must ensure that the ground electrodes at a surface mine and at the surface of an underground mine are inspected and tested every 12 months.

570(2) An employer must ensure that a record of the tests required under subsection (1) is

    (a)   kept at the mine for two years following the activity, and

    (b)   available for inspection at the mine by an officer.

Electric welding

571   An employer must ensure that a worker who uses a welding unit in a mine uses a current return wire from the welding unit to the work area that has the same cross-sectional area as the power lead wire.

Hand held electrical drills

572   An employer must ensure that if the power switch is released on a hand held drill used by a worker in a mine,

    (a)   the power to the drill is interrupted, and

    (b)   the drill stops operating.

Rubber-Tired, Self-Propelled Machines

Approval

573(1) An employer must not use a rubber-tired, self-propelled machine with a GVW of more than 32,000 kilograms at a mine site unless the Director has approved it or a representative unit for use in Alberta.

573(2) Despite subsection (1),

    (a)   the Director may request that any rubber-tired, self-propelled machine at a mine site be tested and approved for use,

    (b)   all rubber-tired, self-propelled machines must meet the applicable requirements of sections 577 through 596, and

    (c)   any machine approved under the *Traffic Safety Act* is approved for use in a mine.

573(3) An employer may operate a rubber-tired, self-propelled machine with a load that weighs more than the manufacturer's specifications for the maximum weight of a load if the employer

    (a)   prepares a report of the employer's assessment of the hazards relating to the operation of the machine, and

    (b)   develops procedures

        (i)   that ensure the safe operation of the machine, and

        (ii)   that are approved by the Director.

Standards

574(1) An employer must ensure that rubber-tired, self-propelled machines used in an underground mine meet the requirements of CSA Standard CAN/CSA M424.3-M90 (R2007), *Braking Performance — Rubber-Tired, Self-Propelled Underground Mining Machines.*

574(2) The Director may exempt a rubber-tired, self-propelled machine from subsection (1).

Prototype machine

575(1) This section applies to a prototype machine that is (a)　a new or used, rubber-tired, self-propelled, machine unit referred to in ISO Standard 6165: 2006, *Earth-moving machinery — Basic types — Vocabulary*,

(b)　intended for use at surface mines or at surface operations related to underground mines, and

(c)　brought into Alberta for the first time.

575(2) An employer must ensure that a prototype machine meets the requirements of the braking performance set by ISO Standard 3450: 1996, *Earth-moving machinery — Braking systems of rubber-tyred machines — Systems and performance requirements and test procedures.*

575(3) Repealed

575(4) Repealed

575(5) An employer must ensure that the manufacturer of a prototype self-propelled machine or a professional engineer certifies that the prototype self-propelled machine meets or exceeds the requirements of this section.

575(6) An employer must ensure that a copy of the "Test Report" referred to in clause 8 of ISO Standard 3450: 1996, on the prototype machine is given to the Director.

Representative machines

576(1) This section applies to a type of rubber-tired, self-propelled machine that

(a)　is not included in ISO Standard 6165: 2006, *Earth-moving machinery — Basic types — Vocabulary,*

(b)　has a GVW of more than 32,000 kilograms, and

(c)　is proposed by an employer for use in surface mines or at surface operations related to underground mines.

576(2) An employer must ensure that a machine is not used in Alberta unless

(a)　the braking systems of a representative unit of each type of machine are tested,

(b)　the machine manufacturer or a professional engineer certifies that the machine meets or exceeds the stopping performance specified in section 7.6 of ISO Standard 3450: 1996, and

(c)　a copy of the "Test Report" referred to in clause 8 of ISO Standard 3450: 1996 on the representative machine is given to the Director.

Emergency energy

577　An employer must ensure that a rubber-tired, self-propelled machine fitted with an air or air-over-hydraulic braking system has an emergency source of energy that can

(a)　apply the service brake, and

(b)　safely stop and hold the machine on all grades over which it operates.

Hydraulic brakes

578　An employer must ensure that a rubber-tired, self-propelled machine with hydraulically activated service brakes

(a)　has a hydraulic system divided into two or more separate circuits that are independently activated, and

    (b)   meets the requirements of ISO Standard 3450: 1996.

Dual brake systems

579   An employer must ensure that a rubber-tired, self-propelled machine fitted with a divided or dual braking system has a visible or audible warning device that effectively alerts the operator when a part of the system stops working as designed.

Emergency brakes

580   If the emergency braking system of a rubber-tired, self-propelled machine is arranged to cause an automatic application of the service brakes when there is an accidental loss of air pressure in the main brake actuating system, an employer must ensure that the available brake application pressure does not fall below 415 kilopascals.

Air brakes

581   An employer must ensure that if air or air-over-hydraulic brake systems are fitted to a rubber-tired, self-propelled machine,

    (a)   all non-braking secondary air circuits are supplied through check valves that isolate the secondary circuit involved if there is a sudden pressure drop in the main circuit,

    (b)   the total volume of air available in the main circuit for normal service brake application is not less than 12 times the total displacement volume of all brake actuators at full travel,

    (c)   a wet reservoir with an automatic water ejection valve or an air-drying system is fitted between the compressor and the first brake service reservoir,

    (d)   the machine has gauges that

        (i)   meet the requirements of

            (A)   SAE Standard J209 (2003), *Instrument Face Design and Location for Construction and Industrial Equipment*, or

            (B)   SAE Standard J209 JAN87, *Instrument Face Design and Location for Construction and Industrial Equipment*,

        (ii)   are visible to the operator, and

        (iii)   show the air pressure in the main and emergency air circuits and the brake application pressure,

    (e)   the machine has a visible or audible warning device that effectively alerts the operator when the air pressure in the main service brake circuit falls below a predetermined pressure, and

    (f)   check valves protect air reservoirs from loss of pressure if the supply side leaks.

Auxiliary air reservoirs

582   If a rubber-tired, self-propelled machine has auxiliary air reservoirs for modulated emergency brake application under driver control, an employer must ensure that the volume of air in the auxiliary reservoirs is not less than six times the total displacement volume of all brake actuators used to develop the emergency brake force.

Front wheel brake control

583   An employer must ensure that a rubber-tired, self-propelled machine used in a surface mine with a GVW of more than 32,000 kilograms and an air or air-over-hydraulic brake system has front wheel brake control that allows the operator to reduce the front wheel brake effort according to road conditions.

Parking brakes

584(1) An employer must ensure that a rubber-tired, self-propelled machine used in a surface mine or a surface operation related to underground mines has a mechanically activated parking brake that can hold the machine on a 15 percent grade when the machine is loaded to the machine's GVW.

584(2) An employer must ensure that the performance of a parking brake system is not affected

(a)   if any of the air pressure in the system is lost, or

(b)   if there is a dimensional change in the brake's components.

Periodic service brake testing

585(1) Subject to subsections (3) and (4), an employer must ensure that the service brakes are tested at regular intervals on a rubber-tired, self-propelled machine

(a)   that has a GVW of more than 32,000 kilograms, and

(b)   that travels at a speed of more than 10 kilometres per hour in normal operations.

585(2) If the Director requests the testing, an employer must ensure that service brakes are tested at regular intervals on a rubber-tired, self-propelled machine that is not referred to in subsection (1).

585(3) An employer must ensure that the service brakes of at least 30 percent of the machines referred to in subsections (1) and (2) in the employer's fleet are tested in each year.

585(4) An employer must ensure that the service brakes of all machines referred to in subsections (1) and (2) in the employer's fleet are tested within a three year period.

585(5) If a rubber-tired, self-propelled machine does not meet the minimum brake performance requirements as determined by the employer or an officer, the employer must remove it from service until it meets the requirements.

585(6) Despite subsections (3) and (4), an officer may request, at any time, that the service brakes of a vehicle be tested.

Tests

586(1) An employer must ensure that the service brakes of a machine referred to in section 585 are tested under the supervision of a competent worker.

586(2) An employer must ensure that the service brakes of a machine referred to in section 585 are tested

(a)   at the machine's normal operation speed,

(b)   with the machine loaded to approximately the manufacturer's specified maximum load weight, and

(c)   on a straight, level road with a hard, dry surface.

586(3) An employer must ensure that the following are measured and recorded when service brakes are tested:

(a) the distance travelled by the machine after the service brakes are applied to the maximum extent possible;

(b) the forward speed of the machine at the time the service brakes are applied.

Maintenance records

587(1) An employer must ensure that a maintenance record is kept on each rubber-tired, self-propelled machine that includes

(a) all unsafe conditions of the machine,

(b) repairs to the machine, and

(c) copies of the machine's periodic service brake tests if required by section 585.

587(2) An employer must ensure that the maintenance record

(a) is kept at the mine for three years following the activity, and

(b) is available for inspection at the mine by an officer.

Auxiliary steering

588(1) An employer must ensure that a rubber-tired, self-propelled machine has an auxiliary power source that enables the operator to steer the machine to a safe stop if

(a) the machine depends on hydraulic power for steering, and

(b) the loss of hydraulic power might prevent the machine from being steered.

588(2) Despite subsection (1), a rubber-tired, self-propelled machine does not require auxiliary steering if

(a) it is restricted to underground use, and

(b) it has a maximum speed of 20 kilometres per hour.

Auxiliary pump

589   An employer must ensure that the hydraulic fluid supply to an auxiliary hydraulic pump used to provide the emergency steering capability on a rubber-tired, self-propelled machine comes from a separate reservoir or from an isolated section of the main reservoir.

Auxiliary steering standards

590(1) An employer must ensure that an auxiliary steering system on a rubber-tired, self-propelled machine conforms to the requirements of SAE Standard J1511 FEB94/ISO 5010, *Steering for Off-Road, Rubber-Tired Machines*.

590(2) The auxiliary steering system must

(a) come into use automatically or be activated manually if the power source fails, and

(b) operate a visible or audible warning device that effectively alerts the operator that steering power or power assistance is not available and emergency steering is being used.

Design safety factors

591(1) An employer must ensure that a rubber-tired, self-propelled machine has

    (a)   shock-absorbing seats,

    (b)   a fail-safe means of preventing unintentional movement when the machine is parked, and

    (c)   an interlock system that prevents the engine from starting when the transmission is engaged.

591(2) An employer must ensure that all haulage trucks fitted with rear dump boxes

    (a)   have a calculated centre of gravity, and

    (b)   will maintain all wheels in contact with the ground during normal operation when loaded to the manufacturer's specified maximum load weight.

591(3) If the load characteristics cause the front wheels of a rubber-tired, self-propelled machine to lift off the ground, an employer must develop procedures to protect workers from the related hazards.

Clearance lights

592(1) An employer must ensure that a rubber-tired, self-propelled machine has clearance lights that

    (a)   indicate clearly from both the front and rear of the machine the overall width of the machine, and

    (b)   meet the requirements of

        (i)   SAE Standard J2042 July2006, *Clearance, Sidemarker, and Identification Lamps for Use on Motor Vehicles 2032 mm or More in Overall Width,* or

        (ii)   SAE Standard J2042 (2003), *Clearance, Sidemarker, and Identification Lamps for Use on Motor Vehicles 2032 mm or More in Overall Width.*

592(2) An employer must ensure that the clearance lights of a rubber-tired, self-propelled machine are on when the machine's engine is on.

592(3) For the purpose of subsection (1), the overall width does not include

    (a)   blades on motor graders or rubber-tired dozers, or

    (b)   buckets on front-end loaders.

Clear view

593   An employer must ensure that means are provided to enhance or improve the operator's line of sight if a rubber-tired, self-propelled machine restricts the operator's ability to safely operate the machine.

Lights

594(1) An employer must ensure that a rubber-tired, self-propelled machine has headlights, reversing lights, tail lights, retarder lights and brake lights, where applicable.

594(2) An employer must ensure that headlights on a rubber-tired, self-propelled machine are properly aligned.

Clearances

595(1) An employer must ensure that, in an underground coal mine

    (a)   the sum of the horizontal clearances on each side of a rubber-tired, self-propelled machine is not less than 2 metres, and

    (b)   the vertical clearance between the highest point of a rubber-tired, self-propelled machine or its load and the lowest overhead obstruction is not less than 0.3 metres.

595(2) The Director may exempt an underground coal mine from the clearances under subsection (1).

Unattended machines

596(1) A worker must not leave a rubber-tired, self-propelled machine unattended underground unless the engine is turned off.

596(2) A worker must not leave a rubber-tired, self-propelled machine unattended underground unless it is parked

    (a)   on level ground,

    (b)   with its downhill end turned into the rib, or

    (c)   with its wheels turned towards the rib and blocked.

Diesel Power

Diesel powered machine

597(1) An employer must ensure that a diesel powered machine used in an underground coal mine meets the requirements of CSA Standard CAN/CSA-M424.1-88 (R2007), *Flameproof Non-Rail-Bound, Diesel-Powered Machines for Use in Gassy Underground Coal Mines*, unless this Code or some other equivalent standard approved by the Director requires otherwise.

597(2) An employer must ensure that a diesel powered machine used in an underground mine, other than a coal mine, meets the requirements of CSA Standard CAN/CSA-M424.2-M90 (R2007), *Non-Rail-Bound Diesel-Powered Machines for Use in Non-Gassy Underground Mines*, or other equivalent standard approved by the Director.

Conveyors

Fire resistance

598   An employer must ensure that, in a hazardous location,

    (a)   all conveyor belting meets the requirements of CSA Standard CAN/CSA-M422-M87 (R2007), *Fire Performance and Anti-static Requirements for Conveyor Belting*, or an equivalent standard approved by the Director, and

    (b)   the conveyor belt system is fitted with a fire suppression system approved by the Director.

Stopping

599(1) An employer must ensure that a section of a conveyor belt system that is accessible to workers has

    (a)   a pull cord to stop the conveyor belt system in an emergency, and

(b) controls that must be reset manually before the conveyor belt system can be restarted after an emergency stop.

599(2) An employer must ensure that a switch is installed on each conveyor belt that

(a) is sensitive to belt travel, and

(b) stops the drive motor if the belt or transfer chute or both are blocked or slip.

Travelling room

600 An employer must ensure that each part of an underground mine over which coal or another mineral is moved by a conveyor belt system has travelling room of at least 1 metre between a side of the conveyor belt and the edge of the roadway on the same side.

Combustible dust

601(1) An employer must ensure that, in hazardous locations, no combustible dust accumulates at or near the conveyor belt, the belt support rollers, the conveyor belt drive and tail or the belt take-up drums.

601(2) An employer must ensure that, if dust may be a hazard, a belt conveyor discharge is constructed so that the amount of dust spilled or dispersed into the air is minimized or eliminated.

Clearances

602(1) An employer must ensure the following clearances are maintained along a conveyor belt:

(a) on the travelling side, if rubber-tired vehicles are used, at least 2 metres more than the maximum width of the vehicle;

(b) on the travelling side, if track-guided vehicles are used, not less than 0.3 metres between the vehicle and the conveyor belt;

(c) on the blind side, not less than 0.3 metres.

602(2) An employer must ensure that there is a clearance of not less than 0.3 metres between the roof supports and the top of the load carried by a conveyor belt.

Riding conveyor belts

603(1) A worker must not ride on a conveyor belt unless the conveyor installation is certified by a professional engineer and designated by the employer as a riding conveyor belt.

603(2) An employer must ensure that a conveyor designated as a riding conveyor belt complies with the following:

(a) it is at no place steeper than 15 degrees from the horizontal plane;

(b) it has head room clearance along its entire length of at least 0.9 metres;

(c) it has a maximum belt speed of 2.65 metres per second;

(d) it has a belt width of not less than 915 millimetres;

(e) it has mounting platforms with non-slip surfaces that

(i) are not less than 1.5 metres long and 0.6 metres wide, and

(ii) have a clearance of 2.4 metres above the platform for the length of the platform plus 10 metres beyond the platform in the direction the belt travels;

(f) it has dismounting platforms with non-slip surfaces that

(i) are not less than 15 metres long and 0.6 metres wide,

(ii) are fitted with a handrail, and

(iii) have adequate head room clearance to allow workers to dismount without stooping;

(g) the mounting and dismounting platforms are electrically illuminated;

(h) it has reflective signs that clearly indicate

(i) the mounting platforms,

(ii) the dismounting platforms, and

(iii) the approaches to dismounting platforms at 30 metres, 20 metres and 10 metres from the dismounting place;

(i) it has a safety device that automatically stops the belt if a worker travels beyond the dismounting platform;

(j) it has automatic brakes that apply when the belt is stopping; and

(k) it has a safety device that automatically stops the belt if a tear or split in the belt is detected.

603(3) An employer must develop safe operating procedures for workers who are required to travel on a riding conveyor belt.

603(4) An employer must post the safe operating procedures for a riding conveyor belt in conspicuous and appropriate locations.

Examination

604 In an underground coal mine, the employer must ensure that a belt line is examined by a worker

(a) at least once during every work shift, and

(b) following the last work shift if there is an interruption in the work.

Carbon monoxide monitors

605 An employer must ensure that conveyor belt systems installed in an underground coal mine have carbon monoxide monitors that are linked to the fire detection system.

Conveyor roadways

606(1) An employer must ensure that conveyor roadways are kept clear of obstructions.

606(2) An employer must ensure that conveyor roadways in an underground mine are at least 1.5 metres high.

606(3) A worker must travel only in the clear space on the conveyor roadway.

Division 2:   Explosives

Theft of explosives

607(1) A mine blaster must immediately report to the employer

(a) the suspected, attempted or known unlawful entry into a magazine, or

(b) the unlawful removal of explosives or detonators from a mine site.

607(2) An employer must immediately report to the Director

(a) the suspected, attempted or known unlawful entry into a magazine, or

(b) the unlawful removal of explosives or detonators from a mine site.

Non-sparking tools

608(1) An employer must provide workers with tools made of non-sparking material for

(a) opening containers or packages of explosives,

(b) preparing explosives, and

(c) loading holes with explosives.

608(2) A worker must use tools made of non-sparking material for

(a) opening containers or packages of explosives,

(b) preparing explosives, and

(c) loading holes with explosives.

Underground mine blaster

609(1) An employer must not allow a worker to handle an explosive or a misfire in an underground mine unless the worker

(a) is an underground mine blaster, or

(b) works under the direct supervision of an underground mine blaster.

609(2) A worker who is not referred to in subsection (1) must not handle an explosive or a misfire in an underground mine.

Surface mine blaster

610(1) An employer must not allow a worker to handle an explosive at a surface mine unless the worker

(a) is a surface mine blaster, or

(b) works under the direct supervision of a surface mine blaster.

610(2) A worker who is not referred to in subsection (1) must not handle an explosive at a surface mine.

Magazines

611   An employer must ensure that magazines in an underground mine are

(a) located and certified by a professional engineer, and

(b) approved by the Director.

Illumination of magazines

612   An employer must ensure that

(a) a permanent illumination system is installed in a magazine, or

(b) only portable lights designed for use in hazardous locations are taken into a magazine.

Stored explosives

613   An employer must ensure that

(a) stored explosives are examined often enough to ensure that no hazardous conditions arise because an explosive has deteriorated,

(b) all deteriorated or damaged explosives are removed from storage, and

(c) all deteriorated or damaged explosives are destroyed in accordance with the manufacturer's specifications.

Electric detonators

614 An employer must ensure that electric detonators are stored and transported with the leg wires coiled and shunted in the manner in which they are supplied by the manufacturer.

Access to explosives

615(1) An employer must ensure that only a mine blaster designated by the employer, or a worker working under the direct supervision of the designated mine blaster, has access to magazines.

615(2) An employer must ensure that no worker, except a mine blaster or a worker working under the direct supervision of the designated mine blaster, has

(a) blasting apparatus at a mine site, or

(b) a key to a case, canister, storage box or magazine at a mine site.

Removal from magazine

616(1) A mine blaster must ensure that, until the explosive is about to be primed, explosives or detonators that are removed from a magazine are

(a) kept in separate containers, and

(b) separated so that one cannot affect the other.

616(2) An employer must ensure that the containers referred to in subsection (1) are

(a) lined with non-conductive material,

(b) secured against unintentional movement or unauthorized access, and

(c) weatherproof.

616(3) An employer must ensure that the explosives in a container are arranged and protected to ensure that they do not contact anything that may cause premature detonation.

616(4) A mine blaster must ensure that the leg wires of electric detonators that are removed from a magazine are shunted until immediately before the detonator is connected to the blasting circuit.

Priority of use

617 An employer and a mine blaster must ensure that the oldest explosives in a magazine are removed for use first and are used first.

Magazine record

618(1) An employer must ensure that a magazine record is kept at each magazine in which the mine blaster records

(a) immediately all explosives placed into or removed from a magazine,

(b) the number of failures of explosive charges at the end of each shift, and

(c) immediately all cartridges that are destroyed.

618(2) An employer must retain the magazine record for at least three years from the date of the last entry.

Explosive location

619(1) A worker must not take explosives into a building at a mine site other than a magazine.

619(2) A worker must get a mine blaster to remove explosives that are in a building other than a magazine.

619(3) If workers have explosives in their possession at the end of the work shift, the workers must return the explosives to a magazine.

Transportation

Removal and transfer

620(1) An employer must ensure that explosives are removed from a magazine and transported to a work area by a worker authorized by the mine manager.

620(2) An employer must ensure that explosives are removed from a magazine and transported to a work area without undue delay.

Restriction on open flames

621 A worker must not smoke tobacco or have an open flame or smouldering substance within 8 metres of a vehicle transporting explosives.

Vehicle requirements

622(1) An employer must ensure that a vehicle used to transport explosives complies with the following:

    (a) it is not loaded until the vehicle is fully serviced, including fuelling;

    (b) it has separate compartments for the explosives and detonators that prevent them from coming into contact with any metals or with each other;

    (c) it is constructed so that the explosives cannot fall from the vehicle;

    (d) is maintained in good working order.

622(2) An employer must ensure that a vehicle used to transport explosives is operated by a mine blaster or by a worker authorized by the mine blaster.

622(3) An employer must ensure that a vehicle used to transport explosives is equipped with at least two 9 kilogram ABC type fire extinguishers.

622(4) An employer must ensure that a vehicle that is transporting more than 25 kilograms of explosives shows placards clearly marked "Explosives" in letters that are not less than 150 millimetres high.

Protection from weather

623 An employer must ensure that explosives being transported are protected from rain and snow.

Original packaging

624 An employer must ensure that explosives are transported in their original packaging.

Detonators

625(1) An employer must ensure that detonators transported in a vehicle are separated from other explosives by a solid partition of wood or its equivalent that

(a) provides a distance of not less than 150 millimetres between the detonators and other explosives, and

(b) extends at least 150 millimetres above the highest level to which explosives are packed in the vehicle.

625(2) An employer must ensure that a radio transmitter in a vehicle transporting electric detonators is switched off while the detonators are being placed into or removed from the containment areas.

Vehicle breakdown

626(1) If a vehicle transporting explosives breaks down, repairs may be made to the vehicle without unloading the explosives if, in the opinion of the operator of the vehicle,

(a) the repairs are minor, and

(b) the repairs can be made without creating a hazard.

626(2) If a vehicle transporting explosives breaks down, the explosives must be transferred to another vehicle or be removed from the vehicle if, in the opinion of the operator of the vehicle,

(a) the repairs are major, or

(b) the repairs cannot be made without creating a hazard.

626(3) An employer must ensure that explosives removed from a vehicle that has broken down are placed under proper security

(a) at a safe distance from the track, road or highway, and

(b) not less than 300 metres from an inhabited building or a work area.

Operational Procedures

Manufacturer's specifications

627(1) An employer must ensure that explosives are handled, stored, used and destroyed in accordance with the manufacturer's specifications.

627(2) A worker must handle, store, use and destroy explosives in accordance with the manufacturer's specifications.

Unsafe explosives

628 A mine blaster must not use, or permit another worker to use, an explosive that, in the mine blaster's opinion, is deteriorated, damaged or otherwise unsafe to use.

Blast area control

629(1) An employer must ensure that the blast area is under the direction and control of a mine blaster.

629(2) If there are two or more mine blasters at a blast area, an employer must designate one mine blaster to be the blaster-in-charge of all blasting operations at the blast area.

Access to blast area

630 A worker must not approach, enter or remain in a blast area unless authorized to do so by the mine blaster.

General duties

631(1) An employer and a mine blaster must ensure that

    (a)   the blasting operation and related activities are performed safely,

    (b)   all primers are made up at the blast area,

    (c)   only sufficient primers for the number of shots to be fired are made up prior to the loading,

    (d)   no explosive is forcibly pressed into a hole of insufficient size,

    (e)   before a charge is fired, explosives not required for the blast are removed from the blast area,

    (f)   workers who are not required for loading operations are outside the blast area during loading operations, and

    (g)   the firing lines and lead-in lines required for electric detonation are in good condition.

631(2) A mine blaster must supervise, where applicable, the connection of

    (a)   the detonator to the detonating cord,

    (b)   the blasting cable to the detonator wires, and

    (c)   the non-electric lead-in line detonator to the blast pattern.

631(3) A mine blaster must, before the blast is fired, ensure that all workers are out of danger from the effects of the blast.

631(4) A mine blaster must, before blasting, ensure that

    (a)   entrances and approaches to the blast area are effectively guarded to prevent unauthorized workers entering or remaining in the blast area, and

    (b)   the guards or equipment guarding the blast area remain in position until the blast area is cleared and work can resume safely.

631(5) A mine blaster must give due warning of a blast.

631(6) After the blast is fired, a mine blaster must

    (a)   examine the blast area, including blasting cables affected by the blasting, and

    (b)   take whatever action is necessary to allow work to be safely resumed.

Secondary blasting

632   A mine blaster must ensure that if secondary blasting is practised,

    (a)   blockholes are used whenever reasonably practicable,

    (b)   the blockholes are deep enough to accommodate both the charge of explosive and sufficient stemming to confine the charge, and

    (c)   two or more charges are not used on the same boulder unless the charges are detonated simultaneously.

Mine blaster's record

633   A mine blaster must keep, in a log book that is kept at the mine for that purpose, a daily record at the end of the mine blaster's shift showing the following:

    (a)   the number of holes charged;

    (b)   the number of detonators used;

(c) the number of holes blasted;

(d) the kind and amount of explosives used;

(e) the kind and quantity of explosives taken from the magazines;

(f) the number and location of misfires;

(g) the kind and quantity of explosives returned to the magazines;

(h) the number and location of any charges left unfired.

Damaged blasting wires

634 If a worker drives over or damages blasting lead wires or lines, that worker must immediately advise the mine blaster and the employer.

Blasting machine control

635 An employer must ensure that a blasting machine is under the direct supervision and control of a mine blaster while it is in the blast area.

Undetonated or Abandoned Explosives

Unused explosives

636(1) An employer and a mine blaster must ensure that

(a) explosives are not abandoned,

(b) a misfire that can be safely detonated or removed from its hole is not abandoned, and

(c) unused explosives are returned to their magazine or destroyed in accordance with the manufacturer's specifications.

636(2) An employer must ensure that, before a blast area is defined as safe,

(a) all portions of charges that have been blown from the blast area are treated as misfires, and

(b) all wrappings or containers used in the handling of the explosives are destroyed.

Misfire procedures

637(1) A mine blaster must not abandon a misfire unless it cannot be safely detonated or removed from its hole.

637(2) An employer must ensure that safe work procedures are developed for handling of misfires.

Abandoned explosive

638(1) A worker who finds an abandoned explosive must

(a) take all reasonable action to ensure that other workers who may be exposed to it are made aware of it, and

(b) report the find to the employer or to a mine blaster.

638(2) An employer or mine blaster to whom an abandoned explosive is reported must

(a) take immediate steps to ensure that workers are protected from the hazards associated with the abandoned explosive, and

(b) notify the Director of the abandoned explosive.

Blasting Machines and Circuits

Testing and initiation

639 An employer must ensure that a worker who initiates and tests a blasting circuit uses

(a) explosive initiating and testing devices designed and manufactured for that purpose, and

(b) explosive initiating and testing devices approved by CANMET or by the Director in a location where an explosion or fire hazard exists or may exist.

Blasting apparatus

640(1) An employer must ensure that a blasting machine is clearly marked with its capacity.

640(2) A mine blaster must ensure that a blasting machine is tested before it is used for a blast that may require the machine's maximum capacity.

Circuit testing

641(1) A mine blaster must ensure that

(a) all workers are outside the blast area before an electrical blasting circuit is tested, and

(b) an electrical blasting circuit is tested before firing to confirm that the circuit is complete.

641(2) If electric blasting is performed with delayed-action detonators, a worker must not return to the scene of the blasting operation until at least 10 minutes after the blasting circuit is closed.

Circuit requirement

642(1) A mine blaster must ensure that

(a) power circuits used for blasting meet the requirements of clause 3.7 of CSA Standard CAN/CSA-M421-00 (R2007), *Use of Electricity in Mines*,

(b) the blasting machine or power source has adequate capacity for the number of detonators involved, and

(c) circuits supplying electricity for blasting are fed from

    (i) a blasting machine,

    (ii) an isolating transformer, or

    (iii) a power source that does not supply any other equipment.

642(2) A mine blaster must ensure that lead wires between the blasting machine and the zone of blasting operations

(a) are not less than No. 16 AWG in size,

(b) are readily identifiable as being for blasting use,

(c) are waterproof,

(d) consist of two insulated conductors,

(e) are used only for blasting,

(f)   are kept at a distance of not less than 1.5 metres from a power or lighting cable, and

(g)   are installed so that they do not touch pipes, rails or other electrically conductive materials.

642(3) A mine blaster must ensure that expendable connecting wires used from the lead wires to the leg wires of the electric detonator are not less than No. 20 AWG in size.

Surface Mines

Application

643   Sections 644 to 657 apply to explosives used at surface mines.

Signs

644(1) An employer must ensure that the blast area is clearly identified by posted signs, flagging or other means approved by the Director.

644(2) An employer must ensure that unauthorized mobile equipment, vehicles and workers do not inadvertently enter a blast area.

Blast holes

645(1) A surface mine blaster must ensure that holes are stemmed.

645(2) Subsection (1) does not apply to controlled blasting holes.

Electrical storm

646   If an electrical storm is approaching the blast area, a surface mine blaster must ensure that

(a)   no attempt is made to connect or fire a blast,

(b)   all loading operations are stopped and workers are withdrawn to a safe distance from the blast area, and

(c)   if charges are loaded and connected, workers are posted to prevent access to the blast area until the storm passes.

Detonating cord

647(1) A surface mine blaster must ensure that, if drill holes are being primed, detonating cord

(a)   is cut from the reel and the reel moved away before other explosives are loaded,

(b)   extends at least 1 metre from the hole in the case of holes that are 3 metres or more deep, and

(c)   is drawn taut and made secure at the top of the hole.

647(2) A surface mine blaster must ensure that inserting detonating cords, loading the hole and stemming is as continuous an operation as is practically possible.

647(3) A surface mine blaster must ensure that

(a)   no splices in the detonating cord are inserted within a blast hole,

(b)   detonating cords are not coupled to a trunk line, charged hole or delay or relay until final blast preparation,

(c)   the main or trunk line splices

(i)   are tight square knots, or

(ii)   are spliced by another method acceptable to the manufacturer,

(d) the trunk lines are free from kinks or coils when laid out,

(e) main or trunk lines are not laid out from a moving vehicle unless

(i)   the surface mine blaster is in attendance at the rear of the vehicle, or

(ii)   the vehicle is moving at idle speed,

(f) all connections in the line, other than splices, are tight and at right angles,

(g) detonators are not attached to the detonating cord until everything else is ready for blast initiation, and

(h) the detonator is attached to the detonating cord by a method acceptable to the manufacturer.

Ignition precautions

648(1) An employer must ensure that only machinery directly involved in loading an explosive is operated within 8 metres of a hole being loaded with explosive.

648(2) A worker must not load a hole or prime an explosive charge if machinery other than that directly involved in the loading is operating within 8 metres of the hole or the explosive charge.

648(3) A worker must not smoke tobacco or allow an open flame or other possible means of ignition within 8 metres of a blast area.

Safety fuses

649   A surface mine blaster must ensure that safety fuses protrude at least 1.5 metres from the drill hole.

Electrical cables and wires

650   A surface mine blaster must ensure that

(a) the blasting cable assembly is not grounded,

(b) the insulation of the blasting cable is kept in good condition to avoid grounding, and

(c) the splice connections between detonator wires and the blasting cable are kept clear of the ground or otherwise protected to prevent grounding.

Electric blasting

651(1) This section applies to electric blasting in the presence of electromagnetic radiation.

651(2) If blasting is within 60 metres of an overhead power line, a surface mine blaster must ensure that precautions are taken to prevent

(a) an electrical charge build-up in the blasting circuit, and

(b) damage or short-circuiting of the overhead power line.

651(3) An employer must ensure that electric detonators are not used at a blast area if radiofrequency transmitters or other radiofrequency fields are closer than the distances listed in Schedule 11, Tables 1 and 2.

651(4) A surface mine blaster must ensure that lead wires laid out from the connecting wires are not within 1 metre of any trailing cables.

Burning explosives

652 If a surface mine blaster is of the opinion that explosives are burning in a drill hole, the surface mine blaster must not allow a worker to return to the area of the hole until the surface mine blaster is of the opinion that it is safe to return.

Misfires

653(1) An employer must ensure that a misfire identified by a worker is not dug out by an excavator except under the direction of a surface mine blaster or a competent worker appointed by the employer.

653(2) An employer must ensure that a hole drilled in order to blast or disperse a misfired charge is drilled under the direction of a surface mine blaster or a competent worker appointed by the employer.

Drilling near explosives

654(1) Subject to section 653(2), an employer must ensure that workers do not drill within 5 metres of a charged blast hole.

654(2) If a charge or shot has been fired, an employer must ensure that workers do not drill until the area to be drilled is examined by a surface mine blaster for misfires and cut-off holes.

Storage

655(1) An employer must ensure that only sufficient explosives are taken to a mine to provide a 24-hour supply.

655(2) A surface mine blaster must ensure that explosives and detonators, including detonating relays, are stored in separate operation storage boxes that are kept not less than 8 metres apart.

655(3) An employer must ensure that the operation storage boxes are a type 6 magazine, as defined in the *Storage Standards for Industrial Explosives* (M81-7/2001E), published by Natural Resources Canada.

655(4) An employer must ensure that operation storage boxes are

    (a) locked at all times when not in use,

    (b) placed not less than 60 metres from a blasting area or an operating unit of equipment,

    (c) placed not less than 8 metres from a track, roadway, travel way or power cable, and

    (d) identified by a luminous or reflecting sign reading "Danger Explosives."

Blasting warnings

656(1) Before an electric blasting system is connected, a surface mine blaster must ensure that signs are posted around the blast area warning that mobile radio transmitters must be turned off within 20 metres of the blast area.

656(2) If electric blasting is being conducted near a public road, an employer must ensure that an approach sign is posted on the road that reads as follows:

BLASTING

DRIVERS MUST TURN OFF MOBILE TRANSMITTERS UNTIL FURTHER POSTED NOTICE

WATCH FOR IT ON THE RIGHT SIDE

656(3) If electric blasting is being conducted near a public road, an employer must ensure that a departure sign is posted on the road that reads as follows:

YOU MAY RESUME TRANSMITTING

THANK YOU

Charged holes

657   A surface mine blaster must ensure that a charged hole is not left unattended unless

(a)   if an electric detonator is being used, the ends of the electric detonator wires are shorted, and

(b)   a warning sign is posted that reads as follows:

DANGER: CHARGED SHOT HOLES

Underground Mines and Tunnels

Application

658   Sections 659 to 679 apply to explosives used in underground mines or tunnels.

Permitted explosives

659(1) An employer must ensure that a worker in an underground coal mine uses explosives or detonators that are classed as "permitted explosives" by a laboratory approved by the Director.

659(2) Despite subsection (1), the Director may authorize a worker in an underground coal mine to use explosives that are not classed as "permitted explosives" if

(a)   the proposed blasting is to be performed in solid rock,

(b)   an application is made to the Director using the form in Schedule 11, Table 3, and

(c)   the employer puts in place safety measures certified by a professional engineer and approved by the Director.

659(3) An employer must ensure that a worker does not take into an underground coal mine explosives that the worker cannot use under subsection (1) or (2).

Electric conveyance

660   An employer must ensure that explosives are not transported on an electric locomotive, on a conveyance moved by an electric locomotive or wire rope, on a conveyor or in a shuttle car unless the explosives

(a)   are in special closed containers, and

(b)   the Director gives permission in writing.

Mine shaft conveyance

661 An employer must not allow workers to transport explosives on a hoist in a mine shaft unless procedures are developed to ensure the safe transport of the explosives.

Transport underground

662(1) An employer must ensure that explosives taken underground are

    (a) in a secure case or canister with detonators kept separately from the explosives, and

    (b) in a quantity sufficient for a working shift.

662(2) The Director may exempt an underground mine from subsection (1).

662(3) An underground mine blaster must ensure that a case or canister

    (a) is kept closed until immediately before the shot hole is charged, and

    (b) is closed immediately after the shot hole is charged.

662(4) Repealed

662(5) If there are two or more cases or canisters containing explosives at a working face because two or more workers are working together, the underground mine blaster must ensure the cases or canisters are kept as far apart as is reasonably practicable.

662(6) A worker carrying electric detonators must not enter a room where lamps or batteries are charged.

Drilling distances

663 An employer must ensure that a worker does not drill a hole within 300 millimetres of a hole that has contained explosives.

Underground mine blaster

664(1) An underground mine blaster must

    (a) personally prepare all primer charges,

    (b) make tests for the presence of flammable gas immediately

        (i) before the holes are charged,

        (ii) before the round is fired, and

        (iii) after returning to the working face when a shot is fired,

    (c) regulate the quantity of explosive used in each hole, and

    (d) ensure that blasting cable is

        (i) disconnected and short-circuited and kept short-circuited at the blasting apparatus end until ready to attach the blasting apparatus, and

        (ii) staggered in length, at the detonator end, to prevent short-circuiting.

664(2) An underground mine blaster must not load or fire explosives if, within 25 metres of a hole,

    (a) the atmosphere contains more than 1 percent of methane or 20 percent of the lower explosive limit of a flammable gas,

(b) there is coal dust that has not been treated with a minimum of 6 kilograms of incombustible dust per hole or 75 kilograms of incombustible dust per working face, whichever is greater, or

(c) the area has been thoroughly wetted.

664(3) If the atmosphere within 25 metres of a hole contains more than 1 percent of methane or 20 percent of the lower explosive limit of a flammable gas, the underground mine blaster

(a) must not load the blast hole, and

(b) must fill the blast hole with stemming material.

664(4) Before firing a round, an underground mine blaster must

(a) post guards not less than 75 metres from the blast area to stop workers from approaching the blast area while the shot is fired and the guards must remain in position until released by the blaster,

(b) couple the cables to the detonator and blasting apparatus, and

(c) take refuge in a manhole or other safe place not less than 75 metres from the blast area.

664(5) An underground mine blaster must not allow a worker to return to the face after a blast until the expiration of a waiting period of at least 10 minutes or for a longer period determined by the underground mine blaster.

Blasting cable

665(1) An underground mine blaster must use a blasting cable

(a) designed for that purpose, and

(b) with a resistance of less than 2 ohms.

665(2) An underground mine blaster must ensure that a cable used in blasting

(a) is not less than 75 metres long, and

(b) reaches from the blast area to a suitable refuge for the underground mine blaster.

Use of detonators

666 A worker charging the shot hole must insert the detonator in the primer cartridge and insert the primer cartridge first with the detonator at the back of the hole.

Same manufacturer

667 An underground mine blaster must ensure that all the electric detonators used in the same round are made by a single manufacturer.

Series connection

668 An underground mine blaster must ensure that all the charges to be fired in the same round are connected in series, except in shaft excavation work.

Water

669 An underground mine blaster must ensure that only a water-resistant explosive, or an explosive sheathed to make it waterproof, is used if water may enter the hole before it is fired.

Stemming

670(1) An underground mine blaster must ensure that

   (a)   all blast holes are stemmed,

   (b)   stemming is to the collar in shot holes, and

   (c)   a non-flammable substance or material is used for stemming.

670(2) If water stemming is used, the underground mine blaster must ensure that

   (a)   a layer of clay at least 100 millimetres thick is tamped into the hole between the charge and the stemming, or

   (b)   the water is in at least two separate packings.

Firing in the same round

671   An underground mine blaster must ensure that only holes to be fired in the same round are charged and tamped before the round is fired.

Misfires

672(1) A mine manager must ensure that a misfire is handled under the direct supervision of an underground mine blaster.

672(2) If a misfire occurs, the underground mine blaster must ensure that

   (a)   no worker returns to the working face until the expiration of a waiting period of at least 10 minutes, and

   (b)   the blasting cable is disconnected from the blasting apparatus and the cable ends short-circuited before a worker examines the misfire to determine the cause of the misfire.

672(3) An underground mine blaster must ensure that a worker removes an explosive from a loaded blast hole only by using a jet of water.

672(4) A worker must not pull a detonator lead wire from a charged blast hole.

Misfire detonation

673(1) An attempt to detonate a misfire must be done as a single hole blast.

673(2) If the attempt to detonate a misfire is unsuccessful, an underground mine blaster must ensure that the worker deactivating the misfire

   (a)   removes the minimum amount of stemming material from the misfired hole required to establish the true direction of the hole,

   (b)   fires a separate charge parallel to the misfired charge and no closer to it than 300 millimetres,

   (c)   after detonating the parallel hole, exercises extra caution while the rock broken by the blast is loaded out of the working face, and

   (d)   searches for cartridges, their parts or detonators during and after the rock loading is complete.

673(3) If there is a faulty electric detonator, an underground mine blaster must ensure that a worker short-circuits the leg wires.

Leaving a misfire

674(1) If a misfire is not deactivated in the same work shift as the one in which it occurred, the underground mine blaster must erect a warning board or fence bearing a sign "DO NOT ENTER — MISFIRE" across the whole width of the tunnel or location of the blast area before leaving the misfire unattended.

674(2) An underground mine blaster must report to the blaster's supervisor the location of a misfire that is not deactivated.

Compressed air

675   If compressed air is used to break coal, an employer must ensure that a professional engineer prepares a detailed procedure to be used and certifies it as safe.

Shock blasting

676(1) If an area of an underground mine is subject to sudden outbursts of gas or coal, the Director, on written application by the employer, may allow shock blasting.

676(2) An application to the Director to allow shock blasting under subsection (1) must be prepared by a professional engineer and must include

    (a)   the location in the underground mine where the shock blasting will take place,

    (b)   detailed reasons for shock blasting, and

    (c)   the proposed safety procedures.

Surface shots

677   An employer must ensure that no worker remains in an underground mine at the time an underground blast is fired from the surface.

Permanent firing station

678(1) When shots are fired from a permanent underground firing station, an employer must ensure that the only workers remaining in the blast area at the time of firing are

    (a)   the underground mine blaster, and

    (b)   not more than two blast guards appointed by the employer.

678(2) When shots are fired from a permanent underground firing station, an employer must ensure that no worker, other than the underground mine blaster and blast guards, is downwind from where the shots are fired.

Secondary blasting

679(1) If charges are placed directly on top of the material being blasted in an underground mine, an underground mine blaster must ensure that

    (a)   the charges weigh not more than 0.5 kilograms,

    (b)   not more than two charges are fired at any one time,

    (c)   only instantaneous detonators are used,

    (d)   the surrounding area within a radius of 10 metres is clear of coal dust and dusted with incombustible dust, and

    (e)   each charge is covered with stemming material and not less than 10 kilograms of incombustible dust.

679(2) An underground mine blaster must ensure that, if charges are placed directly on top of the material being blasted in an underground mine, the charges are not fired if the methane content in the surrounding area is more than 0.3 percent (6 percent of the lower explosive limit).

679(3) An underground mine blaster must ensure that if charges are placed directly on top of the material being blasted in an underground mine, a refuge or shelter for the blaster is located not less than 150 metres away from the charges

Division 3:   Underground Coal Mines

Application

680   This Division applies to underground coal mines.

Annual plan

681   An employer must ensure that the following mine plans, certified by a professional engineer, are submitted to the Director before the last day in September in each year for review:

    (a)   a proposed underground operations working plan for the next year's operation;

    (b)   a ventilation plan for operations in the next year of operation.

Underground coal mine surveyor

682(1) An employer must appoint a worker as an underground coal mine surveyor.

682(2) An underground coal mine surveyor must make all surveys and mine plans required under this Part.

682(3) All survey plans for an underground coal mine must be approved by a professional engineer.

Mine Workers

Supervision

683   An employer at an underground coal mine must ensure that a worker employed underground is under the supervision of the holder of an underground coal mine manager's certificate or an underground coal mine foreman's certificate.

Required qualifications

684(1) An employer must not appoint a worker as an underground coal mine manager or acting underground coal mine manager unless the worker holds an underground coal mine manager's certificate issued under the *Occupational Health and Safety Regulation.*

684(2) An employer must not appoint a worker as an underground coal mine foreman or acting underground coal mine foreman unless the worker holds an underground coal mine foreman's certificate issued under the *Occupational Health and Safety Regulation.*

684(3) An employer must not appoint a worker as underground coal mine electrical superintendent or acting underground coal mine electrical superintendent unless the worker holds an underground coal mine electrical superintendent's certificate issued under the *Occupational Health and Safety Regulation.*

Mine manager

685(1) An employer must

(a) appoint an underground coal mine manager to supervise daily activities at an underground coal mine, and

(b) notify the Director of the appointment without undue delay.

(c) **Repealed**

685(2) An employer may appoint an underground coal mine foreman as a temporary underground coal mine manager if

(a) the foreman holds an underground coal mine foreman's certificate,

(b) not more than 30 workers in total are working underground at any one time, and

(c) the appointment is for a period that does not exceed seven calendar days.

685(3) An employer must ensure that whenever the underground coal mine manager is absent from the mine site for a period not exceeding seven calendar days, the underground coal mine manager maintains, as far as is reasonably practicable, constant communication with the mine site.

685(4) An employer must appoint an acting underground coal mine manager for any absence of the underground coal mine manager that exceeds seven calendar days but is less than 90 calendar days.

685(5) An employer must

(a) appoint a new underground coal mine manager for any absence of the underground coal mine manager that exceeds 90 calendar days, and

(b) inform the Director of the appointment as soon as possible.

Combined operations

686(1) If surface mining operations and underground coal mining operations with the same owner take place simultaneously and are in such proximity that mining in one may affect the safety of workers in the other, they must be declared a "combined operation" by

(a) the owner,

(b) an employer of the surface mine or an employer of the underground coal mine, or

(c) the Director.

686(2) If surface mining operations and underground coal mining operations are declared to be a combined operation, overall control of the mining activities must be coordinated under the direction of a single mine manager, who may be the underground coal mine manager or the manager of the surface mine, without either being relieved of the responsibility for their separate mines.

686(3) Nothing in subsection (2) shall be construed to mean that only one mine manager is required under this Code for two or more mining operations.

Working alone

687(1) Only a worker who is sampling, testing or inspecting at a working face may work alone at a working face.

687(2) Subject to subsection (1), an underground coal mine manager must ensure that no worker works at producing coal while alone at a working face.

Unsafe conditions

688(1) A worker in a mine must immediately notify the workers and a mine official if the workers are exposed to a hazard if the worker discovers the following:

    (a) the ventilation is interrupted;

    (b) an air crossing, door, stopping, brattice or duct is damaged;

    (c) an air flow in an air course is reduced by a disruption;

    (d) a weakness in a roof or rib;

    (e) a deficiency of a roof or rib;

    (f) evidence of movement in a roof or rib;

    (g) smoke or fire;

    (h) an accumulation of gas or water;

    (i) any other hazard to workers.

688(2) If a worker at the surface of a mine discovers a hazard to workers in the mine, the worker must immediately notify a mine official.

688(3) A mine official to whom a hazard to workers is reported under subsection (1) or (2) must

    (a) take immediate steps to withdraw workers exposed to a hazard until the defect is remedied, and

    (b) assess the hazard and remedy it if possible.

688(4) The mine official must record an incident reported under subsection (1) or (2) and the record must be available for workers at the mine.

Shift change

689 An underground coal mine foreman must ensure that entrances to any place found unsafe during a work shift are fenced, cordoned or taped off and signed at sufficient distances to prevent workers from entering the unsafe place.

Shift report

690(1) An employer must ensure that a shift report is completed by an underground coal mine foreman at a mine.

690(2) At the beginning of a work shift, an underground coal mine foreman must read and initial the reports of the underground coal mine foreman of the immediately preceding shift and note whether a hazard has been reported.

690(3) Before work begins, an underground coal mine foreman must inspect that section of the mine assigned to the underground coal mine foreman unless an inspection was carried out by an underground coal mine foreman within the immediately preceding four hours.

690(4) Immediately at the end of a work shift, an underground coal mine foreman must post an inspection report that includes the names of workers remaining in the foreman's section of the mine at the end of the work shift.

690(5) The report posted under subsection (4) must be in the designated place and accessible to anyone who might need to determine the location and number of workers who are still underground.

Record of workers

691   An employer must ensure a daily report is kept in the shift report of

(a)   the times at which each worker checked in and out of the mine, and

(b)   the name of each worker who remains in the mine beyond the end of the regular shift.

Self rescuers

692   An employer must

(a)   provide or make available to each worker who goes underground, an approved self-contained self rescuer device, rated at a minimum of one hour,

(b)   require that each worker be in possession of a self rescuer at all times when underground,

(c)   ensure that each worker receives training in

(i)   the proper procedures for use, donning and switch-over of the self rescuer during an emergency, and

(ii)   the location of underground caches of additional self rescuers,

(d)   ensure that each worker receives refresher training every three months in the subjects referred to in (c),

(e)   ensure that a record of the training is maintained at the mine for at least three years and is available to an officer upon request, and

(f)   store and strategically locate as many additional units as may be required by workers walking from the most distant working face to the defined emergency exit during a mine emergency.

Means of ignition

693(1) An employer must

(a)   ensure that workers entering a mine do not take smoking materials, matches or other means of ignition into the mine,

(b)   direct all workers who enter a mine, or such number of workers as may be selected using a system approved by the Director, to be searched to confirm that they are not carrying any prohibited means of ignition, and

(c)   ensure that any worker who refuses to be searched is refused entry into the mine.

693(2) Workers must not have in their possession, or otherwise transport, smoking materials, matches or other means of ignition when they enter a mine.

693(3) A worker must not use smoking materials, matches or other means of ignition in a mine.

693(4) Subsections (1) to (3) do not prohibit a worker from taking an approved explosive initiating apparatus or cutting equipment specifically permitted by this Code into a mine, or from using it.

No smoking warnings

694   An employer must ensure that areas at the surface in which tobacco or matches or other means of ignition are not allowed are clearly marked as no smoking areas.

Mine equipment

Recognizing international standards

694.1 Equipment for use in underground coal mines that is approved to a current, relevant standard in another country can be used subject to the approval of the Director.

Propane installations

695(1) An employer must ensure that propane installations in proximity to underground workings are installed and maintained in accordance with the manufacturer's specifications and the *Safety Codes Act*.

695(2) An employer must ensure that precautions are taken to prevent

(a) moving vehicles from contacting propane installations, and

(b) propane from collecting in low areas.

695(3) An employer must ensure that propane installations are inspected once each week by a competent worker to ensure the propane does not leak into an underground working or ventilation system of the mine or a building or other structure.

695(4) An employer must ensure that, as part of the mine maintenance scheme, a competent worker examines the burners, relighters, vapourizers, storage tanks and all associated protective devices every three months to ensure the equipment is functioning and there is no leakage of propane.

695(5) An employer must ensure that a detection system operates at all times that

(a) will detect propane from leaking into the ventilation system of a mine, and

(b) visibly or audibly warns workers of the leak.

695(6) An employer must ensure that no furnace or device for heating mine air is installed without the written approval of the Director.

Bulk fuel storage

696(1) An employer must ensure that bulk fuel storage facilities are located on ground that is impervious to the substances being stored.

696(2) An employer must ensure that bulk fuel storage facilities are

(a) located at a lower ground elevation than the entrance to an underground working,

(b) placed in a secondary containment structure, or

(c) protected by an earthen berm to prevent propane or other fuel from entering the underground working.

Voice communication

697(1) An employer must ensure that a mine has a voice communication system between the surface and underground that consists of interconnected voice communication stations.

697(2) Subsection (1) does not apply to exploration drivages from the surface that are not more than 60 metres long.

697(3) An employer must ensure that a voice communication system has a separate back-up power supply that operates if there is a power failure.

Location

698(1) An employer must ensure that interconnected voice communication stations in a mine are located at the following:

(a) the top and bottom of mine shafts and mine tunnel outlets and main hoisting and haulage engines;

(b) main electrical distribution centres, both at the surface and underground;

(c) main pumping stations;

(d) refuge stations;

(e) at the drive of a conveyor belt and, if the conveyor belt is more than 60 metres long, at the tail end of the conveyor belt;

(f) booster fans;

(g) underground garages and repair shops;

(h) a mining section as close as is practicable to the working face and, in the case of a longwall face, to each end of the working face;

(i) permanently attended surface stations.

698(2) The Director may require an employer to locate interconnected voice communication stations in a mine at a place not referred to in subsection (1).

Permanently attended stations

699(1) An employer must ensure that a permanently attended surface communication station in the voice communication system of a mine has a telephone connection to the public telephone system.

699(2) An employer must ensure that a communication station in the voice communication system of a mine has an audible alarm that is

(a) initiated from the permanently attended surface communication station, and

(b) sounded in case of emergency.

Portal

700(1) An employer must ensure that all parts of a portal are constructed of non-flammable materials.

700(2) An employer must ensure, before a portal is constructed, that a professional engineer prepares and certifies a portal construction plan that

(a) includes drawings, diagrams and instructions detailing the design of the portal, and

(b) specifies how the portal is to be safely constructed and positioned while protecting workers from falling or collapsing ground.

Mine outlets

701(1) An employer must ensure that there are at least two separate and independent mine openings or outlets by which workers can leave a mine.

701(2) An employer must ensure that the mine openings

(a) **Repealed**

(b) are connected to the mine voice communication system.

701(2.1)   An employer must ensure that the mine openings or outlets are certified by a professional engineer so that in the event of any reasonably foreseeable incident, at least one opening will allow egress of workers.

701(3) Subsection (1) does not apply to the following:

  (a) a new mine where mine openings are being constructed;

  (b) a location where the mine voice communication system is in the process of being constructed between mine openings;

  (c) a location where ground is being excavated for the purposes of searching for or proving mineral deposits.

701(4) If there is only a single means of exit in an underground working, an employer must ensure that the number of workers in the working is never greater than nine in total, unless others are needed to secure the health and safety of those nine workers in an emergency.

Escape ways

702(1) The underground coal mine manager must ensure that shafts, tunnels, levels, ladders, stairs and similar installations used as escape ways

  (a) are kept free from accumulations of ice and obstructions of every kind, and

  (b) have signs posted where necessary to show the direction to the surface outlet, and

  (c) are provided with continuous directional guide lines or equivalent devices that are

  (i)   installed and maintained throughout the entire length of each escapeway,

  (ii) made of durable material,

  (iii) marked with reflective material every 8 metres,

  (iv) located in a manner that allows effective escape,

  (v)   equipped with directional indicators, signifying the route of escape, and placed at intervals not exceeding 30 metres, and

  (vi) securely attached to, and marked to show the location of, any self-contained, self rescuer storage locations in the escapeways.

702(2) An underground coal mine manager must ensure that all water is conducted away from stairways.

702(3) An employer must ensure that shafts, tunnels and slopes used as escape ways and inclined at more than 30 degrees from horizontal have ladders, walkways or other apparatus that

  (a) are designed to allow workers to leave the mine safely,

  (b) are kept in good repair, and

  (c) lead to the mine opening.

702(4) An employer must ensure that the airway and travelling road of an escapeway are not less than 2 metres high and 2 metres wide.

Manholes

703(1) An employer must ensure that a haulage mine level or tunnel in which workers normally travel has manholes or places of refuge at intervals of not more than 20 metres.

703(2) Despite subsection (1), manholes or places of refuge are not required if

(a)   the speed of haulage does not exceed 8 kilometres per hour, and

(b)   there is clear standing room of at least 1 metre between the side of the equipment and the side of the road.

703(3) An employer must ensure that a manhole or place of refuge is

(a)   at least 1 metre wide, 1.3 metres deep and 1.8 metres high,

(b)   kept clear at all times,

(c)   clearly identified as a manhole or place of refuge, and

(d)   numbered.

Vehicles

Underground fuel stations

704(1) An underground coal mine manager must ensure that diesel fuel tanks of vehicles filled underground are filled at designated fuel stations certified by a professional engineer.

704(2) An employer must ensure that an underground fuel station

(a)   has a smooth concrete floor,

(b)   is constructed of non-flammable material,

(c)   has fireproof doors with the door nearest the fueling point opening outwards, and

(d)   has a sump in the floor, or collecting pans, at possible spillage points.

704(3) An employer must ensure that an underground fuel station has appropriate fire fighting equipment.

Diesel fuel

705(1) An employer must ensure that diesel fuel supplied at a fuel station

(a)   at least meets the requirements of CGSB Standard CAN/CGSB 3.16-99 AMEND, *Mining Diesel Fuel*, and

(b)   is not stored underground in quantities greater than the quantity required for 24 hour's work unless permission to store more is given by the Director.

705(2) An employer must ensure that workers take precautions to prevent the diesel fuel from spilling while the fuel tanks are filled.

705(3) An employer must ensure that all empty diesel fuel containers are removed from the mine daily.

705(4) An underground coal mine manager must ensure that spilled oil and diesel fuel is immediately taken up with a non-flammable absorbent material that is

(a)   deposited in a fireproof receptacle, and

(b)   removed from the mine at intervals of not more than every three days.

705(5) An employer must ensure that a copy of subsections (1) to (4) is posted in a conspicuous place at an underground fuel station.

Control of equipment

706(1) An employer must ensure that the control levers of storage battery locomotives, trolley locomotives and vehicles are designed so that the levers

    (a)   can only be removed when the lever is in the neutral position, and

    (b)   are spring-loaded or biased to return to the neutral position.

706(2) If remote controlled equipment is used at a mine site, the employer must ensure it is used in accordance with the manufacturer's specifications.

Roof and Side Support

Support system

707(1) If an entry or roadway is to be excavated in an underground coal mine, an employer must ensure that a geotechnical analysis of the strata and structures is conducted by a professional engineer to determine the effects of the strata and structures on the entry or roadway excavation.

707(2) An employer must ensure that a professional engineer certifies

    (a)   the support system of the roof and sides of a roadway, and

    (b)   the dimensions of all support pillars.

707(3) The professional engineer referred to in subsection (2) must take into consideration the following:

    (a)   the depth of cover and stratigraphy;

    (b)   the nature and character of the strata immediately above the roof horizon, the further overlying strata and the floor strata;

    (c)   the strength characteristics of the roof, sides, floor strata and the coal seam;

    (d)   the thickness and sequence of bedding planes and other planes of weakness in relation to the application of supports;

    (e)   the local hydrogeology;

    (f)   the structural control including faults, synclines, anticlines and other known abnormalities;

    (g)   the proximity of any surface glacial deposits and their stability;

    (h)   the possible interaction between underlying and overlying coal seams, mine workings, pillars, aquifers, geological features and the proposed mine workings;

    (i)   the mining sequence;

    (j)   with respect to the general roadways layout and related extraction, the possible impact at the surface area and its infrastructure;

    (k)   the geotechnical analysis referred to in subsection (1); and

    (l)   the propensity of the coal and surrounding strata for sudden bursts of solids and/or gas.

707(4) Nothing in this section prevents a worker from setting additional supports if the worker considers them to be necessary for safety.

Extractions

708(1) If solid mineral pillars or blocks are to be extracted from a mine, an employer must ensure that a systematic method and sequence of extraction is prepared in which

    (a) workers are not required to work beneath an unsupported roof, and

    (b) workers are not subjected to the hazard of the collapse of a side or rib.

708(2) The method and sequence of extraction must be certified by a professional engineer.

Operating procedures

709(1) An employer must prepare a code of practice for installing and maintaining or removing ground supports that prescribes the procedures to be followed by workers.

709(2) A mine official must post a copy of the code of practice prepared under subsection (1) in a conspicuous location at the mine.

Removal of ground supports

710(1) A worker must not remove a ground support without the permission of a mine official.

710(2) If work requires the removal of ground supports prescribed by this Code, the underground coal mine manager must ensure that there are temporary supports in place.

710(3) Despite subsection (2), other supports must not be used to protect workers from falling ground if

    (a) supports are withdrawn from the gob, or

    (b) supports are withdrawn under a roof that appears to the mine official to be insecure.

710(4) A professional engineer must certify the means to be used to protect workers from falling ground if

    (a) supports are withdrawn from the gob, or

    (b) supports are withdrawn under a roof that appears to the mine official to be insecure.

Ventilation System

Ventilation system

711(1) An employer must ensure that a mine has a mechanical ventilation system, certified by a professional engineer, that

    (a) dilutes, displaces, eliminates or otherwise renders harmless all noxious or flammable gases and harmful substances,

    (b) keeps work areas and accessible roads fit for workers to work or travel in,

    (c) ensures that the air contains at least 19.5 percent oxygen by volume and not more than 0.5 percent carbon dioxide by volume, and

    (d) ensures that a minimum volume of 1.9 cubic metres per second of air passes active working headings.

711(2) An employer must develop safe operating procedures for the ventilation system that are certified by a professional engineer.

711(3) An employer must ensure that

(a) the ventilation system is designed to prevent the raising of dust, and

(b) compressed air is not used for ventilation.

Air velocity

712(1) An employer must ensure that a ventilation system in a mine maintains a minimum air velocity at working faces of 0.3 metres per second.

712(2) An employer must ensure that a ventilation system maintains a minimum air velocity in roadways, other than working headings, of 0.3 metres per second unless methane layering is occurring, in which case the air velocity must be increased to prevent the methane layering.

712(3) An employer must ensure that the velocity of the air in a ventilation system is not more than

(a) **Repealed**

(b) 5 metres per second in a coal conveyor road, and

(c) 8 metres per second in other roadways.

712(4) The Director may grant an acceptance changing the requirements of subsections (2) or (3) only after reviewing a proposal certified by a professional engineer.

Return airway

713 An employer must ensure that underground oil transformers rated at more than 1000 kilovoltamperes, garages, bulk oil storage areas and fuel stations are ventilated by air that flows directly to the return airway.

Doors

714(1) An employer must ensure that airlock doors

(a) remain open no longer than is necessary for workers or vehicles to pass through,

(b) are designed to be self-closing, and

(c) operate in such a way that if one door of the airlock system is open, the other door remains closed.

714(2) A worker must not, without the authority of the employer,

(a) leave a ventilation door open that the worker found shut, or

(b) leave a ventilation door closed that the worker found open.

714(3) An employer must ensure that an airlock located in major connections between the main air intake and the air return has a door system in which at least one door remains closed if there is an air reversal.

Stoppings

715 An employer must ensure that

(a) ventilation stoppings between intake and return airways prevent air leaks,

(b) the space between the faces of ventilation stoppings and roadways is kept free of obstructions, and

(c) ventilation stoppings are constructed at crosscuts on each side of the conveyor system up to the last crosscut before the tail end of the last conveyor in order to minimize the potential contamination of those airways.

Seals

716(1) An employer must ensure that worked out or inaccessible parts of a mine are sealed off unless otherwise approved by the Director.

716(1.1) The seals referred to in subsection (1) must withstand an overpressure of at least 345 kilopascals.

716(2) An employer must ensure that a worked out district is sealed off within three months after mining stops in the district unless otherwise approved by the Director.

716(3) An employer must ensure that workers monitor conditions at a seal to ensure that a hazardous condition does not develop.

716(4) An employer must ensure that a seal constructed to contain fire, spontaneous heating or another similar hazard is

(a) certified by a professional engineer,

(b) constructed to withstand the force of an explosion in the sealed off area, and

(c) has a method of sampling the atmosphere and draining water from behind the seal.

Chutes

717   An employer must ensure that, in a system with chutes passing from an upper to a lower mine level, mineral or rock is kept in the chutes above the bulkhead to prevent any passage of air.

Splits

718(1) An employer must ensure that a coal mine is divided into splits.

718(2) An employer must ensure that each split and each working face in a split is supplied with a separate current of fresh air.

718(3) An employer must ensure that the return air from a working split goes directly to the return airway.

Fans

719(1) An employer must ensure that

(a) all main fans in a mine have an automatic ventilating pressure recording device that is always operating and monitored daily,

(b) a mine has a standby main fan, and

(c) a mine has an emergency power supply capable of running the main fan if the principle source of power fails.

719(2) An employer must keep a record of the ventilating pressures taken and the dates on which they were taken.

Reverse flows

720(1) Repealed

720(2) A worker must not reverse the air flow of a main fan without the underground coal mine manager's authorization.

Surface fans

721(1) An employer must ensure that the main surface ventilating fans

    (a)   are offset by not less than 5 metres from the nearest side of the mine opening, and

    (b)   have non-combustible air ducts and housing.

721(2) An employer must ensure that the mine opening referred to in subsection (1) is protected by one or more weak walls or explosion doors, or a combination of weak walls and explosion doors, located in direct line with possible explosive forces.

721(3) Despite subsection (1), the main surface ventilating fan may be located directly in front of or over a mine opening if

    (a)   the opening is not in a direct line with possible air blasts coming out of the mine, and

    (b)   there is another opening not less than 5 metres and not more than 30 metres from the fan opening that

        (i)   is in a direct line with possible air blasts coming out of the mine, and

        (ii)   has explosion doors.

Booster fans

722   An employer must ensure that a booster fan

    (a)   does not restrict the free passage of air delivered by a main fan if the booster fans stops,

    (b)   stops if a main fan stops, and

    (c)   is continuously monitored by a system that alarms at a permanently attended monitoring station if the fan stops or its performance falls below an established efficiency level.

Auxiliary fans

723(1) An employer must ensure that an auxiliary fan used in a mine is electrically grounded.

723(2) An employer must ensure that a heading that is advanced more than 10 metres from the main ventilation circuit and a raise or sub-drift that is more than 10 metres from the main ventilation circuit has an auxiliary ventilation system, or a system of line brattices, to direct ventilation so that the face of the heading is swept by the ventilating air supply.

723(3) The distance referred to in subsection (2) must be measured from the nearest rib.

723(4) If a heading to be ventilated is less than 200 metres long, the auxiliary fan interlock requirement of Clause 6.2.3 of CSA Standard M421-00 (R2007), *Use of Electricity in Mines*, does not apply.

Brattice, vent tubes

724(1) If brattice or vent tubes are used to ventilate the working face, an employer must ensure that the brattice or vent tubes are kept advanced as close as possible to the working face.

724(2) An employer must ensure that brattice or vent tubes used in a mine are constructed of materials that meet the requirements of CSA Standard CAN/CSA M427-M91 (R2001), *Fire-Performance and Antistatic Requirements for Ventilation Materials.*

Operating procedures for booster and auxiliary fans

725(1) An employer must ensure that

    (a)   if a booster fan or auxiliary fan stops, workers in an area that is affected by the stopping move to a place that is adequately ventilated, and

    (b)   a competent worker tests the affected area to ensure it is adequately ventilated before other workers enter the area.

725(2) An employer must ensure that an auxiliary fan is not restarted unless a competent worker has

    (a)   inspected the area underground that is serviced by the auxiliary fan and has tested for flammable gases,

    (b)   declared in writing that it is safe to restart the auxiliary fan, and

    (c)   included a copy of the declaration in the supervisor's shift report.

725(3) An employer must develop a code of practice to be followed if a booster fan or an auxiliary fan stops and post it at a conspicuous location at the surface of the mine.

725(4) Repealed

Stopping fan

726(1) A worker must not stop a fan that provides ventilation for a mine without the consent of the mine official in charge.

726(2) If workers withdraw because a fan stops or there is a decrease in ventilation, an employer must ensure that no worker is re-admitted to the mine, to part of the mine or to a split until

    (a)   the fan is in operation and ventilation is restored,

    (b)   the work areas are examined by a mine official,

    (c)   a report that the workings are safe is made by a mine official in a book that is kept at the mine for that purpose, and

    (d)   a copy of the report is posted in a conspicuous location.

726(3) Subsection (2) does not apply to the mine official examining the work area.

Ventilation monitoring

727(1) An employer must appoint a competent worker who must measure the barometric pressure outside the mine and the velocity and quantity of air in all airways and old workings of the mine that are accessible to workers.

727(2) An employer must ensure that measurements under subsection (1) are, at a minimum, taken

(a) at the main airway as near as is reasonably practicable to the point at which the air enters or leaves the mine,

(b) within each split or part of the mine

    (i) as near as reasonably practicable to the points at which air enters and leaves the split or part of the mine, and

    (ii) in longwall workings, within 10 metres of the working face in the intake and return airways,

(c) in other mining methods, as near as is reasonably practicable to the last open cross cut,

(d) as near as is reasonably practicable to the working face of each active heading, and

(e) at seals along intake air courses where intake air passes by a seal to ventilate active working sections.

727(3) The appointed worker must notify the mine manager of any abnormalities in the barometric pressure or the velocity and quantity of air.

727(4) An employer must ensure that the measurements under subsection (1) are taken at least once a week.

727(5) If the quality or quantity of air passing a place where the measurements are taken may be substantially affected because the ventilation system of a mine is altered, an employer must ensure that the appointed worker repeats the measurements as soon as the effect of the alteration would be apparent.

727(6) An underground coal mine manager must ensure that before the commencement of each work shift, the appointed worker takes temperature and barometric pressure readings outside the mine.

727(7) An appointed worker must

(a) record the results of the measurements taken under this section in the log book provided by the employer for that purpose,

(b) sign each entry, and

(c) post a copy of the results at the portal.

Cross cuts

728(1) Repealed

728(2) An employer must ensure that all cross-cuts except the one nearest to the working face are securely stopped off.

728(3) If an employer applies to the Director with specifications certified by a professional engineer, the Director may give an exemption from subsection (2).

Operating in split

729 An employer must ensure that not more than one coal mining machine operates in one split.

Gas and Dust Control

Gas inspections

730(1) An underground coal mine manager must ensure that a mine official

(a) always carries an approved gas testing device for methane, carbon monoxide and oxygen when underground, and

   (b) within four hours of each shift commencing work, inspects, with the device referred to in (a), that part of the mine being worked, or intended to be worked, and all related roadways.

730(2) A mine official must inspect for gas at the working face of every work area, at the edge of the gob, in roof cavities and anywhere else that gas may accumulate.

730(3) A mine official who makes the inspection must

   (a) report to the mine manager on the conditions of the part of the mine, the roadways and the explosion barriers inspected for gas and ventilation, and

   (b) enter and sign a detailed report of the inspection in a book kept at the mine for that purpose.

730(4) An underground coal mine manager must ensure that a copy of the report is immediately posted at a conspicuous location at the mine or the entrance to the inspected part of the mine, or at a place designated by the underground coal mine manager.

730(5) The report referred to in subsection (3)(b) must be examined and countersigned by the underground coal mine manager or designate at least once every day.

Flammable gas levels

731(1) An underground coal mine manager must ensure that workers are withdrawn from a work area if the amount of flammable gas in the general body of the air exceeds 40 percent of the lower explosive limit.

731(2) An underground coal mine manager must ensure that the supply of electrical power is automatically cut off if the amount of flammable gas in the general body of air exceeds 25 percent of the lower explosive limit.

731(3) An underground coal mine manager must ensure that workers do not blast if the amount of flammable gas in the general body of air exceeds 20 percent of the lower explosive limit.

731(4) An underground coal mine manager must ensure that workers do not operate diesel engines if the amount of flammable gas in the general body of air exceeds 20 percent of the lower explosive limit.

731(5) An underground coal mine manager must ensure that a bleeder system is designed such that the flammable gas level does not exceed 40 percent of the lower explosive limit.

Diesel vehicle roads

732(1) If workers operate a diesel vehicle in an underground coal mine, the underground coal mine manager must ensure that a worker measures the air flow and the percentage of flammable gas present in the general body of air at all points that the underground coal mine manager or the Director specify.

732(2) Repealed

732(3) An underground coal mine manager must ensure that a worker takes the measurements required under subsection (1)

   (a) at least once each week, and

   (b) whenever an alteration is made in the quantity of air circulating.

732(4) If the percentage of flammable gas measured under subsection (1) exceeds 15 percent of the lower explosive limit, the underground coal mine manager must appoint a competent worker who must

(a) take further measurements under subsection (1), and

(b) immediately submit a written report of the results to the mine manager.

732(5) If the percentage of flammable gas measured under subsection (1) exceeds 15 percent of the lower explosive limit continuously over a 24-hour period, the employer must install a system of continuous methane monitoring.

732(6) The measurements required by subsection (4) must continue to be taken until

(a) the percentage of flammable gas measured is less than 15 percent of the lower explosive limit, or

(b) a system of continuous methane monitoring is installed.

Degassing procedures

733(1) An employer must ensure that procedures for degassing headings are prepared and certified by a professional engineer.

733(2) An employer must ensure that a copy of the procedures for degassing headings is posted at a conspicuous location at the mine.

Gas removal

734 An employer must ensure that workers remove standing gas in a mine under the direct supervision of a mine official.

Unused areas

735(1) An employer must ensure that parts of a mine that are not being worked are, so far as is reasonably practicable, kept free of dangerous gases.

735(2) Repealed

Sealed off areas

736(1) An employer must ensure that parts of a mine that cannot be kept free of accumulations of gas are fenced off.

736(2) If an accumulation of gas cannot be safely removed, an employer must ensure that the affected parts are sealed in accordance with section 716.

Approval of devices for testing and measuring

737 An employer must ensure that combustible gas detectors and other devices used for testing and measuring air quality, velocity, and volume in a mine are approved for use in coal mines by one of the following:

(a) the United States Mines Safety and Health Administration, or its predecessors or successors in administration;

(b) the Ministry of Power of the Government of Great Britain, or its predecessors or successors in administration;

(c) the Department of Natural Resources, Canada, or its predecessors or successors in administration; or

(d) another organization or combination of organizations approved by the Director.

Combustible gas detector

738(1) An employer must ensure that a coal cutting machine is equipped with a combustible gas detector.

738(2) A worker operating a coal cutting machine must keep the combustible gas detector operating at all times.

738(3) An employer must ensure that the sensing device of a combustible gas detector is installed

    (a) as close to the cutting head as is reasonably practicable, and

    (b) not more than 3 metres from the cutting head.

738(4) Despite subsection (3), the Director may approve a distance of more than 3 metres from the cutting head.

738(5) An employer must ensure that the combustible gas detector

    (a) **Repealed**

    (b) has a distinct and separate visible or audible warning that is activated if the level of flammable gas reaches 20 percent of the lower explosive limit, and

    (c) automatically cuts off power to the cutting head if the level of flammable gas reaches 25 percent of the lower explosive limit.

738(6) If power to the cutting head is cut off, the operator must back the coal cutting machine out of the face and turn off the power to the machine.

Portable detector

739(1) A worker must not use a portable combustible gas detector unless an underground coal mine manager authorizes its use.

739(2) An underground coal mine manager may authorize a competent worker to use a portable combustible gas detector.

739(3) A portable combustible gas detector must comply with section 737.

739(4) An employer must ensure that before each shift, a portable combustible gas detector to be used underground is tested for accuracy and calibrated according to the manufacturer's specifications.

Breakdown of detector

740(1) A worker may continue to operate a coal cutting machine that has a broken combustible gas detector if

    (a) there is a continual monitoring by another combustible gas detector operated by a worker authorized under section 739, and

    (b) the flammable gas reading at the operator's cab does not exceed 15 percent of the lower explosive limit.

740(2) A worker must not operate a coal cutting machine that has a broken combustible gas detector after the end of the work shift in which it broke down.

Roof bolting

741(1) An employer must ensure that a worker operating a roof bolter

    (a) is competent to use a combustible gas detector,

    (b) carries a combustible gas detector, and

    (c) takes flammable gas readings at roof level.

741(2) An employer must ensure that workers do not drill or install bolts at a location where methane readings exceed 25 percent of the lower explosive limit.

741(3) Subsections (1)(a) and (b) do not apply if a working flammable gas monitor is installed on the bolter at roof level.

Airborne dust

742(1) An employer must ensure that there is a water supply designed to suppress airborne dust

    (a) at a location where mineral is transferred from one conveyor to another conveyor, a chute or a vehicle, and

    (b) at the cutting teeth or picks of a coal cutting machine.

742(2) Subsection (1) does not apply to a location where mineral is conveyed from the conveyor of a mobile unit.

742(3) An employer must ensure that a roadway used by rubber-tired vehicles is treated or wetted to minimize the creation of airborne dust.

742(4) An employer must ensure that there is an ongoing program for monitoring the concentration of respirable dust to which workers are exposed.

742(5) The Director may require an employer to install dust collection devices on exhaust fans if the Director considers that conditions warrant doing so.

Incombustible dust

743(1) This section does not apply to the part of a roadway within 10 metres of the working face while coal cutting is in progress.

743(1.1) If reasonably practicable, an employer must ensure that every area in an underground coal mine is kept free of accumulations of coal dust.

743(1.2) An employer must file with the Director a copy of a stone dusting program for the mine, including the method and frequency of testing.

743(2) An employer must ensure that the floor, roof and sides of a roadway that is accessible to workers are treated with

    (a) incombustible dust, or

    (b) other methods and mine materials for dust stabilization or consolidation in a manner approved by the Director.

743(3) An employer must ensure that the dust on the floor, roof and sides consists of at least 80 percent of incombustible matter.

743(4) Subsections (2) and (3) do not apply if the dust mixture on the floor, sides, timbers and roof of the roadway consists of at least 30 percent by weight of water.

743(5) An employer must ensure that the minimum amount of incombustible matter prescribed by subsection (3) is increased by 1 percent for each 0.1 percent of flammable gas in the atmosphere if there is flammable gas in the ventilating current.

743(6) Repealed

743(7) An underground coal mine manager must ensure that a part of a roadway is cleaned as thoroughly as is possible of all combustible dust before it is dusted for the first time with incombustible dust.

Sampling of settled dust

744 An employer must

   (a) put in place and maintain sampling procedures acceptable to the Director to ensure the requirements of section 743 are met, and

   (b) keep a record of the results at the mine site.

Explosion Control

Explosion barriers

745(1) An employer must develop an explosion prevention plan acceptable to the Director and certified by a professional engineer for the design, erection, location and maintenance of any explosion barriers included in it.

745(2) An employer must ensure that the position of any explosion barrier is shown on the mine ventilation and emergency response plans.

Welding, cutting and soldering

746(1) An employer must ensure that a worker does not weld, cut or solder using an arc or flame.

746(2) Despite subsection (1), if an employer deems hot work essential, the employer may develop and submit to the Director for approval, a plan for safe working procedures in accordance with section 169.

746(2.1) An employer must report to the Director all hot work performed underground.

746(3) Repealed

Pillars

747(1) The owners or prime contractors of adjoining underground properties must ensure that a pillar is left in each seam along the boundary line common to the adjoining properties.

747(2) The owners or prime contractors of adjoining underground properties must ensure that together the pillars are a sufficient barrier to ensure the safety of workers in each mine.

747(3) A professional engineer must determine the width of the pillar required to be left under subsection (1).

747(4) An employer must not conduct mining operations within 100 metres of the boundary line of an underground mine referred to in subsection (1) until the determination is made under subsection (3).

747(5) An employer must ensure that no mining is performed in the barrier pillar.

747(6) The underground coal mine surveyor of one mine may enter an adjoining mine to survey the working face of that mine along the barrier pillar.

747(7) An employer must

   (a) ensure that an underground coal mine surveyor prepares plans of the survey of the working faces along the barrier pillar within 60 days of the extraction of coal adjoining the barrier pillar, and

   (b) file the plans with the Director immediately after they are prepared.

Drill holes

748   An employer must ensure that workers do not mine coal within 100 metres of a drill hole drilled or being drilled for oil or gas, unless the Director approves the mining.

Water or gas

749(1) An employer must apply to the Director for an approval if a working face approaches to within 50 metres of the surface or to within 100 metres horizontally of

(a) a projection onto the working face of a place that is likely to contain a dangerous accumulation of water or gas,

(b) inactive workings that have not been examined and found free from accumulations of water or gas, or

(c) the seam outcrop or subcrop.

749(2) An application for an approval under subsection (1) must include a scheme certified by a professional engineer.

749(3) A working face referred to in subsection (1) may not be advanced unless the Director has issued an approval.

Shaft access and hoisting equipment

749.1 An employer intending to use shaft access and mine hoisting equipment, including rope haulage, must prepare designs, plans and procedures, certified by a professional engineer, and submit them to the Director prior to beginning construction.

Part 37   Oil and Gas Wells

Application

750 This Part applies to activities and auxiliary processes associated with exploring for and drilling, operating or servicing wells for gas, crude oil or geothermal energy.

Competent supervisor

751(1) An employer must appoint a supervisor to supervise an exploration, drilling, servicing, snubbing, testing or production operation.

751(2) An employer must ensure the supervisor is competent in each of the following that is within the supervisor's area of responsibility:

(a) safe work practices, including the safe operation of a plant at the work site;

(b) the safe handling, use and storage of hazardous substances;

(c) well control and blow out prevention;

(d) detecting and controlling worker exposure to hydrogen sulphide;

(e) handling, using, maintaining and storing personal protective equipment;

(f) appropriate responses to emergencies at the work site;

(g) the duties and responsibilities of all workers supervised by the supervisor;

(h) training workers supervised by the supervisor in safe work practices and procedures;

(i) health and safety programs.

Breathing equipment

752(1) If a worker is undertaking emergency response activities at a well site and the worker may be exposed to a harmful substance in excess of its occupational exposure limit, an employer must ensure that sufficient self-contained breathing apparatus units that comply with section 251 are provided, based on the hazard assessment required by Part 2 and the emergency response plan required by Part 7.

752(2) Despite subsection (1), if there is only one worker at the well site, an employer may use alternate means to protect the worker to ensure that the worker is not exposed to a harmful substance in excess of its occupational exposure limit.

Operating load of derrick or mast

753(1) An employer must ensure that the maximum safe operating load of a derrick or mast

(a) is specified in the manufacturer's specifications or specifications certified by a professional engineer,

(b) is prominently displayed on the derrick or mast, and

(c) is not exceeded.

753(2) If a structural modification or repair is made to a derrick or mast, an employer must ensure that

(a) the structural modification or repair is certified by a professional engineer,

(b) the maximum safe operating load of the derrick or mast is determined and certified by a professional engineer, and

(c) the load marking on the derrick or mast is replaced if the maximum safe operating load is changed.

Derricks and masts

754(1) An employer must ensure that, before a derrick or mast is erected or brought down, a competent worker inspects all of its parts in accordance with

(a) the manufacturer's specifications, or

(b) procedures approved by a Director of Inspection.

754(2) An employer must ensure that

(a) a competent worker is in charge of a derrick or mast and present when a derrick or mast is erected or brought down, and

(b) a derrick or mast is erected or brought down in a manner that does not create a danger to workers.

Log book

755(1) An employer must ensure that inspections and repairs on a derrick or mast are recorded in a log book issued by the Canadian Association of Oil Well Drilling Contractors or its equivalent.

755(2) An employer must ensure that the log book is available at the work site for review by an officer.

Drillers

756(1) An employer must ensure that the driller's position on a drilling or service rig is protected or guarded from hazards created by the cathead or tong lines.

756(2) An employer must ensure that workers do not slide down a pipe, kelly hose, cable or rope on a derrick or mast unless the line is part of a means of escape and there is an emergency.

756(3) A worker must not slide down a pipe, kelly hose, cable or rope on a derrick or mast unless the line is part of a means of escape and there is an emergency.

Geophysical operations

757 An employer must ensure that, during operations involving shot hole drilling,

(a) **Repealed**

(b) the mast of the seismic drill is lowered if the equipment being moved is in danger of contacting an overhead power line or losing its stability, and

(c) the seismic drill has an emergency stopping device at the driller's console.

Drilling rig, service rig, and snubbing unit inspections

758(1) An employer must ensure that the drilling rig, service rig or snubbing unit is inspected by a competent worker

(a) before it is placed into service, and

(b) every seventh day on which it is used for as long as it is in service.

758(2) The competent worker must prepare a report of the inspection and the employer must keep a copy of the report

(a) at the work site where the drilling rig, service rig or snubbing unit is in service, and

(b) at the employer's principal place of business in Alberta for at least one year from the date of the inspection.

Overloaded service rig trucks

759   An employer may operate a service rig truck with a load that exceeds the manufacturer's specifications for the maximum weight of the load if the employer

(a) prepares a written assessment of the hazards relating to the operation of the truck, and

(b) implements controls that ensure the safe operation of the truck.

Safety check

760   An employer must ensure that no worker services or works on a drilling rig, service rig or snubbing unit until a competent worker ensures that

(a) all guards are installed and secure,

(b) all platforms, stairways, handrails and guardrails are installed and secure,

(c) the emergency escape line and its components are installed and secure, and

(d) all fastening devices required in the erection of the rig and its substructure are installed and secure.

Exits from enclosures

761(1) An employer must ensure that a drilling rig, service rig or snubbing unit floor enclosure has exits to ground level that

(a) are located on at least two sides of the drilling or service rig floor,

(b) open away from the drill hole, and

(c) have no obstacles that would hinder or prevent a worker who is leaving in an emergency.

761(2) An employer must ensure that a pumphouse enclosure has at least two exits leading in different directions to the outside.

761(3) An employer must ensure that a catwalk on a drilling rig, service rig or snubbing unit has a stairway at the end farthest from the drill hole.

Emergency escape route

762(1) If a primary exit from the principal working platform above the drill floor may be blocked or otherwise compromised, an employer must ensure there is an emergency means of escape from the principal working platform that

(a) is visually inspected by a competent worker at least once a week, and

(b) is kept free of obstructions.

762(2) If the emergency means of escape includes using an anchored line, the employer must ensure the line is

(a)   installed, tested and maintained according to the manufacturer's specifications, and

(b)   able to successfully withstand a pull-test load of 13.3 kilonewtons at the time of its installation.

762(3) If an emergency escape safety buggy is used as part of the emergency means of escape, the employer must ensure it is

(a)   installed and maintained according to the manufacturer's specifications,

(b)   kept at the principal working platform when not in use, and

(c)   easily accessible to workers in an emergency.

Guy lines

763(1) An employer must ensure that derrick, mast or self-contained snubbing unit guy lines are installed in accordance with

(a)   the manufacturer's specifications, or

(b)   API Recommended Practice RP 4G, *Recommended Practice for Maintenance and Use of Drilling and Well Servicing Structures* (2004).

763(2) An employer must ensure that the specifications applied under subsection (1) for the correct number and proper spacing of guy lines are on a plate attached to the derrick, mast or self-contained snubbing unit.

Ground anchors

764(1) An employer must ensure that ground anchors are pull-tested annually in accordance with

(a)   API Recommended Practice RP 4G, *Recommended Practice for Maintenance and Use of Drilling and Well Servicing Structures* (2004), or

(b)   the manufacturer's specifications, or

(c)   specifications certified by a professional engineer.

764(2) An employer must ensure that the pull-test charts for temporary and permanent ground anchors are readily available for inspection by an officer.

Trailer pipe rack

765(1) An employer must ensure that a trailer that is used as a pipe rack

(a)   has guardrails and toe boards along the full length of both sides of the trailer,

(b)   has a stairway at the end farthest from the drilling or service rig floor, and

(c)   is constructed so that the lower end of the pipe does not roll off the trailer when the pipe is hoisted into the derrick.

765(2) An employer must ensure that a trailer used as a pipe rack is secured from movement.

(3)   **Moved to section 762(3).**

Drawworks

766(1) An employer must ensure that the function or action of each operating control on a drilling rig, service rig or self-contained snubbing unit is clearly marked on or near the control.

766(2) A worker in charge of the drawworks must ensure that all other workers are clear of the machinery and lines before the drawworks is put into motion.

Brakes

767(1) An employer must ensure that a mechanism used to hold the drawworks brakes of a drilling or service rig in the "on" position is designed so that the brakes cannot be accidentally disengaged.

767(2) An employer must ensure that the drawworks brakes of a drilling or service rig are tested at the beginning of each crew shift and examined at least weekly to ensure they are in good working order.

767(3) Unless drawworks have an automatic feed control, an employer must ensure that drawworks brakes are not left unattended without first being secured in the "on" position.

767(4) An employer must ensure that, except during drilling, drawworks controls are not left unattended while the hoisting drum is in motion.

Weight indicators

768   An employer must ensure that the hoist mechanism of a drilling or service rig has a reliable weight indicator that

    (a)   is secured against falling by a secondary cable or chain if it is hung above the derrick or mast floor, and

    (b)   is calibrated in accordance with the manufacturer's specifications or at least annually if a minimum interval between calibrations is not stated by the manufacturer.

Travelling blocks

769(1) An employer must ensure that each hook of a travelling block has a safety latch, mousing, shackle or equivalent positive locking device.

769(2) An employer must ensure that the travelling block and each hook, elevator, elevator link and unit of travelling equipment is free from projecting bolts, nuts, pins or other parts.

769(3) An employer must ensure that an upward travel limiting device

    (a)   is installed on every drilling or service rig and is tested at least once during each shift, and

    (b)   prevents the travelling block from contacting the crown structure by disengaging the power to the hoisting drum and applying brakes.

Tugger or travelling block

770(1) Subject to subsection (2), an employer must ensure that a worker does not use a travelling block or a tugger to raise or lower a worker unless the manufacturer's specifications allow the travelling block or tugger to be used in that way.

770(2) Subsection (1) does not apply in an emergency if

(a) an injured worker is lowered from a derrick using a travelling block or a tugger,

(b) the rotary table is stopped, and

(c) a competent worker trained in emergency procedures operates the control of the travelling block or tugger.

Catheads

771(1) An employer must ensure that workers do not use a rope-operated friction cathead on a drilling or service rig.

771(2) A worker must not use a rope-operated friction cathead on a drilling or service rig.

771(3) An employer must ensure that each automatic cathead has a separate control unless

(a) the cathead has dual purpose controls, and

(b) a locking device is installed to prevent one cathead from being engaged accidentally while another cathead is in operation.

771(4) Despite subsections (1) and (2), a worker may use a rope-operated friction cathead for hoisting before January 1, 2005 if

(a) a cathead on which a rope is manually operated has a blunt, smooth-edged rope divider,

(b) the clearance between a rope divider and the friction surface of a cathead is not more than 7 millimetres,

(c) every key seat and projecting key on a cathead is covered with a smooth thimble or plate,

(d) the clearance between the outer flange of a cathead and any substructure, guardrail or wall is at least 500 millimetres,

(e) a competent worker handles the drawworks control while a cathead is in use,

(f) the operating area of a manually operated cathead is kept clear at all times, and

(g) the portion of a rope or line that is not being used is coiled or spooled.

771(5) A worker who operates a rope-operated friction cathead must not

(a) leave a rope or line wrapped around or in contact with an unattended cathead, or

(b) allow a splice to come in contact with the friction surface of the cathead.

Racking pipes

772(1) An employer must ensure that provision is made for completely draining fluids from standing drill pipes, drill collars and tubing racked in a derrick.

772(2) An employer must ensure that drill pipes, drill collars, tubing, casing and rods racked in a derrick or mast are secured and cannot fall out of or across the derrick or mast.

Rotary table danger zone

773(1) An employer must ensure that a danger zone is established and clearly marked around a rotary table used in a drilling operation.

773(2) When a rotary table is in motion during an operation, a worker must not enter the danger zone or allow other equipment or loose materials to enter the danger zone.

773(3) Despite subsection (2), a worker is permitted within the rotary table danger zone only during non-drilling operations and only once a hazard assessment as required by Part 2 is completed.

773(4) If a worker is within the rotary table danger zone while the rotary table is in motion, the employer must ensure that

(a) the table is restricted to a slow rate of speed and is under the continuous control of a designated driller positioned at the table controls,

(b) the area around the rotary table is clear of any equipment that may contact the rotating equipment,

(c) all workers positioning slips or tongs remain clear of rotating equipment,

(d) all lines attached to tongs are placed outside of the direct line of rotating slips,

(e) the worker's clothing and personal protective equipment is in good repair and fits closely to the body, and

(f) the worker does not wear bracelets, rings, dangling neckwear, a wristwatch, or similar articles.

773(5) Prior to initiating or resuming drilling operations, the employer must ensure that all workers are positioned outside of the rotary table danger zone and that all auxiliary equipment is stored clear of the danger zone.

Tong safety

774   An employer must ensure that a rotary tong has

(a) a primary device that prevents uncontrolled movement of the tong, and

(b) a safety device that prevents uncontrolled movement of the tong if the primary device fails.

Counterweights

775   An employer must ensure that a counterweight above a derrick or mast floor cannot come within 2.3 metres of the floor if the counterweight is not

(a) fully encased, or

(b) running in permanent guides.

Drilling fluid

776(1) An employer must ensure that, when workers are pumping drilling fluid,

(a) a positive displacement pump and its attachments have valves, pipes and fittings rated equal to or greater than the pump's maximum working pressure,

(b) a positive displacement pump is protected against freezing,

(c) a pressure relief device is installed on the discharge side of a positive displacement pump,

(d) a valve is not installed between a pressure relief device and a positive displacement pump,

    (e) piping on the discharge side of a pressure relief device does not have a valve,

    (f) a pressure relief device is set to discharge at a pressure that is not more than the maximum working pressure recommended by the manufacturer for the drilling fluid pump, connecting pipes and fittings,

    (g) shear pins used in a pressure relief device are of the design and strength specified in the manufacturer's specifications,

    (h) the fluids or materials discharged through a pressure relief device are piped to a place where they will not endanger workers,

    (i) piping connected to the pressure side and discharge side of a pressure relief device is not smaller than the normal pipe size openings of the device,

    (j) piping on the discharge side of the pressure relief device is secured,

    (k) piping from the discharge side of the pressure relief device is continuously sloped to drain liquids, and

    (l) piping going vertically on a relief line is heated or installed in a heated environment.

776(2) An employer must ensure that the manufacturer's specifications and recommendations are followed under subsection (1) unless a professional engineer certifies otherwise.

776(3) An employer must ensure that a mud gun used for jetting is secured to prevent movement.

776(4) An employer must ensure that a worker does not use a "quick closing" type of valve on the discharge line of a positive displacement pump.

776(5) A worker must not use a "quick closing" type of valve on the discharge line of a positive displacement pump.

Rig tank or pit enclosures

777(1) An employer must ensure that a rig tank or pit used for the circulation of drilling fluids containing flammable or combustible material is protected from sources of ignition.

777(2) An employer must ensure that a rig tank or pit that is enclosed

    (a) is properly vented, and

    (b) that vented vapours are directed away from ignition sources.

Prohibition on fuel storage

778(1) An employer must ensure that fuel is not stored within 25 metres of a well.

778(2) A worker must not store fuel within 25 metres of a well.

778(3) Subsections (1) and (2) do not apply to diesel fuel provided that

    (a) it is used solely as fuel for machinery operating at the well,

    (b) it is stored in fully enclosed storage containers,

    (c) no more than 8000 litres total is stored in the storage containers, and

    (d) it is more than 7 metres away from the well.

Drill stem testing

779(1) This section applies to drill stem testing operations.

779(2) An employer must ensure that after fluids are encountered while tripping out, workers use the mud can and test plug on every joint of pipe disconnected, unless the drill stem contents have been pumped out and replaced with drilling fluid.

779(3) An employer must ensure that

    (a)   workers test for the presence of hydrogen sulphide and hydrocarbons if oil, water or gas is encountered during the drill stem testing, and

    (b)   if hydrogen sulphide is present, the sour fluids in the drill stem are displaced with drilling fluid and circulated to a flare pit or a holding tank that is at least 50 metres from the well.

779(4) An employer must ensure that

    (a)   motors and engines not required in the testing operation are shut off, and

    (b)   there are no motor vehicles within 25 metres of the well bore.

779(5) An employer must ensure that, if swivel joints are used in the piping system, workers secure the source and discharge ends of the piping system in a manner that prevents pipes that are separated from the source or discharge connection from whipping or flailing.

779(6) An employer must ensure that, if test fluid recovery is encountered during darkness,

    (a)   liquids are reverse circulated, or

    (b)   if reverse circulation is not practicable because the pump-out sub has failed, additional drill pipe is not pulled and disconnected until daylight.

Well swabbing

780(1) This section applies to well swabbing operations.

780(2) An employer must ensure that during swabbing operations,

    (a)   workers anchor auxiliary swabbing units securely against movement,

    (b)   fluids are piped directly to a battery, skid tank, mobile trailer or tank truck, and

    (c)   the battery, skid tank, mobile trailer or tank truck is at least 50 metres from the well bore.

780(3) An employer must ensure that if fluids are piped to a tank truck during swabbing operations,

    (a)   the engine of the truck is shut off, and

    (b)   the driver is not in the cab of the truck while fluids are transferred.

780(4) A person must not be in the cab of a truck while fluids are transferred to the truck during swabbing operations.

780(5) Repealed

780(6) If workers are well swabbing during darkness, an employer must ensure that

(a) there is auxiliary lighting providing a minimum illumination level of 54 lux measured 500 millimetres above the travel surface,

(b) rig lighting is turned off if it is not designed for use in an explosive atmosphere,

(c) sandline flags are illuminated and acid resistant,

(d) wind direction indicators are illuminated and appropriately located around the site, and

(e) workers use atmospheric monitoring equipment.

Well servicing

781(1) This section applies to well servicing operations.

781(2) An employer must ensure that

(a) when circulating hydrocarbons, the air intake and exhaust of the pump motor are located at least 6 metres away from the rig tank,

(b) if a tank truck is being loaded or unloaded, it is at least 6 metres away from the rig tank in a direction away from the well bore, and

(c) carbon dioxide suction lines are secured to the supply vehicle and pumping unit.

781(3) An employer must ensure that, before pressurization begins, warning signs prohibiting the presence of workers in the area and complying with CSA Standard CAN/CSA-Z321-96 (R2006), *Signs and Symbols for the Workplace*, are positioned along the discharge pipelines.

781(4) An employer must ensure that, before fluids are unloaded into the well-head, workers hydraulically pressure test the lines between the pump and the well-head for 10 minutes

(a) to at least 10 percent above the maximum pressure anticipated during service, but

(b) not above the working pressure rating of the line.

781(5) An employer must ensure that the controls on oil savers can be readily operated by a worker on the rig floor.

781(6) An employer must ensure that when a snubbing unit conducts gas-assisted sand clean-out, it is done only by a competent worker, during daylight hours, and using equipment intended for that activity.

Well stimulation

782(1) This section applies to well stimulation or a similar operation.

782(2) An employer must ensure that if a working pressure of 2000 kilopascals or more is applied to the piping system,

(a) workers establish the area between a pump or sand concentrator and the well-head as a potential danger area,

(b) workers control equipment located between a pump or sand concentrator and the well-head outside the potential danger area, and

(c) subject to subsection (3), workers do not enter that potential danger area when the system is pressurized.

782(3) Subject to section 188, an employer may permit a worker to enter the potential danger area to operate the bleed-off valve or squeeze manifold if the pump is disengaged before that worker enters the potential danger area.

782(4) An employer must ensure that

(a) while workers are using liquid carbon dioxide or liquid nitrogen, the pumping unit is positioned so that the valve controls are on the side opposite to the pipe supplying the well,

(b) a check valve is installed as close as is practical to the well-head except while cementing or selective acidizing is occurring,

(c) if flammable fluids are being pumped during fracturing and acidizing treatment, fire protection equipment capable of extinguishing a fire that may occur is provided on pumping units, including blenders and coiled tubing units,

(d) a worker does not use the mud line from the cement truck in place of the circulating line, and

(e) a bleed-off valve is installed between a check valve and the well-head.

Well site piping system

783(1) An employer must ensure that piping systems installed and maintained at a well site

(a) are designed, constructed, installed, operated and maintained to safely contain any material at the maximum operating pressures anticipated,

(b) meet the requirements of ANSI/ASME Standard B1.20.1-1983 (R2006), *Pipe Threads, General Purpose (Inch)*, for threaded connections,

(c) are anchored during well testing, servicing and flowback in accordance with section 188, and

(d) have connections that are welded, flanged or hammer unions if pressures exceed 3000 kilopascals.

783(2) Subsection (1) does not apply to low pressure water, steam, fuel, lubrication, pneumatic or conduit lines if the low pressure lines are clearly distinguishable from high pressure lines.

Gas sample containers

784 An employer must ensure that containers, piping and fittings used in collecting gas samples are

(a) strong enough to withstand all the pressures to which they may be subjected, and

(b) designed, used and transported in such a way that their contents cannot be released accidentally.

Part 38   Residential Roofing — Expired

Application
  785   Expired

Expiration of Part
  786   This Part expired on April 30, 2007.

Daily inspection
  787   Expired

Placement of materials
  788   Expired

Securing roof brackets
  789   Expired

Slide guard height
  790   Expired

Roof slopes
  791   Expired

Part 39   Tree Care Operations

Application

792   This Part applies to arboriculture activities that involve pruning, repairing, maintaining or removing trees or cutting brush if a worker works at height and depends on the tree for support.

Safe work practices

793(1) An employer must develop and implement safe work practices and procedures that include

    (a)   the assessment of hazards at the work site,

    (b)   worker training, including hazard recognition,

    (c)   the selection, limitation, operation and maintenance of tools and equipment,

    (d)   work positioning and fall protection, and

    (e)   emergency rescue.

793(2) If reasonably practicable, an employer must involve affected workers in the development and implementation of the safe work practices and procedures.

Fall protection and work positioning

794(1) If it is not reasonably practicable to comply with the fall protection requirements of section 139, an employer must ensure that a worker uses a work positioning system.

794(2) A worker must use or wear the work positioning or fall protection system the employer requires the worker to use or wear.

Harness standards

795(1) An employer must ensure that a harness manufactured on or after July1, 2009 and used as part of a work positioning system is approved to

    (a)   NFPA Standard 1983, *Standard on Fire Service Life Safety Rope and System Components*, 2006 Edition, as a Class II or Class III life safety harness,

    (b)   CEN Standard EN 813: 1997, *Personal protective equipment for prevention of falls from a height — Sit harnesses*,

    (c)   CSA Standard CAN/CSA-Z259.10-06, *Full Body Harnesses*,

    (d)   ANSI/ASSE Standard Z359.1-2007, *Safety requirements for personal fall arrest systems, subsystems and components*, or

    (e)   CEN Standard EN 361: 2007, *Personal protective equipment against falls from a height — Full body harnesses*.

795(2) Subsection (1) does not apply to harnesses in use before April 30, 2004.

Knot exemption

796   Section 150.3 does not apply to arboriculture activities to which this Part applies.

Part 40   Utility Workers — Electrical

Application

797   If a requirement of this Part conflicts with a requirement elsewhere in this Code, the requirement of this Part prevails.

798   If a term is defined in both this Code and the *Alberta Electrical and Communication Utility Code,* published by the Safety Codes Council, Second Edition, 2002, the definition appearing in the *Alberta Electrical and Communication Utility Code* prevails.

Protective devices or equipment

799(1) An employer must ensure that a protective device and protective equipment required by this Part meets the requirements of the following applicable standards:

(a)   CAN/ULC-60832-99, *Insulating Poles (Insulating Sticks) and Universal Tool Attachments (Fittings) for Live Workings*;

(b)   CAN/ULC-D60855-00, *Live Working — Insulating Foam-Filled Tubes and Solid Rods for Live Working*;

(c)   CAN/ULC-60895-04, *Live Working — Conductive Clothing for Use at Nominal Voltage Up to 800 kV A.C. and +/- 600 kV D.C.*;

(d)   CAN/ULC-60900-99, *Hand Tools for Live Working up to 1000 V a.c. and 1500 V d.c.;*

(e)   CAN/ULC-60903-04, *Live Working — Gloves of Insulating Materials*;

(f)   CAN/ULC-D60984-00, *Sleeves of Insulating Material for Live Working;*

(g)   CAN/ULC-D61112-01, *Blankets of Insulating Material for Electrical Purposes;*

(h)   CAN/ULC-D61229-00, *Rigid Protective Covers for Live Working on a.c. Installations;*

(i)   CAN/ULC-61236-99, *Saddles, Pole Clamps (Stick Clamps) and Accessories for Live Working*;

(j)   CAN/CSA-C225-00 (R2005), *Vehicle-Mounted Aerial Devices.*

799(2) Subsection (1) applies only to new protective devices and protective equipment put into service as of the effective date of this Code.

799(3) A laboratory that performs electrical insulating materials testing to the standards listed in subsection (1) must meet the requirements of ASTM Standard D2865-06, *Standard Practice for Calibration of Standards and Equipment for Electrical Insulating Materials Testing.*

Safe work practices for electric utilities and rural electrification associations

800(1) An electric utility and a rural electrification association must ensure that all work performed by utility employees is in accordance with the requirements of section 4 of the *Alberta Electrical and Communication Utility Code*, published by the Safety Codes Council, Second Edition, 2002.

800(2) Despite subsection (1), rules 4-040(1)(a) and (b), 4-044(a), 4-048, 4-126, 4-160, 4-162, 4-164 and 4-176 of the *Alberta Electrical and Communication Utility Code* do not apply.

Safe work practices for industrial power producers

801   An industrial power producer must

    (a) complete a written assessment of hazards associated with the production of electrical energy,

    (b) implement written safe work procedures that are made available to utility employees, and

    (c) ensure all work performed by utility employees is in accordance with the safe work procedures required by subsection (b).

Coordinated work

802   If utility employees

    (a) perform work on or near a power system, and

    (b) their work activities may affect or be affected by a utility employee of another electric utility, industrial power producer or rural electrification association,

the involved electric utilities, industrial power producers or rural electrification associations must jointly develop and follow one agreed-upon set of safe work procedures for isolating electrical equipment and lines or blocking reclosing devices.

Communication lines, cables

803   A utility employee stringing or removing communication lines or cables near any electric utility facility must ensure that

    (a) the limit of approach distances required by Rule 4-130 of the *Alberta Electrical and Communication Utility Code* between the communication lines or cables and energized equipment or lines are met,

    (b) the communication lines or cables are prevented from contacting overhead electrical lines,

    (c) the work is done under the control of the operator of the electric utility system, and

    (d) the work method is acceptable to the operator of the electric utility system.

Work on energized electrical equipment or lines (above 750 volts)

804(1) If work is performed on energized electrical equipment or lines, an employer must ensure that

    (a) a minimum of two qualified utility employees are used to perform the work and an additional utility employee is at ground level,

    (b) aerial devices are equipped with both upper and lower controls, and

    (c) if an aerial device is used to perform the work, either an additional utility employee qualified to operate the lower controls is present at the work site at ground level or the utility employee already at the work site is qualified to operate the lower controls.

804(2) Despite subsection (1), subsections (1)(a) and (1)(c) do not apply if

    (a) a professional engineer certifies that an alternative live line work procedure provides adequate utility employee protection,

(b) the live line work on the electrical equipment or lines is performed by one qualified utility employee, and

(c) a second qualified utility employee is present at the work site at ground level.

804(3) Subsections (1) and (2) do not apply to

(a) switching work,

(b) fuse replacement work,

(c) phasing work,

(d) measuring clearances with live line tools,

(e) power quality measurements with live line tools, and

(f) emergency situations in which, in order to protect life or property, a qualified utility employee performs work to eliminate the electrical hazards.

Part 41   Work Requiring Rope Access

General Requirements

Exemptions

805   Workers involved in training for occupational rope access work or performing occupational rope access work may use equipment and practices other than those specified in Part 9.

806   Workers involved in emergency rescue services or training for the purpose of emergency rescue may use equipment and practices other than those specified in this Part.

807   This Part does not apply to workers using fall protection systems specified in Part 9.

Rope access safe work plan

808   An employer must develop an occupational rope access safe work plan for a work site if

(a)   a worker at the work site may fall 3 metres or more, or

(b)   there is an unusual possibility of injury if a worker falls less than 3 metres.

809   An occupational rope access safe work plan must specify the following:

(a)   the hazards associated with the work to be performed;

(b)   how the hazards will be eliminated or controlled;

(c)   the rope access system to be used at the work site;

(d)   the procedures used to assemble, maintain, inspect, use and disassemble the rope access system;

(e)   the members of the work team by name, and their duties;

(f)   the appropriate personal protective equipment to be used;

(g)   an emergency response plan.

810   An employer must ensure that an occupational rope access safe work plan is available at the work site before work with a risk of falling begins.

Safe work practices

811   An employer must develop and implement safe work practices that include

(a)   the assessment of hazards at the work site in accordance with Part 2,

(b)   worker training, including hazard recognition and the selection, limitations, operation, inspection and maintenance of tools and equipment,

(c)   work positioning and fall protection, and

(d)   the rescue procedures to be used in case of equipment malfunction, a fall or injury that leaves a worker suspended and requiring rescue.

Instruction of workers

812   An employer must ensure that a worker is trained in the rope access safe work plan, the safe work practices and the safe use of the rope access system before allowing the worker to work in an area where a rope access system is to be used.

Tools and equipment

813(1) An employer must ensure that equipment to be used by a worker during occupational rope access work activities is not suspended from the worker's working line or safety line.

813(2) An employer must ensure that equipment weighing more than 8 kilograms and to be used by a worker during occupational rope access work activities is suspended from a separate line secured to a suitable anchorage.

Equipment compatibility

814 An employer must ensure that all components of an occupational rope access system are compatible with one another and with the environment in which they are used.

Inspection and maintenance

815 An employer must ensure that the components of an occupational rope access system are

(a) inspected by the worker as required by the manufacturer before the system is used on each work shift,

(b) kept free from substances and conditions that could contribute to their deterioration, and

(c) re-certified as specified by the manufacturer.

Low stretch (static) and high stretch (dynamic) rope

816 An employer must ensure that the working line and safety line of an occupational rope access system are the same diameter.

817 An employer must ensure that low stretch or static rope manufactured on or after July1, 2009 and used in an occupational rope access system is approved to

(a) CEN Standard EN 1891: 1998, *Personal protective equipment for the prevention of falls from a height — Low stretch kernmantel ropes*, and is a Type A rope as classified by the standard,

(b) NFPA Standard 1983, *Standard on Fire Service Life Safety Rope, Harness, and Hardware*, 2006 Edition, or

(c) UIAA Standard 107: 2004, *Mountaineering and Climbing Equipment — Low Stretch Ropes*, and is a Type A rope as classified by the standard.

818 An employee must ensure that high stretch or dynamic rope used in an occupational rope access system is approved to

(a) CEN Standard EN 892: 2004, *Mountaineering equipment — Dynamic mountaineering ropes — Safety requirements and test methods*, or

(b) UIAA Standard 101: 2004, *Mountaineering and Climbing Equipment — Dynamic Ropes.*

Cow's tail

819(1) If a cow's tail is made of dynamic rope, an employer must ensure that the rope is approved to

(a) CEN Standard EN 892: 2004, *Mountaineering equipment — Dynamic mountaineering ropes — Safety requirements and test methods*, or

(b) UIAA Standard 101: 2004, *Mountaineering and Climbing Equipment — Dynamic Ropes.*

819(2) If a cow's tail is not made of dynamic rope, an employer must ensure that the cow's tail is approved to CEN Standard EN 354: 2002, *Personal protective equipment against falls from a height — Lanyards.*

Removal from service

820(1) An employer must ensure that equipment used as part of an occupational rope access system is removed from service

(a) as specified by the manufacturer, or

(b) if it is defective,

and returned to the manufacturer, destroyed, or rendered unusable.

820(2) An employer must ensure that equipment used as part of an occupational rope access system that is removed from service is not returned to service unless a professional engineer or the manufacturer certifies that the equipment is safe to use.

Worker rescue

821　　An employer must ensure that a worker can be promptly rescued in case of equipment malfunction, fall or injury.

822　　An employer must ensure that a worker is trained to perform self-rescue on the equipment.

Industrial Rope Access Work

Safe work practices

823　　An employer must ensure that one of the following safe work practices for industrial rope access work is followed:

(a) *International guidelines on the use of rope access methods for industrial purposes*, July2001, published by the Industrial Rope Access Trade Association;

(b) *Safe Practices for Rope Access Work*, October 2003, published by the Society of Professional Rope Access Technicians;

(c) *Industrial Rope Access Technique*, ARAA Industry Code, September 2000, published by the Australian Rope Access Association.

824　　If the requirements of section 823 conflict with requirements elsewhere in this Code, the requirements of this Code prevail.

825　　An employer must ensure that at least two workers trained in industrial rope access work are present when rope access equipment and techniques are used.

Worker competency

826　　An employer must ensure that the training required to comply with section 812 includes the applicable skills and practical experience hours described in

   (a) Clauses 15.3, 16.3 or 17.3 as appropriate, of *General requirements for certification of personnel engaged in industrial rope access methods*, 2005, published by the Industrial Rope Access Trade Association,

   (b) Clause 7 of *Certification Requirements for Rope Access Work*, January 2005, published by the Society of Professional Rope Access Technicians, or

   (c) Appendix D of *Industrial Rope Access Technique*, ARAA Industry Code, September 2000, published by the Australian Rope Access Association.

Worker's personal logbook

827(1) A worker performing industrial rope access work must have a personal logbook containing a record of the industrial rope access work performed by that worker.

827(2) Records in the worker's personal logbook must be in chronological order and each entry must be verified and signed by the rope access supervisor or worksite manager.

827(3) Each record of work must include

   (a) the date the work was performed,

   (b) the type of work performed, including the access method used,

   (c) the type of structure worked on, and

   (d) the hours worked using industrial rope access techniques.

827(4) The worker must ensure that the personal logbook is current and available at the worksite for inspection by an officer.

Maximum arrest force, clearance, anchor strength

828   An employer must ensure that a rope access system used for industrial rope access work

   (a) limits the maximum arresting force on a worker to 6 kilonewtons,

   (b) prevents the worker from striking a lower surface that could cause injury, unless doing so exposes the worker to other greater hazards, and

   (c) minimizes the hazards of swinging and striking an object that could injure the worker.

829(1) An employer must ensure that an anchor to which an industrial rope access system is attached has an ultimate breaking strength of at least 16 kilonewtons per worker attached, in the direction in which the load may be applied.

829(2) Despite subsection (1), if it is not practicable for the anchor to have the specified ultimate breaking strength, an anchor may be used that has an ultimate breaking strength per attached worker of two times the estimated maximum arresting force created by a fall in the direction of the rope pull, unless doing so exposes the worker to other greater hazards.

Safety line

830(1) An employer must ensure that a safety, secondary, belay or backup line is used when the working line is the primary means of support.

830(2) An employer must ensure that the safety line and the working line are each provided with a separate anchorage connection and are separately fixed to the worker's harness.

830(3) Subsections (1) and (2) do not prohibit both the working line and safety line from being attached to single harness attachment point.

830(4) An employer may allow a worker to connect the safety line to the sternal or frontal attachment point of the worker's full body harness in accordance with the harness manufacturer's specifications.

Head protection

831(1) Despite section 234, if there is a foreseeable danger of injury to a worker's head while the worker is performing industrial rope access work, and there is a significant possibility of lateral impact to the worker's head, an employer must ensure that the worker wears protective headwear that is appropriate to the hazards and meets the requirements of

    (a) CSA Standard Z94.1-05, *Industrial Protective Headwear*,

    (b) ANSI Standard Z89.1-2003, *American National Standard for Industrial Head Protection*, for Type II helmets,

    (c) CEN Standard EN 12492: 2000, *Mountaineering equipment — Helmets for mountaineers — Safety requirements and test methods*, if the manufacturer's specifications allow the helmet to be used for industrial work at height, or

    (d) UIAA Standard 106: 2004, *Mountaineering and Climbing Equipment — Helmets,* if the manufacturer's specifications allow the helmet to be used for industrial work at height,

if the protective headwear was manufactured on or after July1, 2009.

831(2) Despite section 234, if there is a foreseeable danger of injury to a worker's head while the worker is performing industrial rope access work, and the possibility of lateral impact to the worker's head is unlikely, an employer must ensure that the worker wears protective headwear that is appropriate to the hazards and meets the requirements of

    (a) CSA Standard Z94.1-05, *Industrial Protective Headwear*,

    (b) ANSI Standard Z89.1-2003, *American National Standard for Industrial Head Protection*, for Type I or Type II helmets,

    (c) CEN Standard EN 397: 2006, *Specification for industrial safety helmets,*

    (d) CEN Standard EN 12492: 2000, *Mountaineering equipment — Helmets for mountaineers — Safety requirements and test methods*, if the manufacturer's specifications allow the helmet to be used for industrial work at height, or

    (e) UIAA Standard 106: 2004, *Mountaineering and Climbing Equipment — Helmets,* if the manufacturer's specifications allow the helmet to be used for industrial work at height,

if the protective headwear was manufactured on or after July1, 2009.

832   An employer must ensure that the protective headwear required by section 831 is equipped with a retention system having at least three separate points of attachment to the helmet shell, and includes a chin strap.

833   An employer must ensure that a worker secures the protective headwear according to the manufacturer's specifications.

Full body harness

834   An employer must ensure that a full body harness is used during industrial rope access work and if manufactured on or after July1, 2009 is approved to

    (a)   NFPA Standard 1983, *Standard on Fire Service Life Safety Rope and System Components*, 2006 Edition, as a Class III safety harness,

    (b)   CEN Standard EN 361: 2007, *Personal protective equipment against falls from a height — Full body harnesses*, or

    (c)   ANSI/ASSE Standard Z359.1-2007, *Safety requirements for personal fall arrest systems, subsystems and components.*

Connecting components

835   An employer must ensure that connecting components manufactured on or after July1, 2009 used in industrial rope access work consist of carabiners, D-rings, O-rings, oval rings and self-locking connectors approved to

    (a)   CEN Standard EN 362: 2004, *Personal protective equipment against falls from height. Connectors,*

    (b)   CEN Standard EN 12275: 1998, *Mountaineering equipment — Connector — Safety requirements and test methods,*

    (c)   UIAA Standard 121: 2004, *Mountaineering and Climbing Equipment — Connectors,*

    (d)   CSA Standard Z259.12-01 (R2006), *Connecting Components for Personal Fall-Arrest Systems*, or

    (e)   NFPA Standard 1983, *Standard on Fire Service Life Safety Rope, Harness, and Hardware*, 2006 Edition.

836   An employer must ensure that carabiners used as part of an industrial rope access system are

    (a)   a screw-gate type, or

    (b)   self-locking and self-closing, requiring at least two consecutive, deliberate actions to open.

Ascenders

837   An employer must ensure that an ascender manufactured on or after July1, 2009 used in an industrial rope access system is approved to

    (a)   CEN Standard EN 567: 1997, *Mountaineering equipment — Rope clamps — Safety requirements and test methods,*

    (b)   UIAA Standard 126: 2004, *Mountaineering and Climbing Equipment — Rope Clamps*, or

    (c)   NFPA Standard 1983, *Standard on Fire Service Life Safety Rope, Harness, and Hardware*, 2006 Edition.

Back-up devices

838   An employer must ensure that a back-up device manufactured on or after July1, 2009 used in an industrial rope access system is approved to

(a) CEN Standard EN 353-2: 2002, *Personal protective equipment against falls from a height — Part 2: Guided type fall arresters including a flexible anchor line,*

(b) CEN Standard EN 567: 1997, *Mountaineering equipment — Rope clamps — Safety requirements and test methods,*

(c) UIAA Standard 126: 2004, *Mountaineering and Climbing Equipment — Rope Clamps,* or

(d) ANSI Standard Z359.1-2007, *Safety requirements for personal fall arrest systems, subsystems and components.*

Descenders

839   An employer must ensure that a descender manufactured on or after July1, 2009 used in an industrial rope access system is approved to

(a) CEN Standard EN 341: 1997, *Personal protective equipment against falls from height — Descender devices,* as a Class A device, or

(b) NFPA Standard 1983, *Standard on Fire Service Life Safety Rope, Harness and Hardware,* 2006 Edition.

Non-industrial Rope Access Work

Safe work practices

840   An employer must ensure that a Director of Inspection approves the safe work practices for non-industrial rope access work.

Worker competency

841   An employer must ensure that the training required to comply with section 812 includes the applicable skills described in

(a) *Technical Handbook for Professional Mountain Guides* (July1999), published by the Association of Canadian Mountain Guides (ACMG), if the work involves guiding activities within the scope of the publication,

(b) *Climbing Gym Instructor Technical Manual* (July2003), published by the Association of Canadian Mountain Guides (ACMG), if the work involves climbing activities within the scope of the publication, or

(c) if this work involves caving activities within the scope of these publications,

   (i) *Cave Guiding Standards for British Columbia and Alberta* (March 2003), published by the Canadian Cave Conservancy, and

   (ii) *British Columbia Cave Rescue Companion Rescue Workshop* (2005), published by British Columbia Cave Rescue.

Fall factor, clearance, anchorage strength

842   An employer must ensure that a rope system used for non-industrial rope access work

(a) limits the fall factor on a worker to 1.78, unless doing so exposes the worker to other greater hazards,

(b) prevents the worker from striking a lower surface that could cause injury, unless doing so exposes the worker to other greater hazards, and

(c) minimizes the hazards of swinging and striking an object that could injure the worker.

843(1) An employer must ensure that an anchor used for non-industrial rope access work has an ultimate breaking strength of at least 16 kilonewtons per worker attached, in the direction in which the load may be applied.

843(2) Despite subsection (1), if it is not practicable for the anchor to have the specified ultimate breaking strength, an anchor may be used that has an ultimate breaking strength per attached worker of two times the estimated maximum arresting force created by a fall in the direction of the rope pull, unless doing so exposes the worker to other greater hazards.

Head protection

844   Despite section 234, if there is a foreseeable danger of injury to a worker's head while performing non-industrial rope access work, an employer must ensure that a worker wears protective headwear that is appropriate to the hazards and meets the requirements of

(a) CEN Standard EN 12492: 2000, *Mountaineering equipment — Helmets for mountaineers — Safety requirements and test methods*,

(b) UIAA Standard 106: 2004, *Mountaineering and Climbing Equipment — Helmets,* or

(c) ANSI Standard Z89.1-2003, *American National Standard for Industrial Head Protection,* for Type II helmets,

if the protective headwear was manufactured on or after July 1, 2009.

845   An employer must ensure that a worker secures the protective headwear according to the manufacturer's specifications.

846   Protective headwear in good condition meeting an earlier edition of a standard listed in section 844 may remain in service.

Sit harness

847   An employer must ensure that a sit harness used for non-industrial rope access work is approved to

(a) CEN Standard EN 813: 1997, *Personal protective equipment for prevention of falls from a height — Sit harnesses*,

(b) CEN Standard EN 12277: 1998, *Mountaineering equipment — Harnesses — Safety requirements and test methods*, or

(c) UIAA Standard 105: 2004, *Mountaineering and Climbing Equipment — Harnesses.*

Full body harness

848   An employer must ensure that a full body harness used during non-industrial rope access work is approved to

(a) CEN Standard EN 361: 2007, *Personal protective equipment against falls from a height — Full body harnesses*, or

(b) ANSI/ASSE Standard Z359.1-2007, *Safety requirements for personal fall arrest systems, subsystems and components.*

if the full body harness was manufactured on or after July 1, 2009.

Connecting components

849   An employer must ensure that connecting components used during non-industrial rope access work are approved to

(a)   CEN Standard EN 12275: 1998, *Mountaineering equipment — Connectors — Safety requirements and test methods*, or

(b)   UIAA Standard 121: 2004, *Mountaineering and Climbing Equipment — Connectors.*

Schedules

Schedule 1   Chemical Substances

Table 1   Substances and processes requiring a code of practice

[See subsection 26(1)]

- Arsenic and arsenic compounds
- Asbestos
- Benzene
- Beryllium
- 1,3-Butadiene
- Cadmium
- Coal tar pitch volatiles
- 1,2-Dibromoethane (Ethylene dibromide)
- Ethylene oxide
- Hexachlorobutadiene
- Hydrazines
- Hydrogen sulphide
- Isocyanates
- Lead and lead compounds
- Methyl bromide
- Methyl hydrazine
- Perchlorates
- Silica-crystalline, respirable
- Styrene in styrene resin fabrication
- Vinyl chloride (Chloroethylene)
- Zinc chromate

Table 2   Occupational exposure limits for chemical substances

(1) A person using this Table may apply either the "mg/m³" or "ppm" measure defined as follows:

"mg/m³" means milligrams of substance per cubic metre of air measured at ambient work site conditions;

"ppm" (parts per million) means parts of a vapour or gas by volume at standard conditions (25°C and an absolute barometric pressure of 101.3 kilopascals) per parts of contaminated air by volume at ambient work site conditions.

(2) "f/cc" means fibres per cubic centimetre of air; "CAS" means Chemical Abstracts Service.

(3) The numbers 1, 2 and 3 in the "Substance Interaction" column have the following meanings:

1 — substance may be readily absorbed through intact skin;

2 — substance is a simple asphyxiant that may create an atmosphere deficient in oxygen; available oxygen in the range of 19.5 percent to 23 percent by volume must be present.

3 — occupational exposure limit is based on irritation effects and its adjustment to compensate for unusual work schedules is not required.

(4) A carcinogen is defined as "an agent capable of inducing benign or malignant neoplasms." Based on the weight of evidence from epidemiologic studies, "A1" would be a Confirmed Human Carcinogen and means that the agent is carcinogenic to humans. "A2" would be a Suspected Human Carcinogen and means that human data are accepted as adequate in quality but are conflicting or insufficient to classify the agent as A1 (*American Conference of Governmental Industrial Hygienists*).

| Substance | CAS number | 8-hour occupational exposure limit | | | 15-minute or ceiling (c) occupational exposure limit | | Substance interaction 1, 2, 3 | Carcino-genicity A1, A2 |
		ppm	mg/m³	f/cc	ppm	mg/m³		
Acetaldehyde	75-07-0	—	—	—	(c) 25	(c) 45	3	
Acetic acid	64-19-7	10	25	—	15	37	—	
Acetic anhydride	108-24-7	—	—	—	(c) 5	(c) 21	3	
Acetone	67-64-1	500	1200	—	750	1800	—	
Acetone cyanohydrin	75-86-5	—	—	—	—	(c) 5	1	
Acetonitrile	75-05-8	20	34	—	—	—	3	
Acetophenone	98-86-2	10	49	—	—	—	3	
Acetylene	74-86-2	—	—	—	—	—	2	

Substance	CAS number	8-hour occupational exposure limit			15-minute or ceiling (c) occupational exposure limit		Substance interaction 1, 2, 3	Carcinogenicity A1, A2
		ppm	mg/m³	f/cc	ppm	mg/m³		
Acetylene dichloride (1,2-Dichloroethylene)	540-59-0 156-59-2 156-60-5	200	793	—	—	—	—	
Acetylene tetrabromide (1,1,2,2-Tetrabromoethane)	79-27-6	0.1	1.4	—	—	—	—	
Acetylene tetrachloride (1,1,2,2-Tetrachloroethane)	79-34-5	1	6.9	—	—	—	1	
Acetylsalicylic acid (Aspirin)	50-78-2	—	5	—	—	—	3	
Acrolein	107-02-8	—	—	—	(c) 0.1	(c) 0.2	1	
Acrylamide	79-06-1	—	0.03	—	—	—	1	
Acrylic acid	79-10-7	2	5.9	—	—	—	1,3	
Acrylic acid, n-butyl ester (n-Butyl acrylate)	141-32-2	2	10	—	—	—	3	
Acrylic acid, ethyl ester (Ethyl acrylate)	140-88-5	5	20	—	15	61	—	
Acrylic acid, methyl ester (Methyl acrylate)	96-33-3	2	7	—	—	—	1	
Acrylonitrile (Vinyl cyanide)	107-13-1	2	4.3	—	—	—	1	
Adipic acid	124-04-9	—	5	—	—	—	—	
Adiponitrile	111-69-3	2	8.8	—	—	—	1	

Substance	CAS number	8-hour occupational exposure limit			15-minute or ceiling (c) occupational exposure limit		Substance interaction 1, 2, 3	Carcinogenicity A1, A2
		ppm	mg/m³	f/cc	ppm	mg/m³		
Aldrin	309-00-2	—	0.25	—	—	—	1	
Aliphatic Hydrocarbon gases, Alkane (C2-C4)	—	1000	—	—	—	—	—	—
Allyl alcohol	107-18-6	0.5	1.2	—	—	—	1, 3	
Allyl chloride	107-05-1	1	3.1	—	2	6.2	—	
Allyl glycidyl ether	106-92-3	1	4.7	—	—	—	—	
Allyl propyl disulfide	2179-59-1	0.5	3	—	—	—	3	
Alumina (Aluminum oxide)	1344-28-1	—	10	—	—	—	—	
Aluminum	7429-90-5			—				
Metal Dust		—	10		—	—	3	
Pyro powders, as Al		—	5		—	—		
Soluble salts, as Al		—	2		—	—	3	
Alkyls, not otherwise specified as Al		—	2		—	—	3	
Aluminum oxide (Alumina)	1344-28-1	—	10	—	—	—	—	
Aminoethanol (Ethanolamine)	141-43-5	3	7.5	—	6	15	3	
Aminopyridine	504-29-0	0.5	1.9	—	—	—	—	
Amino-1,2,4 triazole (Amitrole)	61-82-5	—	0.2	—	—	—	—	
Amitrole	61-82-5	—	0.2	—	—	—	—	

Substance	CAS number	8-hour occupational exposure limit			15-minute or ceiling (c) occupational exposure limit		Substance interaction 1, 2, 3	Carcino-genicity A1, A2
		ppm	mg/m³	f/cc	ppm	mg/m³		
Ammonia	7664-41-7	25	17	—	35	24	—	
Ammonium chloride fume	12125-02-9	—	10	—	—	20	3	
Ammonium perfluorooctanoate	3825-26-1	—	0.01	—	—	—	1	
Ammonium persulfate (Persulfates)	7727-54-0	—	0.1	—	—	—	3	
Ammonium sulfamate	7773-06-0	—	10	—	—	—	—	
Amosite (Asbestos)	12172-73-5	—	—	0.1	—	—	—	A1
n-Amyl acetate (1-Pentyl acetate)	628-63-7	50	266	—	100	532	3	
Sec-Amyl acetate (2-Pentyl acetate)	626-38-0	50	266	—	100	532	3	
Tert-Amyl acetate (1,1-dimethylpropyl acetate)	625-16-1	50	266	—	100	532	3	
Aniline	62-53-3	2	7.6	—	—	—	1	
o-Anisidine	90-04-0	—	0.5	—	—	—	1	
p-Anisidine	104-94-9	—	0.5	—	—	—	1	
Antimony & compounds, as Sb	7440-36-0	—	0.5	—	—	—	3	
Antimony hydride	7803-52-3	0.1	0.5	—	—	—	—	
ANTU (α-Naphthylthiourea)	86-88-4	—	0.3	—	—	—	—	
Argon	7440-37-1	—	—	—	—	—	2	

Substance	CAS number	8-hour occupational exposure limit			15-minute or ceiling (c) occupational exposure limit		Substance interaction 1, 2, 3	Carcinogenicity A1, A2
		ppm	mg/m³	f/cc	ppm	mg/m³		
Arsenic, elemental & inorganic compounds as As	7440-38-2	—	0.01	—	—	—	—	A1
Arsine	7784-42-1	0.05	0.2	—	—	—	—	
Asbestos, all forms	1332-21-4 12172-73-5 12001-29-5 12172-67-7	—	—	0.1	—	—	—	A1
Asphalt (Petroleum; Bitumen) fume	8052-42-4	—	5	—	—	—	3	
Atrazine	1912-24-9	—	5	—	—	—	3	
Azinphos-methyl (Guthion)	86-50-0	—	0.2	—	—	—	1	
Barium and soluble compounds, as Ba	7440-39-3	—	0.5	—	—	—	—	
Barium sulfate	7727-43-7	—	10	—	—	—	—	
Benomyl	17804-35-2	0.84	10	—	—	—	3	
Benzene	71-43-2	0.5	1.6	—	2.5	8	1	A1
p-Benzoquinone (Quinone)	106-51-4	0.1	0.4	—	—	—	—	
Benzotrichloride (Benzyl trichloride)	98-07-7	—	—	—	(c) 0.1	(c) 0.8	1	A2
Benzoyl chloride	98-88-4	—	—	—	(c) 0.5	(c) 2.9	3	
Benzoyl peroxide	94-36-0	—	5	—	—	—	3	

Substance	CAS number	8-hour occupational exposure limit			15-minute or ceiling (c) occupational exposure limit		Substance interaction 1, 2, 3	Carcino-genicity A1, A2
		ppm	mg/m³	f/cc	ppm	mg/m³		
Benzyl acetate	140-11-4	10	61	—	—	—	3	
Benzyl chloride	100-44-7	1	5.2	—	—	—	3	
Benzyl trichloride (Benzotrichloride)	98-07-7	—	—	—	(c) 0.1	(c) 0.8	1	A2
Beryllium and compounds, as Be	7440-41-7	—	0.002	—	—	0.01	—	A1
Biphenyl (Diphenyl)	92-52-4	0.2	1.3	—	—	—	—	
Bis (2-dimethylaminoethyl) ether	3033-62-3	0.5	0.3	—	0.15	0.9	1,3	
Bismuth telluride	1304-82-1							
Undoped, as Bi_2Te_3		—	10	—	—	—	—	
Se-doped, as Bi_2Te_3		—	5	—	—	—	—	
Bitumen (Asphalt fume)	8052-42-4	—	5	—	—	—	3	
Borates, tetra, sodium salts,	1303-96-4							
Anhydrous		—	1	—	3	—	3	
Decahydrate		—	1	—	3	—		
Pentahydrate		—	1	—	3	—		
Boron oxide	1303-86-2	—	10	—	—	—	3	
Boron tribromide	10294-33-4	—	—	—	(c) 1	(c) 10	—	
Boron trifluoride	7637-07-2	—	—	—	(c) 1	(c) 2.8	—	
Bromacil	314-40-9	—	10	—	—	—	—	

Substance	CAS number	8-hour occupational exposure limit			15-minute or ceiling (c) occupational exposure limit		Substance interaction 1, 2, 3	Carcino-genicity A1, A2
		ppm	mg/m³	f/cc	ppm	mg/m³		
Bromine	7726-95-6	0.1	0.7	—	0.2	1.3	—	
Bromine pentafluoride	7789-30-2	0.1	0.7	—	—	—	3	
Bromochloromethane (Chlorobromomethane)	74-97-5	200	1060	—	—	—	—	
Bromoethane (Ethyl bromide)	74-96-4	5	22	—	—	—	1	
Bromoform (Tribromomethane)	75-25-2	0.5	5.2	—	—	—	1	
1-Bromopropane	106-44-5	10	50	—	—	—	—	
Bromotrifluoromethane (Trifluorobromomethane)	75-63-8	1000	6090	—	—	—	—	
1,3-Butadiene	106-99-0	2	4.4	—	—	—	—	A2
Butane	106-97-8	1000	—	—	—	—	—	
Butanethiol (n-tyl mercaptan)	109-79-5	0.5	1.8	—	—	—	3	
n-Butanol (n-Butyl alcohol)	71-36-3	20	60	—	—	—	3	
sec-Butanol (sec-Butyl alcohol)	78-92-2	100	303	—	—	—	—	
tert-Butanol (tert-Butyl alcohol)	75-65-0	100	303	—	—	—	—	

Substance	CAS number	8-hour occupational exposure limit			15-minute or ceiling (c) occupational exposure limit			Substance interaction 1, 2, 3	Carcino-genicity A1, A2
		ppm	mg/m^3	f/cc	ppm	mg/m^3			
2-Butanone (Methyl ethyl ketone)	78-93-3	200	590	—	300	885	—	
3-Buten-2-one (Methyl vinyl ketone)	78-94-4	—	—	—	(c) 0.2	(c) 0.6	1	
2-Butoxyethanol (Ethylene glycol monobutyl ether)	111-76-2	20	97	—	—	—	3	
n-Butoxyethyl acetate	112-07-2	20	131	—	—	—	—	
n-Butyl acetate	123-86-4	150	713	—	200	950	3	
sec-Butyl acetate	105-46-4	200	950	—	—	—	3	
tert-Butyl acetate	540-88-5	200	950	—	—	—	3	
n-Butyl acrylate	141-32-2	2	10	—	—	—	—	
n-Butylamine	109-73-9	—	—	—	(c) 5	(c) 15	1	
Butylated hydroxytoluene (BHT) (2,6-Di-tert-butyl-p-cresol)	128-37-0	—	10	—	—	—	3	
tert-Butyl chromate as CrO$_3$	1189-85-1	—	—	—	—	(c) 0.1	1	
n-Butyl glycidyl ether	2426-08-06	3	16	—	—	—	1	
n-Butyl lactate	138-22-7	5	30	—	—	—	—	
Butyl mercaptan (Butanethiol)	109-79-5	0.5	1.8	—	—	—	3	
o-sec-Butylphenol	89-72-5	5	31	—	—	—	1, 3	
p-tert-Butyltoluene	98-51-1	1	6.1	—	—	—	—	

Substance	CAS number	8-hour occupational exposure limit			15-minute or ceiling (c) occupational exposure limit		Substance interaction 1, 2, 3	Carcinogenicity A1, A2
		ppm	mg/m³	f/cc	ppm	mg/m³		
Cadmium, elemental	7440-43-9	—	0.01	—	—	—	—	A2
Cadmium compounds as Cd, respirable			0.002					A2
Calcium carbonate (Aragonite, Calcite, Marble, Vaterite)	1317-65-3 471-34-1	—	10	—	—	—	3	
Calcium chromate, as Cr	13756-19-0	—	0.001	—	—	—	—	A2
Calcium cyanamide	156-62-7	—	0.5	—	—	—	3	
Calcium hydroxide	1305-62-0	—	5	—	—	—	3	
Calcium oxide	1305-78-8	—	2	—	—	—	3	
Calcium silicate, (synthetic, nonfibrous)	1344-95-2	—	10	—	—	—	3	
Calcium sulphate (Plaster of Paris, Gypsum)	7778-18-9 26499-65-0 13397-24-5	—	10	—	—	—	—	
Camphor, synthetic	76-22-2	2	12	—	3	19	—	
Caprolactam	105-60-2	—	5	—	—	—	—	
Captafol	2425-06-1	—	0.1	—	—	—	1,3	
Captan	133-06-2	—	5	—	—	—	3	
Carbaryl (Sevin®)	63-25-2	—	5	—	—	—	—	
Carbofuran	1563-66-2	—	0.1	—	—	—	—	
Carbon black	1333-86-4	—	3.5	—	—	—	—	

Substance	CAS number	8-hour occupational exposure limit			15-minute or ceiling (c) occupational exposure limit		Substance interaction 1, 2, 3	Carcino-genicity A1, A2
		ppm	mg/m³	f/cc	ppm	mg/m³		
Carbon dioxide	124-38-9	5000	9000	—	30,000	54,000	—	
Carbon disulfide	75-15-0	1	3.1	—	—	—	1	
Carbon monoxide	630-08-0	25	29	—	—	—	—	
Carbon tetrabromide	558-13-4	0.1	1.4	—	0.3	4.1	—	
Carbon tetrachloride (Tetrachloromethane)	56-23-5	5	31	—	10	63	1	A2
Carbonyl chloride (Phosgene)	75-44-3	0.1	0.4	—	—	—	—	
Carbonyl fluoride	353-50-4	2	5.4	—	5	13	—	
Catechol	120-80-9	5	23	—	—	—	1	
Cellulose	9004-34-6	—	10	—	—	—	3	
Cesium hydroxide	21351-79-1	—	2	—	—	—	3	
Chlordane	57-74-9	—	0.5	—	—	—	1	
Chlorinated camphene (Toxaphene)	8001-35-2	—	0.5	—	—	1	1	
Chlorinated diphenyl oxide	31242-93-0	—	0.5	—	—	—	—	
Chlorine	7782-50-5	0.5	1.5	—	1	2.9	3	
Chlorine dioxide	10049-04-4	0.1	0.3	—	0.3	0.8	—	
Chlorine trifluoride	7790-91-2	—	—	—	(c) 0.1	(c) 0.4	—	
Chloroacetaldehyde	107-20-0	—	—	—	(c) 1	(c) 0.4	3	
Chloroacetone	78-95-5	—	—	—	(c) 1	(c) 3.8	1, 3	

Substance	CAS number	8-hour occupational exposure limit			15-minute or ceiling (c) occupational exposure limit		Substance interaction 1, 2, 3	Carcino-genicity A1, A2
		ppm	mg/m³	f/cc	ppm	mg/m³		
2-Chloroacetophenone (Phenacyl chloride)	532-27-4	0.05	0.3	—	—	—	3	
Chloroacetyl chloride	79-04-9	0.05	0.2	—	0.15	0.7	1,3	
Chlorobenzene	108-90-7	10	46	—	—	—	—	
o-Chlorobenzylidene malononitrile	2698-41-1	—	—	—	(c) 0.05	(c) 0.4	1	
Chlorobromomethane	74-97-5	200	1060	—	—	—	—	
2-Chloro-1,3-butadiene (β-Chloroprene)	126-99-8	10	36	—	—	—	1,3	
Chlorodifluoromethane	75-45-6	1000	3500	—	—	—	1	
Chlorodiphenyl (42 percent chlorine) (PCBs, Polychlorinated biphenyls — 42 percent chlorine)	53469-21-9	—	1	—	—	—	1	
Chlorodiphenyl (54 percent chlorine) (PCBs, Polychlorinated biphenyls — 54 percent chlorine)	11097-69-1	—	0.5	—	—	—	1	
1-Chloro,2,3-epoxy-propane (Epichlorohydrin)	106-89-8	0.5	1.9	—	—	—	1	
Chloroethane (Ethyl chloride)	75-00-3	100	264	—	—	—	1	

Substance	CAS number	8-hour occupational exposure limit			15-minute or ceiling (c) occupational exposure limit		Substance interaction 1, 2, 3	Carcinogenicity A1, A2
		ppm	mg/m³	f/cc	ppm	mg/m³		
2-Chloroethanol (Ethylene chlorohydrin)	107-07-3	—	—	—	(c) 1	(c) 3.3	1	
Chloroethylene (Vinyl chloride)	75-01-4	1	2.6	—	—	—	—	A1
Chloroform (Trichloromethane)	67-66-3	10	49	—	—	—	—	
Bis(Chloromethyl) ether	542-88-1	0.001	0.005	—	—	—	—	A1
p-Chloronitrobenzene (p-Nitrochlorobenzene)	100-00-5	0.1	0.6	—	—	—	1	
1-Chloro-1-nitropropane	600-25-9	2	10	—	—	—	—	
Chloropentafluoroethane	76-15-3	1000	6300	—	—	—	—	
Chloropicrin (Trichloronitromethane)	76-06-2	0.1	0.7	—	—	—	—	
1-Chloro-2-propanol and 2-Chloro-1-propanol	127-00-4 78-89-7	1	4	—	—	—	1	
β-Chloroprene	126-99-8	10	36	—	—	—	1,3	
2-Chloropropionic acid	598-78-7	0.1	0.4	—	—	—	1	
o-Chlorostyrene	2039-87-4	50	283	—	75	425	—	
o-Chlorotoluene	95-49-8	50	259	—	—	—	3	
2-Chloro-6-(trichloromethyl) pyridine (Nitrapyrin)	1929-82-4	—	10	—	—	20	—	

Substance	CAS number	8-hour occupational exposure limit			15-minute or ceiling (c) occupational exposure limit		Substance interaction 1, 2, 3	Carcino-genicity A1, A2
		ppm	mg/m³	f/cc	ppm	mg/m³		
Chlorpyrifos	2921-88-2	—	0.1	—	—	—	1	
Chromite ore processing (Chromate), as Cr	-	—	0.05	—	—	—	—	A1
Chromium, metal and inorganic compounds, as Cr	7440-47-3							
Metal and Cr III compounds		—	0.5	—	—	—	3	A1
Water-soluble Cr VI compounds		—	0.05	—	—	—	—	
Insoluble Cr VI compounds		—	0.01	—	—	—	—	A1
Chromyl chloride	14977-61-8	0.025	0.2	—	—	—	3	A1
Chrysotile (Asbestos)	12001-29-5	—	—	0.1	—	—	—	A1
Clopidol	2971-90-6	—	10	—	—	—	3	
Coal dust (Respirable particulate) This limit expires on July 1, 2010 and is replaced by the exposure limit shown below		—	2	—	—	—	—	—
Coal dust (Respirable particulate)		—						
Anthracite			0.4					
Bituminous			0.9					
These limits come into effect on July 1, 2010								

Substance	CAS number	8-hour occupational exposure limit			15-minute or ceiling (c) occupational exposure limit		Substance interaction 1, 2, 3	Carcinogenicity A1, A2
		ppm	mg/m³	f/cc	ppm	mg/m³		
Coal tar pitch volatiles, as benzene solubles	65996-93-2	—	0.2	—	—	—	—	A1
Cobalt, elemental inorganic compounds, as Co	7440-48-4	—	0.02	—	—	—	—	
Cobalt carbonyl, as Co	10210-68-1	—	0.1		—	—	—	
Cobalt hydrocarbonyl, as Co	16842-03-8	—	0.1	—	—	—	—	
Copper	7440-50-8							
Fume		—	0.2		—	—	—	
Dusts/mists, as Cu		—	1		—	—	—	
Cotton, dust, raw		—	0.2	—	—	—	—	
Coumaphos (mg/m3)	56-72-4	—	0.5	—	—	—	1	
Cresol, all isomers	1319-77-3 95-48-7 108-39-4 106-44-5	5	22		—	—	1	
Cristobalite, respirable (Silica, crystalline)	14464-46-1	—	0.025	—	—	—	—	A2
Crocidolite (Asbestos)	12001-28-4	—	—	0.1	—	—	—	A1
Crotonaldehyde	4170-30-3	—	—	—	(c) 0.3	(c) 0.9	1, 3	
Cruformate	299-86-5	—	5	—	—	—	—	
Cumene	98-82-8	50	246	—	—	—	—	

Substance	CAS number	8-hour occupational exposure limit			15-minute or ceiling (c) occupational exposure limit		Substance interaction 1, 2, 3	Carcinogenicity A1, A2
		ppm	mg/m³	f/cc	ppm	mg/m³		
Cyanamide	420-04-2	—	2	—	—	—	3	
Cyanide and Cyanide salts and hydrogen cyanide as CN								
Hydrogen cyanide	74-90-8	—	—	—	(c) 4.7	(c) 5.2	1	
Calcium cyanide	592-01-8	—	—	—	—	(c) 5	1	
Potassium cyanide	151-50-8	—	—	—	—	(c) 5	1	
Sodium cyanide	143-33-9	—	—	—	—	(c) 5	1	
Cyanogen	460-19-5	10	21	—	—	—	3	
Cyanogen chloride	506-77-4	—	—	—	(c) 0.3	(c) 0.8	—	
Cyclohexane	110-82-7	100	344	—	—	—	—	
Cyclohexanol	108-93-0	50	205	—	—	—	1	
Cyclohexanone	108-94-1	20	80	—	50	200	1	
Cyclohexene	110-83-8	300	1010	—	—	—	3	
Cyclohexylamine	108-91-8	10	41	—	—	—	3	
Cyclonite (RDX)	121-82-4	—	0.5	—	—	—	1	
Cyclopentadiene	542-92-7	75	203	—	—	—	3	
Cyclopentane	287-92-3	600	1720	—	—	—	—	
Cyhexatin (Tricyclohexyltin hydroxide)	13121-70-5	—	5	—	—	—	—	
2,4-D (2,4-Dichlorophenoxyacetic acid)	94-75-7	—	10	—	—	—	3	

Substance	CAS number	8-hour occupational exposure limit			15-minute or ceiling (c) occupational exposure limit			Substance interaction 1, 2, 3	Carcino-genicity A1, A2
		ppm	mg/m³	f/cc	ppm	mg/m³			
DDT (Dichlorodiphenyl trichloroethane)	50-29-3	—	1	—	—	—		—	
Decaborane	17702-41-9	0.05	0.3	—	0.15	0.8		1	
Demeton (Systox®)	8065-48-3	—	0.05	—	—	—		1	
Demeton-s-methyl (Methyl demeton)	8022-00-2	—	0.05	—	—	—		1	
Diacetone alcohol (4-Hydroxyl-4-methyl-2-pentanone)	123-42-2	50	238	—	—	—		3	
4,4-Diaminodiphenyl-methane (4,4'-Methylene dianiline)	101-77-9	0.1	0.8	—	—	—		1	
1,2-Diaminoethane (Ethylenediamine)	107-15-3	10	25	—	—	—		1	
Diazinon	333-41-5	—	0.01	—	—	—		1	
Diazomethane	334-88-3	0.2	0.3	—	—	—		—	A2
Dibenzoyl peroxide (Benzoyl peroxide)	94-36-0	—	5	—	—	—		3	
Diborane	19287-45-7	0.1	0.1	—	—	—		—	
Dibrom (Naled)	300-76-5	—	0.1	—	—	—		1	
2-N-Dibutylaminoethanol	102-81-8	0.5	3.5	—	—	—		1,3	

Schedule 1

| Substance | CAS number | 8-hour occupational exposure limit | | | 15-minute or ceiling (c) occupational exposure limit | | Substance interaction 1, 2, 3 | Carcino-genicity A1, A2 |
		ppm	mg/m^3	f/cc	ppm	mg/m^3		
2,6-Di-tert-butyl-p-cresol (Butylated hydroxytoluene, BHT)	128-37-0	—	10	—	—	—	3	
Dibutyl phenyl phosphate	2528-36-1	0.3	3.5	—	—	—	1	
Dibutyl phosphate	107-66-4	1	8.6	—	2	17	—	
Dibutyl phthalate	84-74-2	—	5	—	—	—	—	
Dichloroacetic acid	79-43-6	0.5	2.6	—	—	—	1	
Dichloroacetylene	7572-29-4	—	—	—	(c) 0.1	(c) 0.4	—	
o-Dichlorobenzene (1,2-Dichlorobenzene)	95-50-1	25	150	—	50	300	—	
p-Dichlorobenzene (1,4-Dichlorobenzene)	106-46-7	10	60	—	—	—	—	
1,4-Dichloro-2-butene	764-41-0	0.005	0.03	—	—	—	1	A2
Dichlorodifluoromethane	75-71-8	1000	4950	—	—	—	—	
1,3-Dichloro-5,5-dimethyl hydantoin	118-52-5	—	0.2	—	—	0.4	3	
Dichlorodiphenyl-trichloroethane (DDT)	50-29-3	—	1	—	—	—	—	
1,1-Dichloroethane (Ethylidene chloride)	75-34-3	100	405	—	—	—	—	
1,2-Dichloroethane (Ethylene dichloride)	107-06-2	10	40	—	—	—	—	

Substance	CAS number	8-hour occupational exposure limit			15-minute or ceiling (c) occupational exposure limit		Substance interaction 1, 2, 3	Carcino-genicity A1, A2
		ppm	mg/m^3	f/cc	ppm	mg/m^3		
1,1-Dichloroethylene (Vinylidene chloride)	75-35-4	5	20	—	—	—	—	
1,2-Dichloroethylene, all isomers (Acetylene dichloride)	540-59-0 156-59-2 156-60-5	200	793	—	—	—	—	
Dichloroethyl ether (2,2'-Dichlorodiethyl ether)	111-44-4	5	29	—	10	58	1	
Dichlorofluoromethane (Dichloromonofluoromethane)	75-43-4	10	42	—	—	—	—	
Dichloromethane (Methylene chloride)	75-09-4	50	174	—	—	—	—	
1,1-Dichloro-1-nitroethane	594-72-9	2	12	—	—	—	3	
2,4-Diclorophenoxyacetic acid (2,4-D)	94-75-7	—	10	—	—	—	3	
1,2-Dichloropropane (Propylene dichloride)	78-87-5	10	46	—	—	—	—	
1,1-Dichloro-1-nitroethane	594-72-9	2	12	—	—	—	—	
1,3-Dichloropropene	542-75-6	1	4.5	—	—	—	1	
2,2-Dichloropropionic acid	75-99-0	—	5	—	—	—	3	
Dichlorotetrafluoroethane (1,2-Dichloro-1,1,2,2-tetrafluoroethane)	76-14-2	1000	7000	—	—	—	—	

Substance	CAS number	8-hour occupational exposure limit			15-minute or ceiling (c) occupational exposure limit		Substance interaction 1, 2, 3	Carcinogenicity A1, A2
		ppm	mg/m³	f/cc	ppm	mg/m³		
Dichlorvos	62-73-7	—	0.1	—	—	—	1	
Dicrotophos	141-66-2	—	0.05	—	—	—	1	
Dicyclopentadiene	77-73-6	5	27	—	—	—	3	
Dicyclopentadienyl iron (Ferrocene)	102-54-5	—	10	—	—	—	—	
Dieldrin	60-57-1	—	0.25	—	—	—	1	
Diesel fuel, as total hydrocarbons	68334-30-5 68476-30-2 68476-34-6 68476-31-3 77650-28-3	—	100	—	—	—	—	
Diethanolamine	111-42-2	—	2	—	—	—	1	
Diethylamine	109-89-7	5	15	—	15	45	1,3	
2-Diethylaminoethanol	100-37-8	2	9.6	—	—	—	1	
Diethylene dioxide (1,4-Dioxane)	123-91-1	20	72	—	—	—	1	
Diethylene triamine	111-40-0	1	4.2	—	—	—	1,3	
Diethyl ether (Ethyl ether)	60-29-7	400	1210	—	500	1520	—	
Di(2-ethylhexyl)phthalate (DEHP, Di-sec-octyl phthalate)	117-81-7	—	5	—	—	—	3	
Diethyl ketone	96-22-0	200	705	—	300	1060	—	

Substance	CAS number	8-hour occupational exposure limit			15-minute or ceiling (c) occupational exposure limit		Substance interaction 1, 2, 3	Carcino-genicity A1, A2
		ppm	mg/m³	f/cc	ppm	mg/m³		
Diethyl phthalate	84-66-2	—	5	—	—	—	3	
Difluorodibromomethane	75-61-6	100	858	—	—	—	—	
1, 1-Difluoroethylene (Vinylidene fluoride)	75-38-7	500	1310	—	—	—	—	
Diglycidyl ether	2238-07-5	0.1	0.5	—	—	—	—	
Dihydroxybenzene (Hydroquinone)	123-31-9	—	2	—	—	—	—	
Diisobutyl ketone (2,6-Dimethyl-4-heptanone)	108-83-8	25	145	—	—	—	3	
Diisopropylamine	108-18-9	5	21	—	—	—	1	
Dimethoxymethane (Methylal)	109-87-5	1000	3110	—	—	—	—	
N,N-Dimethylacetamide	127-19-5	10	36	—	—	—	1	
Dimethylamine	124-40-3	5	9.2	—	15	28	—	
Dimethylaminobenzene (Xylidine, mixed isomers)	1300-73-8	0.5	2.5	—	—	—	1	
bis(2-Dimethylamino-ethyl) ether (DMAEE)	3033-62-3	0.05	0.3	—	0.15	0.98	1	
Dimethylaniline (N,N-Dimethylaniline)	121-69-7	5	25	—	10	50	1	

Substance	CAS number	8-hour occupational exposure limit			15-minute or ceiling (c) occupational exposure limit		Substance interaction 1, 2, 3	Carcino-genicity A1, A2
		ppm	mg/m³	f/cc	ppm	mg/m³		
Dimethylbenzene (Xylene, o,m & p isomers)	1330-20-7 95-47-6 108-38-3 106-42-3	100	434	—	150	651	—	
Dimethylbutane (Hexane, all isomers, except n-Hexane)	75-83-2 79-29-8	500	1760	—	1000	3500	—	
Dimethyl-1,2-dibromo-2,2-dichloroethyl phosphate (Dibrom, Naled)	300-76-5	—	0.1	—	—	—	1	
Dimethylethoxysilane	14857-34-2	0.5	2.1	—	1.5	6.4	—	
Dimethylformamide	68-12-2	10	30	—	—	—	1	
2,6-Dimethyl-4-heptanone (Diisobutyl ketone)	108-83-8	25	145	—	—	—	3	
1,1-Dimethylhydrazine	57-14-7	0.01	0.02	—	—	—	1	
Dimethyl phthalate	131-11-3	—	5	—	—	—	3	
1,1-Dimethylpropyl acetate (tert-Amyl acetate)	625-16-1	50	266	—	100	532	3	
Dimethyl sulfate	77-78-1	0.1	0.5	—	—	—	1, 3	
Dimethyl sulfide	75-18-3	10	25	—	—	—	3	
Dinitolmide (3,5-Dinitro-o-toluamide)	148-01-6	—	5	—	—	—	—	

Schedule 1

Substance	CAS number	8-hour occupational exposure limit			15-minute or ceiling (c) occupational exposure limit		Substance interaction 1, 2, 3	Carcino-genicity A1, A2
		ppm	mg/m³	f/cc	ppm	mg/m³		
Dinitrobenzene, all isomers	528-29-0 99-65-0 100-25-4 25154-54-5	0.15	1	—	—	—	1	
Dinitro-o-cresol	534-52-1	—	0.2	—	—	—	1	
3,5-Dinitro-o-toluamide (Dinitolmide)	148-01-6	—	5	—	—	—	—	
Dinitrotoluene	25321-14-6	—	0.2	—	—	—	1	
1,4-Dioxane (Diethylene dioxide)	123-91-1	20	72	—	—	—	1	
Dioxathion	78-34-2	—	0.1	—	—	—	1	
1,3-Dioxolane	646-06-0	20	61	—	—	—	—	
Diphenyl (Biphenyl)	92-52-4	0.2	1.3	—	—	—	—	
Diphenylamine	122-39-4	—	10	—	—	—	—	
Diphenyl ether, vapour (Phenyl ether)	101-84-8	1	7	—	2	14	—	
Diphenylmethane-4,4'-diisocyanate (Methylene bisphenyl isocyanate, MDI)	101-68-8	0.005	0.05	—	—	—	—	

Substance	CAS number	8-hour occupational exposure limit			15-minute or ceiling (c) occupational exposure limit		Substance interaction 1, 2, 3	Carcinogenicity A1, A2
		ppm	mg/m³	f/cc	ppm	mg/m³		
Dipropylene glycol methyl ether [(2-Methoxymethylethoxy) propanol, DPGME]	34590-94-8	100	606	—	150	909	1	
Dipropyl ketone	123-19-3	50	235	—	—	—	3	
Diquat	2764-72-9							
Total	85-00-7	—	0.5	—	—	—	1	
Respirable	6385-62-2	—	0.1	—	—	—	1	
Di-sec-octyl-phthalate (DEHP, Di-sec-octyl phthalate)	117-81-7	—	5	—	—	—	3	
Disulfiram	97-77-8	—	2	—	—	—	—	
Disulfoton	298-04-4	—	0.05	—	—	—	1	
Diuron	330-54-1	—	10	—	—	—	3	
Divinyl benzene	1321-74-0	10	53	—	—	—	3	
Dodecyl mercaptan	112-55-0	0.1	0.8	—	—	—	3	
Emery	1302-74-5	—	10	—	—	—	3	
Endosulfan	115-29-7	—	0.1	—	—	—	1	
Endrin	72-20-8	—	0.1	—	—	—	1	
Enflurane	13838-16-9	75	566	—	—	—	—	
Enzymes, proteolytic (Subtilisins)	1395-21-7 9014-01-1	—	—	—	—	(c) 0.00006	—	
Epichlorohydrin (1-Chloro-2,3-epoxypropane)	106-89-8	0.5	1.9	—	—	—	1	

Substance	CAS number	8-hour occupational exposure limit			15-minute or ceiling (c) occupational exposure limit			Substance interaction 1, 2, 3	Carcino-genicity A1, A2
		ppm	mg/m³	f/cc	ppm	mg/m³			
EPN	2104-64-5	—	0.1	—	—	—		1	
1,2-Epoxypropane (Propylene oxide)	75-56-9	2	4.7	—	—	—		—	
2,3-Epoxy-1-propanol (Glycidol)	556-52-5	2	6.1	—	—	—		3	
Ethane	74-84-0	1000	—	—	—	—		—	
Ethanethiol (Ethyl mercaptan)	75-08-1	0.5	1.3	—	—	—		—	
Ethanol (Ethyl alcohol)	64-17-5	1000	1880	—	—	—		—	
Ethanolamine (2-Aminoethanol)	141-43-5	3	7.5	—	6	15		3	
Ethion	563-12-2	—	0.05	—	—	—		1	
2-Ethoxyethanol (Ethylene glycol monoethyl ether)	110-80-5	5	18	—	—	—		1	
2-Ethoxyethyl acetate (Ethylene glycol monoethyl ether acetate)	111-15-9	5	27	—	—	—		1	
Ethyl acetate	141-78-6	400	1440	—	—	—		3	
Ethyl acrylate (Acrylic acid, ethyl ester)	140-88-5	5	20	—	15	61		—	

Substance	CAS number	8-hour occupational exposure limit			15-minute or ceiling (c) occupational exposure limit		Substance interaction 1, 2, 3	Carcinogenicity A1, A2
		ppm	mg/m³	f/cc	ppm	mg/m³		
Ethyl alcohol (Ethanol)	64-17-5	1000	1880	—	—	—	—	
Ethylamine	75-04-7	5	9.2	—	15	28	1	
Ethyl amyl ketone (5-Methyl-3-heptanone)	541-85-5	25	131	—	—	—	—	
Ethyl benzene	100-41-4	100	434	—	125	543	—	
Ethyl bromide (Bromoethane)	74-96-4	5	22	—	—	—	1	
Ethyl tert-butyl ether (ETBE)	637-92-3	5	21	—	—	—	—	
Ethyl butyl ketone (3-Heptanone)	106-35-4	50	234	—	75	350	1	
Ethyl chloride (Chloroethane)	795-00-3	100	264	—	—	—	1	
Ethyl cyanoacrylate (Ethyl-2-cyanoacrylate)	7085-85-0	0.2	1	—	—	—	—	
Ethylene chlorohydrin (2-chloroethanol)	107-07-3	—	—	—	(c) 1	(c) 3.3	1	
Ethylenediamine (1,2-Diaminoethane)	107-15-3	10	25	—	—	—	1	
Ethylene dichloride (1,2-Dichloroethane)	107-06-2	10	40	—	—	—	—	

Substance	CAS number	8-hour occupational exposure limit			15-minute or ceiling (c) occupational exposure limit		Substance interaction 1, 2, 3	Carcino-genicity A1, A2
		ppm	mg/m^3	f/cc	ppm	mg/m^3		
Ethylene	74-85-1	200	229	—	—	—	—	
Ethylene glycol	107-21-1	—	—	—	—	(c) 100	3	
Ethylene glycol dinitrate (EGDN)	628-96-6	0.05	0.3	—	—	—	1	
Ethylene glycol isopropyl ether (2-Isopropoxyethanol)	109-59-1	25	106	—	—	—	1	
Ethylene glycol methyl ether acetate (2-Methoxyethyl acetate)	110-49-6	0.1	0.5	—	—	—	1	
Ethylene glycol monobutyl ether (2-Butoxyethanol)	111-76-2	20	97	—	—	—	3	
Ethylene glycol monoethyl ether (2-Ethoxyethanol)	110-80-5	0.1	0.4	—	—	—	1	
Ethylene glycol monoethyl ether acetate (2-Ethoxyethyl acetate)	111-15-9	5	27	—	—	—	1	
Ethylene glycol monomethyl ether (2-Methoxyethanol)	109-86-4	0.1	0.3	—	—	—	1	
Ethylene oxide	75-21-8	1	1.8	—	—	—	—	A2
Ethylenimine	151-56-4	0.5	0.9	—	—	—	1	
Ethyl ether (Diethyl ether)	60-29-7	400	1210	—	500	1520	—	

Substance	CAS number	8-hour occupational exposure limit			15-minute or ceiling (c) occupational exposure limit		Substance interaction 1, 2, 3	Carcino-genicity A1, A2
		ppm	mg/m³	f/cc	ppm	mg/m³		
Ethyl formate (Formic acid, ethyl ester)	109-94-4	100	303	—	—	—	3	
2-Ethylhexanoic acid	149-57-5	—	5	—	—	—	—	
Ethylidene chloride (1,1-Dichloroethane)	75-34-3	100	405	—	—	—	—	
Ethylidene norbornene	16219-75-3	—	—	—	(c) 5	(c) 25	3	
Ethyl mercaptan	75-08-1	0.5	1.3	—	—	—	—	
N-Ethylmorpholine	100-74-3	5	24	—	—	—	1	
Ethyl silicate (Silicic acid, tetraethyl ester)	78-10-4	10	85	—	—	—	—	
Fenamiphos	22224-92-6	—	0.05	—	—	—	1	
Fensulfothion	115-90-2	—	0.01	—	—	—	1	
Fenthion	55-38-9	—	0.05	—	—	—	1	
Ferbam	14484-64-1	—	10	—	—	—	3	
Ferrocene (Dicyclopentadienyl iron)	102-54-5	—	10	—	—	—	—	
Ferrovanadium dust	12604-58-9	—	1	—	—	3	3	
Flour dust (Total particulate)		—	0.5	—	—	—	—	
Fluorides, as F		—	2.5	—	—	—	—	
Fluorine	7782-41-4	1	1.6	—	2	3.1	3	

Substance	CAS number	8-hour occupational exposure limit			15-minute or ceiling (c) occupational exposure limit			Substance interaction 1, 2, 3	Carcino-genicity A1, A2
		ppm	mg/m³	f/cc	ppm	mg/m³			
Fluorotrichloromethane (Trichlorofluoromethane)	75-69-4	—	—	—	(c) 1000	(c) 5620	—	
Fonofos	944-22-9	—	0.01	—	—	—	1	
Formaldehyde	50-00-0	0.75	0.9	—	(c) 1	(c) 1.3	—	A2
Formamide	75-12-7	10	18	—	—	—	1	
Formic acid	64-18-6	5	9.4	—	10	19	3	
Formic acid, ethyl ester (Ethyl formate)	109-94-4	100	303	—	—	—	3	
Formic acid, methyl ester (Methyl formate)	107-31-3	100	246	—	150	368	3	
Furfural	98-01-1	2	7.9	—	—	—	1, 3	
Furfuryl alcohol	98-00-0	10	40	—	15	60	1, 3	
Gallium arsenide, respirable particulate	1303-00-0	—	0.0003	—	—	—	3	
Gasoline	86290-81-5	300	—	—	500	—	—	
Germanium tetrahydride	7782-65-2	0.2	0.6	—	—	—	—	
Glass Fibres								
Continuous filament		—	—	1	—	—	3	
Continuous filament, total		—	5	—	—	—	3	
Glass Wool		—	—	1	—	—	—	
Special purpose		—	—	1	—	—	3	

Substance	CAS number	8-hour occupational exposure limit			15-minute or ceiling (c) occupational exposure limit		Substance interaction 1, 2, 3	Carcinogenicity A1, A2
		ppm	mg/m³	f/cc	ppm	mg/m³		
Glutaraldehyde, activated and inactivated	111-30-8	—	—	—	(c) 0.05	(c) 0.2	—	
Glycerin mist	56-81-5	—	10	—	—	—	3	
Glycidol (2,3-Epoxy-1-propanol)	556-52-5	2	6.1	—	—	—	3	
Glycol monoethyl ether (2-Ethoxyethanol)	110-80-5	5	18	—	—	—	1	
Glyoxal	107-22-2	—	0.1	—	—	—	—	
Grain dust (oat, wheat, barley)		—	4	—	—	—	—	
Graphite, respirable (all forms except graphite fibres)	7782-42-5	—	2	—	—	—	—	
Guthion® (Azinphos-methyl)	86-50-0	—	0.2	—	—	—	1	
Gypsum (Calcium sulphate)	13397-24-5	—	10	—	—	—	—	
Hafnium and compounds, as Hf	7440-58-6	—	0.5	—	—	—	—	
Halothane	151-67-7	50	404	—	—	—	—	
Helium	7440-59-7	—	—	—	—	—	2	
Heptachlor and Heptachlor epoxide	76-44-8 1024-57-3	—	0.05	—	—	—	1	

Substance	CAS number	8-hour occupational exposure limit			15-minute or ceiling (c) occupational exposure limit		Substance interaction 1, 2, 3	Carcinogenicity A1, A2
		ppm	mg/m³	f/cc	ppm	mg/m³		
Heptane, all isomers	142-82-5 590-35-2 565-59-3 108-08-7 591-76-4 589-34-4	400	1640	—	500	2050	—	
2-Heptanone (Methyl n-amyl ketone)	110-43-0	50	233	—	—	—	3	
3-Heptanone (Ethyl butyl ketone)	106-35-4	50	234	—	75	350	—	
Hexachlorobenzene	118-74-1	—	0.002	—	—	—	1	
Hexachlorobutadiene	87-68-3	0.02	0.2	—	—	—	1	
γ-Hexachlorocyclohexane (Lindane)	58-89-9	—	0.5	—	—	—	1	
Hexachlorocyclopentadiene	77-47-4	0.01	0.1	—	—	—	3	
Hexachloroethane	67-72-1	1	9.7	—	—	—	1	
Hexachloronaphthalene	1335-87-1	—	0.2	—	—	—	1	
Hexafluoroacetone	684-16-2	0.1	0.7	—	—	—	1	
Hexahydrophthalic anhydride, all isomers	85-42-7 13149-00-3 14166-21-3	—	—	—	—	(c) 0.005	—	
1,6-Hexamethylene diisocyanate	822-06-0	0.005	0.03	—	—	—	—	

Substance	CAS number	8-hour occupational exposure limit			15-minute or ceiling (c) occupational exposure limit		Substance interaction 1, 2, 3	Carcinogenicity A1, A2
		ppm	mg/m³	f/cc	ppm	mg/m³		
n-Hexane	110-54-3	50	176	—	—	—	1	
Hexane (all isomers except n-hexane)	107-83-5 96-14-0 75-83-2 79-29-8	500	1760	—	1000	3500	—	
1,6-Hexanediamine	124-09-4	0.5	2.4	—	—	—	3	
2-Hexanone (Methyl n-butyl ketone)	591-78-6	5	20	—	10	40	1	
1-Hexene	592-41-6	50	172	—	—	—	—	
Hexone (Methyl isobutyl ketone)	108-10-1	50	205	—	75	307	—	
Sec-Hexyl acetate	108-84-9	50	295	—	—	—	3	
Hexylene glycol	107-41-5	—	—	—	(c) 25	(c) 121	3	
Hydrazine	302-01-2	0.01	0.01	—	—	—	1	
HCFC-123 1,1,1-trifluoro-2,2-dichloroethane	306-83-2	50	310	—	—	—	—	
Hydrogen	1333-74-0	—	—	—	—	—	2	
Hydrogenated terphenyls	61788-32-7	0.5	4.9	—	—	—		
Hydrogen bromide	10035-10-6	—	—	—	(c) 2	(c) 6.6	3	
Hydrogen chloride	7647-01-0	—	—	—	(c) 2	(c) 3	3	

Substance	CAS number	8-hour occupational exposure limit			15-minute or ceiling (c) occupational exposure limit		Substance interaction 1, 2, 3	Carcino-genicity A1, A2
		ppm	mg/m³	f/cc	ppm	mg/m³		
Hydrogen cyanide and cyanide salts, as CN								
Hydrogen cyanide	74-90-8	—	—	—	(c) 4.7	(c) 5.2	1	
Calcium cyanide	592-01-8	—	—	—	—	(c) 5	1	
Potassium cyanide	151-50-8	—	—	—	—	(c) 5	1	
Sodium cyanide	143-33-9	—	—	—	—	(c) 5	1	
Hydrogen fluoride, as F	7664-39-3	0.5	0.4	—	(c) 2	(c) 1.6	—	
Hydrogen peroxide	7722-84-1	1	1.4	—	—	—	3	
Hydrogen selenide, as Se	7783-07-5	0.05	0.2	—	—	—	—	
Hydrogen sulphide	7783-06-4	10	14	—	(c) 15	(c) 21	—	
Hydroquinone (Dihydroxybenzene)	123-31-9	—	2	—	—	—	—	
4-Hydroxy-4-methyl-2-pentanone (Diacetone alcohol)	123-42-2	50	238	—	—	—	3	
2-Hydroxypropyl acrylate	999-61-1	0.5	2.7	—	—	—	1	
Indene	95-13-6	10	48	—	—	—	—	
Indium & compounds, as In	7440-74-6	—	0.1	—	—	—	3	
Iodine	7553-56-2	—	—	—	(c) 0.1	(c) 1	—	
Iodoform	75-47-8	0.6	9.7	—	—	—	3	
Iron oxide (Fe₂O₃), Respirable	1309-37-1	—	5	—	—	—	—	
Iron pentacarbonyl, as Fe	13463-40-6	0.1	0.8	—	0.2	1.6	—	
Iron salts, soluble, as Fe	-	—	1	—	—	—	3	

Substance	CAS number	8-hour occupational exposure limit			15-minute or ceiling (c) occupational exposure limit		Substance interaction 1, 2, 3	Carcinogenicity A1, A2
		ppm	mg/m³	f/cc	ppm	mg/m³		
Isoamyl acetate (Isopentyl acetate)	123-92-2	50	266	—	100	532	3	
Isoamyl alcohol	123-51-3	100	361	—	125	451	3	
Isobutyl acetate	110-19-0	150	713	—	—	—	3	
Isobutyl alcohol	78-83-1	50	152	—	—	—	3	
Isobutyl nitrite	542-56-3	—	—	—	(c) 1	4.2	—	
Isooctyl alcohol	26952-21-6	50	266	—	—	—	1, 3	
Isopentane (Pentane, all isomers)	78-78-4	600	1770	—	—	—	—	
Isopentyl acetate (Isoamyl acetate)	123-92-2	50	266	—	100	532	3	
Isophorone	78-59-1	—	—	—	(c) 5	(c) 28	—	
Isophorone diisocyanate	4098-71-9	0.005	0.05	—	—	—	—	
Isopropanol (2-Propanol, Isopropyl alcohol)	67-63-0	200	492	—	400	984	—	
Isopropoxyethanol	109-59-1	25	106	—	—	—	1	
Isopropyl acetate	108-21-4	100	416	—	200	832	1	
Isopropyl alcohol (2-Propanol, Isopropanol)	67-63-0	200	492	—	400	984	—	
Isopropylamine	75-31-0	5	12	—	10	24	—	
N-Isopropylaniline	768-52-5	2	11	—	—	—	1	
Isopropyl ether	108-20-3	250	1040	—	310	1300	3	

Substance	CAS number	8-hour occupational exposure limit			15-minute or ceiling (c) occupational exposure limit		Substance interaction 1, 2, 3	Carcinogenicity A1, A2
		ppm	mg/m³	f/cc	ppm	mg/m³		
Isopropyl glycidyl ether (IGE)	4016-14-2	50	238	—	75	356	—	
Kaolin Respirable	1332-58-7	—	2	—	—	—	—	
Kerosene/Jet fuels, as total hydrocarbon vapour	8008-20-6 64742-81-0	—	200	—	—	—	1	
Ketene	463-51-4	0.5	0.9	—	1.5	2.6	—	
Lead elemental & inorganic compounds, as Pb	7439-92-1	—	0.05	—	—	—	—	
Lead arsenate, as Pb(AsO$_4$)$_2$	7784-40-9	—	0.15	—	—	—	—	
Lead chromate, as Pb as Cr	7758-97-6	—	0.05 0.012	—	—	—	—	A2
Limestone (Calcium carbonate)	1317-65-3	—	10	—	—	—	3	
Lindane (γ-Hexachlorocyclohexane)	58-89-9	—	0.5	—	—	—	1	
Lithium hydride	7580-67-8	—	0.025	—	—	—	3	
L.P.G. (Liquified petroleum gas)	68476-85-7	1000	—	—	1500	—	—	
Magnesium oxide fume	1309-48-4	—	10	—	—	—	—	
Malathion	121-75-5	—	1	—	—	—	1	
Maleic anhydride	108-31-6	0.1	0.4	—	—	—	—	

Substance	CAS number	8-hour occupational exposure limit			15-minute or ceiling (c) occupational exposure limit		Substance interaction 1, 2, 3	Carcino-genicity A1, A2
		ppm	mg/m³	f/cc	ppm	mg/m³		
Manganese, elemental & inorganic compounds, as Mn	7439-96-5	—	0.2	—	—	—	—	
Manganese cyclopentadienyl tricarbonyl, as Mn	12079-65-1	—	0.1	—	—	—	1	
Marble (Calcium carbonate)	1317-65-3	—	10	—	—	—	3	
Mercury, as Hg in	7439-97-6							
Alkyl compounds,			0.01	—	—	—	1	
Aryl compounds			0.1	—	—	0.03	1	
Inorganic compounds, including metallic mercury			0.025	—	—	—	1	
Mesityl oxide	141-79-7	15	60	—	25	100	—	
Methacrylic acid	79-41-4	20	70	—	—	—	3	
Methacrylic acid, methyl ester (Methyl methacrylate)	80-62-6	50	205	—	100	410	—	
Methanethiol (Methyl mercaptan)	74-93-1	0.5	1.0	—	—	—	—	
Methanol (Methyl alcohol)	67-56-1	200	262	—	250	328	1	
Methomyl	16752-77-5	—	2.5	—	—	—	—	
Methoxychlor	72-43-5	—	10	—	—	—	—	
2-Methoxyethanol (Ethylene glycol monomethyl ether)	109-86-4	0.1	0.3	—	—	—	1	

Substance	CAS number	8-hour occupational exposure limit			15-minute or ceiling (c) occupational exposure limit			Substance interaction 1, 2, 3	Carcino-genicity A1, A2
		ppm	mg/m³	f/cc	ppm	mg/m³			
2-Methoxyethyl acetate (Ethylene glycol monomethyl ether acetate)	110-49-6	0.1	0.5	—	—	—		1	
(2-Methoxymethylethoxy) propanol (DPGME)	34590-94-8	100	606	—	150	909		—	
4-Methoxyphenol	150-76-5	—	5	—	—	—		—	
1-Methoxy-2-propanol (Propylene glycol monomethyl ether)	107-98-2	100	369	—	150	553		—	
Methyl acetate	79-20-9	200	606	—	250	757		—	
Methyl acetylene (Propyne)	74-99-7	1000	1640	—	—	—		—	
Methyl acetylene-propadiene mixture (MAPP)	59355-75-8	1000	1640	—	1250	2050		—	
Methyl acrylate (Acrylic acid, methyl ester)	96-33-3	2	7	—	—	—		1	
Methylacrylonitrile	126-98-7	1	2.7	—	—	—		1	
Methylal (Dimethoxymethane)	109-87-5	1000	3110	—	—	—		—	
Methyl alcohol (Methanol)	67-56-1	200	262	—	250	328		1	
Methylamine	74-89-5	5	6.4	—	15	19		3	

Substance	CAS number	8-hour occupational exposure limit			15-minute or ceiling (c) occupational exposure limit		Substance interaction 1, 2, 3	Carcino-genicity A1, A2
		ppm	mg/m³	f/cc	ppm	mg/m³		
Methyl amyl alcohol (Methyl isobutyl carbinol; 4-Methyl-2-pentanol)	108-11-2	25	104	—	40	167	1	
Methyl n-amyl ketone (2-Heptanone)	110-43-0	50	233	—	—	—	3	
N-Methyl aniline (Monomethyl aniline)	100-61-8	0.5	2.2	—	—	—	1	
2-Methylaziridine (Propyleneimine)	75-55-8	2	4.7	—	—	—	1,3	
Methyl bromide	74-83-9	1	3.9	—	—	—	1,3	
1-Methylbutyl acetate (2-Pentyl acetate, sec-amyl acetate)	626-38-0	50	266	—	100	532	3	
3-Methylbutyl acetate (Isopentyl acetate, isoamyl acetate)	123-92-2	50	266	—	100	532	3	
Methyl-tert-butyl ether (MTBE)	1634-04-4	50	180	—	—	—	—	
Methyl n-butyl ketone (2-Hexanone)	591-78-6	5	20	—	10	40	1	
Methyl Cellosolve (2-Methoxyethanol)	109-86-4	0.1	0.3	—	—	—	1	
Methyl Cellosolve acetate (2-Methoxyethyl acetate)	110-49-6	0.1	0.5	—	—	—	1	

Substance	CAS number	8-hour occupational exposure limit			15-minute or ceiling (c) occupational exposure limit		Substance interaction 1, 2, 3	Carcino- genicity A1, A2
		ppm	mg/m³	f/cc	ppm	mg/m³		
Methyl chloride	74-87-3	50	103	—	100	207	1	
Methyl chloroform (1,1,1-Trichloroethane)	71-55-6	350	1910	—	450	2460	—	
Methyl-2-cyanoacrylate	137-05-3	0.2	0.9	—	—	—	3	
Methylcyclohexane	108-87-2	400	1610	—	—	—	—	
Methylcyclohexanol	25639-42-3	50	234	—	—	—	3	
o-Methylcyclohexanone	583-60-8	50	229	—	75	344	1	
2-Methylcyclopentadienyl manganese tricarbonyl, as Mn	12108-13-3	—	0.2	—	—	—	1	
Methyl demeton (Demeton-methyl)	8022-00-2	—	0.5	—	—	—	1	
Methylene bisphenyl isocyanate (Diphenylmethane-4,4'-diisocyanate; MDI)	101-68-8	0.005	0.05	—	—	—	—	
Methylene chloride (Dichloromethane)	75-09-2	50	174	—	—	—	—	
4,4'-Methylene bis (2-chloroaniline) (MBOCA)	101-14-4	0.01	0.1	—	—	—	1	
Methylene bis(4-cyclohexylisocyanate)	5124-30-1	0.005	0.05	—	—	—	—	
4,4'-Methylene dianiline (4,4'-Diaminodiphenylmethane)	101-77-9	0.1	0.8	—	—	—	1	

Substance	CAS number	8-hour occupational exposure limit			15-minute or ceiling (c) occupational exposure limit		Substance interaction 1, 2, 3	Carcino-genicity A1, A2
		ppm	mg/m³	f/cc	ppm	mg/m³		
Methyl ethyl ketone (MEK; 2-Butanone)	78-93-3	200	590	—	300	885	—	
Methyl ethyl ketone peroxide	1338-23-4	—	—	—	(c) 0.2	(c) 1.4	3	
Methyl formate (Formic acid, methyl ester)	107-31-3	100	246	—	150	368	3	
5-Methyl-3-heptanone (Ethyl amyl ketone)	541-85-5	25	131	—	—	—	—	
Methyl hydrazine	60-34-4	0.01	0.02	—	—	—	1	
Methyl iodide	74-88-4	2	12	—	—	—	1	
Methyl isoamyl ketone	110-12-3	50	234	—	—	—	—	
Methyl isobutyl carbinol (Methyl amyl alcohol)	108-11-2	25	104	—	40	167	1	
Methyl isobutyl ketone (Hexone)	108-10-1	50	205	—	75	307	—	
Methyl isocyanate	624-83-9	0.02	0.05	—	—	—	1,3	
Methyl isopropyl ketone	563-80-4	200	705	—	—	—	3	
Methyl mercaptan (Methanethiol)	74-93-1	0.5	1	—	—	—	—	
Methyl mercury, as Hg (mercury, alkyl compounds)	22967-92-6	—	0.01	—	—	0.03	1	
Methyl methacrylate	80-62-6	50	205	—	100	410	—	
Methyl parathion	298-00-0	—	0.2	—	—	—	1	

Substance	CAS number	8-hour occupational exposure limit			15-minute or ceiling (c) occupational exposure limit		Substance interaction 1, 2, 3	Carcino- genicity A1, A2
		ppm	mg/m³	f/cc	ppm	mg/m³		
2-Methylpentane (all isomers except n-hexane, isohexane) (hexane)	107-83-5	500	1760	—	1000	3500	—	
3-Methylpentane (all isomers except n-hexane) (hexane)	96-14-0	500	1760	—	1000	3500	—	
4-Methyl-2-pentanol (Methyl amyl alcohol)	108-11-2	25	104	—	40	167	1	
Methyl propyl ketone (2-Pentanone)	107-87-9	200	705	—	250	881	—	
Methyl silicate	681-84-5	1	6	—	—	—	—	
α-Methyl styrene	98-83-9	50	242	—	100	483	—	
Methyl styrene (all isomers) (Vinyl toluene, α-methyl styrene)	25013-15-4 98-83-9 1319-73-9	50	242	—	100	483	—	
N-Methyl-N,2,4,6-tetranitroaniline (Tetryl)	479-45-8	—	1.5	—	—	—	3	
Methyl vinyl ketone (3-Buten-2-one)	78-94-4	—	—	—	(c) 0.2	(c) 0.6	1	
Metribuzin	21087-64-9	—	5	—	—	—		
Mevinphos	7786-34-7	—	0.01	—	—	—	1	

Substance	CAS number	8-hour occupational exposure limit			15-minute or ceiling (c) occupational exposure limit		Substance interaction 1, 2, 3	Carcino-genicity A1, A2
		ppm	mg/m³	f/cc	ppm	mg/m³		
Mica	12001-26-2							
Respirable		—	3	—	—	—	—	
Molybdenum, as Mo	7439-98-7							
Soluble compounds, respirable		—	0.5	—	—	—	3	
Metal and insoluble compounds, respirable		—	3	—	—	—	—	
Metal and insoluble compounds, total		—	10	—	—	—		
Monochloroacetic acid	79-11-8	0.5	1.9	—	—	—	1,3	
Monochlorobenzene (Chlorobenzene)	108-90-7	10	46	—	—	—	—	
Monocrotophos	6923-22-4	—	0.05	—	—	—	1	
Morpholine	110-91-8	20	71	—	—	—	1	
Naled (Dibrom)	300-76-5	—	0.1	—	—	—	1	
Naphtha (Rubber solvent)	8030-30-6	400	1590	—	—	—	—	
Naphthalene	91-20-3	10	52	—	15	79	1	
α-Naphthylthiourea (ANTU)	86-88-4	—	0.3	—	—	—	—	
Natural Rubber latex, as total proteins	9006-04-6	—	0.001	—	—	—	1	

Substance	CAS number	8-hour occupational exposure limit			15-minute or ceiling (c) occupational exposure limit			Substance interaction 1, 2, 3	Carcino-genicity A1, A2
		ppm	mg/m^3	f/cc	ppm	mg/m^3			
Neon	7440-01-9	—	—	—	—	—		2	
Nickel									
Elemental/metal	7440-02-0	—	1.5	—	—	—		—	A1
Insoluble compounds, as Ni		—	0.2	—	—	—		—	
Soluble compounds, as Ni		—	0.1	—	—	—		—	
Nickel carbonyl, as Ni	13463-39-3	0.05	0.3	—	—	—		—	
Nickel subsulfide, as Ni	12035-72-2	—	0.1	—	—	—		—	A1
Nicotine	54-11-5	—	0.5	—	—	—		1	
Nitrapyrin (2-Chloro-6-trichloromethyl pyridine)	1929-82-4	—	10	—	—	20		—	
Nitric acid	7697-37-2	2	5.2	—	4	10		—	
Nitric oxide	10102-43-9	25	31	—	—	—		1	
p-Nitroaniline	100-01-6	—	3	—	—	—		1	
Nitrobenzene	98-95-3	1	5	—	—	—		1	
p-Nitrochlorobenzene	100-00-5	0.1	0.6	—	—	—		—	
Nitroethane	79-24-3	100	307	—	—	—		2	
Nitrogen	7727-37-9	—	—	—	—	—		3	
Nitrogen dioxide	10102-44-0	3	5.6	—	5	9.4		—	
Nitrogen trifluoride	7783-54-2	10	29	—	—	—		1	
Nitroglycerin (NG)	55-63-0	0.05	0.5	—	—	—		—	
Nitromethane	75-52-5	20	50	—	—	—		—	

| Substance | CAS number | 8-hour occupational exposure limit | | | 15-minute or ceiling (c) occupational exposure limit | | Substance interaction 1, 2, 3 | Carcino- genicity A1, A2 |
		ppm	mg/m³	f/cc	ppm	mg/m³		
1-Nitropropane	108-03-2	25	91	—	—	—	—	
2-Nitropropane	79-46-9	10	36	—	—	—	—	
Nitrotoluene, all isomers	88-72-2 99-08-1 99-99-0	2	11	—			1	
Nitrotrichloromethane (Chloropicrin, trichloronitromethane)	76-06-2	0.1	0.7	—	—	—	—	
Nitrous oxide	10024-97-2	50	90	—	—	—	—	
Nonane, all isomers	111-84-2	200	1050	—	—	—	—	
Octachloronaphthalene	2234-13-1	—	0.1	—	—	0.3	1	
Octane, all isomers	111-65-9	300	1400	—	—	—	3	
Oil mist, mineral	—	—	5	—	—	10	—	
Osmium tetroxide, as Os	20816-12-0	0.0002	0.002	—	0.0006	0.006	3	
Oxalic acid	144-62-7	—	1	—	—	2	3	
Oxygen difluoride	7783-41-7	—	—	—	(c) 0.05	(c) 0.1	—	
Ozone	10028-15-6	0.1	0.2	—	0.3	0.6	—	
Paraffin wax fume	8002-74-2	—	2	—	—	—	—	
Paraquat Total Respirable	4685-14-7	— —	0.5 0.1	— —				
Parathion	56-38-2	—	0.05	—	—	—	1	

Substance	CAS number	8-hour occupational exposure limit			15-minute or ceiling (c) occupational exposure limit		Substance interaction 1, 2, 3	Carcino-genicity A1, A2
		ppm	mg/m³	f/cc	ppm	mg/m³		
Particulate polycyclic aromatic hydrocarbons (PPAH; Coal tar pitch volatiles)	65996-93-2	—	0.2	—	—	—	—	A1
Particulate Not Otherwise Regulated Total Respirable		— —	10 3	— —	— —	— —	3	
PCBs, Polychlorinated biphenyls —42 percent chlorine (Chlorodiphenyl — 42 percent chlorine)	53469-21-9	—	1	—	—	—	1	
PCBs, Polychlorinated biphenyls —54 percent chlorine (Chlorodiphenyl — 54 percent chlorine)	11097-69-1	—	0.5	—	—	—	1	
Pentaborane	19624-22-7	0.005	0.01	—	0.015	0.04	—	
Pentachloronaphthalene	1321-64-8	—	0.5	—	—	—	1	
Pentachloronitrobenzene	82-68-8	—	0.5	—	—	—	—	
Pentachlorophenol	87-86-5	—	0.5	—	—	—	1	
Pentaerythritol	115-77-5	—	10	—	—	—	3	
Pentane, all isomers	78-78-4 109-66-0 463-82-1	600	1770	—	—	—	—	

Substance	CAS number	8-hour occupational exposure limit			15-minute or ceiling (c) occupational exposure limit		Substance interaction 1, 2, 3	Carcinogenicity A1, A2
		ppm	mg/m^3	f/cc	ppm	mg/m^3		
2-Pentanone (Methyl propyl ketone)	107-87-9	200	705	—	250	881	—	
1-Pentyl acetate (n-Amyl acetate)	628-63-7	50	266	—	100	532	3	
2-Pentyl acetate (sec-Amyl acetate)	626-38-0	50	266	—	100	532	3	
Perchloroethylene (Tetrachloroethylene)	127-18-4	25	170	—	100	678	—	
Perchloromethyl mercaptan	594-42-3	0.1	0.8	—	—	—	3	
Perchloryl fluoride	7616-94-6	3	13	—	6	25	—	
Perfluorobutyl ethylene	19430-93-4	100	1010	—	—	—	—	
Perfluoroisobutylene	382-21-8	—	—	—	(c) 0.01	(c) 0.08	—	
Persulphates								
Ammonium persulphate	7727-54-0	—	0.1	—	—	—	3	
Potassium persulphate	7727-21-1	—	0.1	—	—	—	3	
Sodium persulphate	7775-27-1	—	0.1	—	—	—	3	
Phenacyl chloride (2-Chloroacetophenone)	532-27-4	0.05	0.3	—	—	—	3	
Phenol	108-95-2	5	19	—	—	—	1	
Phenothiazine	92-84-2	—	5	—	—	—	1	
o-Phenylenediamine	95-54-5	—	0.1	—	—	—	—	
m-Phenylenediamine	108-45-2	—	0.1	—	—	—	—	

| Substance | CAS number | 8-hour occupational exposure limit | | | 15-minute or ceiling (c) occupational exposure limit | | Substance interaction 1, 2, 3 | Carcino-genicity A1, A2 |
		ppm	mg/m³	f/cc	ppm	mg/m³		
p-Phenylenediamine	106-50-3	—	0.1	—	—	—	—	
Phenyl ether, vapour	101-84-8	1	7	—	2	14	—	
Phenylethylene (Styrene, monomer)	100-42-5	20	85	—	40	170	—	
Phenyl glycidyl ether (PGE)	122-60-1	0.1	0.6	—	—	—	1	
Phenylhydrazine	100-63-0	0.1	0.4	—	—	—	1	
Phenyl mercaptan	108-98-5	0.1	0.5	—	—	—	1	
Phenylphosphine	638-21-1	—	—	—	(c) 0.05	(c) 0.2	—	
Phorate	298-02-2	—	0.05	—	—	—	1	
Phosgene (Carbonyl chloride)	75-44-5	0.1	0.4	—	—	—	—	
Phosphine	7803-51-2	0.3	0.4	—	1	1.4	—	
Phosphoric acid	7664-38-2	—	1	—	—	3	3	
Phosphorous (yellow)	7723-14-0	—	0.1	—	—	—	—	
Phosphorus oxychloride	10025-87-3	0.1	0.6	—	—	—	3	
Phosphorus pentachloride	10026-13-8	0.1	0.9	—	—	—	3	
Phosphorus pentasulphide	1314-80-3	—	1	—	—	3	3	
Phosphorus trichloride	7719-12-2	0.2	1.1	—	0.5	2.8	3	
Phthalic anhydride	85-44-9	1	6.1	—	—	—	—	
m-Phthalodinitrile	626-17-5	—	5	—	—	—	3	
Picloram	1918-02-1	—	10	—	—	—	—	

Substance	CAS number	8-hour occupational exposure limit			15-minute or ceiling (c) occupational exposure limit		Substance interaction 1, 2, 3	Carcinogenicity A1, A2
		ppm	mg/m³	f/cc	ppm	mg/m³		
Picric acid (2,4,6-Trinitrophenol)	88-89-1	—	0.1	—	—	—	—	
Pindone (2-Pivalyl-1,3-indandione)	83-26-1	—	0.1	—	—	—	—	
Piperazine dihydrochloride	142-64-3	—	5	—	—	—	—	
2-Pivalyl-1,3-indandione (Pindone)	83-26-1	—	0.1	—	—	—	—	
Plaster of Paris (Calcium sulfate; Gypsum)	26499-65-0	—	10	—	—	—	—	
Platinum	7440-06-4							
Metal		—	1	—	—	—	—	
Soluble salts, as Pt		—	0.002	—	—	—	—	
Polymethylene polyphenyl isocyanate (PAPI)	9016-87-9	0.005	0.07	—	—	—	—	
Portland cement	65997-15-1	—	10	—	—	—	3	
Potassium hydroxide	1310-58-3	—	—	—	—	(c) 2	3	
Potassium persulfate (Persulfates)	7727-21-1	—	0.1	—	—	—	3	
Propane	74-98-6	1000	—	—	—	—	—	
n-Propanol (n-Propyl alcohol)	71-23-8	200	492	—	400	984	3	

Substance	CAS number	8-hour occupational exposure limit			15-minute or ceiling (c) occupational exposure limit		Substance interaction 1, 2, 3	Carcino-genicity A1, A2
		ppm	mg/m³	f/cc	ppm	mg/m³		
2-Propanol (Isopropyl alcohol, isopropanol)	67-63-0	200	492	—	400	984	—	
Propargyl alcohol	107-19-7	1	2.3	—	—	—	1	
β-Propiolactone	57-57-8	0.5	1.5	—	—	—		
Propionaldehyde	123-38-6	20	48	—	—	—	3	
Propionic acid	79-09-4	10	30	—	—	—	3	
Propoxur	114-26-1	—	0.5	—	—	—	—	
n-Propyl acetate	109-60-4	200	835	—	250	1040	3	
n-Propyl alcohol (n-Propanol)	71-23-8	200	492	—	400	984	3	
Propylene	115-07-1	500	860	—	—	—	—	
Propylene dichloride (1,2-Dichloropropane)	78-87-5	10	46	—	—	—	1	
Propylene glycol dinitrate	6423-43-4	0.05	0.3	—	—	—	1	
Propylene glycol monomethyl ether	107-98-2	100	369	—	150	553	—	
Propyleneimine (2-Methylaziridine)	75-55-8	2	4.7	—	—	—	1,3	
Propylene oxide (1,2-Epoxypropane)	75-56-9	2	4.7	—	—	—	—	
n-Propyl nitrate	627-13-4	25	107	—	40	172	—	

| Substance | CAS number | 8-hour occupational exposure limit | | | 15-minute or ceiling (c) occupational exposure limit | | Substance interaction 1, 2, 3 | Carcinogenicity A1, A2 |
		ppm	mg/m^3	f/cc	ppm	mg/m^3		
Propyne (Methyl acetylene)	74-99-7	1000	1640	—	—	—	—	
Pyrethrum	8003-34-7	—	5	—	—	—	—	
Pyridine	110-86-1	1	3.2	—	—	—	1	
Pyrocatechol (Catechol)	120-80-9	5	23	—	—	—	—	
Quartz Respirable particulate	14808-60-7	—	0.025	—	—	—	—	A2
Quinone	106-51-4	0.1	0.4	—	—	—	—	
RCF (Refractory Ceramic Fibres)	-	—	—	0.2	—	—	—	A2
RDX (Cyclonite)	121-82-4	—	0.5	—	—	—	1	
Refractory Ceramic Fibres (RCF)	-	—	—	0.2	—	—	—	A2
Resorcinol	108-46-3	10	45	—	20	90	3	
Rhodium, as Rh Metal and Insoluble compounds,	7440-16-6	—	1	—	—	—	3	
Soluble compounds		—	0.01	—	—	—	—	
Rock Wool Fibres		—	—	1	—	—	—	
Ronnel	299-84-3	—	5	—	—	—	—	

Substance	CAS number	8-hour occupational exposure limit			15-minute or ceiling (c) occupational exposure limit		Substance interaction 1, 2, 3	Carcinogenicity A1, A2
		ppm	mg/m³	f/cc	ppm	mg/m³		
Rotenone (commercial)	83-79-4	—	5	—	—	—	—	
Rubber solvent (Naphtha)	8030-30-6	400	1590	—	—	—	—	
Selenium and compounds, as Se	7782-49-2	—	0.2	—	—	—	3	
Selenium hexafluoride	7783-79-1	0.05	0.4	—	—	—	—	
Sesone (Sodium-2-4-dichlorophenoxyethyl sulphate)	136-78-7	—	10	—	—	—	3	
Silane (Silicon tetrahydride)	7803-62-5	5	6.6	—	—	—	3	
Silica-Crystalline, Respirable particulate								
Cristobalite	14464-46-1	—	0.025	—	—	—	—	A2
Quartz	14808-60-7	—	0.025	—	—	—	—	A2
Silicic acid, tetraethyl ester (Ethyl silicate)	78-10-4	10	85	—	—	—	—	
Silicon carbide, nonfibrous **Total particulate**	409-21-2	—	10	—	—	—	3	
Respirable particulate		—	3	—	—	—	3	
Silicon carbide, fibrous (including whiskers)	409-21-2	—	—	0.1	—	—	—	A2

Substance	CAS number	8-hour occupational exposure limit			15-minute or ceiling (c) occupational exposure limit		Substance interaction 1, 2, 3	Carcinogenicity A1, A2
		ppm	mg/m³	f/cc	ppm	mg/m³		
Silicon tetrahydride (Silane)	7803-62-5	5	6.6	—	—	—	3	
Silver	7440-22-4							
Metal		—	0.1	—	—	—	—	
Soluble compounds, as Ag		—	0.01	—	—	—	—	
Slag Wool Fibres		—	—	1	—	—	—	
Soapstone								
Total (no asbestos and less than 1% crystalline silica)		—	6	—	—	—	3	
Respirable		—	3	—	—	—	3	
Sodium azide	26628-22-8							
As Sodium azide		—	—	—	—	(c) 0.29	—	
As Hydrazoic acid vapour		—	—	—	(c) 0.11	0.3	—	
Sodium bisulfite	7631-90-5	—	5	—	—	—	3	
Sodium-2,4-dichlorophenoxyethyl sulfate (Sesone)	136-78-7	—	10	—	—	—	3	
Sodium fluoroacetate	62-74-8	—	0.05	—	—	—	1	
Sodium hydroxide	1310-73-2	—	—	—	—	(c) 2	3	
Sodium metabisulfite	7681-57-4	—	5	—	—	—	3	
Sodium persulfate (Persulfates)	7775-27-1	—	0.1	—	—	—	3	

Substance	CAS number	8-hour occupational exposure limit			15-minute or ceiling (c) occupational exposure limit		Substance interaction 1, 2, 3	Carcinogenicity A1, A2
		ppm	mg/m³	f/cc	ppm	mg/m³		
Starch	9005-25-8	—	10	—	—	—	—	
Stearates, excludes stearates of toxic metals		—	10	—	—	—	3	
Stibine (Antimony hydride)	7803-52-3	0.1	0.5	—	—	—	—	
Stoddard solvent	8052-41-3	100	572	—	—	—	—	
Strontium chromate, as Cr	7789-06-2	—	0.0005	—	—	—	—	A2
Strychnine	57-24-9	—	0.15	—	—	—	—	
Styrene, monomer (Phenylethylene; Vinyl benzene)	100-42-5	20	85	—	40	170	—	
Subtilisins (as 100 percent pure crystalline enzyme)	1395-21-7 9014-01-1	—	—	—	—	(c) 0.00006	—	
Sucrose	57-50-1	—	10	—	—	—	—	
Sulfometuron methyl	74222-97-2	—	5	—	—	—	—	
Sulfotep (TEDP)	3689-24-5	—	0.1	—	—	—	1	
Sulphur	7704-34-9 63705-05-5	—	10	—	—	—	—	
Sulphur dioxide	7446-09-5	2	5.2	—	5	13	3	
Sulphur hexafluoride	2551-62-4	1000	5970	—	—	—	—	
Sulphuric acid	7664-93-9	—	1	—	—	3	—	A2
Sulphur monochloride	10025-67-9	—	—	—	(c) 1	(c) 5.5	—	

Substance	CAS number	8-hour occupational exposure limit			15-minute or ceiling (c) occupational exposure limit		Substance interaction 1, 2, 3	Carcinogenicity A1, A2
		ppm	mg/m³	f/cc	ppm	mg/m³		
Sulphur pentafluoride	5714-22-7	—	—	—	(c) 0.01	(c) 0.1	3	
Sulphur tetrafluoride	7783-60-0	—	—	—	(c) 0.1	(c) 0.4	—	
Sulphuryl fluoride	2699-79-8	5	21	—	10	42	—	
Sulprofos	35400-43-2	—	1	—	—	—	—	
Synthetic Vitreous Fibres:								
Glass fibres, continuous filament		—	—	1	—	—	3	—
Glass fibres, continuous filament, total particulate		—	5	—	—	—	3	—
Glass fibres, special purpose		—	—	1	—	—	—	—
Glass wool fibres		—	—	1	—	—	—	—
Refractory ceramic fibres (RCF)		—	—	0.2	—	—	—	A2
Rock wool fibres		—	—	1	—	—	—	—
Slag wool fibres		—	—	1	—	—	—	—
Systox ® (Demeton)	8065-48-3	—	0.05	—	—	—	1	—
2,4,5-T (2,4,5-Trichlorophenoxyacetic acid)	93-76-5	—	10	—	—	—	—	—
Talc Respirable particulate containing no asbestos fibres	14807-96-6	—	2	—	—	—	—	—

Substance	CAS number	8-hour occupational exposure limit			15-minute or ceiling (c) occupational exposure limit		Substance interaction 1, 2, 3	Carcino-genicity A1, A2
		ppm	mg/m³	f/cc	ppm	mg/m³		
Tantalum metal and oxide dusts, as Ta	7440-25-7 1314-61-0	—	5	—	—	—	3	
TEDP (Sulfotep)	3689-24-5	—	0.1		—	—	1	
Tellurium & compounds, except hydrogen telluride, as Te	13494-80-9	—	0.1	—	—	—	—	
Tellurium hexafluoride	7783-80-4	0.02	0.2		—	—	3	
Temephos	3383-96-8	—	1		—	—	1	
TEPP (Tetraethyl pyrophosphate)	107-49-3	—	0.05	—	—	—	1	
Terbufos	13071-79-9	—	0.01	—	—	—	1	
Terephthalic acid	100-21-0	—	10	—	—	—	—	
Terphenyls	26140-60-3	—	—	—	—	(c) 5	3	
1,1,2,2-Tetrabromoethane (Acetylene tetrabromide)	79-27-6	0.1	1.4	—	—	—	—	
1,1,1,2-Tetrachloro-2,2-difluoroethane	76-11-9	500	4170		—	—	—	
1,1,2,2-Tetrachloro-1,2-difluoroethane	76-12-0	500	4170	—	—	—	—	
1,1,2,2-Tetrachloroethane	79-34-5	1	6.9	—	—	—	1	
Tetrachloroethylene (Perchloroethylene)	127-18-4	25	170	—	100	678	—	

Substance	CAS number	8-hour occupational exposure limit			15-minute or ceiling (c) occupational exposure limit		Substance interaction 1, 2, 3	Carcinogenicity A1, A2
		ppm	mg/m³	f/cc	ppm	mg/m³		
Tetrachloromethane (Carbon tetrachloride)	56-23-5	5	31	—	10	63	1	A2
Tetrachloronaphthalene	1335-88-2	—	2	—	—	—	—	
Tetraethyl lead, as Pb	78-00-2	—	0.1	—	—	—	1	
Tetraethyl pyrophosphate (TEPP)	107-49-3	—	0.05	—	—	—	1	
Tetrafluoroethylene	116-14-3	2	8.2	—	—	—	—	
Tetrahydrofuran	109-99-9	50	147	—	100	295	1	
Tetrakis (hydroxymethyl) phosphonium salts								
–**Tetrakis (hydroxymethyl) phosphonium chloride**	124-64-1	—	2	—	—	—	3	
–**Tetrakis (hydroxymethyl) phosphonium sulfate**	55566-30-8	—	2	—	—	—	3	
Tetramethyl lead, as Pb	75-74-1	—	0.15	—	—	—	1	
Tetramethyl succinonitrile	3333-52-6	0.5	2.8	—	—	—	1	
Tetranitromethane	509-14-8	0.005	0.04	—	—	—	3	
Tetryl (2,4,6-Trinitrophenylmethylnitramine)	479-45-8	—	1.5	—	—	—	3	
Thallium, elemental, and soluble compounds, as Tl	7440-28-0	—	0.1	—	—	—	1	

Substance	CAS number	8-hour occupational exposure limit			15-minute or ceiling (c) occupational exposure limit			Substance interaction 1, 2, 3	Carcino-genicity A1, A2
		ppm	mg/m^3	f/cc	ppm	mg/m^3			
4,4'-Thiobis (6-tert-butyl-m-cresol)	96-69-5	—	10	—	—	—	—		
Thioglycolic acid	68-11-1	1	3.8	—	—	—	1,3		
Thionyl chloride	7719-09-7	—	—	—	(c) 1	(c) 4.9	3		
Thiram	137-26-8	—	1	—	—	—	—		
Tin, as Sn	7440-31-5								
Metal		—	2	—	—	—	—		
Oxide and inorganic compounds except tin hydride		—	2	—	—	—	—		
Organic compounds		—	0.1	—	—	0.2	1		
Titanium dioxide	13463-67-7	—	10	—	—	—	3		
Toluene	108-88-3	50	188	—	—	—	1		
(Toluol)									
Toluene-2,4 or 2,6-diisocyanate (or as mixture) (TDI)	584-84-9 91-08-7	0.005	0.04	—	(c) 0.02	(c) 0.1	—		
o-Toluidine	95-53-4	2	8.8	—	—	—	1		
m-Toluidine	108-44-1	2	8.8	—	—	—	1		
p-Toluidine	106-49-0	2	8.8	—	—	—	1		
Toluol	108-88-3	50	188	—	—	—	1		
(Toluene)									

Schedule 1

Substance	CAS number	8-hour occupational exposure limit			15-minute or ceiling (c) occupational exposure limit		Substance interaction 1, 2, 3	Carcinogenicity A1, A2
		ppm	mg/m³	f/cc	ppm	mg/m³		
Toxaphene (Chlorinated camphene)	8001-35-2	—	0.5	—	—	1	1	
Tremolite (Asbestos)	1332-21-4	—	—	0.1	—	—	—	A1
Tribromomethane (Bromoform)	75-25-2	0.5	5.2	—	—	—	1	
Tributyl phosphate	126-73-8	0.2	2.2	—	—	—	—	
Trichloroacetic acid	76-03-9	1	6.7	—	—	—	3	
1,2,4-Trichlorobenzene	120-82-1	—	—	—	(c) 5	(c) 37	3	
1,1,1-Trichloroethane (Methyl chloroform)	71-55-6	350	1910	—	450	2460	—	
1,1,2-Trichloroethane	79-00-5	10	55	—	—	—	1	
Trichloroethylene	79-01-6	50	269	—	100	537	—	
Trichlorofluoromethane (Fluorotrichloromethane)	75-69-4	—	—	—	(c) 1000	(c) 5620	—	
Trichloromethane (Chloroform)	67-66-3	10	49	—	—	—	—	
Trichloronaphthalene	1321-65-9	—	5	—	—	—	1	
Trichloronitromethane (Chloropicrin)	76-06-2	0.1	0.7	—	—	—	—	

Substance	CAS number	8-hour occupational exposure limit			15-minute or ceiling (c) occupational exposure limit		Substance interaction 1, 2, 3	Carcino-genicity A1, A2
		ppm	mg/m³	f/cc	ppm	mg/m³		
2,4,5-Trichlorophenoxy acetic acid (2,4,5-T)	93-76-5	—	10	—	—	—	—	
1,2,3-Trichloropropane	96-18-4	10	60	—	—	—	1	
1,1,2-Trichloro-1,2,2-trifluoroethane	76-13-1	1000	7660	—	1250	9580	—	
Trichlorphon	52-68-6	—	1	—	—	—	—	
Tricyclohexyltin hydroxide (Cyhexatin)	13121-70-5	—	5	—	—	—	—	
Triethanolamine	102-71-6	—	5	—	—	—	3	
Triethylamine	121-44-8	1	4.1	—	3	12	1	
Trifluorobromomethane (Bromotrifluoromethane)	75-63-8	1000	6090	—	—	—	—	
1,1,1-Trifluoro-2,2-dichloroethane (HCFC-123)	306-83-2	50	310	—	—	—	—	
1,3,5-Triglycidyl-s-triazinetrione	2451-62-9	—	0.05	—	—	—	—	
Trimellitic anhydride	552-30-7	—	—	—	—	(c) 0.04	—	
Trimethylamine	75-50-3	5	12	—	15	36	3	
Trimethyl benzene (mixed isomers)	25551-13-7	25	123	—	—	—	—	
Trimethyl phosphite	121-45-9	2	10	—	—	—	—	
2,4,6-Trinitrophenol (Picric acid)	88-89-1	—	0.1	—	—	—	—	

Substance	CAS number	8-hour occupational exposure limit			15-minute or ceiling (c) occupational exposure limit		Substance interaction 1, 2, 3	Carcinogenicity A1, A2
		ppm	mg/m³	f/cc	ppm	mg/m³		
2,4,6-Trinitrophenyl-methylnitramine (Tetryl)	479-45-8	—	1.5	—	—	—	3	
2,4,6-Trinitrotoluene (TNT)	118-96-7	—	0.1	—	—	—	1	
Triorthocresyl phosphate	78-30-8	—	0.1	—	—	—	1	
Triphenyl amine	603-34-9	—	5	—	—	—	3	
Triphenyl phosphate	115-86-6	—	3	—	—	—	—	
Tungsten, as W	7440-33-7							
Metal and insoluble compounds		—	5	—	—	10	3	
Soluble compounds		—	1	—	—	3	—	
Turpentine and selected monoterpenes	8006-64-2 80-56-8 127-91-3 13466-78-9	20	111	—	—	—	3	
Uranium (natural), soluble & insoluble compounds, as U	7440-61-1	—	0.2	—	—	0.6	—	A1
n-Valeraldehyde	110-62-3	50	176	—	—	—	3	
Vanadium pentoxide, as V_2O_5 Respirable particulate or fume	1314-62-1	—	0.05	—	—	—	—	
Vinyl acetate	108-05-4	10	35	—	15	53	—	
Vinyl benzene (Styrene, monomer)	100-42-5	20	85	—	40	170	—	

Substance	CAS number	8-hour occupational exposure limit			15-minute or ceiling (c) occupational exposure limit		Substance interaction 1, 2, 3	Carcinogenicity A1, A2
		ppm	mg/m³	f/cc	ppm	mg/m³		
Vinyl bromide	593-60-2	0.5	2.2	—	—	—	—	A2
Vinyl chloride (Chloroethylene)	75-01-4	1	2.6	—	—	—	—	A1
Vinyl cyanide (Acrylonitrile)	107-13-1	2	4.3	—	—	—	1	
4-Vinyl cyclohexene	100-40-3	0.1	0.4	—	—	—	—	
Vinyl cyclohexene dioxide	106-87-6	0.1	0.6	—	—	—	1	
Vinyl fluoride	75-02-5	1	1.9	—	—	—	—	A2
Vinylidene chloride (1,1-Dichloroethylene)	75-35-4	5	20	—	—	—	—	
Vinylidene fluoride (1,1-Difluoroethylene)	75-38-7	500	1310	—	—	—	—	
N-Vinyl-2-pyrrolidone	88-12-0	0.05	0.2	—	—	—	—	
Vinyl toluene (Methyl styrene, all isomers)	25013-15-4	50	242	—	100	483	—	
VM & P Naphtha	8032-32-4	300	1400	—	—	—	—	
Warfarin	81-81-2	—	0.1	—	—	—	—	

| Substance | CAS number | 8-hour occupational exposure limit | | | 15-minute or ceiling (c) occupational exposure limit | | Substance interaction 1, 2, 3 | Carcino-genicity A1, A2 |
		ppm	mg/m³	f/cc	ppm	mg/m³		
Wood Dust (Total)								
Softwoods and hardwoods except western red cedar		—	5	—	—	—	—	A1 — Oak, beech A2 — Birch, mahogany, teak, walnut
Western red cedar		—	0.5	—	—	—	—	
Xylene (o-,m-,p-isomers)	1330-20-7 95-47-6 108-38-3 106-42-3	100	434	—	150	651	—	
m-Xylene α,α′-diamine	1477-55-0	—	—	—	—	(c) 0.1	1,3	
Xylidine (mixed isomers)	1300-73-8	0.5	2.5	—	—	—	1	
Yttrium metal & compounds, as Y	7440-65-5	—	1	—	—	—	—	
Zinc beryllium silicate, as Be	39413-47-3	—	0.002	—	—	0.01	—	A1
Zinc chloride fume	7646-85-7	—	1	—	—	2	3	
Zinc chromates, as Cr	13530-65-9 11103-86-9 37300-23-5	—	0.01	—	—	—	—	A1
Zinc oxide, respirable	1314-13-2	—	2	—	—	10	—	
Zinc stearate	557-05-1	—	10	—	—	—	3	
Zirconium and compounds, as Zr	7440-67-7	—	5	—	—	10	—	

Schedule 2 First Aid

Table 1 Low hazard work

"Low hazard work" means work at:

(a) administrative sites where the work performed is clerical or administrative in nature;

(b) dispersal sites

(i) where a worker is based,

(ii) where a worker is required to report for instruction, and

(iii) from which a worker is transported to a work site where the work is performed.

Table 2 High hazard work

"High hazard work" means work involving:

(a) construction or demolition, including

(i) industrial and commercial process facilities,

(ii) pipelines and related gas or oil transmission facilities,

(iii) commercial, residential and industrial buildings,

(iv) roads, highways, bridges and related installations,

(v) sewage gathering systems,

(vi) utility installations, and

(vii) water distribution systems;

(b) operation and maintenance of

(i) food packing or processing plants,

(ii) beverage processing plants,

(iii) electrical generation and distribution systems,

(iv) foundries,

(v) industrial heavy equipment repair and service facilities,

(vi) sawmills and lumber processing facilities,

(vii) machine shops,

(viii) metal fabrication shops,

(ix) gas, oil and chemical process plants,

(x) steel and other base metal processing plants, and

(xi) industrial process facilities not elsewhere specified;

(c) woodlands operations;

(d) gas and oil well drilling and servicing operations;

(e) mining and quarrying operations;

(f) seismic operations;

(g) detonation of explosives.

Table 3   First aid equipment and supplies

[See section 178]

(1)   A Number 1 First Aid Kit consists of the following:

  (a)   10   antiseptic cleansing towelettes, individually packaged;

  (b)   25   sterile adhesive dressings, individually packaged;

  (c)   10   10 centimetres x 10 centimetres sterile gauze pads, individually packaged;

  (d)   2   10 centimetres x 10 centimetres sterile compress dressings, with ties, individually packaged;

  (e)   2   15 centimetres x 15 centimetres sterile compress dressings, with ties, individually packaged;

  (f)   2   conform gauze bandages — 75 millimetres wide;

  (g)   3   cotton triangular bandages;

  (h)   5   safety pins — assorted sizes;

  (i)   1   pair of scissors;

  (j)   1   pair of tweezers;

  (k)   1   25 millimetres x 4.5 metres of adhesive tape;

  (l)   1   crepe tension bandage — 75 millimetres wide;

  (m)   1   resuscitation barrier device with a one-way valve;

  (n)   4   pairs of disposable surgical gloves;

  (o)   1   first aid instruction manual (condensed);

  (p)   1   inventory of kit contents;

  (q)   1   waterproof waste bag.

(2)   A Number 2 First Aid Kit consists of the following:

  (a)   10   antiseptic cleansing towelettes, individually packaged;

  (b)   50   sterile adhesive dressings, individually packaged;

  (c)   20   10 centimetres x 10 centimetres sterile gauze pads individually packaged;

  (d)   3   10 centimetres x 10 centimetres sterile compress dressings, with ties, individually packaged;

  (e)   3   15 centimetres x 15 centimetres sterile compress dressings, with ties, individually packaged;

  (f)   1   20 centimetres x 25 centimetres sterile abdominal dressing;

  (g)   2   conform gauze bandages — 75 millimetres wide;

  (h)   4   cotton triangular bandages;

  (i)   8   safety pins — assorted sizes;

  (j)   1   pair of scissors;

  (k)   1   pair of tweezers;

  (l)   1   25 millimetres x 4.5 metres roll of adhesive tape;

  (m)   2   crepe tension bandages — 75 millimetres wide;

  (n)   1   resuscitation barrier device with a one-way valve;

  (o)   6   pairs of disposable surgical gloves;

(p) 1 sterile, dry eye dressing;

(q) 1 first aid instruction manual (condensed);

(r) 1 inventory of kit contents;

(s) 1 waterproof waste bag.

(3) A Number 3 First Aid Kit consists of the following:

(a) 24 antiseptic cleansing towelettes, individually packaged;

(b) 100 sterile adhesive dressings, individually packaged;

(c) 50 10 centimetres x 10 centimetres sterile gauze pads individually packaged;

(d) 6 10 centimetres x 10 centimetres sterile compress dressings, with ties, individually packaged;

(e) 6 15 centimetres x 15 centimetres sterile compress dressings, with ties, individually packaged;

(f) 4 20 centimetres x 25 centimetres sterile abdominal dressings, individually packaged;

(g) 6 conform gauze bandages — 75 millimetres wide;

(h) 12 cotton triangular bandages;

(i) 12 safety pins — assorted sizes;

(j) 1 pair of scissors;

(k) 1 pair of tweezers;

(l) 2 25 millimetres x 4.5 metres rolls of adhesive tape;

(m) 4 crepe tension bandages — 75 millimetres wide;

(n) 1 resuscitation barrier device with a one-way valve;

(o) 12 pairs of disposable surgical gloves;

(p) 2 sterile, dry eye dressings, individually packaged;

(q) 1 tubular finger bandage with applicator;

(r) 1 first aid instruction manual (condensed);

(s) 1 inventory of kit contents;

(t) 2 waterproof waste bags.

(4) A Type P First Aid Kit consists of the following:

(a) 10 sterile adhesive dressings, assorted sizes, individually packaged;

(b) 5 10 centimetres x 10 centimetres sterile gauze pads, individually packaged;

(c) 1 10 centimetres x 10 centimetres sterile compress dressing, with ties;

(d) 5 antiseptic cleansing towelettes, individually packaged;

(e) 1 cotton triangular bandage;

(f) 1 waterproof waste bag;

(g) 1 pair disposable surgical gloves.

Table 4   First aid room requirements

[See section 178]

(1)   If an employer is required to provide a first aid room by Part 11, the employer must ensure that it is

 (a)   located near the work area or areas it is to serve,

 (b)   easily accessible to workers at all times,

 (c)   able to accommodate a stretcher,

 (d)   close to bathroom facilities,

 (e)   of adequate size,

 (f)   kept clean and sanitary,

 (g)   provided with adequate lighting, ventilation and heating,

 (h)   designated as non-smoking,

 (i)   under the supervision of an advanced first aider, a nurse or an Emergency Medical Technician-Paramedic,

 (j)   clearly identified as a first aid facility and appropriately marked with how and where to access the first aider,

 (k)   used only to administer first aid or health related services, and

 (l)   equipped with:

   (i)   a communication system;

   (ii)   a permanently installed sink with hot and cold running water;

   (iii) a cot or bed with a moisture-protected mattress and 2 pillows;

   (iv)   6 towels and 3 blankets;

   (v)   eye wash equipment;

   (vi)   a shower, or is close to a shower facility if it is a work site described in section 24;

   (vii) a Number 3 First Aid Kit.

(2)   A first aid room must contain the following:

 (a)   the supplies of a Number 2 First Aid Kit;

 (b)   space blanket;

 (c)   hot and cold packs;

 (d)   spine board and straps;

 (e)   adjustable cervical collar or set of different sized cervical collars;

 (f)   stretcher;

 (g)   splint set;

 (h)   waterproof waste bag;

 (i)   sphygmomanometer (blood pressure cuff);

 (j)   stethoscope;

 (k)   disposable drinking cups;

 (l)   portable oxygen therapy unit consisting of a cylinder(s) containing compressed oxygen, a pressure regulator, pressure gauge, a flow meter and oxygen delivery equipment;

 (m) flashlight;

 (n)   bandage scissors.

Table 5   First aid requirements for low hazard work

[See sections 178, 181(1)]

Number of workers at work site per shift	Close work site (up to 20 minutes)	Distant work site (20 – 40 minutes)	Isolated work site (more than 40 minutes)
1	Type P First Aid Kit	Type P First Aid Kit	Type P First Aid Kit
2 – 9	No. 1 First Aid Kit	1 Emergency First Aider No. 2 First Aid Kit	1 Standard First Aider No. 2 First Aid Kit
10 – 49	1 Emergency First Aider No. 1 First Aid Kit	1 Emergency First Aider No. 2 First Aid Kit	1 Standard First Aider No. 2 First Aid Kit
50 – 99	1 Emergency First Aider 1 Standard First Aider No. 2 First Aid Kit	1 Emergency First Aider 1 Standard First Aider No. 2 First Aid Kit	2 Standard First Aiders No. 2 First Aid Kit
100 – 199	1 Emergency First Aider 2 Standard First Aiders No. 3 First Aid Kit Designated area for first aid services	1 Emergency First Aider 2 Standard First Aiders No. 3 First Aid Kit 3 blankets, stretcher, splints Designated area for first aid services	3 Standard First Aiders No. 3 First Aid Kit 3 blankets, stretcher, splints Designated area for first aid services
200 or more	1 Emergency First Aider 2 Standard First Aiders **Plus** 1 Standard First Aider for each additional increment of 1 to 100 workers No. 3 First Aid Kit Designated area for first aid services	1 Emergency First Aider 2 Standard First Aiders **Plus** 1 Standard First Aider for each additional increment of 1 to 100 workers No. 3 First Aid Kit 3 blankets, stretcher, splints Designated area for first aid services	3 Standard First Aiders **Plus** 1 Standard First Aider for each additional increment of 1 to 100 workers No. 3 First Aid Kit 3 blankets, stretcher, splints Designated area for first aid services

Note: Number of first aiders indicated is for a shift at all times.

Table 6   First aid requirements for medium hazard work

[See sections 178, 181(1)]

Number of workers at work site per shift	Close work site (up to 20 minutes)	Distant work site (20 – 40 minutes)	Isolated work site (more than 40 minutes)
1	Type P First Aid Kit	Type P First Aid Kit	Type P First Aid Kit
2 – 9	1 Emergency First Aider No. 1 First Aid Kit	1 Standard First Aider No. 2 First Aid Kit 3 blankets	1 Standard First Aider No. 2 First Aid Kit 3 blankets
10 – 19	1 Emergency First Aider 1 Standard First Aider No. 2 First Aid Kit	1 Emergency First Aider 1 Standard First Aider No. 2 First Aid Kit 3 blankets	2 Standard First Aiders No. 2 First Aid Kit 3 blankets
20 – 49	1 Emergency First Aider 1 Standard First Aider No. 2 First Aid Kit	1 Emergency First Aider 1 Standard First Aider No. 2 First Aid Kit 3 blankets	2 Standard First Aiders No. 2 First Aid Kit 3 blankets
50 – 99	2 Emergency First Aiders 1 Standard First Aider No. 3 First Aid Kit	2 Emergency First Aiders 1 Standard First Aider No. 3 First Aid Kit 3 blankets	3 Standard First Aiders No. 3 First Aid Kit 3 blankets
100 – 199	2 Emergency First Aiders 2 Standard First Aiders No. 3 First Aid Kit Designated area for first aid services	2 Emergency First Aiders 2 Standard First Aiders No. 3 First Aid Kit 3 blankets, stretcher, splints Designated area for first aid services	3 Standard First Aiders 1 Advanced First Aider No. 3 First Aid Kit 3 blankets, stretcher, splints Designated area for first aid services
200 or more	2 Emergency First Aiders 2 Standard First Aiders 1 Nurse or 1 EMT-P **Plus** 1 Standard First Aider for each additional increment of 1 to 100 workers First Aid Room	2 Emergency First Aiders 2 Standard First Aiders 1 Nurse or 1 EMT-P **Plus** 1 Standard First Aider for each additional increment of 1 to 100 workers First Aid Room	4 Standard First Aiders 1 Nurse or 1 EMT-P **Plus** 1 Standard First Aider for each additional increment of 1 to 100 workers First Aid Room

Note: Number of first aiders indicated is for a shift at all times.

Table 7　First aid requirements for high hazard work

[See sections 178, 181(1)]

Number of workers at work site per shift	Close work site (up to 20 minutes)	Distant work site (20 – 40 minutes)	Isolated work site (more than 40 minutes)
1	Type P First Aid Kit	Type P First Aid Kit	Type P First Aid Kit
2 – 4	1 Emergency First Aider No. 1 First Aid Kit	1 Standard First Aider No. 2 First Aid Kit 3 blankets	1 Standard First Aider No. 2 First Aid Kit 3 blankets
5 – 9	1 Emergency First Aider 1 Standard First Aider No. 2 First Aid Kit	2 Standard First Aiders No. 2 First Aid Kit 3 blankets	2 Standard First Aiders No. 2 First Aid Kit 3 blankets
10 – 19	1 Emergency First Aider 1 Standard First Aider No. 2 First Aid Kit 3 blankets	2 Standard First Aiders No. 3 First Aid Kit 3 blankets, stretcher, splints	2 Standard First Aiders No. 3 First Aid Kit 3 blankets, stretcher, splints
20 – 49	2 Emergency First Aiders 1 Standard First Aider No. 2 First Aid Kit 3 blankets	3 Standard First Aiders No. 3 First Aid Kit 3 blankets, stretcher, splints	3 Standard First Aiders No. 3 First Aid Kit 3 blankets, stretcher, splints
50 – 99	2 Emergency First Aiders 2 Standard First Aiders No. 3 First Aid Kit 3 blankets	2 Emergency First Aiders 3 Standard First Aiders No. 3 First Aid Kit 3 blankets, stretcher, splints	4 Standard First Aiders 1 Advanced First Aider No. 3 First Aid Kit 3 blankets, stretcher, splints
100 – 199	2 Emergency First Aiders 2 Standard First Aiders 1 Advanced First Aider First Aid Room	4 Standard First Aiders 1 Advanced First Aider First Aid Room	4 Standard First Aiders 1 Advanced First Aider First Aid Room
200 or more	2 Emergency First Aiders 2 Standard First Aiders 1 Nurse or 1 EMT-P **Plus** 1 Standard First Aider for each additional increment of 1 to 100 workers First Aid Room	4 Standard First Aiders 1 Nurse or 1 EMT-P **Plus** 1 Standard First Aider for each additional increment of 1 to 100 workers First Aid Room	4 Standard First Aiders 1 Advanced First Aider 1 Nurse or 1 EMT-P **Plus** 1 Standard First Aider for each additional increment of 1 to 100 workers First Aid Room

Note: Number of first aiders indicated is for a shift at all times.

Schedule 3   Noise

Table 1   Occupational exposure limits for noise
[See sections 218, 219(1)]

Exposure level (dBA)	Exposure duration
82	16 hours
83	12 hours and 41 minutes
84	10 hours and 4 minutes
85	8 hours
88	4 hours
91	2 hours
94	1 hour
97	30 minutes
100	15 minutes
103	8 minutes
106	4 minutes
109	2 minutes
112	56 seconds
115 and greater	0

Note: Exposure levels and exposure durations to be prorated if not specified

Table 2   Selection of hearing protection devices
[See subsection 222(1)]

Maximum equivalent noise level (dBA L_{ex})	CSA Class of hearing protection	CSA Grade of hearing protection
≤ 90	C, B or A	1, 2, 3, or 4
≤ 95	B or A	2, 3, or 4
≤ 100	A	3 or 4
≤ 105	A	4
≤ 110	A earplug + A or B earmuff	3 or 4 earplug + 2, 3, or 4 earmuff
> 110	A earplug + A or B earmuff and limited exposure time to keep sound reaching the worker's ear drum below 85 dBA L_{ex}	3 or 4 earplug + 2, 3, or 4 earmuff and limited exposure time to keep sound reaching the worker's ear drum below 85 dBA L_{ex}

Table 3   Permissible background noise conditions during audiometric testing

[See subsection 223(2)]

Octave band centre frequency (Hz)	Maximum level (dB)
500	22
1000	30
2000	35
4000	42
8000	45

Schedule 4   Safe Limit of Approach Distances

[See sections 225, 226]

Table 1   Safe limit of approach distances from overhead power lines for persons and equipment

Operating voltage between conductors of overhead power line	Safe limit of approach distance for persons and equipment
0-750 volts Insulated or polyethylene covered conductors (1)	300 millimetres
0-750 volts Bare, uninsulated	1.0 metre
Above 750 volts Insulated conductors (1) (2)	1.0 metre
750 volts-40 kilovolts	3.0 metres
69 kilovolts, 72 kilovolts	3.5 metres
138 kilovolts, 144 kilovolts	4.0 metres
230 kilovolts, 260 kilovolts	5.0 metres
500 kilovolts	7.0 metres

Notes:

(1)   Conductors must be insulated or covered throughout their entire length to comply with this group.

(2)   Conductors must be manufactured to rated and tested insulation levels.

Schedule 5　　　Cable Clips on Wire Rope

[See section 300]

Cable clip requirements for wire rope

Diameter of rope (millimetres)	Number of clips	Spacing between clips centre-to-centre (millimetres)	Torque (Newton.metres)
6	2	38	20
8	2	51	40
10	2	57	65
11	2	64	90
12	3	76	90
16	3	102	135
19	4	114	176
22	4	133	305
25	4	152	305
29	5	178	305
32	5	203	488
38	6	229	488
44	7	267	628
50	8	305	881

Schedule 6   Dimensions of Scaffold Members

Table 1   Light duty double-pole scaffolds less than 6 metres in height

[See subsection 333(2)]

Member	Dimensions
Uprights	38 millimetres by 89 millimetres
Ledgers	2 – 21 millimetres by 140 millimetres or 1 – 21 millimetres by 184 millimetres
Ribbons	21 millimetres by 140 millimetres
Braces	21 millimetres by 140 millimetres

Table 2   Light duty double-pole scaffolds 6 metres or more in height

[See subsection 333(2)]

Member	Dimensions
Uprights	89 millimetres by 89 millimetres
Ledgers	2 – 21 millimetres by 140 millimetres or 1 – 21 millimetres by 184 millimetres
Ribbons	21 millimetres by 140 millimetres
Braces	21 millimetres by 140 millimetres

Table 3   Heavy duty double-pole scaffolds less than 6 metres in height

[See subsection 333(2)]

Member	Dimensions
Uprights	38 millimetres by 140 millimetres
Ledgers	2 – 21 millimetres by 140 millimetres or 1 – 38 millimetres by 184 millimetres
Ribbons	21 millimetres by 140 millimetres
Braces	21 millimetres by 140 millimetres

Table 4   Heavy duty double-pole scaffolds 6 metres or more in height

[See subsection 333(2)]

Member	Dimension
Uprights	89 millimetres by 140 millimetres
Ledgers	2 – 21 millimetres by 140 millimetres or 1 – 38 millimetres by 184 millimetres
Ribbons	21 millimetres by 140 millimetres
Braces	21 millimetres by 140 millimetres

Table 5   Half-horse scaffolds less than 3 metres in height

[See subsection 335(2)]

Member	Dimensions
Ledgers	38 millimetres by 140 millimetres
Legs	38 millimetres by 89 millimetres
Braces	21 millimetres by 184 millimetres
Ribbons	21 millimetres by 140 millimetres
Leg spread	1 metre

Table 6   Half-horse scaffolds 3 metres to 5 metres in height

[See subsection 335(2)]

Member	Dimensions
Ledgers	38 millimetres by 140 millimetres
Legs	38 millimetres by 140 millimetres
Braces	21 millimetres by 184 millimetres
Ribbons	21 millimetres by 140 millimetres
Leg spread	1.5 metres

Table 7 Single-pole scaffolds less than 6 metres in height

[See section 340]

Member	Dimensions
Uprights	38 millimetres by 89 millimetres
Ledgers	2 – 21 millimetres by 140 millimetres or 1 – 21 millimetres by 184 millimetres
Ribbons	21 millimetres by 140 millimetres
Braces	21 millimetres by 140 millimetres
Wall scabs	38 millimetres by 140 millimetres

Table 8 Single-pole scaffolds 6 metres to 9 metres in height

[See section 340]

Member	Dimensions
Uprights	89 millimetres by 89 millimetres 91
Ledgers	2 – 21 millimetres by 140 millimetres or 1 – 21 millimetres by 184 millimetres
Ribbons	21 millimetres by 140 millimetres
Braces	21 millimetres by 140 millimetres
Wall scabs	38 millimetres by 140 millimetres

Schedule 7   Toilets at a Work Site

[See subsection 357(1)]

Number of toilets required at a work site

Number of workers of the sex	Minimum number of toilets for that sex
1 – 10	1
11 – 25	2
26 – 50	3
51 – 75	4
76 – 100	5
> 100	6 plus 1 for each additional 30 workers of the sex in excess of 100

Schedule 8   Saw Blade Crack Limits

Table 1   Circular saw blade crack limits

[See subsections 377(1), 377(2)]

Diameter of saw blade (millimetres)	Maximum length of crack (millimetres)
up to 300	13
301 – 610	25
611 – 915	38
916 – 1220	50
1221 – 1525	64
> 1525	76

Table 2   Band saw blade crack limits

[See subsections 378(1), 378(2)]

Width of band saw blade (millimetres)	Maximum length of crack (millimetres)
up to 125	1/10 of saw blade width
126 – 300	13
> 300	19

Schedule 9   Shoring Component Dimensions

[See subsections 457(1), 457(2)]

Shoring components used in excavations, trenches, tunnels and underground shafts

Soil type	Depth of excavation (metres)	Uprights Minimum dimensions (millimetres)	Uprights Maximum horizontal spacing (millimetres)	Stringers Minimum dimensions (millimetres)	Stringers Maximum vertical spacing (millimetres)	Cross-braces Minimum dimensions (millimetres) Width of trench — Less than 1.8 metres	Cross-braces Minimum dimensions (millimetres) Width of trench — 1.8 to 3.7 metres	Cross-braces Maximum spacing (millimetres) Vertical	Cross-braces Maximum spacing (millimetres) Horizontal
Hard and compact	1.5 to 3.0	38 x 235	1800	89 x 140	1200	89 x 89	140 x 140	1200	1800
	More than 3.0 to 4.5	38 x 235	1200	89 x 140	1200	89 x 140	140 x 140	1200	1800
	More than 4.5 to 6.0	38 x 235	10	140 x 140	1200	140 x 184	140 x 184	1200	1800
Likely to crack or crumble	1.5 to 3.0	38 x 235	1200	89 x 140	1200	89 x 140	140 x 140	1200	1800
	More than 3.0 to 4.5	38 x 235	900	140 x 140	1200	140 x 140	140 x 184	1200	1800
	More than 4.5 to 6.0	38 x 235	10	140 x 184	1200	140 x 184	140 x 184	1200	1800
Soft, sandy or loose	1.5 to 3.0	38 x 235	10	140 x 140	1200	140 x 140	140 x 184	1200	1800
	More than 3.0 to 4.5	38 x 235	10	140 x 184	1200	140 x 184	184 x 184	1200	1800
	More than 4.5 to 6.0	38 x 235	10	184 x 184	1200	140 x 184	184 x 235	1200	1800

Schedule 10   Fire Extinguishers and Minimum Separation Distances

Table 1   Fire extinguisher required based on quantity of explosive
[See subsection 473(4)]

Quantity of explosive	Quantity and type of fire extinguisher required
< 25 kilograms	1 — 5 BC fire extinguisher required
25 kg – 2,000 kilograms	1 (minimum) 10 — BC fire extinguisher
> 2,000 kilograms	2 (minimum) 10 — BC fire extinguishers

Table 2   Minimum separation distances between explosives and fixed radiofrequency transmitters
[See subsections 503(1), 503(2)]

Transmitter power (watts)	Minimum separation distance (metres)
25 or less	30
26 – 50	45
51 – 100	65
101 – 250	110
251 – 500	135
501 – 1,000	200
1,001 – 2,500	300
2,501 – 5,000	450
5,001 – 10,000	675
10,001 – 25,000	1,100
25,001 – 50,000	1,500
> 50,000	By extrapolation of this data

Table 3   Minimum separation distances between explosives and mobile radiofrequency transmitters and cellular telephones

[See subsections 503(1), 503(2), 503(4)]

Transmitter power (watts)	Minimum separation distance at selected frequencies (metres)		
	VHF 35 – 36 MHz public use 42 – 44 MHz public use 50 – 54 MHz public use	VHF 144 – 148 MHz amateur 150.8 – 161.6 MHz public use	UHF 450 – 470 MHz public use cellular telephones above 800 MHz
5 or less	25	8	5
6 – 10	35	12	8
11 – 30	57	19	12
31 – 50	80	26	17
51 – 100	115	40	24
101 – 200	160	55	35
201 – 250	180	60	40
251 – 500	250	85	55
501 – 1,000	355	120	75
1,001 – 1,500	435	145	95
1,501 – 10,000	1,115	365	240

Schedule 11   Mining

Table 1   Minimum separation distances between explosives and fixed radio transmitters

[See subsection 651(3)]

Transmitter power (watts)	Minimum separation distance (metres)
5 – 25	30
26 – 50	45
51 – 100	65
101 – 250	110
251 – 500	135
501 – 1000	200
1001 – 2500	300
2501 – 5000	450
5001 – 10,000	675
10,001 – 25,000	1100
25,001 – 50,000	1500
50,001 or more	2000

Table 2   Minimum separation distances between explosives and mobile radio transmitters

[See subsection 651(3)]

Transmitter power (watts)	Minimum separation distance (metres)
1 – 10	4
11 – 30	7
31 – 60	10
61 – 100	20
101 or more	30

Note: The distances specified above are the minimum permissible distances between the nearest part of the vehicle or portable set and the nearest part of the blasting circuit.

Table 3 Application to Director

[See subsection 659(2)]

Pursuant to section 659 of the *Occupational Health and Safety Code*, application is made to the Director on behalf of _Mine Name_ to use an explosive that is not classified as a "permitted explosive" for work in rock.

The following is submitted in support of this application:

(1)   The attached mine plans, sections and notes outline the extent of the proposed work, including appropriate plans to indicate the location and starting point, inclination, size of the heading and the location of adjacent coal seams and the nature of the strata to be penetrated.

(2)   A complete description of the proposed ventilation system, giving direction and volume of air and size and type of fans proposed.

(3)   The details and location of proposed explosive storage, if any.

Mine Manager's Signature

Index

Note: The numbers appearing in this index refer to section or "rule" numbers.

client/resident handling
defined in safe patient/client/resident handling, 1
See also lifting and handling loads
climbable structure
defined, 1
fall protection systems, 154
climbing activities
in definition of non-industrial rope access work, 1
See also rope access work, non-industrial (mountaineering, caving, canyoning, sport climbing)
Climbing Gym Instructor Technical Manual **(Association of Canadian Mountain Guides),** 3, 841(b)
climbing wood poles *See* wood pole climbing
clips, cable, 300
close work site
defined, 1
first aid requirements
low hazard work, Schedule 2, Table 5
medium hazard work, Schedule 2, Table 6
high hazard work, Schedule 2, Table 7
See also first aid and first aiders
clothing *See* foot protection and footwear; head protection and headwear; personal protective clothing; worker's clothing
coal dust
defined
exposed worker, 1
restricted area, 1
building safety, 532
certification by engineer
electrical equipment for surface mines, 563(1)
decontamination methods, 28(c)
Director of Inspection
dust control, alternate protections, approval, 537(2)
dust sampling records, 744(a)
exhaust fans, dust collection devices, order, 742(5)
ignition of dust, report, 544(1)(d)
incombustible dust, approval, 743(1.2)–(2)
documents
dust sampling records, 744
ignition of dust, report, 544(1)(d)
stone dusting program, report, 743(1.2)
dust control in underground coal mines, 742–744
airborne dust, 742
dust sampling, 744
exhaust fans, dust collection devices, 742(5)
housekeeping, 743(1.1)
incombustible dust, 743

monitoring program, 742(4)
roadway used by rubber-tired vehicles, 742(3)
stone dusting program, report, 743(1.2)
water supply to suppress dust, 742(1)–(2)
dust-suppression devices, 548(3)
electrical equipment for surface mines, manufacturer or engineer approval, 563(1)
explosives, 664(2)
health assessment for exposure, 40
costs, 40(11), 40(13)
frequency of assessments, 40(6)–(8)
information to worker, 40(3)
performed during work hours, 40(12)
privacy of information, 40(5)
refusal by worker, 40(9)–(10)
report contents, 40(2)
retention of records, 40(4)
housekeeping, 28(b)
minimization of release, 28(a)
OEL, Schedule 1, Table 2
OEL, amended to come into effect May 1, 2010, 16(2.1)
restricted areas
authorized persons, 29(1), 29(2)(b)
decontamination of workers, 29(4)(c)
emergencies, 29(5)
harmful substances, 29(2)
no eating, drinking or smoking, 29(2)(c)
prohibited activities, 29(2)(c)
protection of worker's street clothing, 29(4)
protective clothing for workers, 29(4)
signs, 29(2)–(3)
signs for restricted area, 29(2)–(3)
coal mines *See* underground coal mines
coal tar pitch volatiles
code of practice required, 26, Schedule 1, Table 1
coats, lab
duty to use, 228
use of, 242–243
See also personal protective clothing
Code
See *Occupational Health and Safety Code*
Code for Electrical Installations at Oil and Gas Facilities **(Alberta Municipal Affairs),** 3, 162.1(1)(b)
Code for Fireworks Display **(NFPA),** 3, 467(2)(a), 499(3)(a)
Code for Tower Cranes **(CSA),** 3, 100
code name and code number *See* Workplace Hazardous Materials Information System (WHMIS)
College and Association of Registered Nurses of Alberta
in definition of nurse, 1

worker on moving platform, prohibition,
348(4)
See also elevating platforms and aerial
devices
forklift trucks, 283–284
load charts, 283
personal fall arrest systems, 156
seat belts, 284
standards, 347(8)
See also powered mobile equipment
forms *See* temporary supporting structures
frames of glasses *See* eye protection
free fall distance *See* personal fall arrest
system (PFAS)
free-standing scaffolds
design, 334(1)
use in demolition work, 422
See also scaffolds and temporary work
platforms
freezing soil for stabilization, 443(2)–(3)
fuel storage
in oil and gas operations, prohibitions, 778
oxygen-fuel systems, prohibitions,
171(1)(b), 171(4)
powered mobile equipment
fuel tank in cab of, 274
portable fuel tanks, 277(1)
refuelling hazards, 279
underground coal mines
bulk fuel storage, 696, 713
diesel fuel, 704–705
fugitive emission
defined, 1
employer's material safety data sheet,
exemption, 405(2)
training in procedures, 397(1)(f), 398(4)(c)
See also Workplace Hazardous Materials
Information System (WHMIS)
full body harness
defined
cow's tail, 1
full body harness, 1
lanyard, 1
in personal fall arrest system, 142
standards
industrial rope access work, 834
standards, 142(1)
wood pole climbing, 149
working positioning systems, tree care,
795
See also personal fall arrest system (PFAS);
sit harness
Full Body Harnesses **(CSA),** 3, 142(1),
795(1)(c)
furnaces *See* industrial furnaces and fired
heaters
fuse assemblies *See* detonators and detonation

G

gallows frame roofer's hoist, 97(6)–(7)
See also roofer's hoists
galvanometer for testing detonators, 495
gantry, overhead cranes, standards, 93–94
gas furnaces *See* industrial furnaces and fired
heaters
gas lines *See* buried or concrete-embedded
facilities
gas monitors, flammable, 543
gas sample containers
oil and gas wells, 784
gas, compressed/liquefied *See*
compressed/liquefied gas
gates *See* safeguards and warnings
General requirements for certification of
personnel engaged in industrial rope
access methods **(International Rope**
Access Trade Association), 3, 826(a)
generic name *See* Workplace Hazardous
Materials Information System
(WHMIS)
geothermal operations *See* oil and gas wells
gin poles
safe practices, 75
girls *See* females
glass windows and windshields
in powered mobile equipment, 265
glasses *See* eye protection
gloves
duty to use, 228
use of, 242–243
gob *See* underground coal mines
goggles *See* eye protection
goods, lifting *See* lifting and handling loads
grain bins *See* confined and restricted spaces
gravitational energy
in definition of hazardous energy, 1
See also hazardous energy control (for
service, repair, tests, adjustments,
inspections)
green tags, scaffolds, 326(1)(a)
grills in powered mobile equipment, 269
grinders, 375
defined
grinder accessory, 1
hand held grinders, 375(1)(c), 375(2)
manufacturer's specifications, 375(1), 375(3)
tool rests, 375(3)–(4)
grinding *See* hot work
ground anchors
oil and gas wells, 764
See also anchors
ground falls
notice to Director of dangerous occurrences
in mines, 544(1)(a)
guardrails, 314–315
bridges for crossing conveyor belts, 373(1)–
(2)

for walkways, runways and ramps, 121(1)(d)

fork-mounted work platforms, fall protection systems, 349(2)(b)

openings and holes, 314

securing of, 315(3)

specifications

guardrails, 315(1)

temporary guardrails, 315(2)

toe boards, 321(1)

toe boards, 321

travel restraint systems in place of, 139(5)–(6)

when required, 139

See also safeguards and warnings

guards *See* safeguards and warnings

guy lines

derrick mast or self-contained snubbing unit, 763

GVW (manufacturer's rated gross vehicle weight)

defined, 1

H

hair

clean shaven for facial seals, 250(2)

contact with equipment and machinery, safety precautions, 362

See also head protection and headwear

half-horse scaffolds

design and specifications, 335

See also scaffolds and temporary work platforms

hand cleaning facilities *See* toilets and washing facilities

hand expose zone

defined, 1

exposing buried facilities, 448(1), 448(3)

See also buried or concrete-embedded facilities

hand held equipment and tools

defined

hand tool, 1

electrical drills, use in mines, 572

grinders, 375

signal lights, 194(6)

hand protection

duty to use, 228

finger rings in contact with machinery, precautions, 362

use of, 242–243

hand shields *See* eye protection

hand signals *See* designated signallers

hand tool *See* hand held equipment and tools

Hand Tools for Live Working up to 1000 V a.c. and 1500 V d.c. **(ULC),** 3, 799(1)

hand-operated hoists

holding suspended load, 80

See also hoists

handling explosives *See* explosives (at mine sites); explosives (other than at mine sites)

handling loads *See* lifting and handling loads

handrails on stairways, 122(2), 123

hard and compact soil *See* soils and soil types

hard hats *See* head protection and headwear

harmful substances

defined, 1

See also occupational exposure limit (OEL)

harness *See* full body harness; sit harness

haul roads

for mines, 539

hazard assessment, elimination and control, 7–11

definitions

hazard, 1

hazard assessment, 1

classification of work sites, 162.1

Director of Inspection

health and safety plan, order, 11

documents

classification of work sites, 162.1(1)(d)

hazard assessment, 7

health and safety plan, 11

prepared by competent person, 162.1(1)(d)

emergency control, 10

hierarchy of elimination and control

elimination, 9(1)

engineering controls, 9(2)

administrative controls, 9(3)

personal protective equipment (PPE), 9(4)

combination of controls and personal protective equipment, 9(5)

prime contractors to inform employers of work site hazards, 7(5)

report of assessment, 7(2)–(3), 10(2)

when to assess, 7(1), 7(4)

worker participation, 8

hazard information *See* Workplace Hazardous Materials Information System (WHMIS)

hazardous energy control (for service, repair, tests, adjustments, inspections), 212–215.5

defined

hazardous energy, 1

isolate, 1

secure, 1

complex group control, 215.1

Director of Inspection, approvals

complex group control processes, 215.1(1)

group control, 215

individual control, 214

isolating piping, 215.4

isolation procedures, 212

duty to report, 182
first aid records, 183–184
musculoskeletal injuries
    prevention, 210–211.1
See also first aid and first aiders; violence,
    workplace
immediately dangerous to life or health
defined, 1
impoundment dike
Director of Inspection
    reports on dangerous occurrences, 544(2)
in-line skates
safety helmets, free of damage or
    modification, 235(1)(b)
safety helmets, standards, 235(1)(a)
inclement weather *See* weather
incombustible dust
defined, 1
in underground coal mines, 743
See also coal dust
Industrial Eye and Face Protectors (CSA), 3,
    229
industrial furnaces and fired heaters, 163,
    168
precautions against fires and explosions
    flammable substances, 163(2)(c)
    ignition after shutdown, 168(3)
    inserted blinds or double block and bleed
        systems, prohibitions, 168(2)
    operations in hazardous locations,
        168(4)–(5)
    other safeguards, 168(1), 168(6)
    standards for classification of hazardous
        locations, 168(4)–(5)
See also fire and explosion hazards
industrial headwear
duty to use, 234
exemption, 239
See also head protection and headwear
industrial minerals *See* mines and mining
industrial power producers
defined
    industrial power producers, 1
    utility employee, 1
coordinated work, 802
safe work practices, 801
See also electrical utilities and utility
    workers
Industrial Protective Headwear (CSA), 3, 234,
    831(1)(a), 831(2)(a)
industrial radiofrequency heaters
electromagnetic radiation
    defined, 1
industrial robot system *See* robots
Industrial Robots and Robot Systems —
    General Safety Requirements (CSA),
    3, 384(1)
Industrial Rope Access Technique (ARAA), 3,
    826(c)

industrial rope access work
in definition of occupational rope access
    work, 1
See also rope access work
industrial tractors, 270–271
rollover protective structures, 270
seatbelts and restraint systems, 271
See also powered mobile equipment
inerting
defined
    inerting, 1
in confined spaces, 54
inflating tires *See* tire servicing
information access and privacy for workers
asbestos, silica or coal dust exposure
    records, 40(5)
audiometric testing records, 223
first aid records, 184
health information in emergencies, 413–414
noise exposure assessment records, 223
information system for hazardous materials
    See Workplace Hazardous Materials
    Information System (WHMIS)
injury *See* illness or injury
inspect machinery, isolating hazardous
    energy to *See* hazardous energy control
    (for service, repair, tests, adjustments,
    inspections)
Installing Poles (Insulating Sticks) and
    Universal Tool Attachments (Fittings)
    for Live Working (ULC), 3, 799(1)
Institut de recherché Robert-Sauvé en santé
    et en sécurité du travail (IRSST)
OEL measurements, 20(1)(e)
instructional signs
logging industry vehicle traffic control,
    525(3)
Instrument Face Design and Location for
    Construction and Industrial
    Equipment (SAE), 3, 581(d)
integrating sound level meter, standards,
    219(3)
interlock barrier
defined, 1
See also robots
internal combustion engines, 166
combustion air intakes and exhaust
    discharges, 163(2)(c)(ii), 166(1)
flammable substances, 163(2)(c), 166(2)–(3)
gas monitoring equipment, 166(6)
hazardous locations, classification of,
    166(5)–(7)
storage of flammable substances, 163(2)
vehicles with, 166(4)–(7)
See also fire and explosion hazards; hot
    work
International Electrotechnical Commission
    (IEC), 3

X

x-rays *See* radiation

Y

yellow tags, scaffolds, 326(1)(b)

Z

zinc chromate
    code of practice required, 26, Schedule 1,
        Table 1